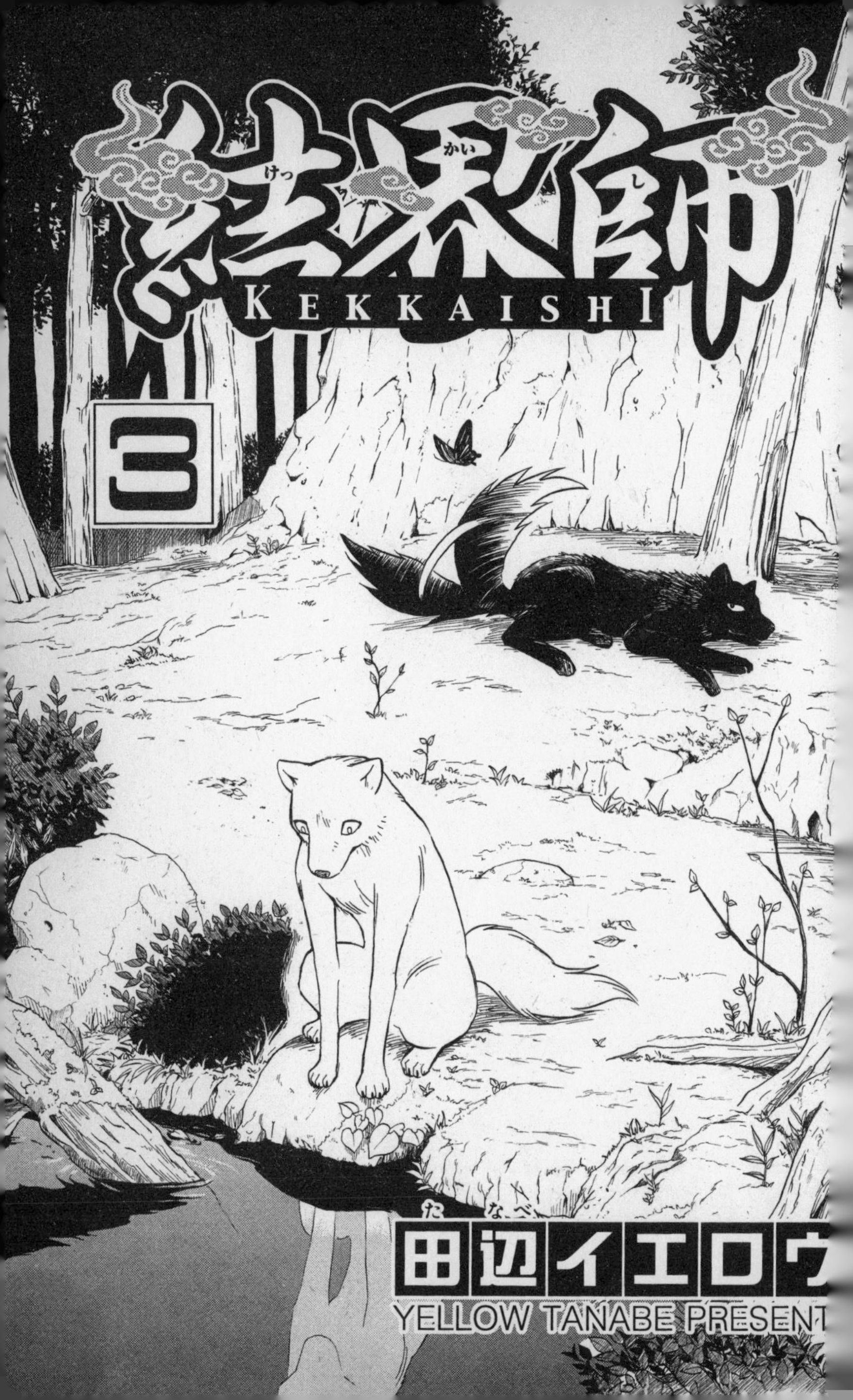
結界師
けっかいし
KEKKAISHI
3
田辺イエロウ
たなべ
YELLOW TANABE PRESENT

THe Story THUS Far

Yoshimori Sumimura and Tokine Yukimura have a special
mission, passed down through their families for
generations. Their mission is to protect Karasumori forest
from supernatural beings called *ayakashi*. People with this
gift for terminating ayakashi are called *kekkaishi*, or barrier
masters.

One night, a demon tamer named Yomi and her demon
servant, Yoki, attempt to take over the Karasumori site for
their own purposes. Aided by the magical power
emanating from the site, Yoki transforms himself into an
extremely powerful demon. Yoshimori and Tokine struggle
to defeat him.

In the midst of the battle, men with magical abilities arrive
from the secretive "shadow organization," which oversees
the work of the kekkaishi and mercilessly destroy Yoki.

The Karasumori site continues to attract ayakashi who wish
to boost their supernatural power. Yoshimori and Tokine
have no idea what forces they will face in their next battle!

KEKKAISHI VOL. 3
TABLE OF CONTENTS

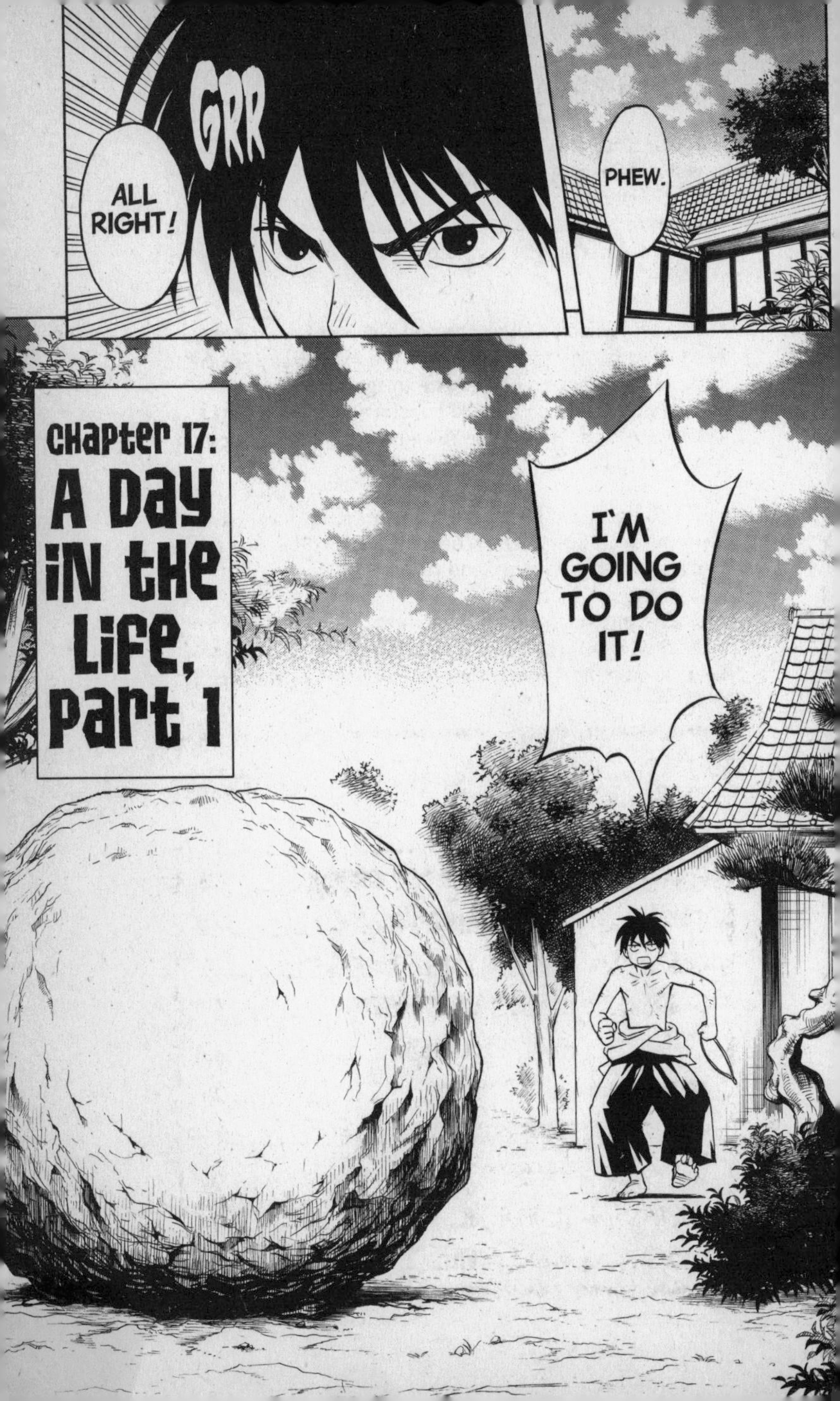
PHEW.
GRR
ALL RIGHT!
I'M GOING TO DO IT!
Chapter 17: A Day in the Life, Part 1

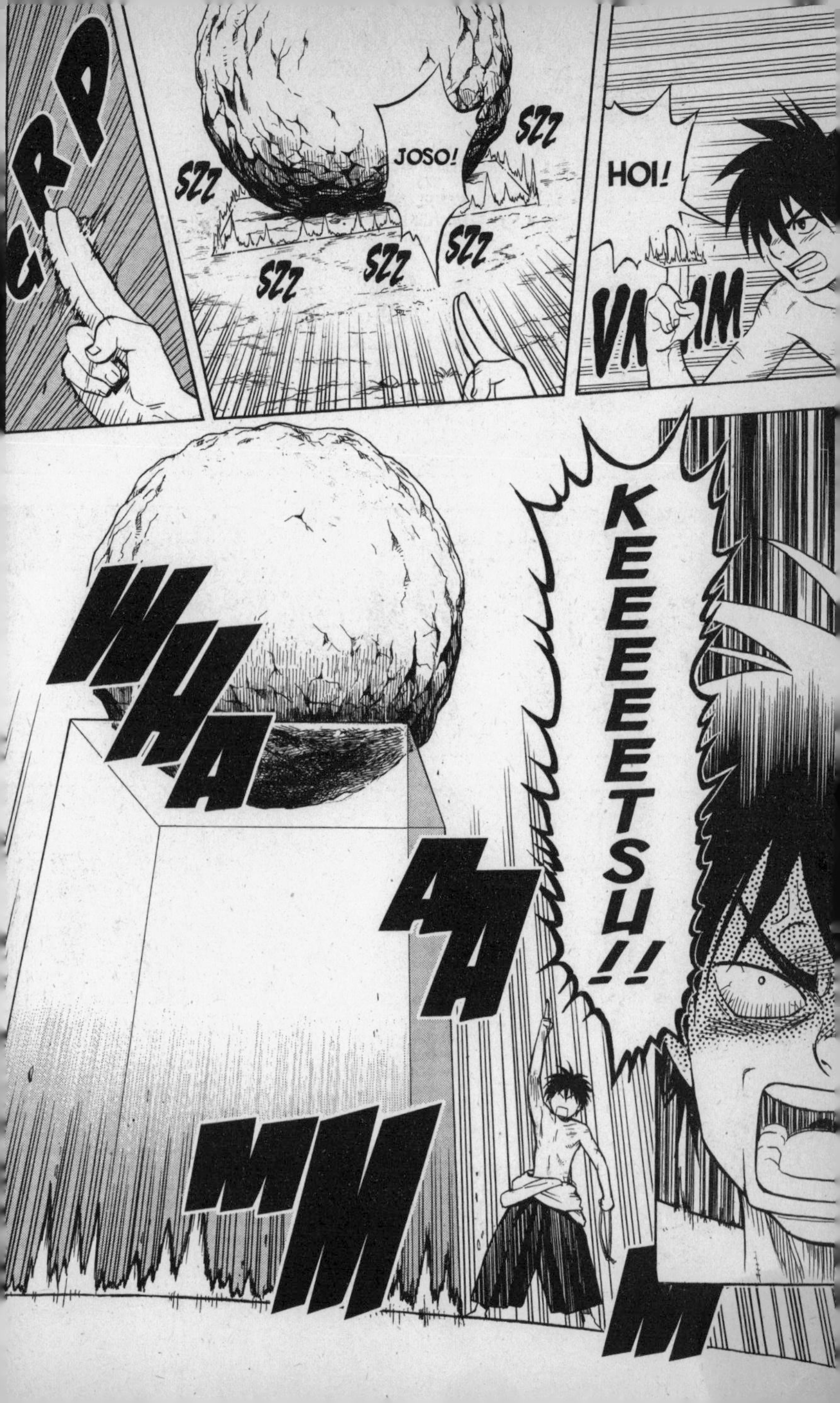
HOI!
VAAM
SZZ
JOSO!
SZZ
SZZ
SZZ
SZZ
CRP
KEEEEEETSU!!
WHAAAMMM

OKAY. NEXT!

PING

KETSU!

IT TOOK ME 2.8 SECONDS TO STABILIZE THE KEKKAI. NOT BAD.

CHK

TAP

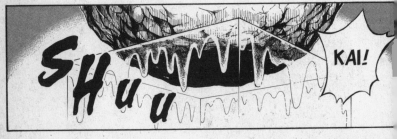

SHUUUU

KAI!

THUD

WHIRR

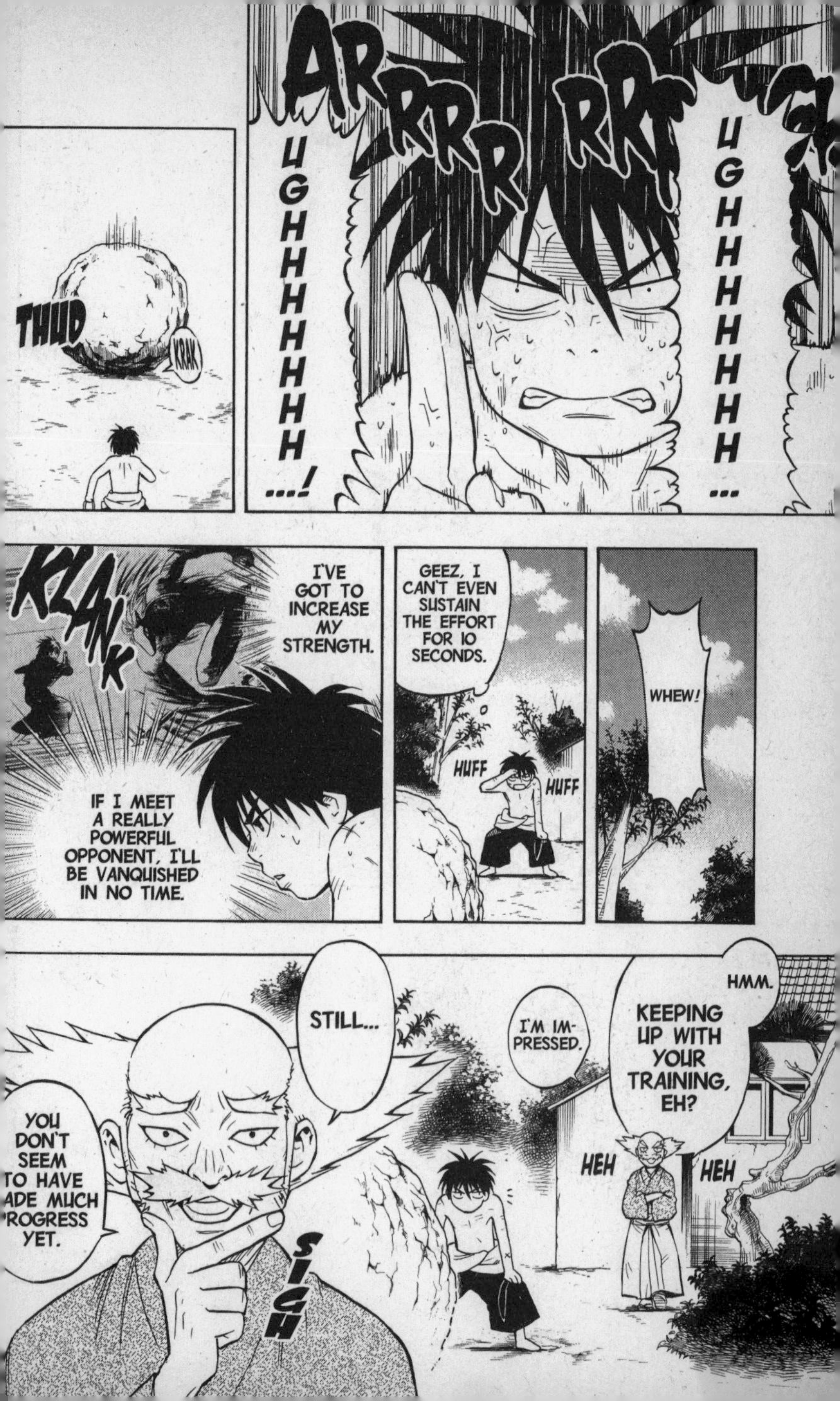
ARRRRRRRRR
UGHHHHHHHH...
UGHHHHHHHH...!
THUD
KRAK
WHEW!
GEEZ, I CAN'T EVEN SUSTAIN THE EFFORT FOR 10 SECONDS.
HUFF
HUFF
I'VE GOT TO INCREASE MY STRENGTH.
IF I MEET A REALLY POWERFUL OPPONENT, I'LL BE VANQUISHED IN NO TIME.
KLANK
HMM.
KEEPING UP WITH YOUR TRAINING, EH?
HEH
HEH
I'M IM-PRESSED.
STILL...
YOU DON'T SEEM TO HAVE
ADE MUCH
ROGRESS YET.
SIGH

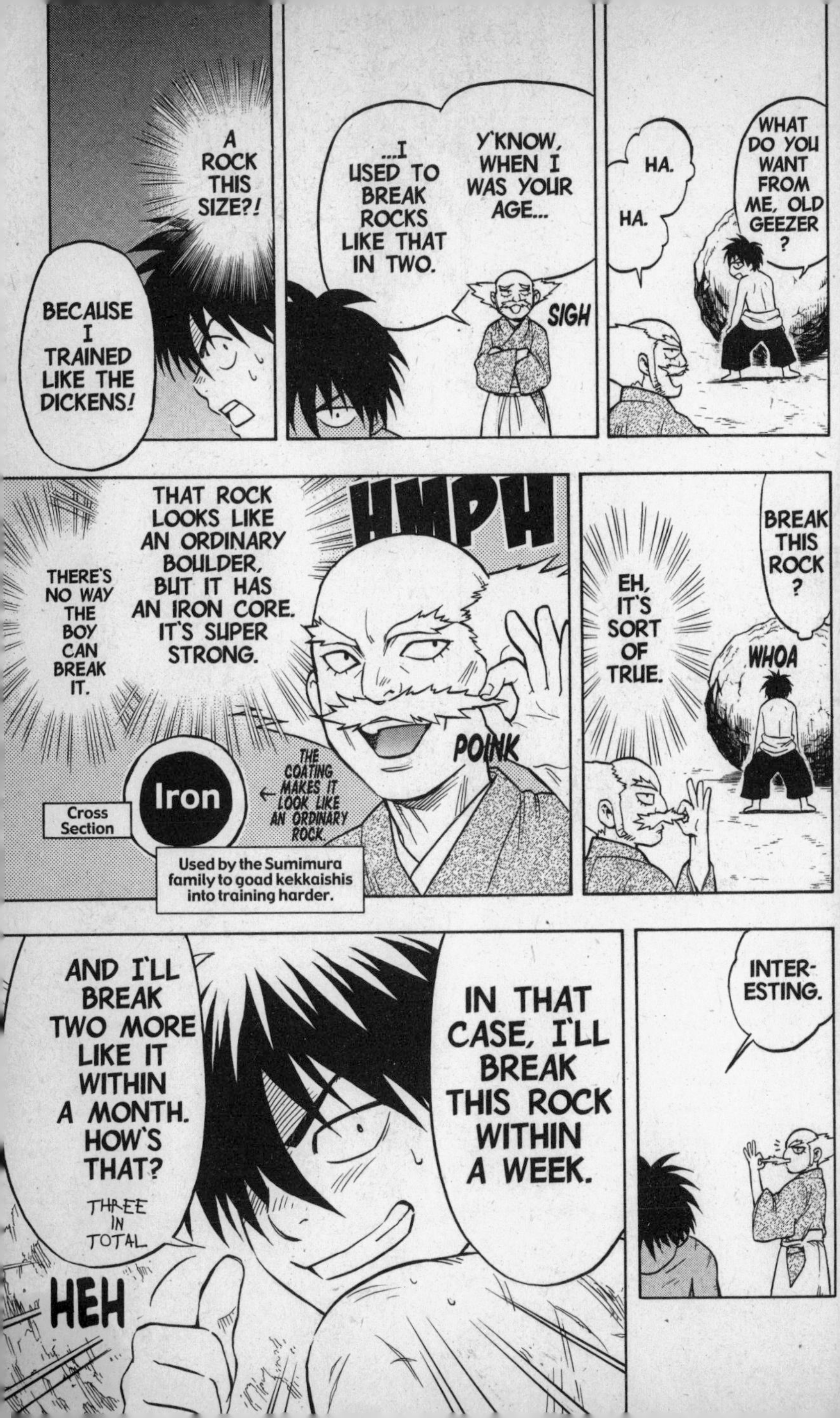
WHAT DO YOU WANT FROM ME, OLD GEEZER?
HA.
HA.
Y'KNOW, WHEN I WAS YOUR AGE...
...I USED TO BREAK ROCKS LIKE THAT IN TWO.
SIGH
A ROCK THIS SIZE?!
BECAUSE I TRAINED LIKE THE DICKENS!
BREAK THIS ROCK?
WHOA
EH, IT'S SORT OF TRUE.
HMPH
THAT ROCK LOOKS LIKE AN ORDINARY BOULDER, BUT IT HAS AN IRON CORE. IT'S SUPER STRONG.
THERE'S NO WAY THE BOY CAN BREAK IT.
POINK
THE COATING MAKES IT LOOK LIKE AN ORDINARY ROCK.
Iron
Cross Section
Used by the Sumimura family to goad kekkaishis into training harder.
INTER-ESTING.
IN THAT CASE, I'LL BREAK THIS ROCK WITHIN A WEEK.
AND I'LL BREAK TWO MORE LIKE IT WITHIN A MONTH. HOW'S THAT?
THREE IN TOTAL
HEH

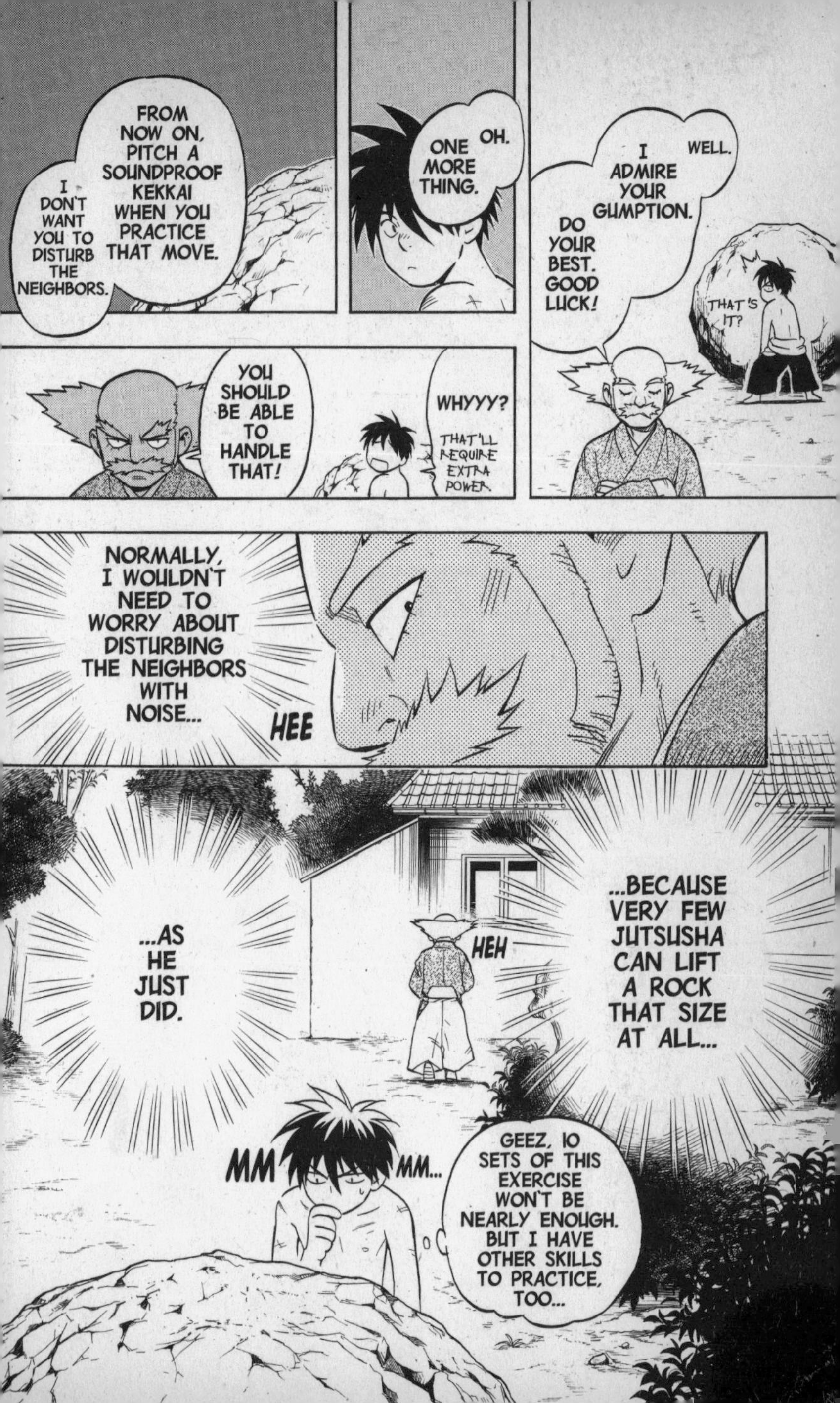
WELL. I ADMIRE YOUR GUMPTION.
DO YOUR BEST. GOOD LUCK!
THAT'S IT?
OH. ONE MORE THING.
FROM NOW ON, PITCH A SOUNDPROOF KEKKAI WHEN YOU PRACTICE THAT MOVE.
I DON'T WANT YOU TO DISTURB THE NEIGHBORS.
WHYYY?
THAT'LL REQUIRE EXTRA POWER.
YOU SHOULD BE ABLE TO HANDLE THAT!
NORMALLY, I WOULDN'T NEED TO WORRY ABOUT DISTURBING THE NEIGHBORS WITH NOISE...
HEE
...BECAUSE VERY FEW JUTSUSHA CAN LIFT A ROCK THAT SIZE AT ALL...
HEH
...AS HE JUST DID.
MM MM...
GEEZ, 10 SETS OF THIS EXERCISE WON'T BE NEARLY ENOUGH. BUT I HAVE OTHER SKILLS TO PRACTICE, TOO...

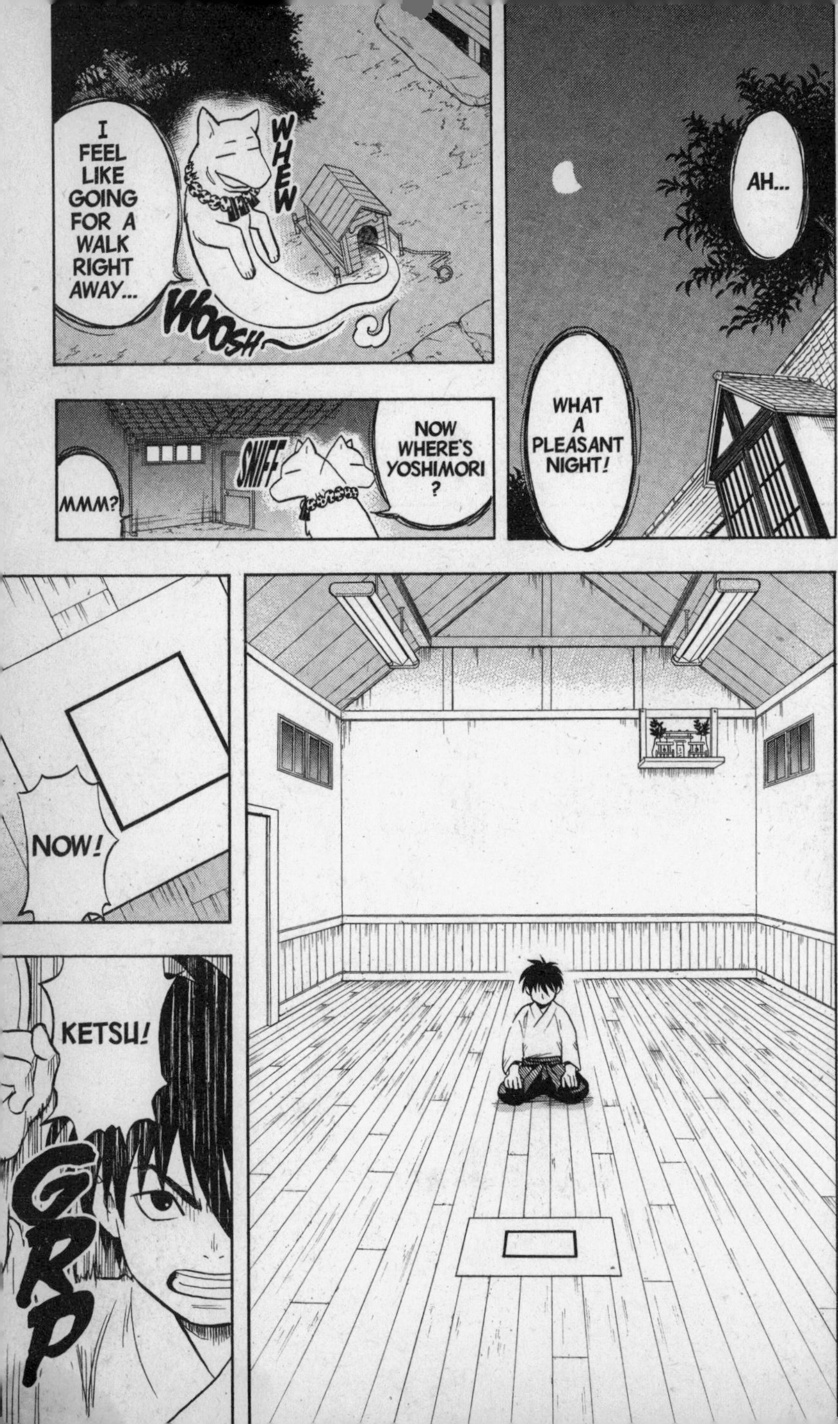
AH...
WHAT A PLEASANT NIGHT!
I FEEL LIKE GOING FOR A WALK RIGHT AWAY...
WHEW
WOOSH
NOW WHERE'S YOSHIMORI?
SNIFF
MMM?
NOW!
KETSU!
GRP

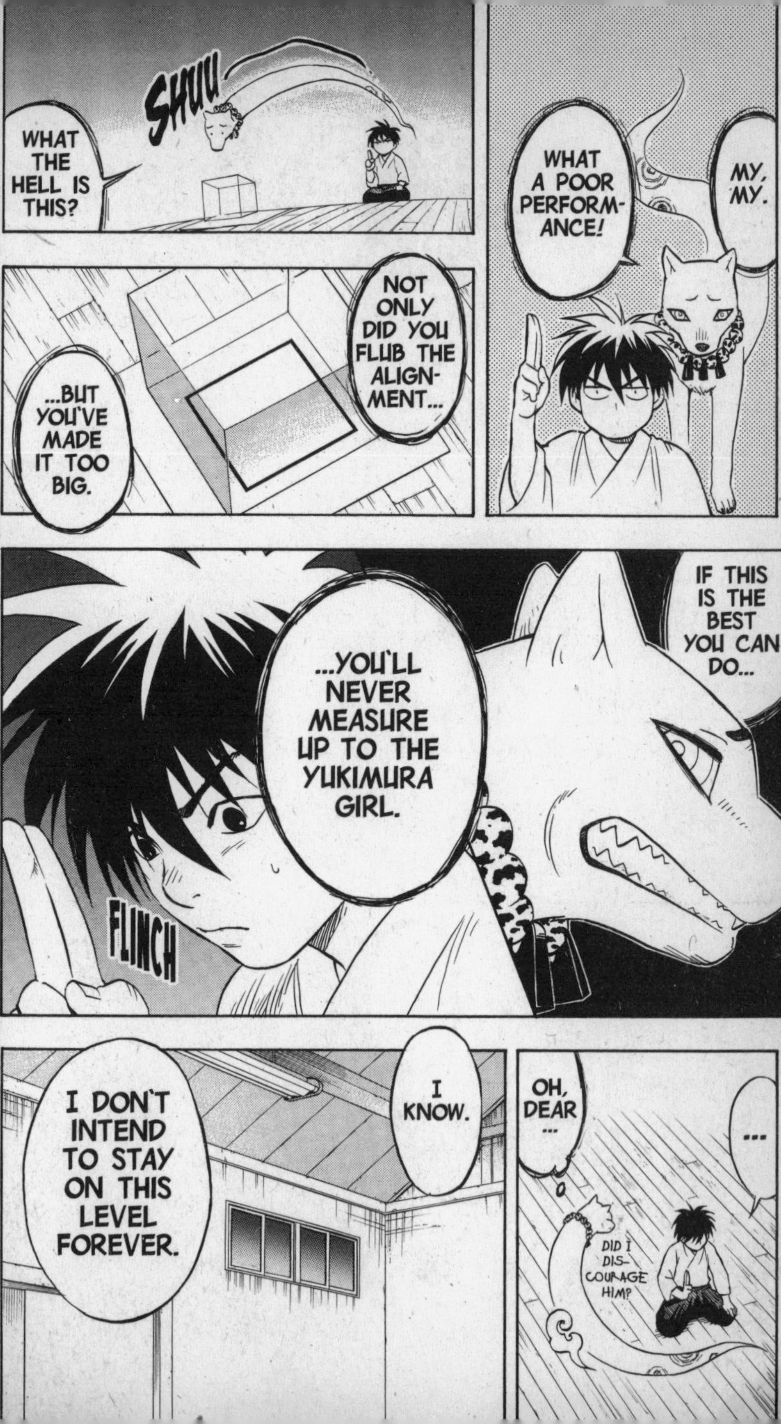
MY, MY.
WHAT A POOR PERFORM-ANCE!
SHUU
WHAT THE HELL IS THIS?
NOT ONLY DID YOU FLUB THE ALIGN-MENT...
...BUT YOU'VE MADE IT TOO BIG.
IF THIS IS THE BEST YOU CAN DO...
...YOU'LL NEVER MEASURE UP TO THE YUKIMURA GIRL.
FLINCH
...
OH, DEAR ...
DID I DIS-COURAGE HIM?
I KNOW.
I DON'T INTEND TO STAY ON THIS LEVEL FOREVER.

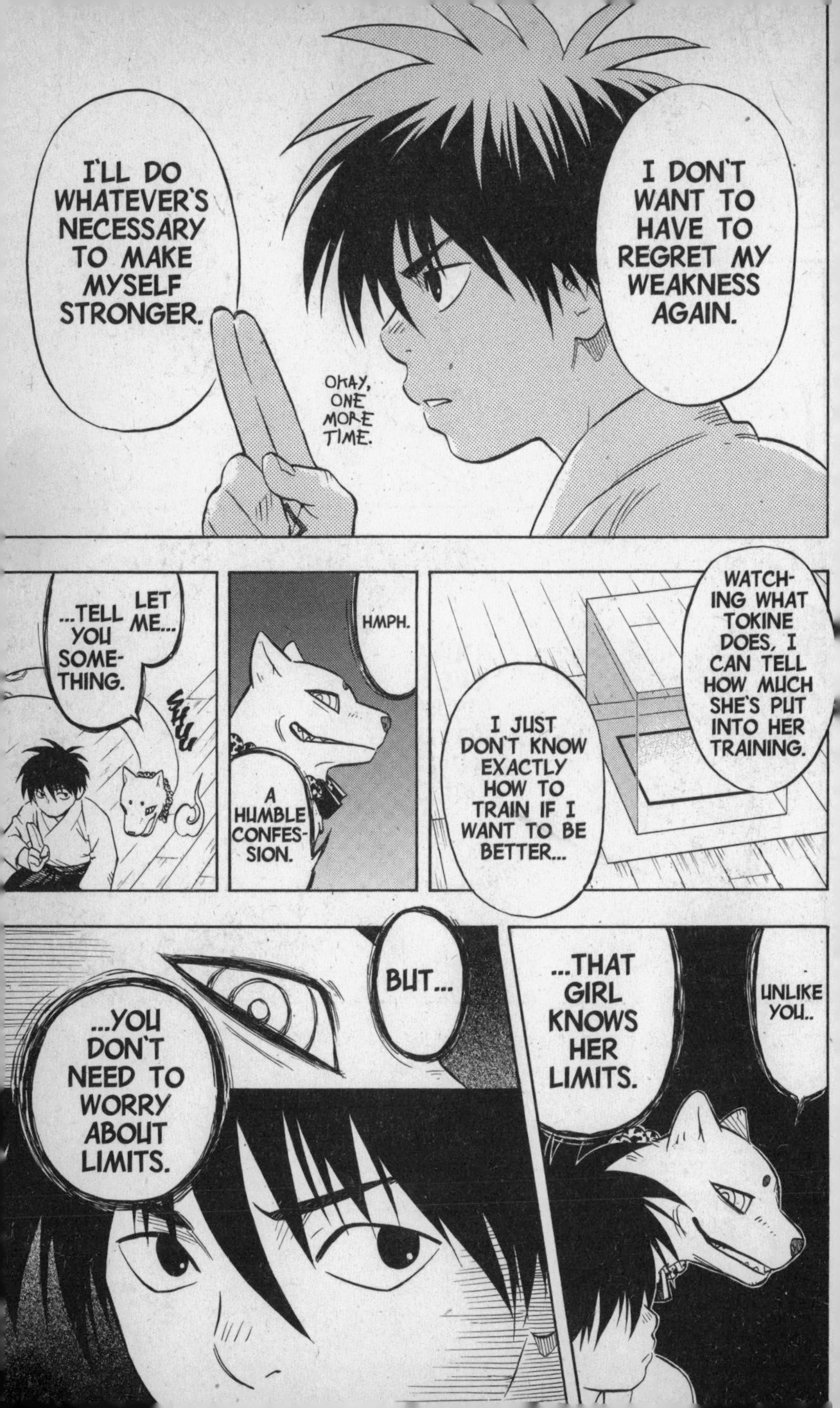
I DON'T WANT TO HAVE TO REGRET MY WEAKNESS AGAIN.
I'LL DO WHATEVER'S NECESSARY TO MAKE MYSELF STRONGER.
OKAY, ONE MORE TIME.
WATCHING WHAT TOKINE DOES, I CAN TELL HOW MUCH SHE'S PUT INTO HER TRAINING.
I JUST DON'T KNOW EXACTLY HOW TO TRAIN IF I WANT TO BE BETTER...
HMPH.
A HUMBLE CONFESSION.
LET ME...
...TELL YOU SOMETHING.
UNLIKE YOU..
...THAT GIRL KNOWS HER LIMITS.
BUT...
...YOU DON'T NEED TO WORRY ABOUT LIMITS.

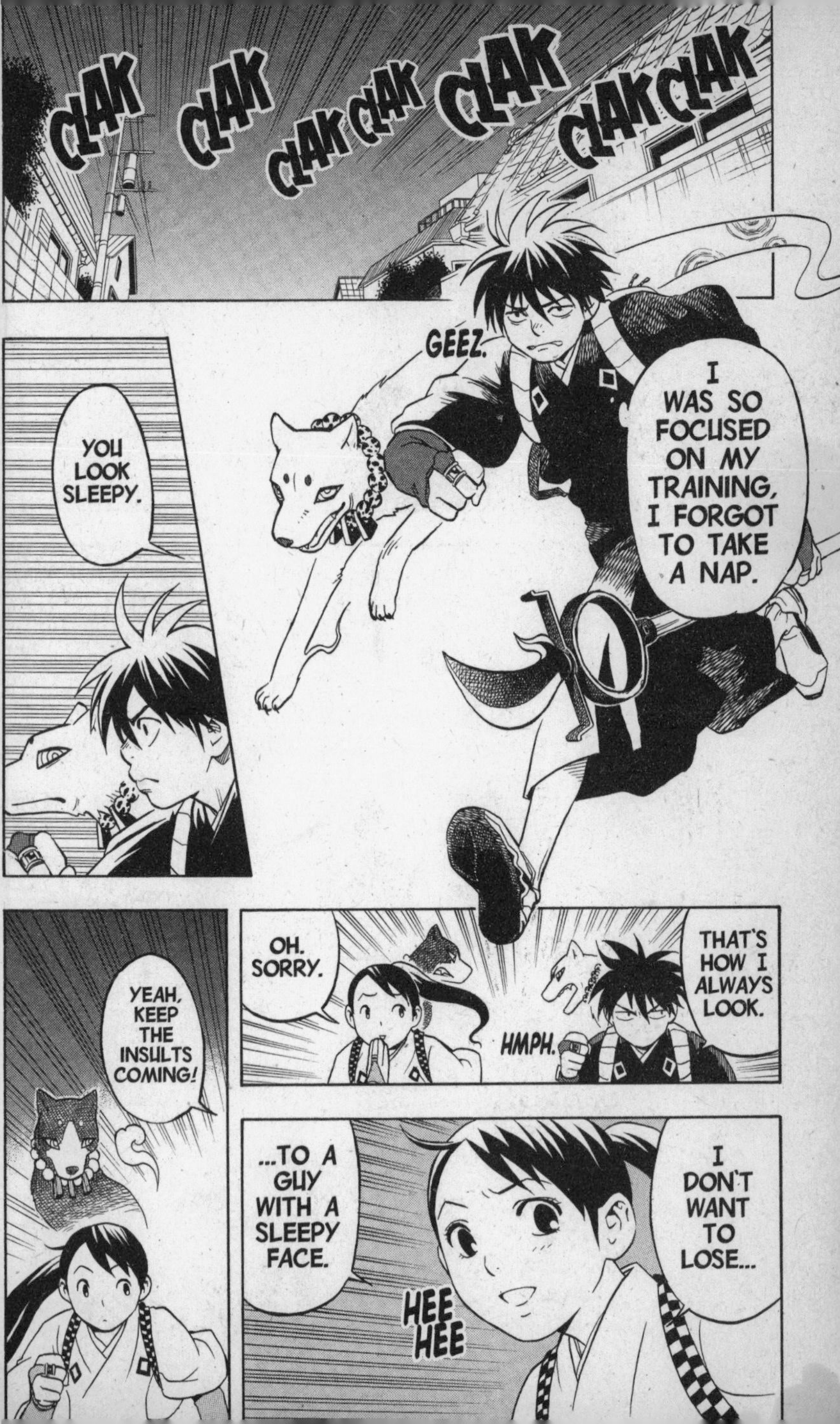
CLAK CLAK CLAK CLAK CLAK CLAK CLAK
GEEZ.
I WAS SO FOCUSED ON MY TRAINING, I FORGOT TO TAKE A NAP.
YOU LOOK SLEEPY.
THAT'S HOW I ALWAYS LOOK.
HMPH.
OH. SORRY.
I DON'T WANT TO LOSE...
...TO A GUY WITH A SLEEPY FACE.
HEE HEE
YEAH, KEEP THE INSULTS COMING!

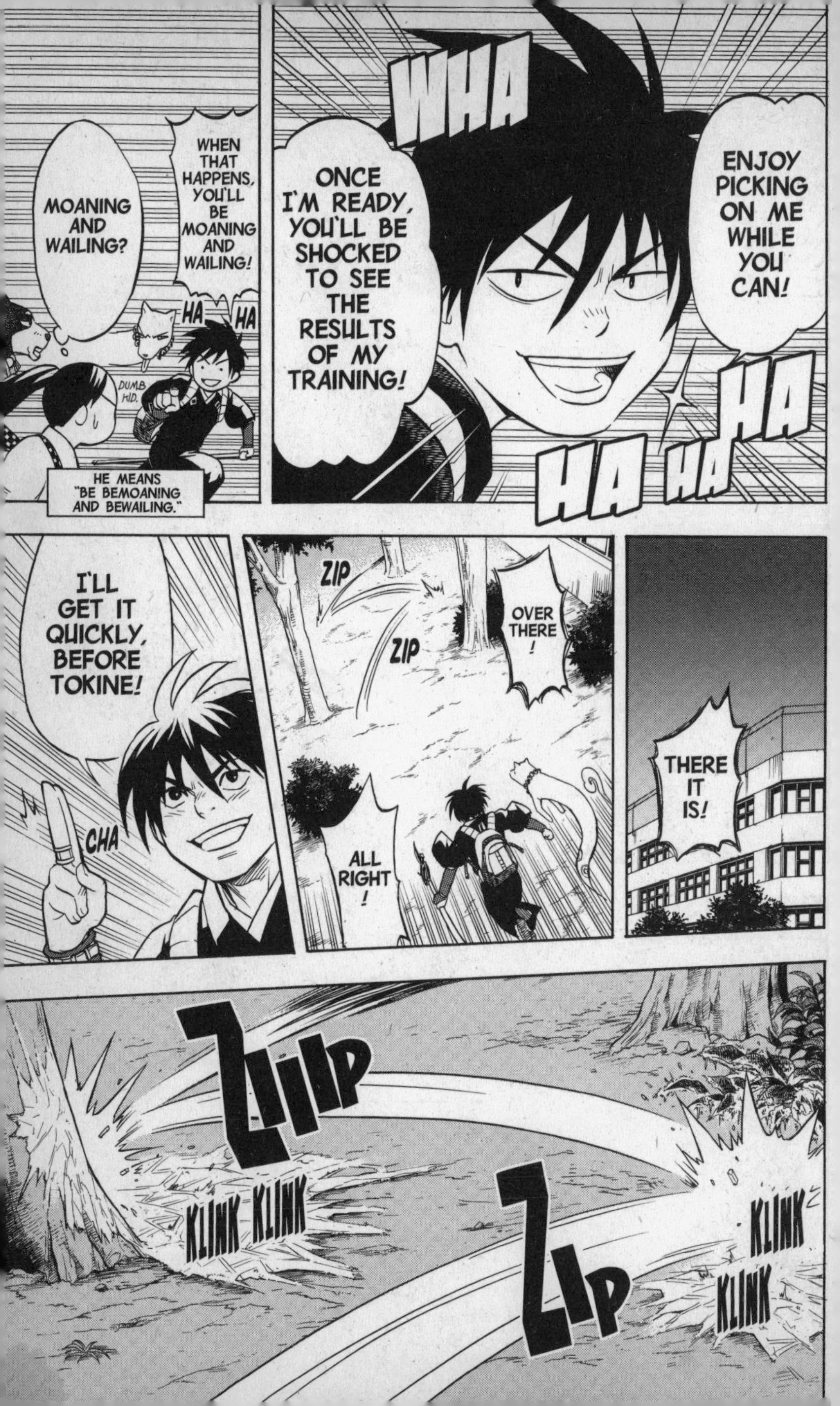

WHA
ENJOY PICKING ON ME WHILE YOU CAN!
ONCE I'M READY, YOU'LL BE SHOCKED TO SEE THE RESULTS OF MY TRAINING!
HA HA HA
WHEN THAT HAPPENS, YOU'LL BE MOANING AND WAILING!
MOANING AND WAILING?
HA HA
DUMB KID.
HE MEANS "BE BEMOANING AND BEWAILING."
THERE IT IS!
OVER THERE!
ZIP
ZIP
ALL RIGHT!
I'LL GET IT QUICKLY, BEFORE TOKINE!
CHA
ZIIIP
KLINK KLINK
ZIP
KLINK KLINK

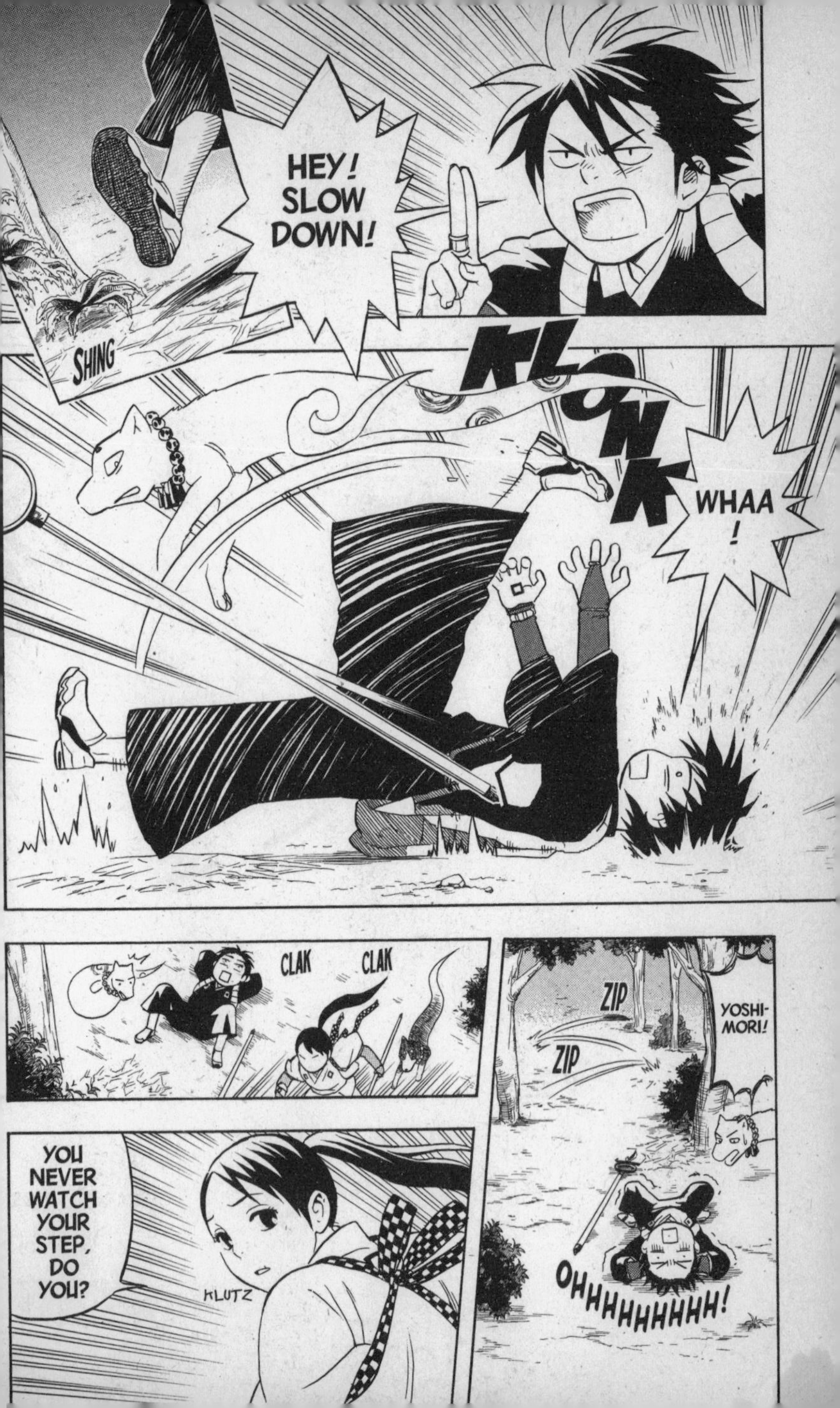
HEY! SLOW DOWN!
SHING
KLONK
WHAA!
YOSHI-MORI!
ZIP
ZIP
OHHHHHHHHH!
CLAK
CLAK
YOU NEVER WATCH YOUR STEP, DO YOU?
KLUTZ

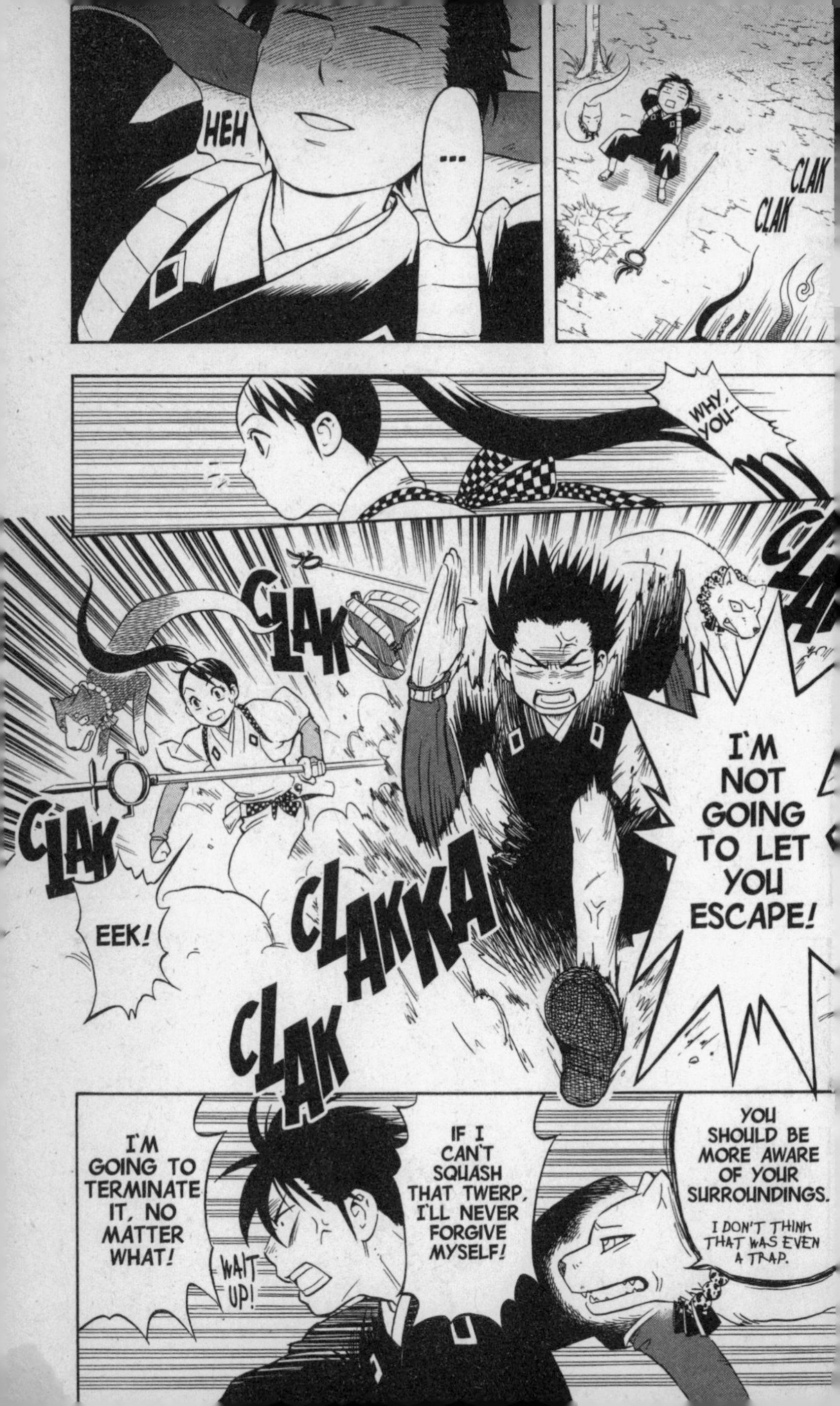
CLAK
CLAK
...
HEH
WHY, YOU--
I'M NOT GOING TO LET YOU ESCAPE!
CLAK
CLAKKA
CLAK
EEK!
CLAK
YOU SHOULD BE MORE AWARE OF YOUR SURROUNDINGS.
I DON'T THINK THAT WAS EVEN A TRAP.
IF I CAN'T SQUASH THAT TWERP, I'LL NEVER FORGIVE MYSELF!
I'M GOING TO TERMINATE IT, NO MATTER WHAT!
WAIT UP!

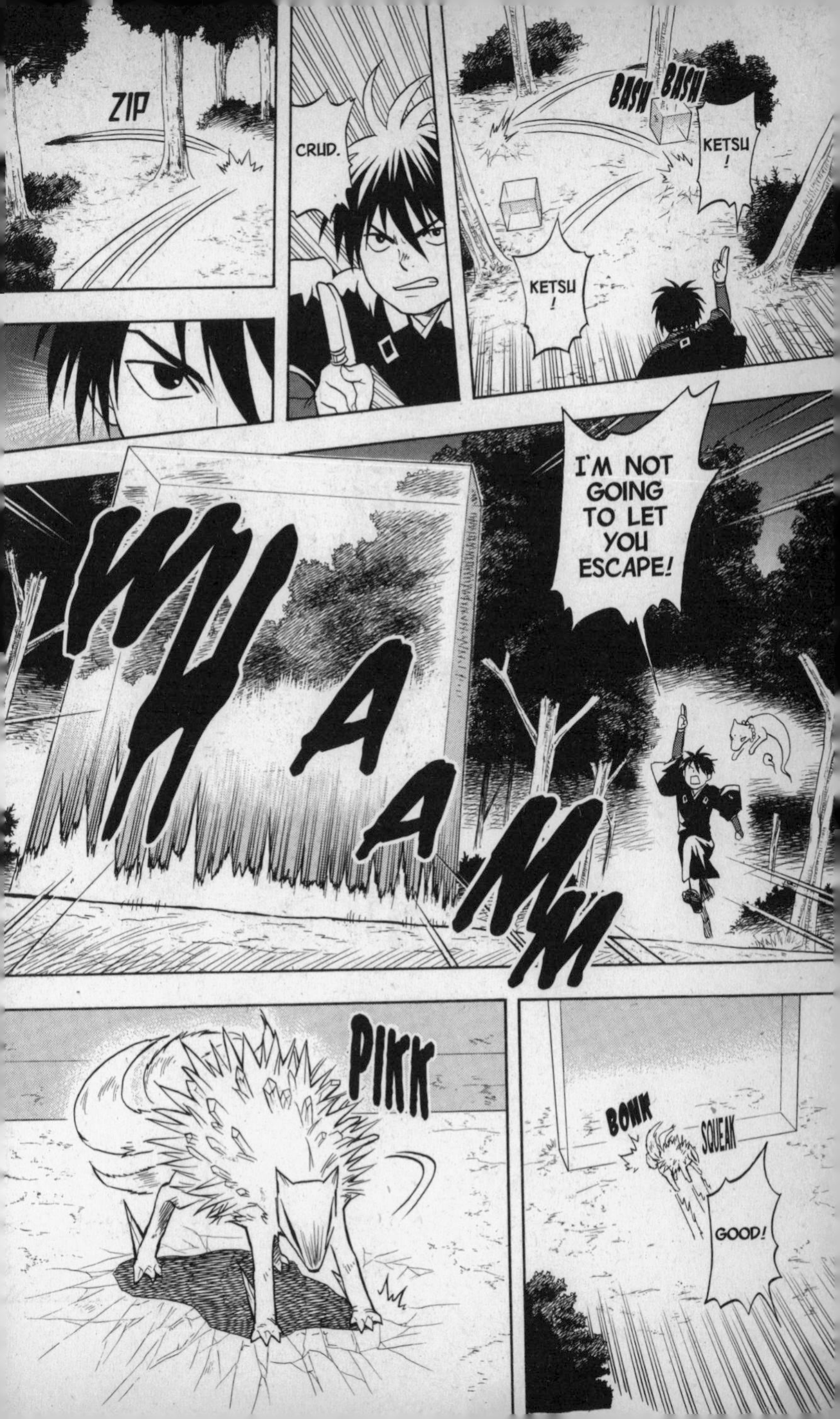
BASH BASH
KETSU!
KETSU!
CRUD.
ZIP
I'M NOT GOING TO LET YOU ESCAPE!
WHAAM
BONK
SQUEAK
GOOD!
PIKK

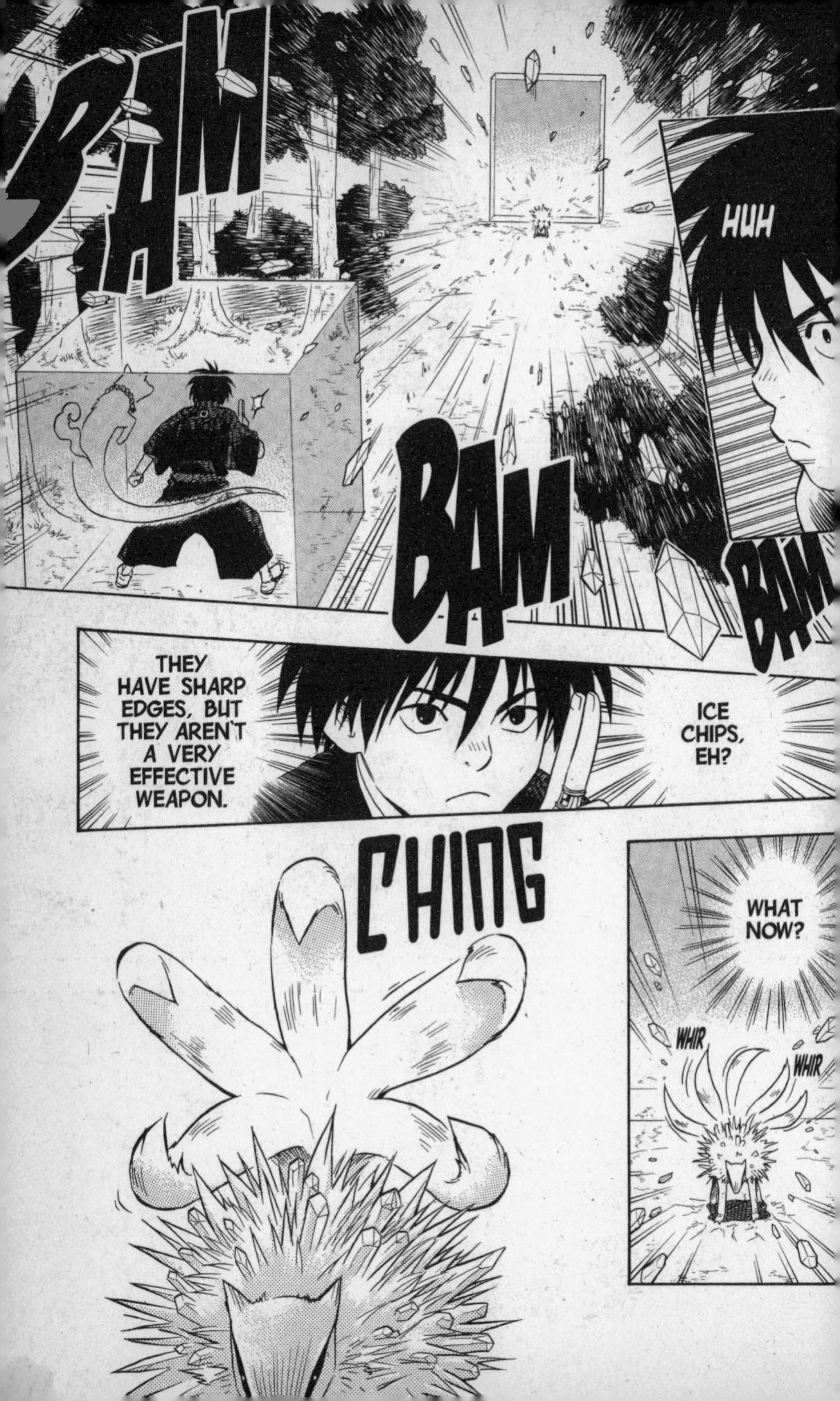
HUH
BAM
BAM
BAM
ICE CHIPS, EH?
THEY HAVE SHARP EDGES, BUT THEY AREN'T A VERY EFFECTIVE WEAPON.
WHAT NOW?
WHIR
WHIR
CHING

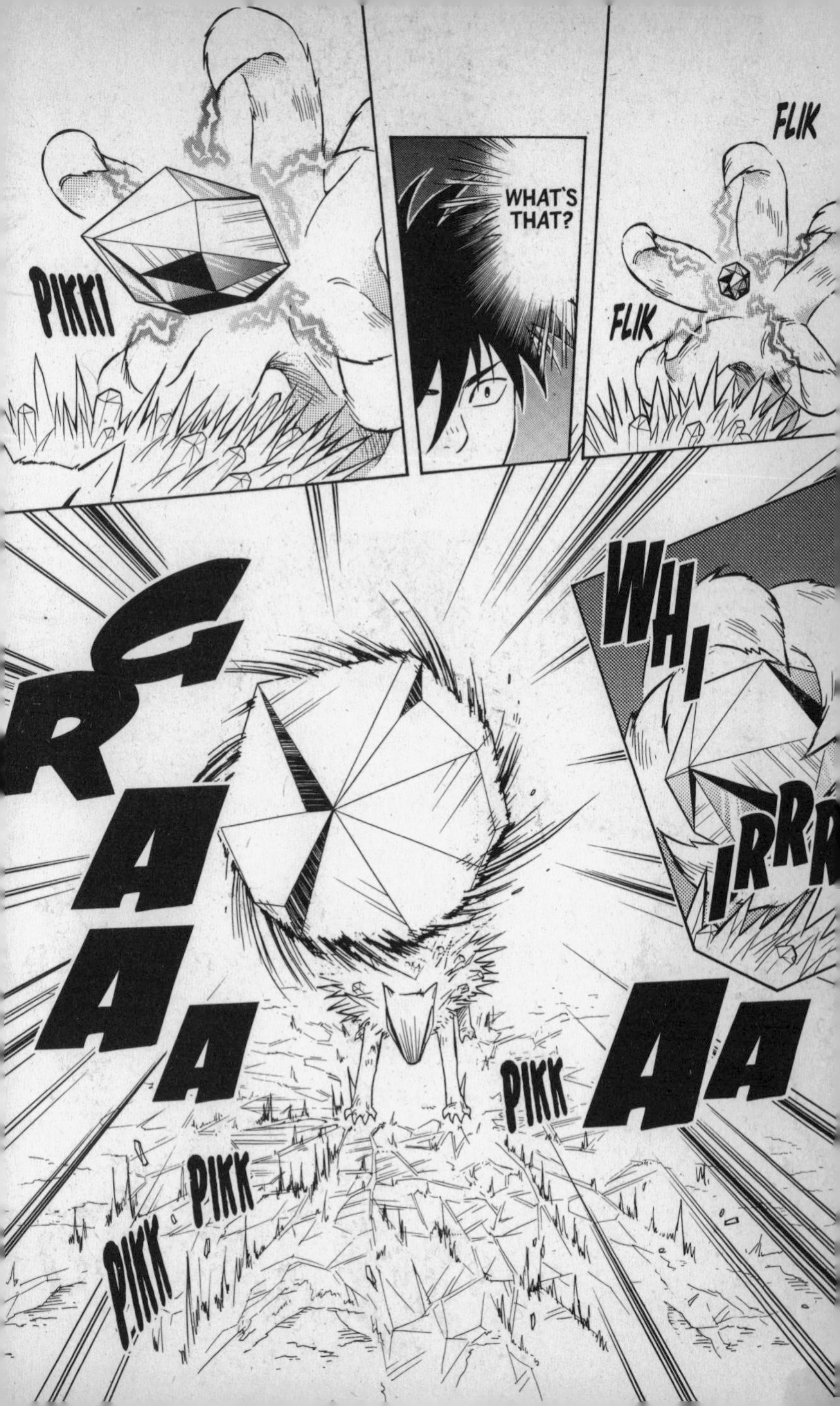
FLIK
FLIK
WHAT'S THAT?
PIKKI
WHI
IRRR
AA
PIKK
GRAAAA
PIKK
PIKK

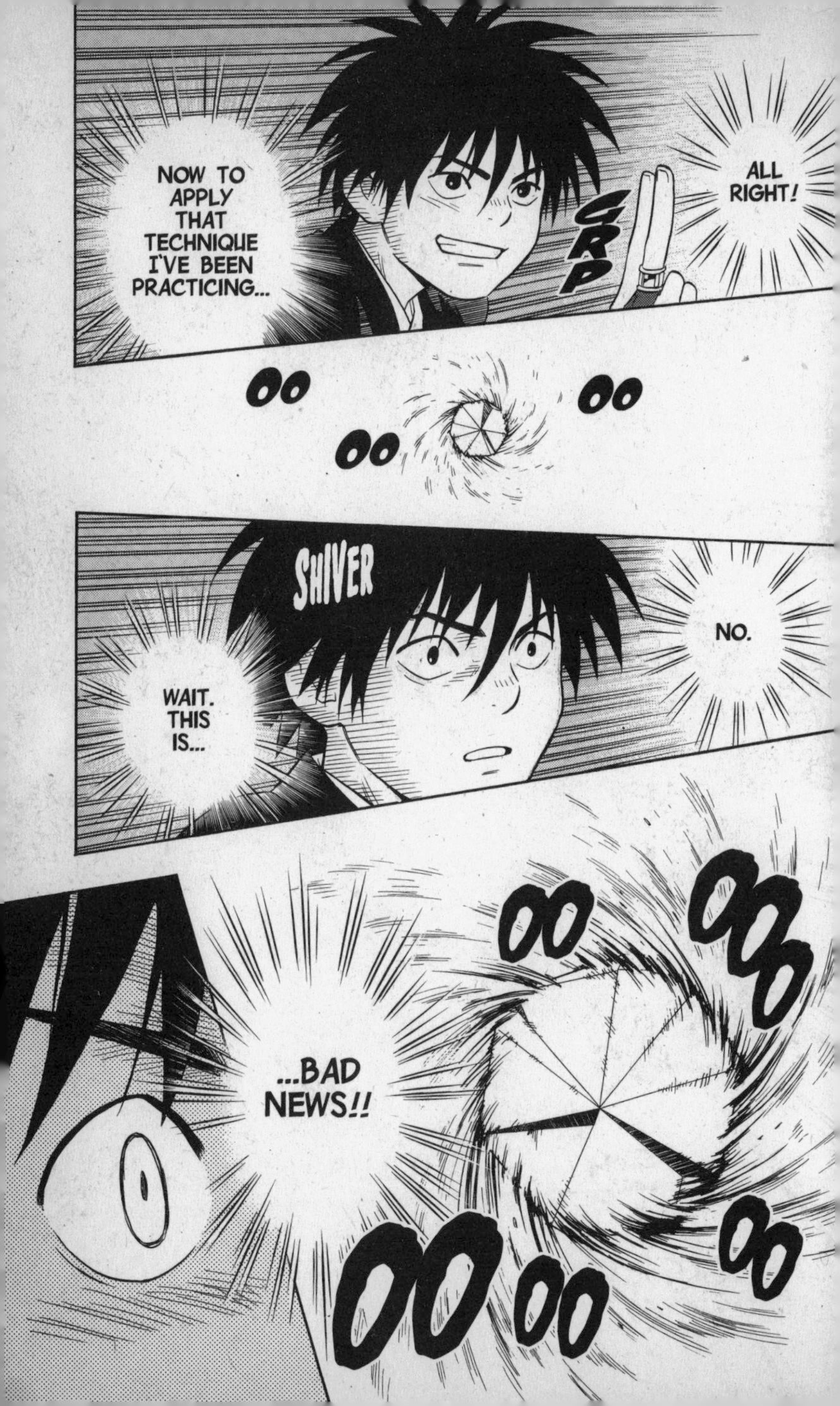
ALL RIGHT!
GRP
NOW TO APPLY THAT TECHNIQUE I'VE BEEN PRACTICING...
OO
OO
OO
NO.
SHIVER
WAIT. THIS IS...
OO
OO
OO
...BAD NEWS!!
OO
OO
OO

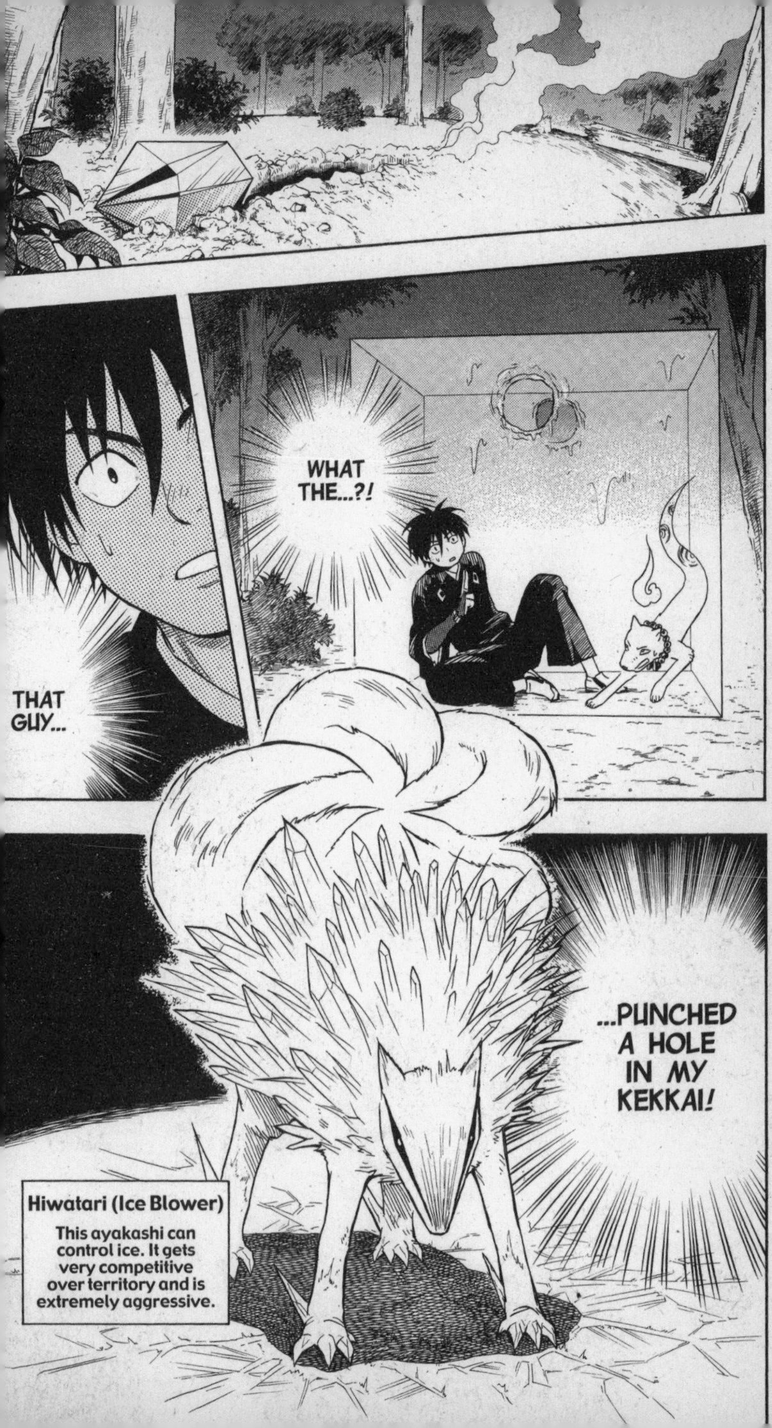
WHAT THE...?!
THAT GUY...
...PUNCHED A HOLE IN MY KEKKAI!
Hiwatari (Ice Blower)
This ayakashi can control ice. It gets very competitive over territory and is extremely aggressive.

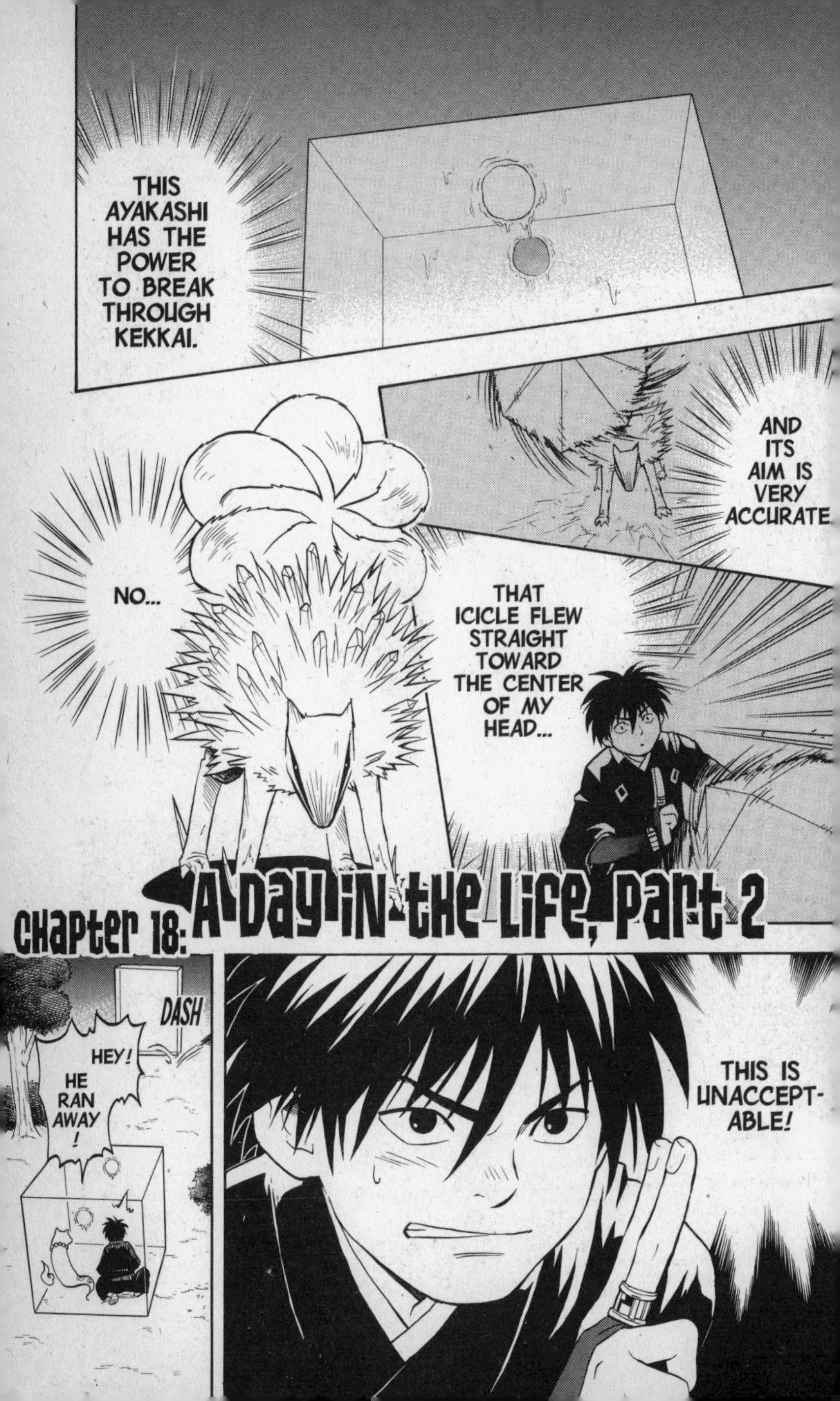
THIS AYAKASHI HAS THE POWER TO BREAK THROUGH KEKKAI.
AND ITS AIM IS VERY ACCURATE.
THAT ICICLE FLEW STRAIGHT TOWARD THE CENTER OF MY HEAD...
NO...
Chapter 18: A Day in the Life, Part 2
THIS IS UNACCEPT-ABLE!
DASH
HEY! HE RAN AWAY!

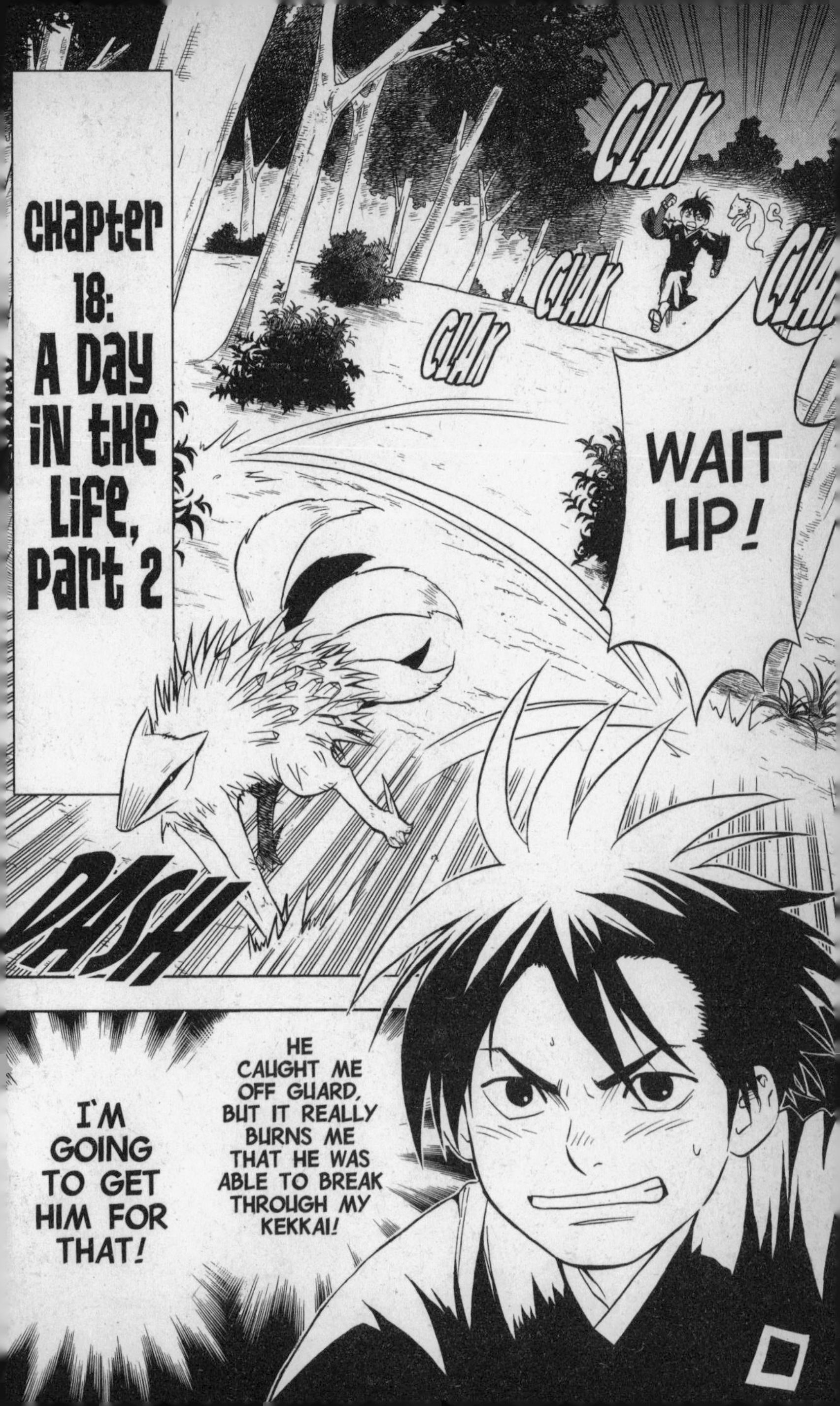
CLAK
CLAK
CLAK
CLAK
WAIT UP!
Chapter 18: A Day in the Life, Part 2
DASH
HE CAUGHT ME OFF GUARD, BUT IT REALLY BURNS ME THAT HE WAS ABLE TO BREAK THROUGH MY KEKKAI!
I'M GOING TO GET HIM FOR THAT!

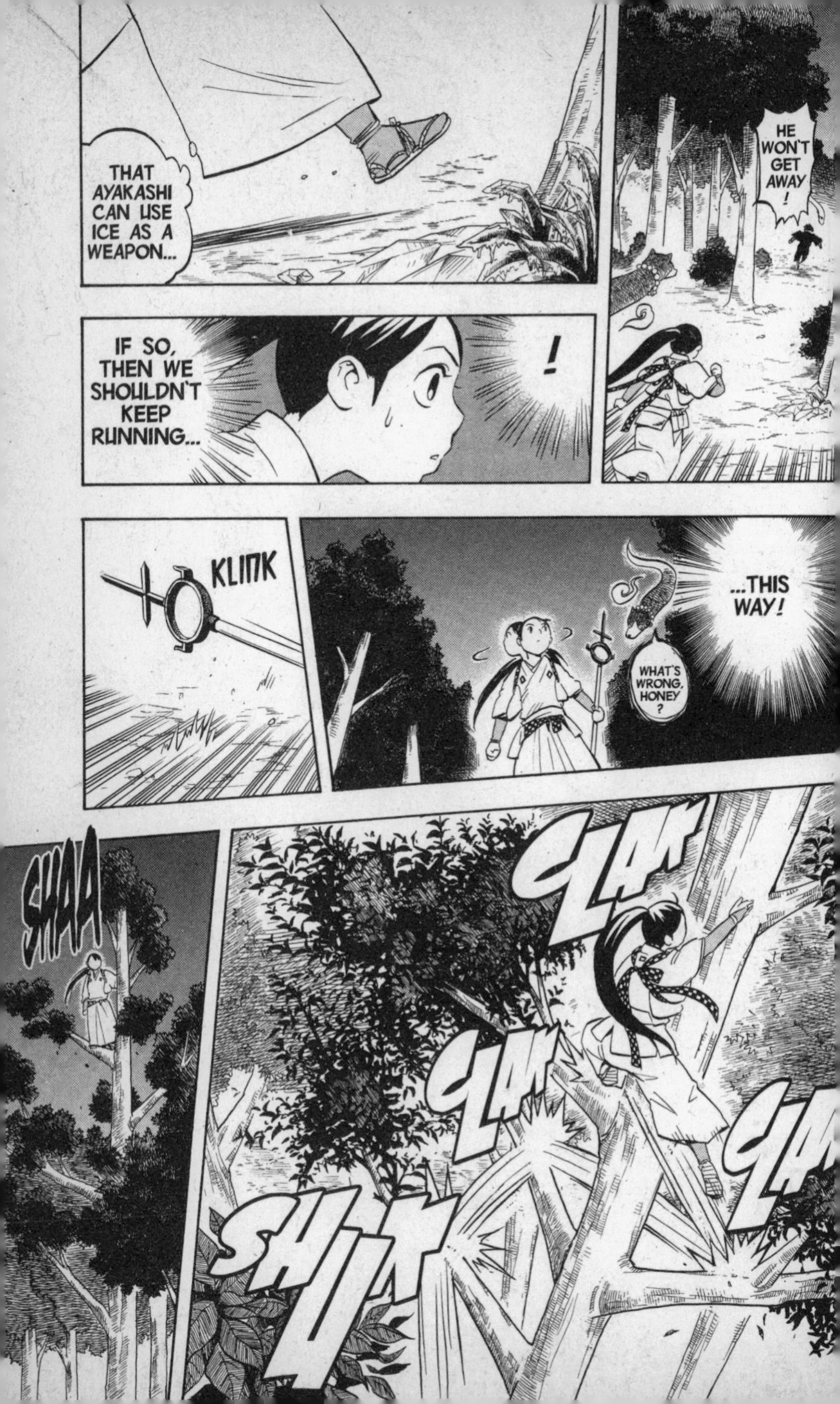

HE WON'T GET AWAY!
THAT AYAKASHI CAN USE ICE AS A WEAPON...
!
IF SO, THEN WE SHOULDN'T KEEP RUNNING...
...THIS WAY!
WHAT'S WRONG, HONEY?
KLINK
CLAK
CLAK
CLA
SHIK
SHAA

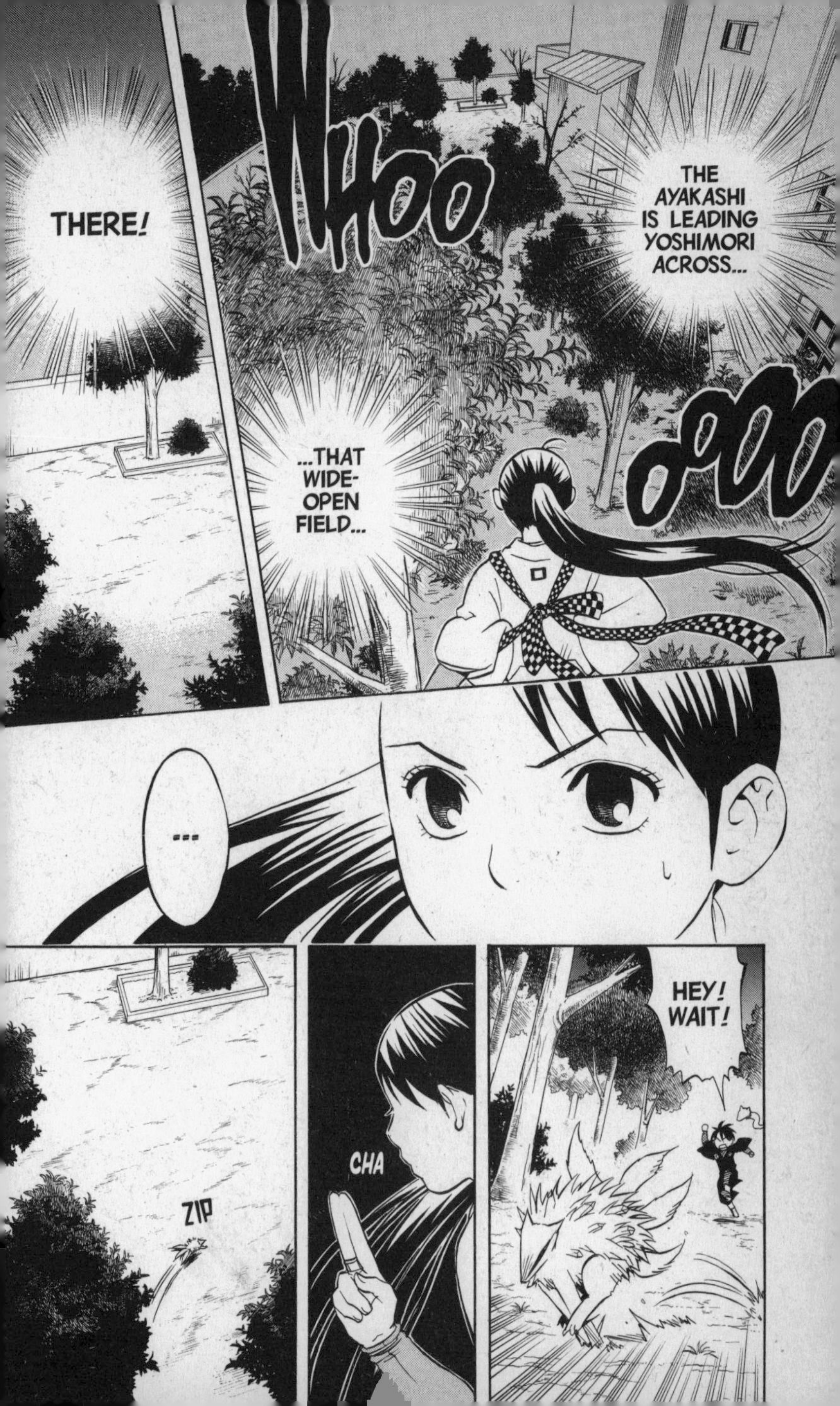
WHOOOOOO
THE AYAKASHI IS LEADING YOSHIMORI ACROSS...
...THAT WIDE-OPEN FIELD...
THERE!
...
HEY! WAIT!
CHA
ZIP

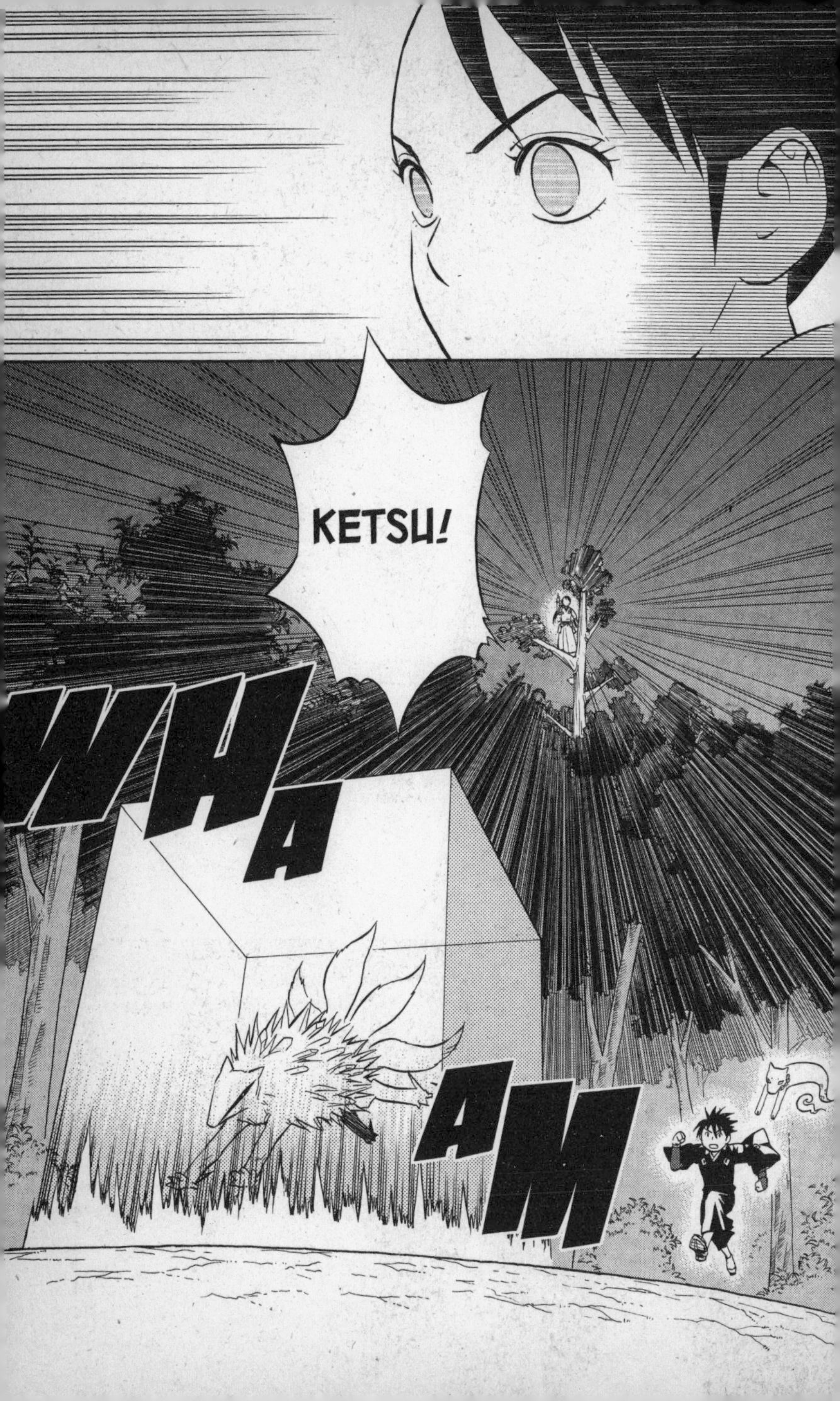
KETSU!
WHAAM

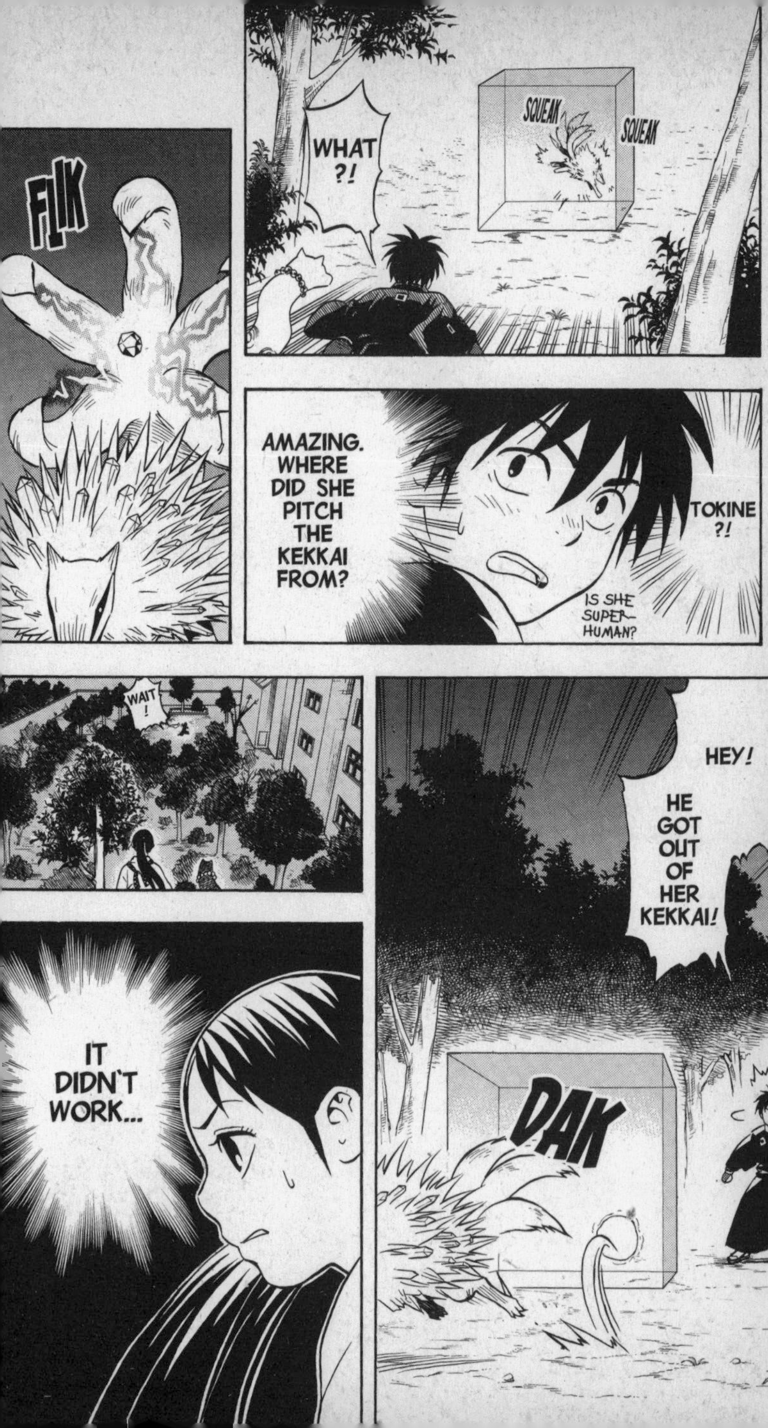
SQUEAK
SQUEAK
WHAT ?!
TOKINE ?!
AMAZING. WHERE DID SHE PITCH THE KEKKAI FROM?
IS SHE SUPER-HUMAN?
FLIK
HEY!
HE GOT OUT OF HER KEKKAI!
DAK
WAIT!
IT DIDN'T WORK...

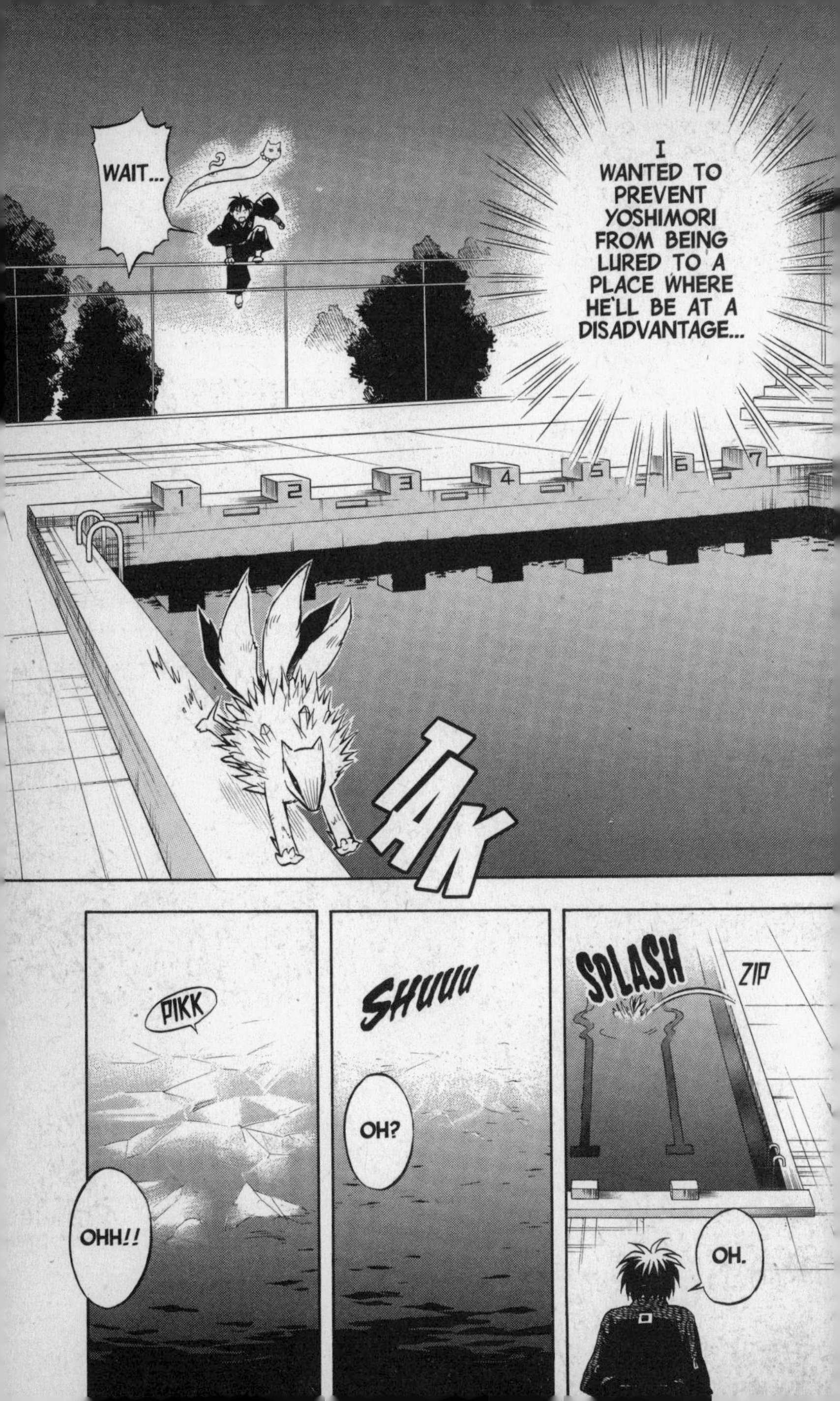
I WANTED TO PREVENT YOSHIMORI FROM BEING LURED TO A PLACE WHERE HE'LL BE AT A DISADVANTAGE...
WAIT...
TAK
SPLASH
ZIP
OH.
SHUUU
OH?
PIKK
OHH!!

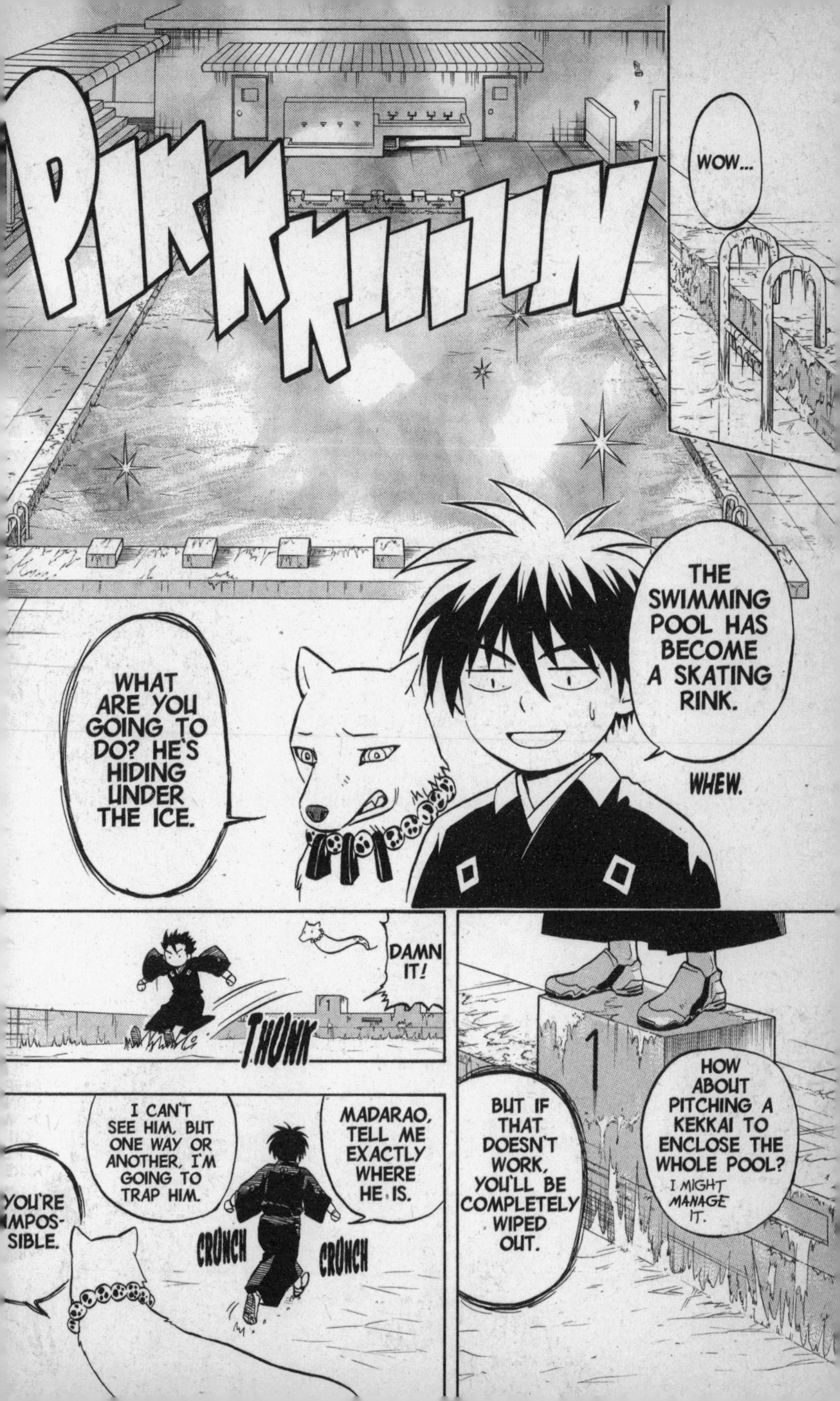
WOW...
PIKKIIIIIIN
THE SWIMMING POOL HAS BECOME A SKATING RINK.
WHEW.
WHAT ARE YOU GOING TO DO? HE'S HIDING UNDER THE ICE.
HOW ABOUT PITCHING A KEKKAI TO ENCLOSE THE WHOLE POOL?
I MIGHT MANAGE IT.
BUT IF THAT DOESN'T WORK, YOU'LL BE COMPLETELY WIPED OUT.
DAMN IT!
THUNK
MADARAO, TELL ME EXACTLY WHERE HE IS.
I CAN'T SEE HIM, BUT ONE WAY OR ANOTHER, I'M GOING TO TRAP HIM.
CRUNCH
CRUNCH
YOU'RE IMPOSSIBLE.

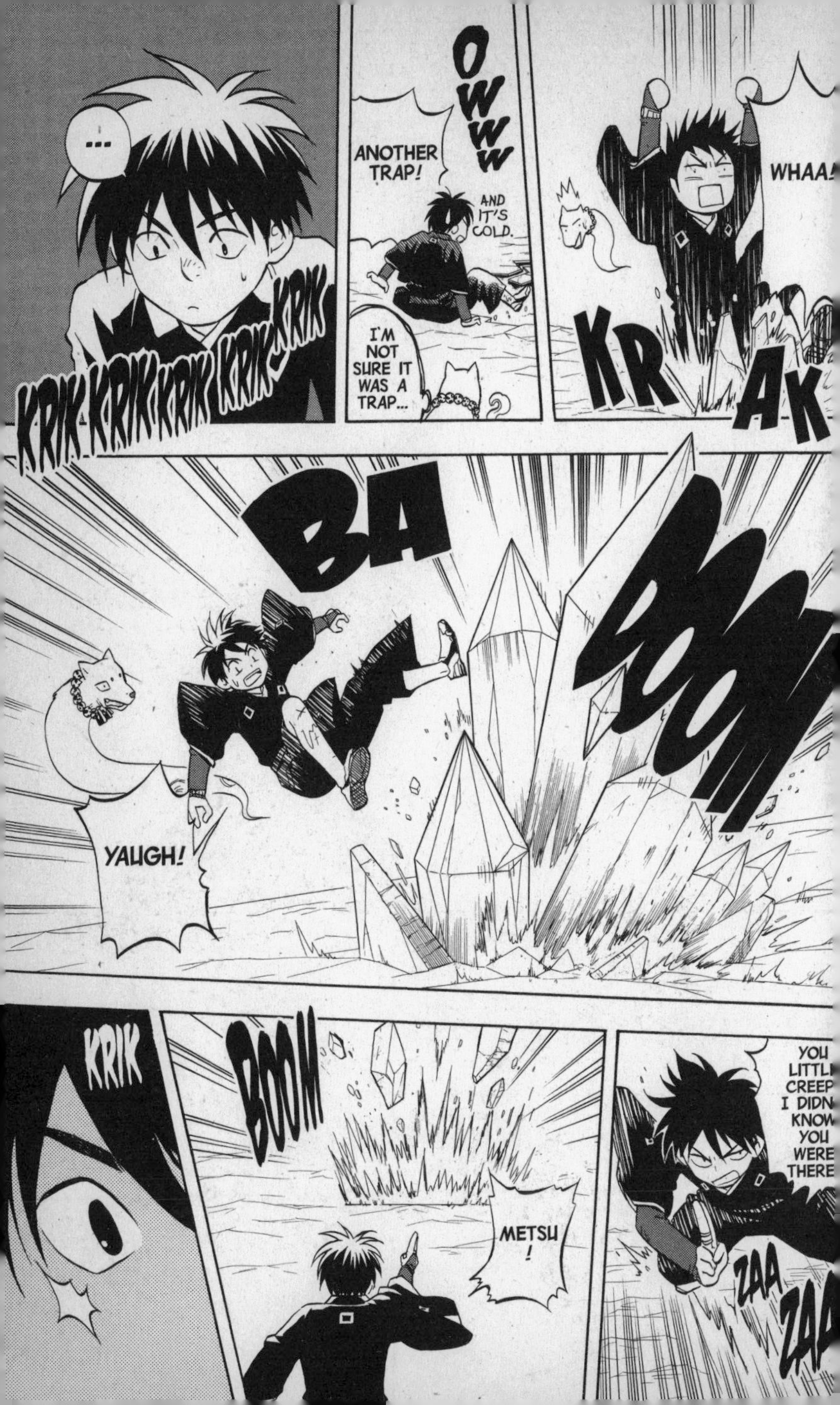

WHAA!
KR AK
OWWW
ANOTHER TRAP!
AND IT'S COLD.
I'M NOT SURE IT WAS A TRAP...
...
KRIK KRIK KRIK KRIK KRIK KRIK
BA BOOM
YAUGH!
YOU LITTL CREEP I DIDN KNOW YOU WERE THERE
ZAA ZAA
BOOM
METSU!
KRIK

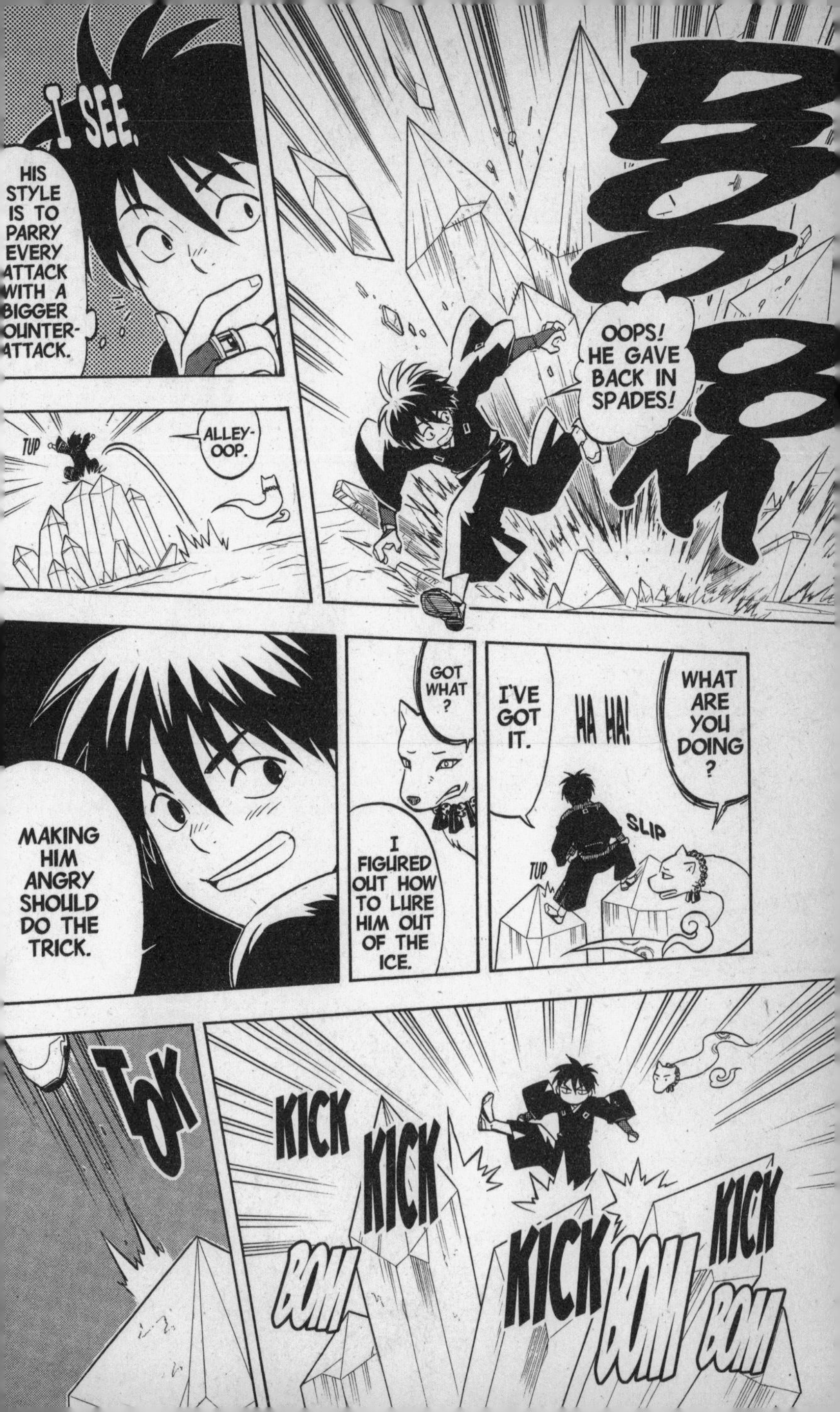
BOOM
OOPS! HE GAVE BACK IN SPADES!
I SEE.
HIS STYLE IS TO PARRY EVERY ATTACK WITH A BIGGER OUNTER-ATTACK.
TUP
ALLEY-OOP.
WHAT ARE YOU DOING?
HA HA!
I'VE GOT IT.
SLIP
TUP
GOT WHAT?
I FIGURED OUT HOW TO LURE HIM OUT OF THE ICE.
MAKING HIM ANGRY SHOULD DO THE TRICK.
KICK
KICK
KICK
KICK
BOM
BOM
BOM
BOM
TOK

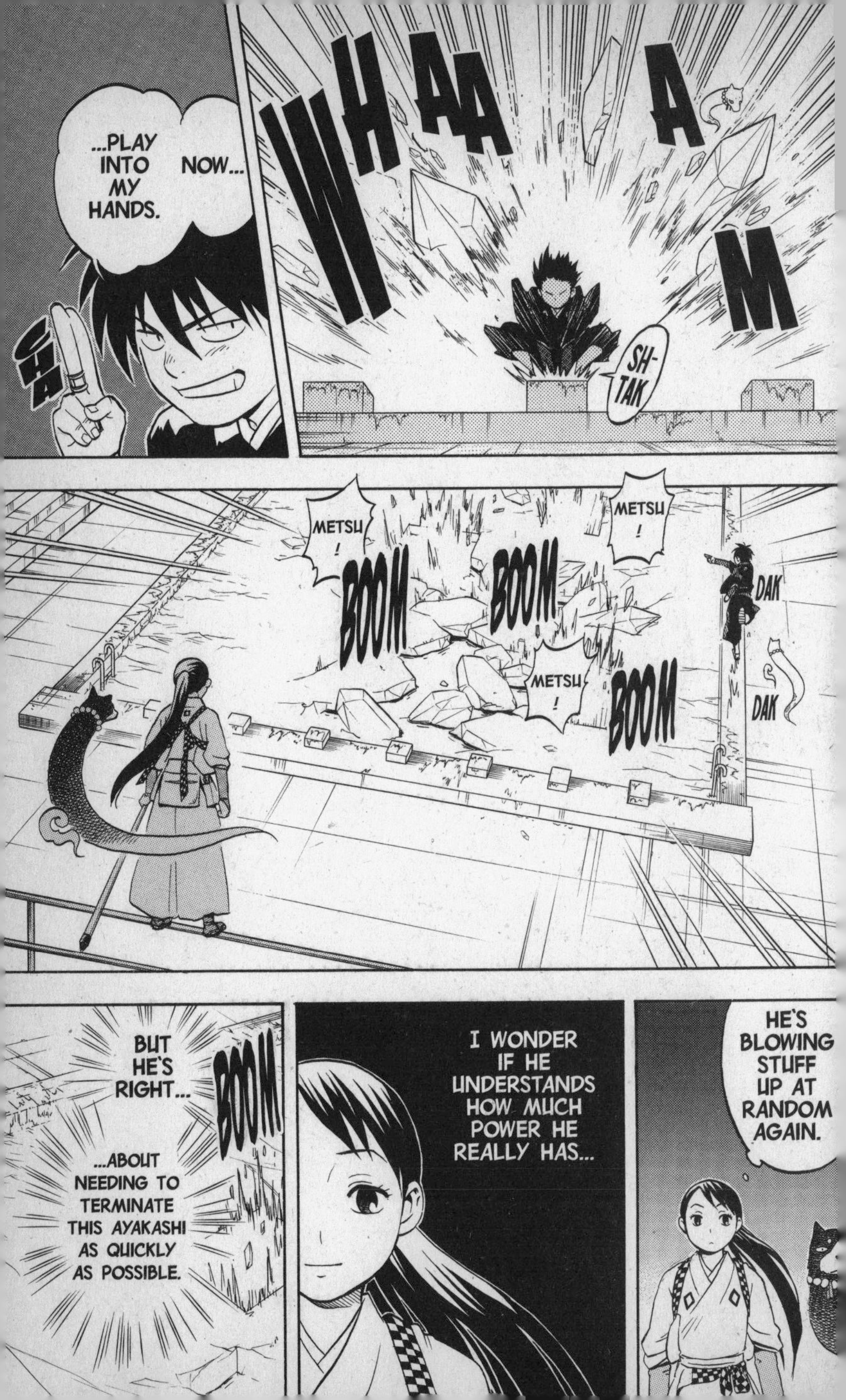
WHAAAAM
SH-TAK
NOW... ...PLAY INTO MY HANDS.
CHA
METSU!
DAK
DAK
BOOM
METSU!
BOOM
METSU!
BOOM
HE'S BLOWING STUFF UP AT RANDOM AGAIN.
I WONDER IF HE UNDERSTANDS HOW MUCH POWER HE REALLY HAS...
BUT HE'S RIGHT...
BOOM
...ABOUT NEEDING TO TERMINATE THIS AYAKASHI AS QUICKLY AS POSSIBLE.

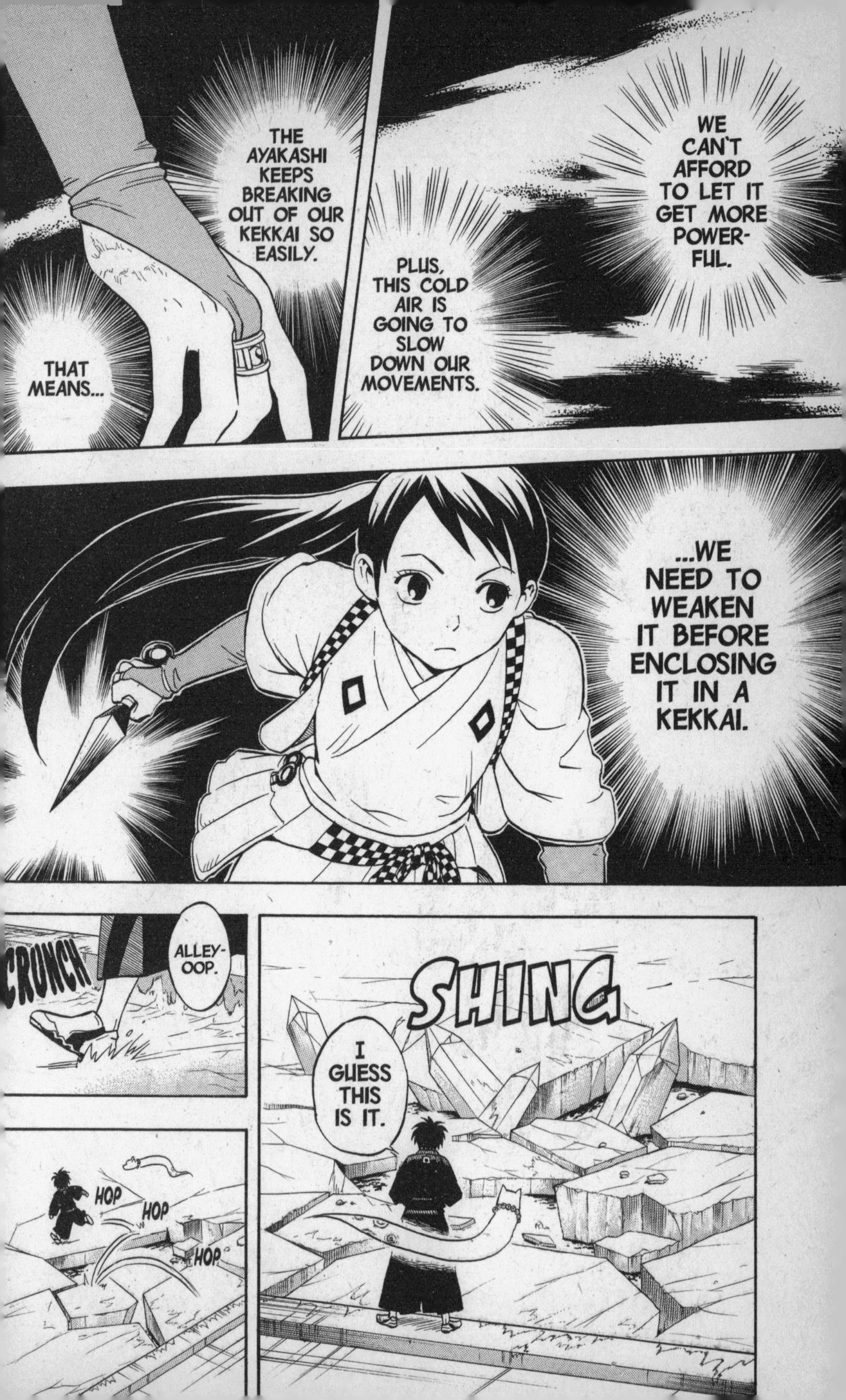
WE CAN'T AFFORD TO LET IT GET MORE POWER-FUL.
PLUS, THIS COLD AIR IS GOING TO SLOW DOWN OUR MOVEMENTS.
THE AYAKASHI KEEPS BREAKING OUT OF OUR KEKKAI SO EASILY.
THAT MEANS...
...WE NEED TO WEAKEN IT BEFORE ENCLOSING IT IN A KEKKAI.
SHING
I GUESS THIS IS IT.
ALLEY-OOP.
CRUNCH
HOP
HOP
HOP

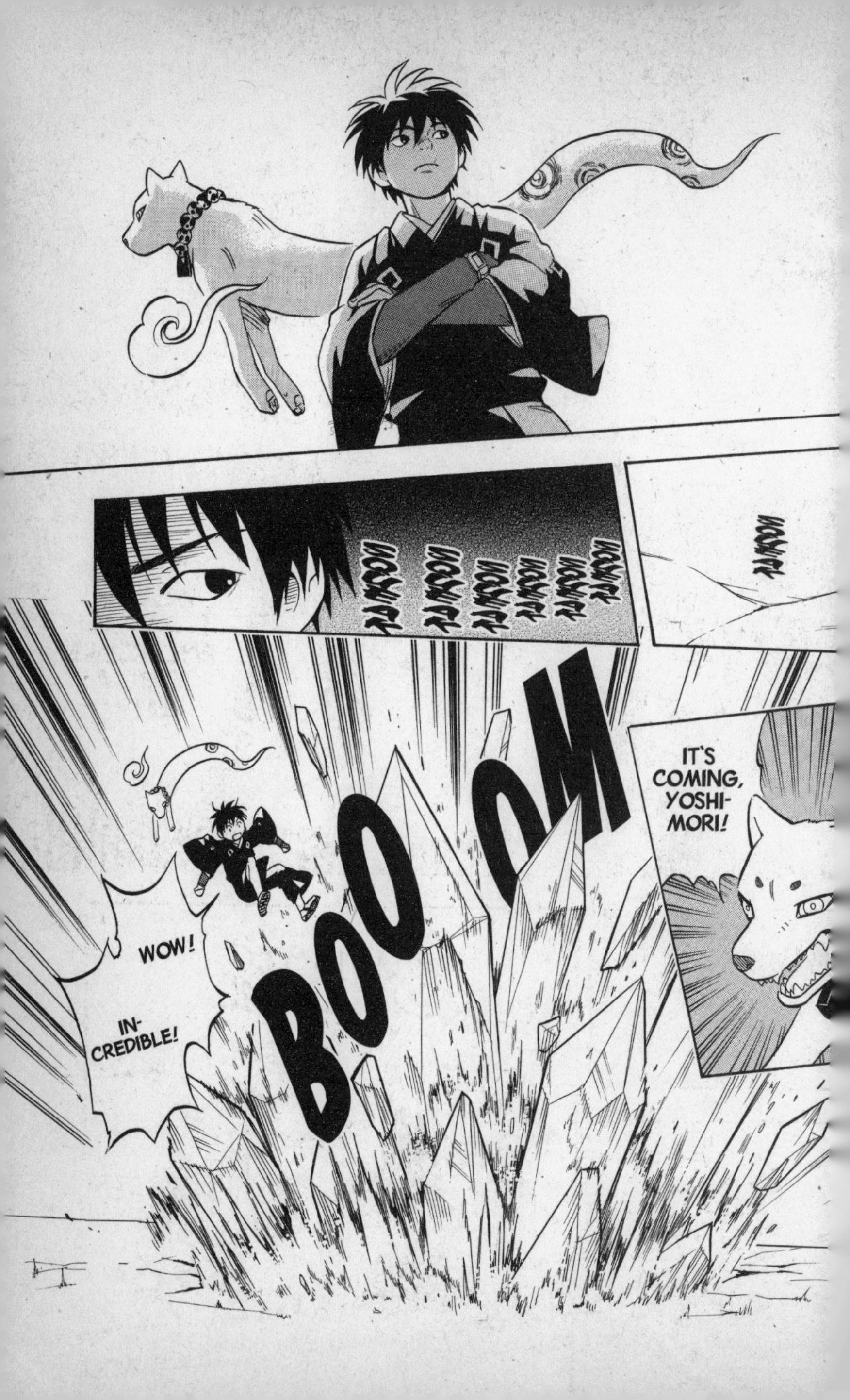
IT'S COMING, YOSHI-MORI!
BOOOM
WOW!
IN-CREDIBLE!

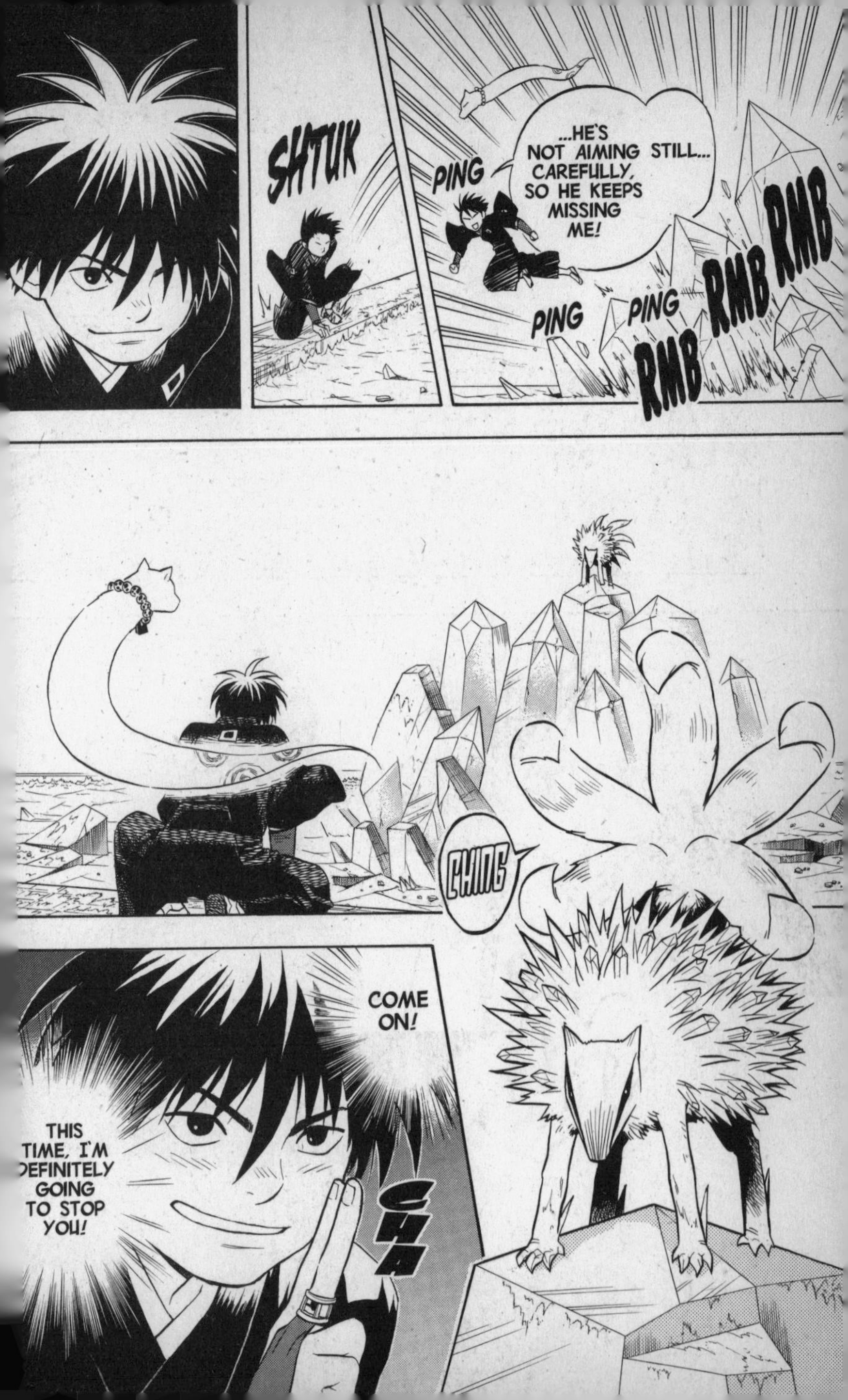
PING
...HE'S NOT AIMING STILL... CAREFULLY, SO HE KEEPS MISSING ME!
PING
PING
RMB RMB RMB
SHTUK
CHING
COME ON!
THIS TIME, I'M DEFINITELY GOING TO STOP YOU!
CHA

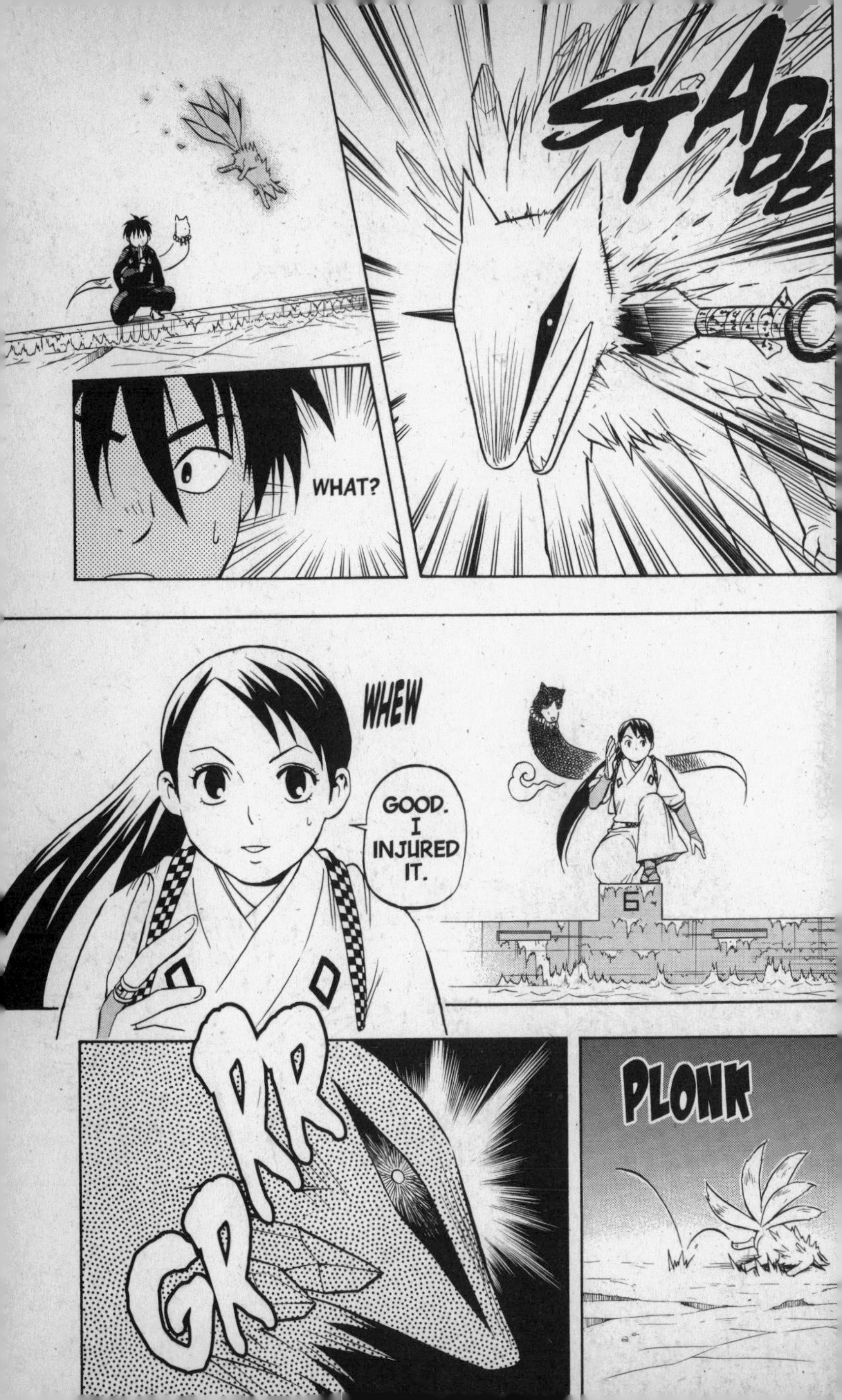
STABB
WHAT?
WHEW
GOOD. I INJURED IT.
PLONK
GRR
GR

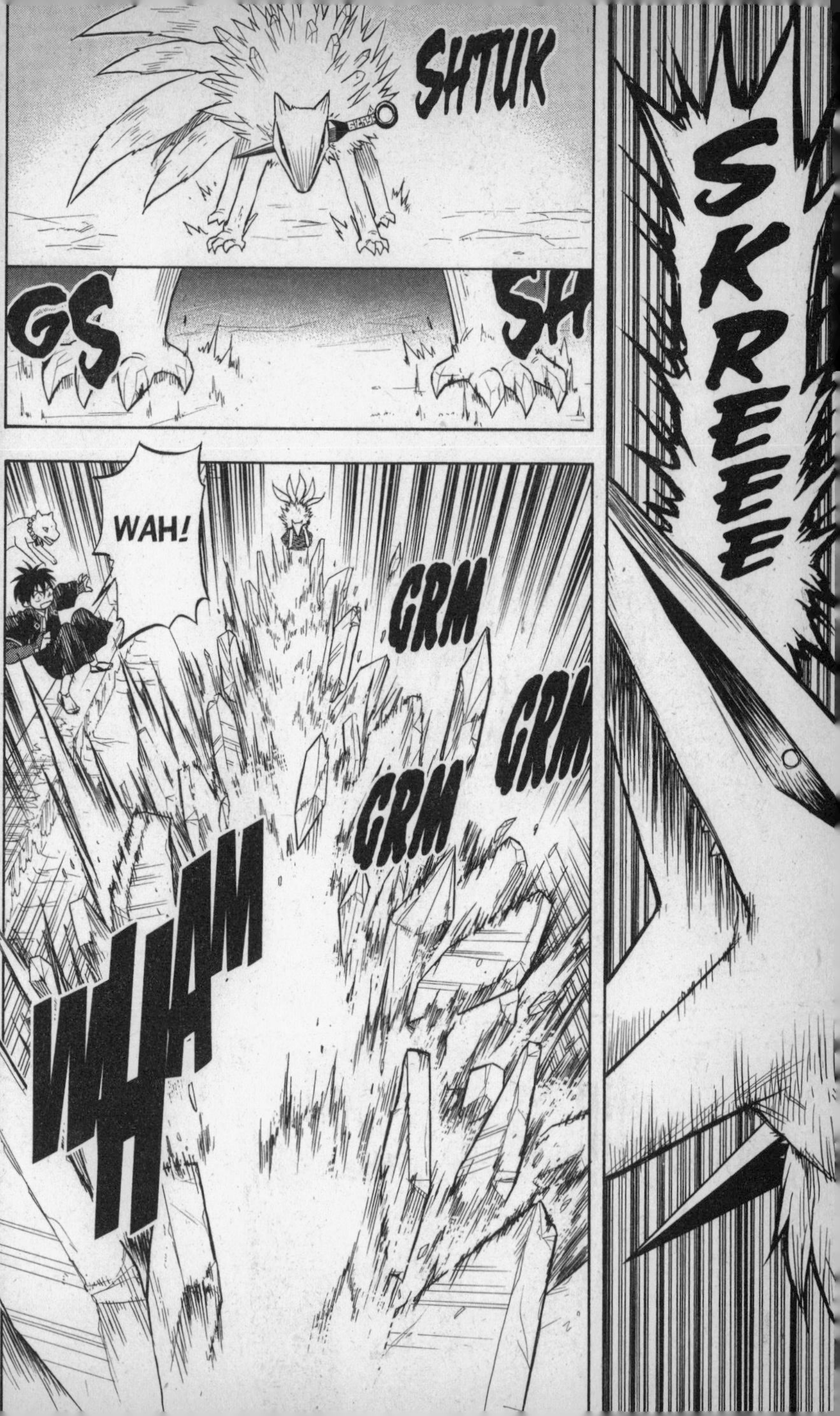
SKREEE
SHTUK
SH
GS
WAH!
GRM
GRM
GRM
WHAM

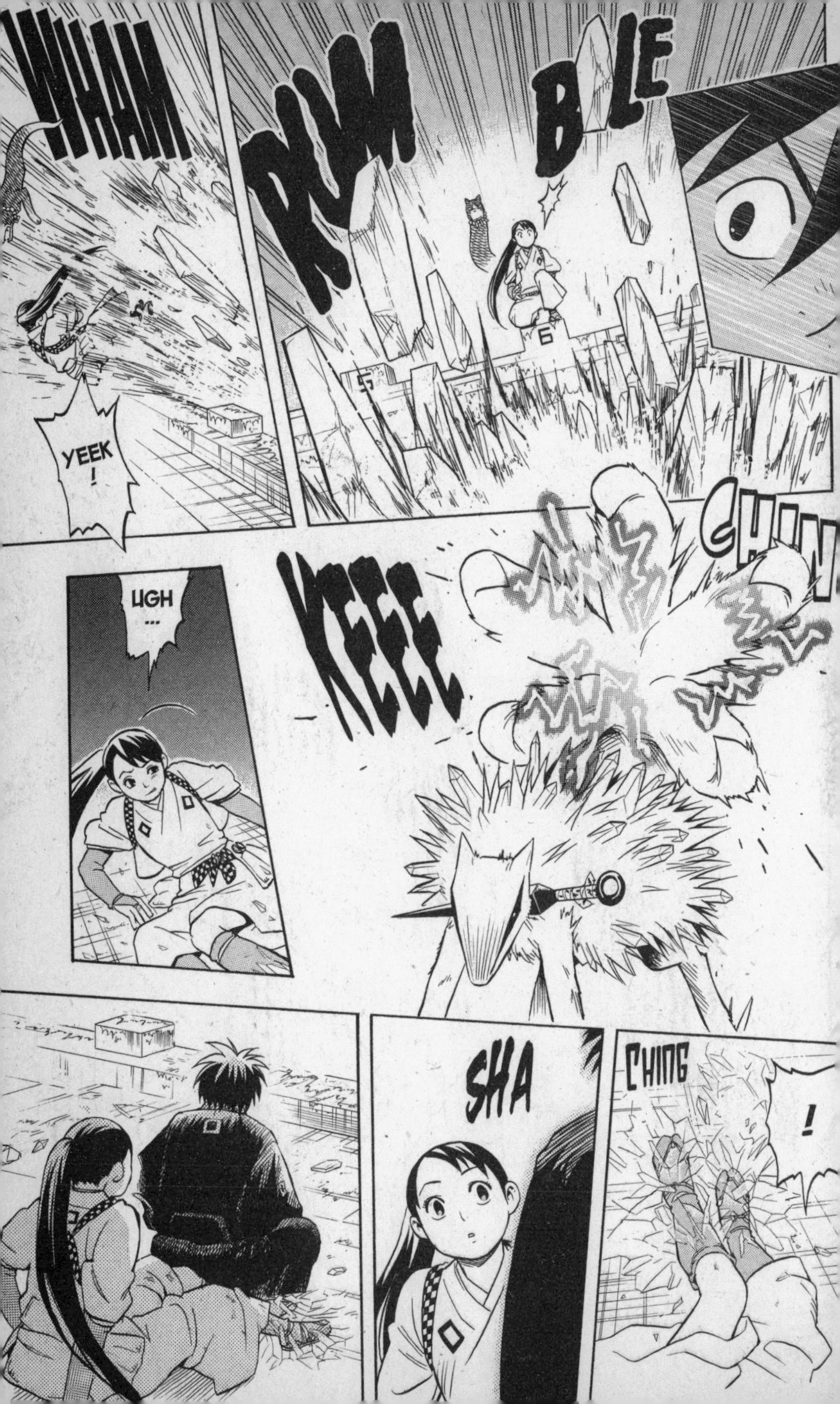
RUMBLE
WHAM
YEEK !
CHIN
KEEE
UGH ...
CHING
!
SHA

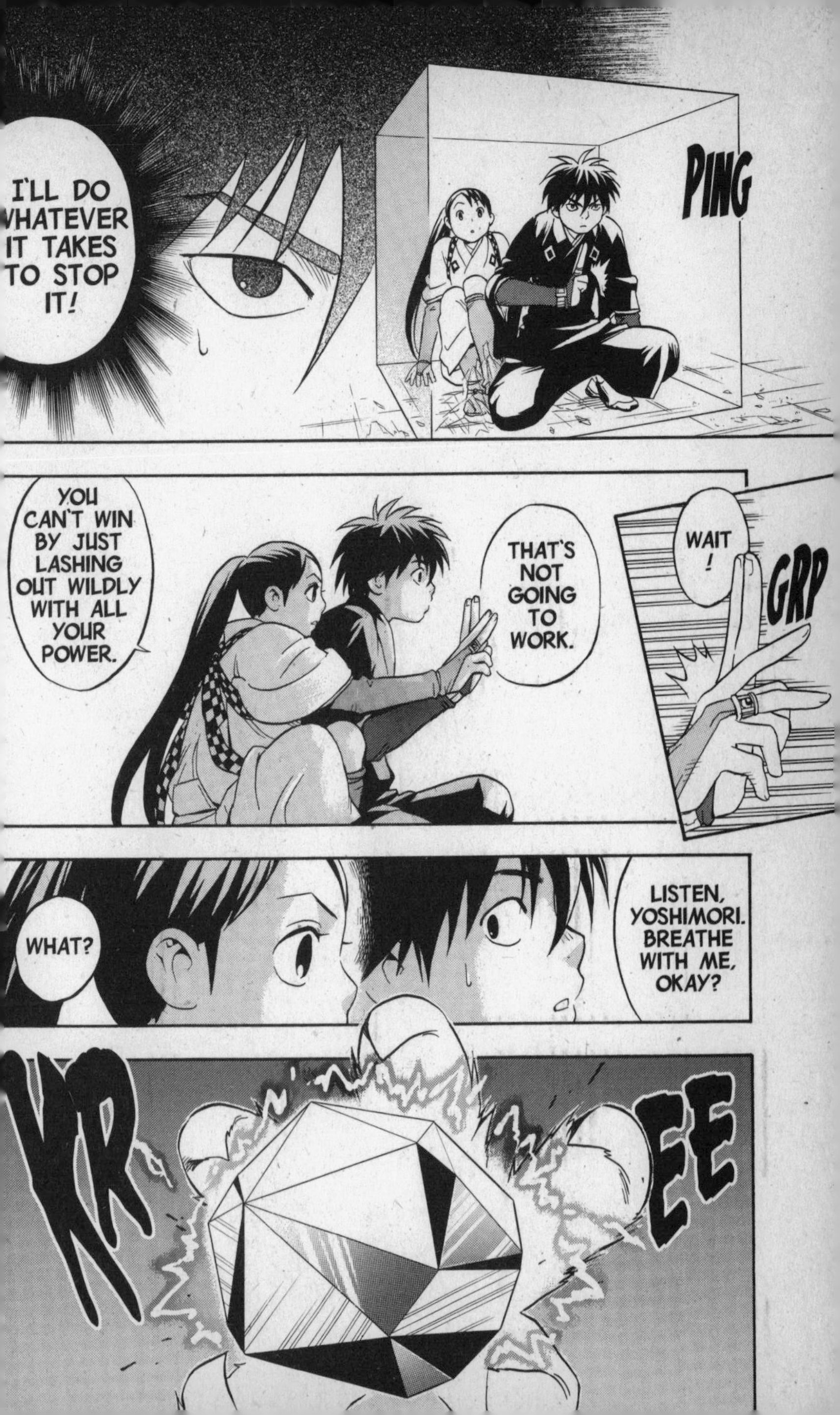
PING
I'LL DO WHATEVER IT TAKES TO STOP IT!
WAIT!
GRP
THAT'S NOT GOING TO WORK.
YOU CAN'T WIN BY JUST LASHING OUT WILDLY WITH ALL YOUR POWER.
LISTEN, YOSHIMORI. BREATHE WITH ME, OKAY?
WHAT?
KR
EE

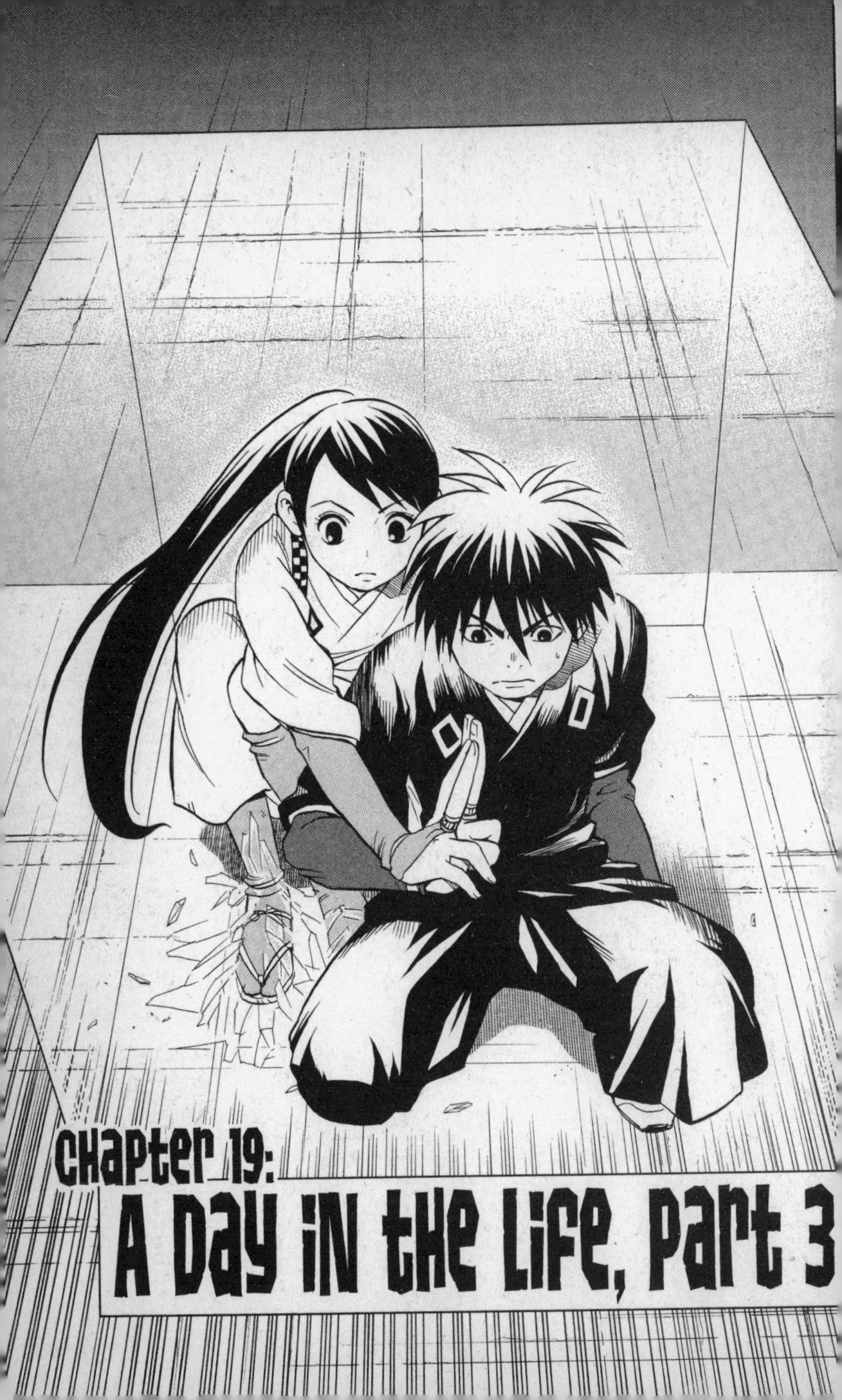

Chapter 19:
A Day in the Life, Part 3

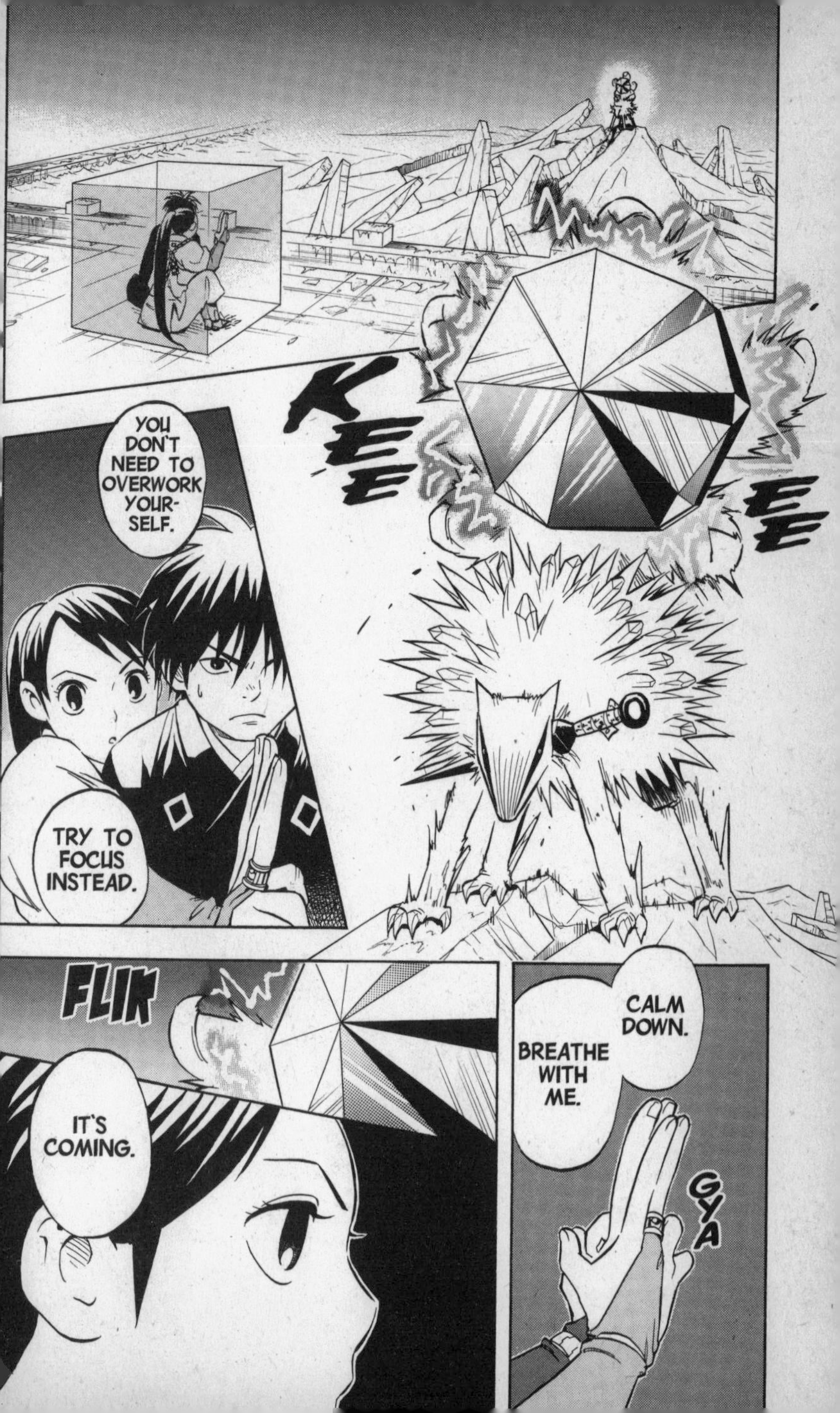

KEE
EE
YOU DON'T NEED TO OVERWORK YOUR-SELF.
TRY TO FOCUS INSTEAD.
CALM DOWN.
BREATHE WITH ME.
GYA
FLIK
IT'S COMING.

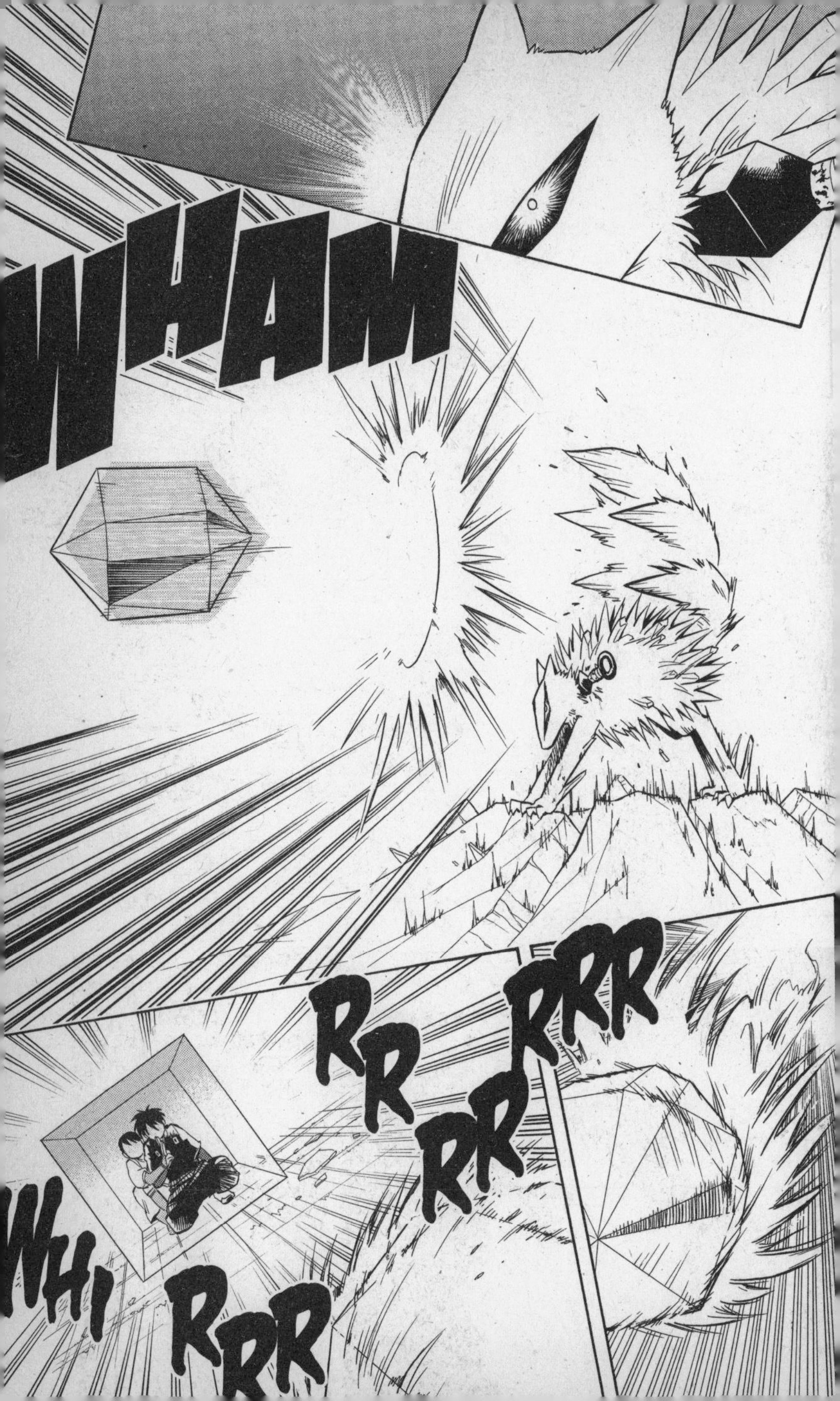
WHAM
RRRRRRR
WHI RRR

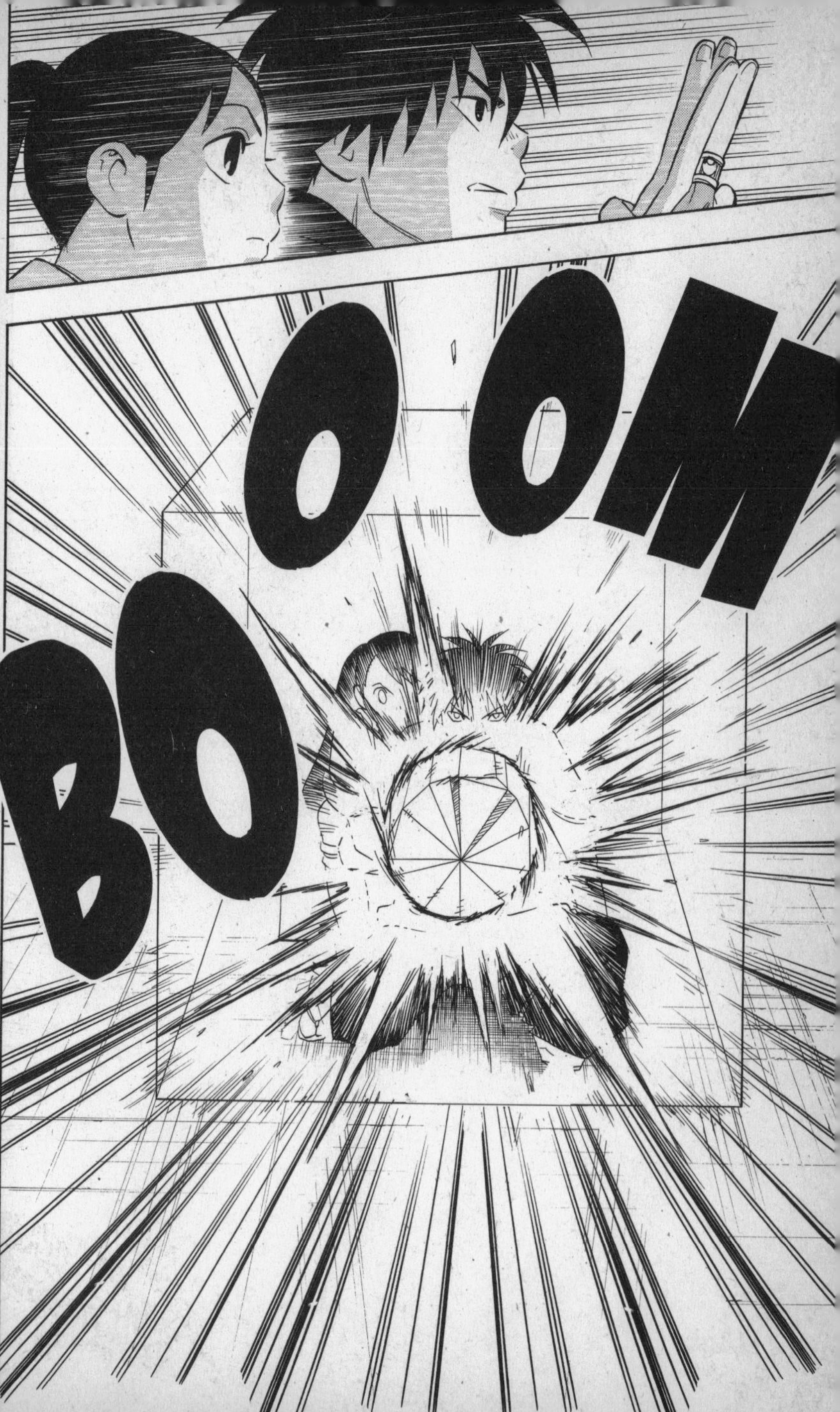
BOOOOM!

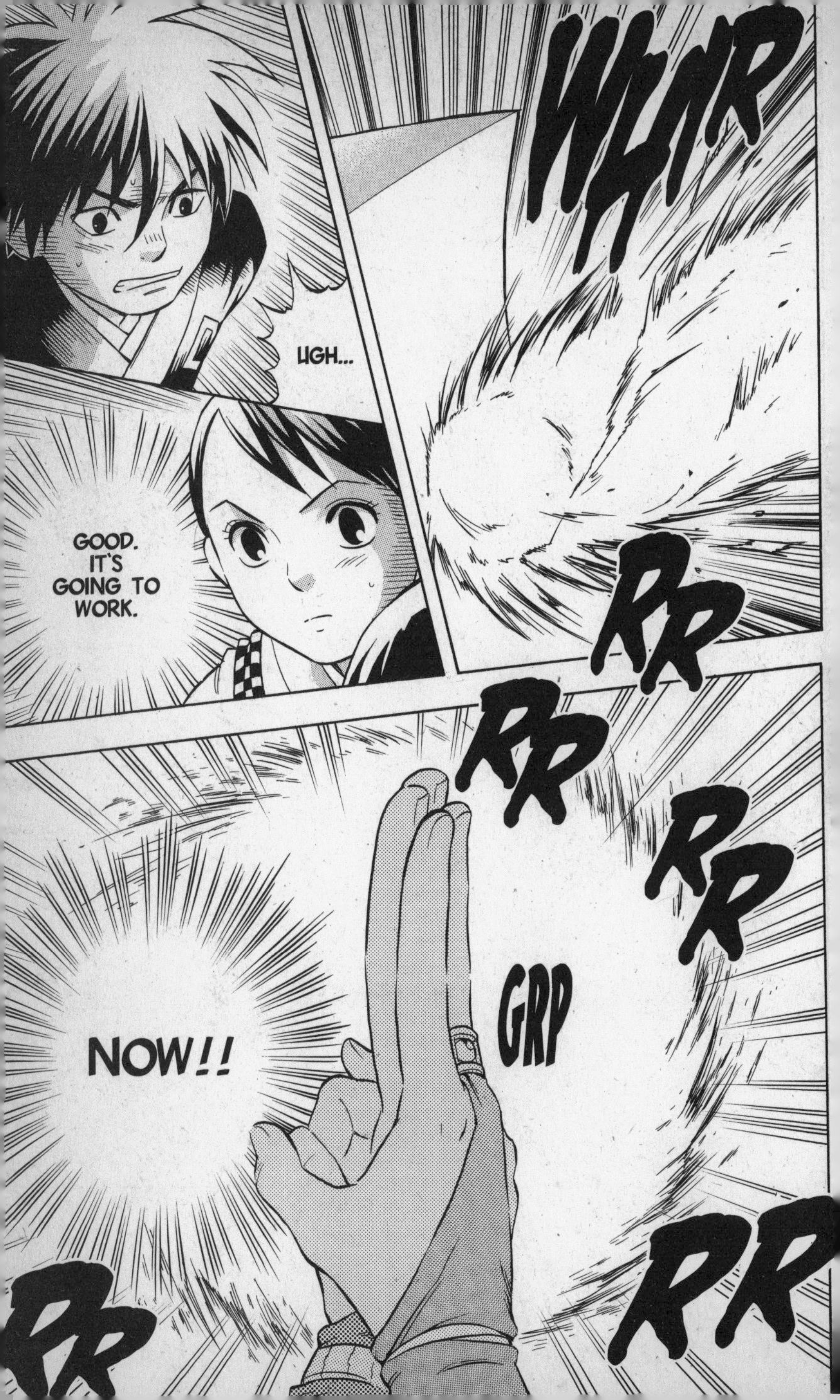
WHIR
RR
UGH...
GOOD. IT'S GOING TO WORK.
RR
RR
GRP
NOW!!
RR
RR

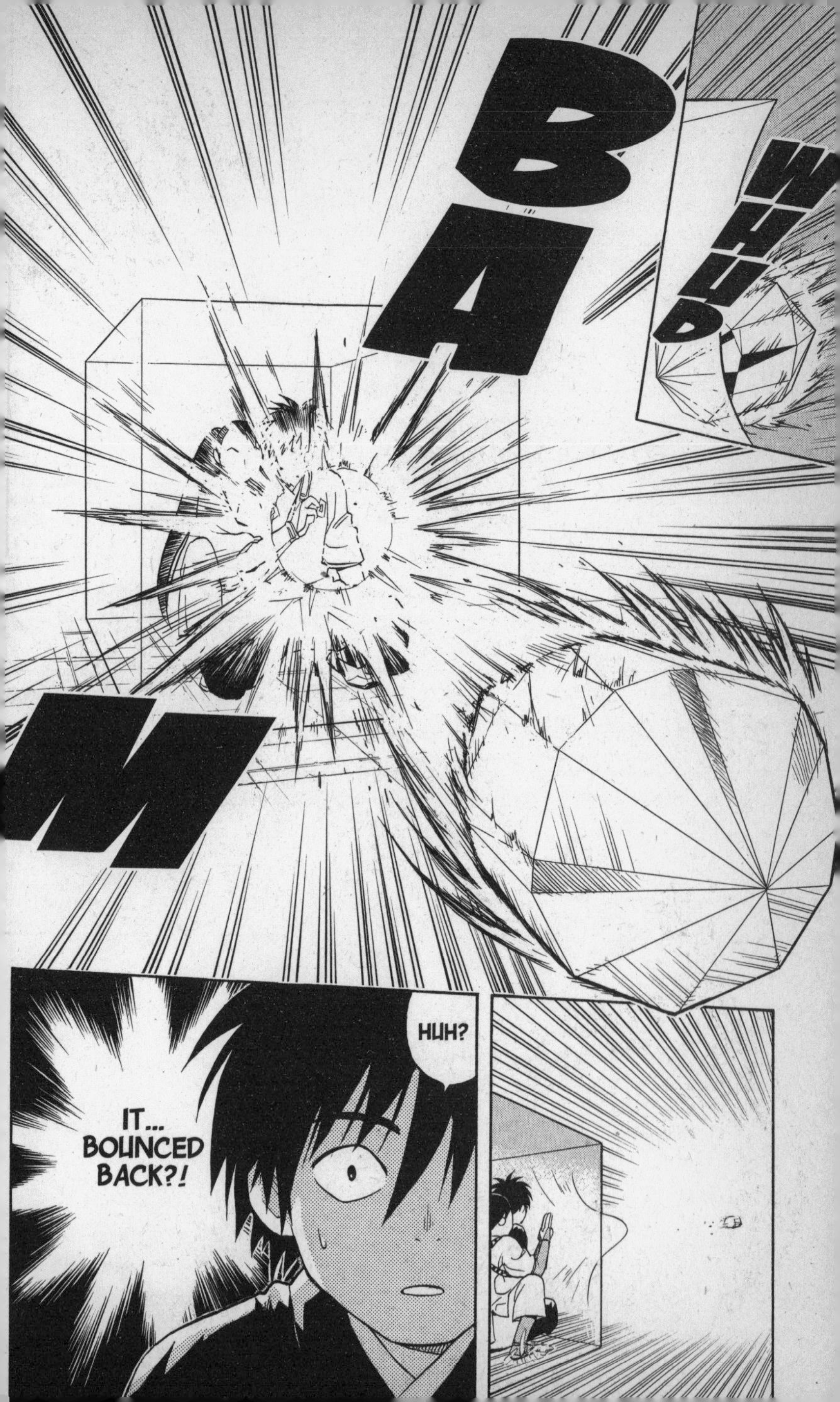
WHUD
BAM
HUH?
IT... BOUNCED BACK?!

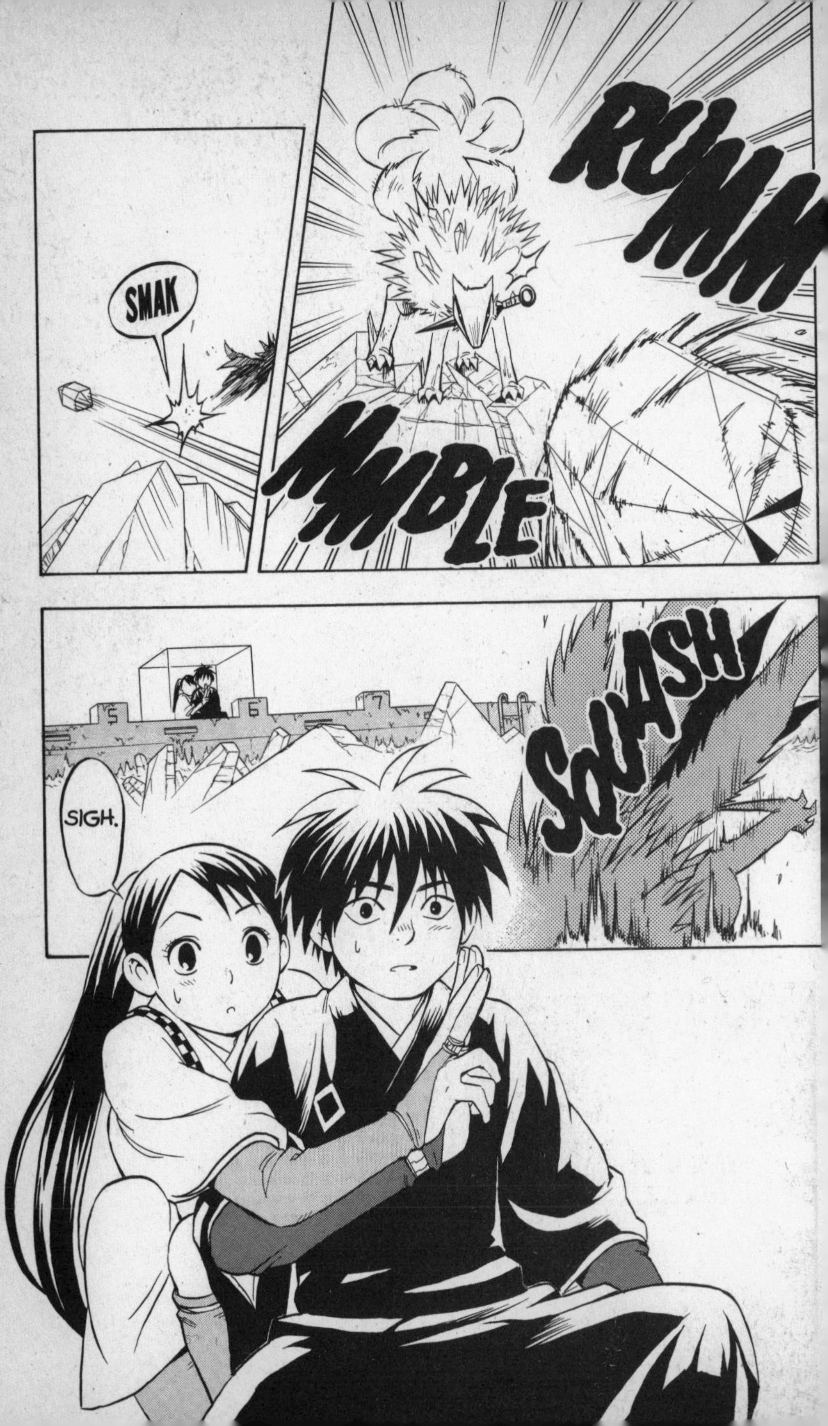
RUMMMBLE
SMAK
SQUASH
SIGH.

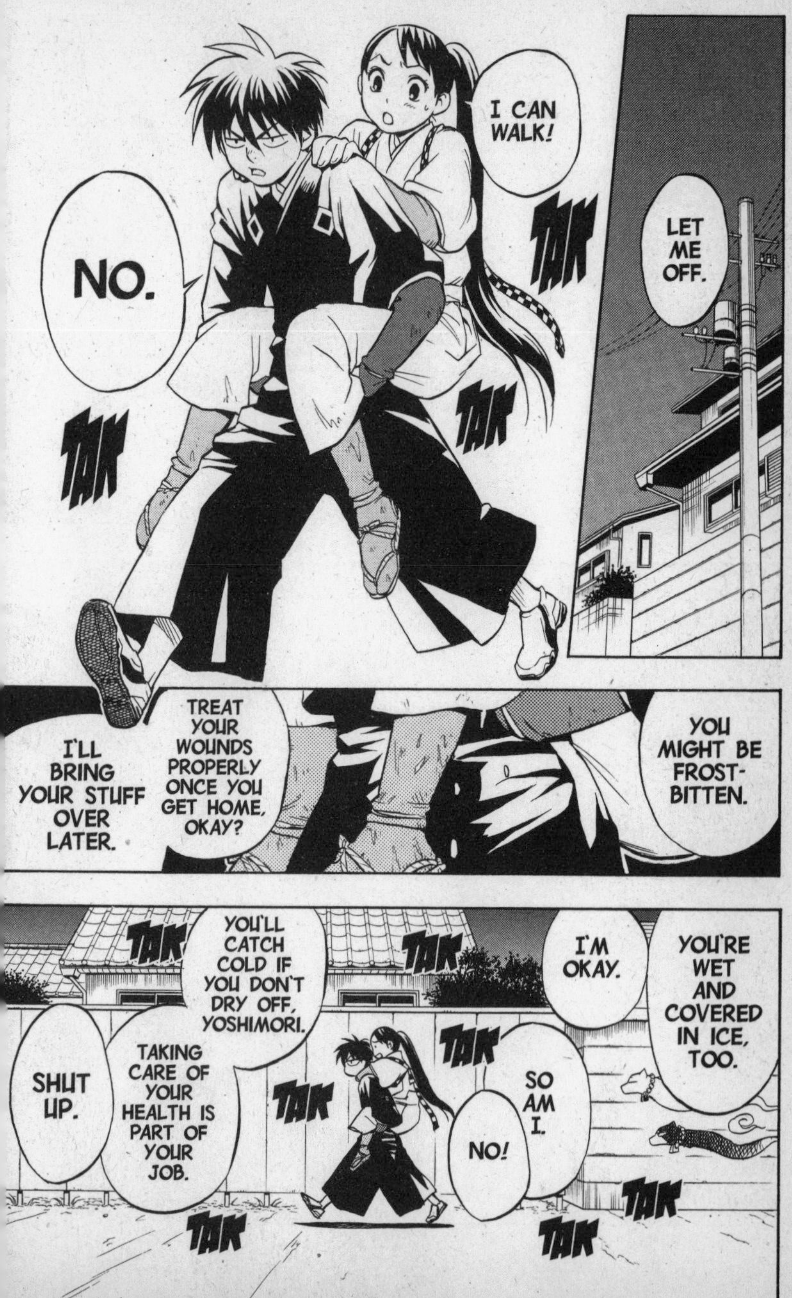
I CAN WALK!
LET ME OFF.
TAK
NO.
TAK
TAK
YOU MIGHT BE FROST-BITTEN.
TREAT YOUR WOUNDS PROPERLY ONCE YOU GET HOME, OKAY?
I'LL BRING YOUR STUFF OVER LATER.
YOU'RE WET AND COVERED IN ICE, TOO.
I'M OKAY.
TAK
SO AM I.
NO!
TAK
YOU'LL CATCH COLD IF YOU DON'T DRY OFF, YOSHIMORI.
TAK
TAKING CARE OF YOUR HEALTH IS PART OF YOUR JOB.
SHUT UP.
TAK
TAK
TAK
TAK

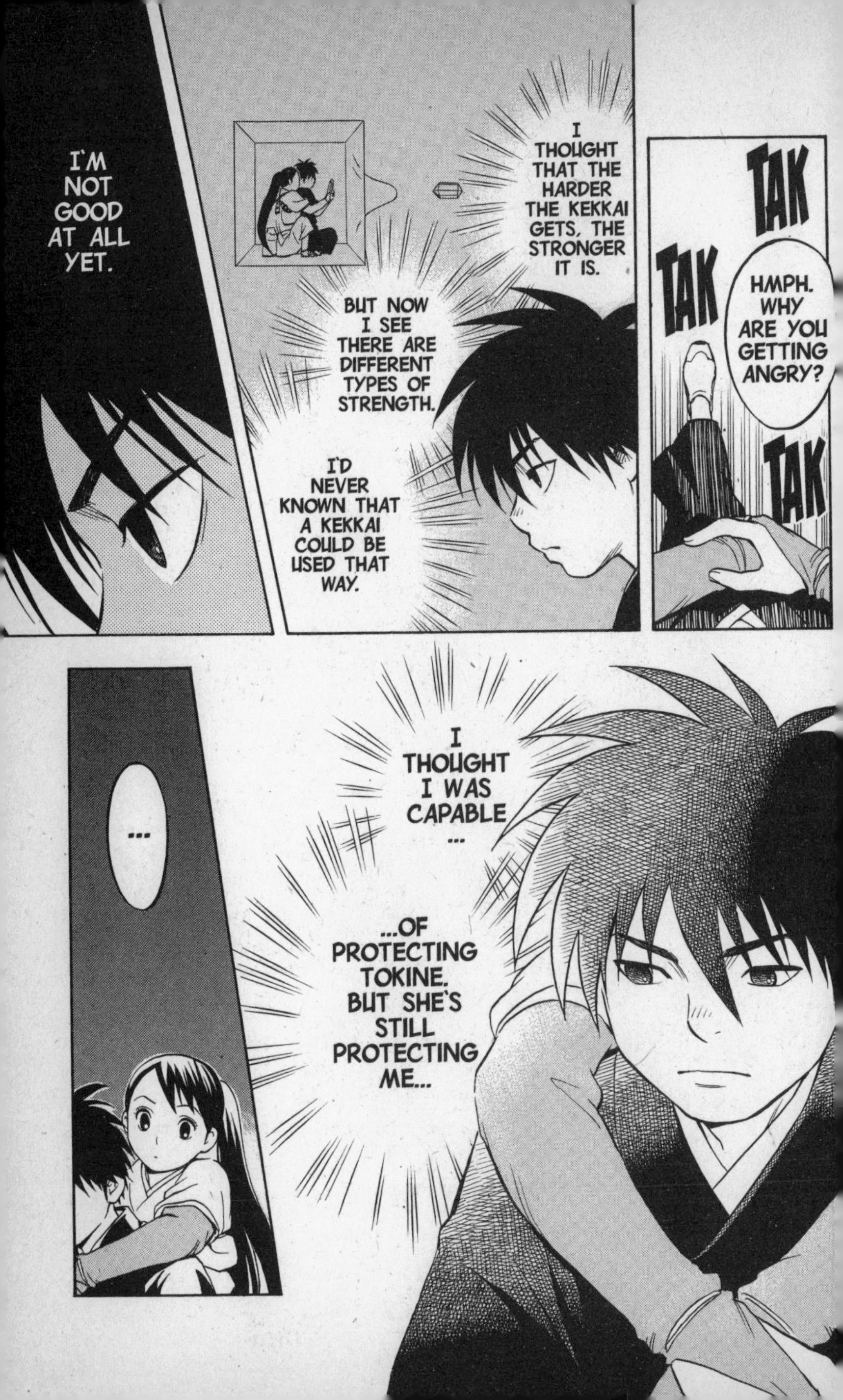
TAK
TAK
HMPH. WHY ARE YOU GETTING ANGRY?
TAK
I THOUGHT THAT THE HARDER THE KEKKAI GETS, THE STRONGER IT IS.
BUT NOW I SEE THERE ARE DIFFERENT TYPES OF STRENGTH.
I'D NEVER KNOWN THAT A KEKKAI COULD BE USED THAT WAY.
I'M NOT GOOD AT ALL YET.
I THOUGHT I WAS CAPABLE ...
...OF PROTECTING TOKINE. BUT SHE'S STILL PROTECTING ME...
...

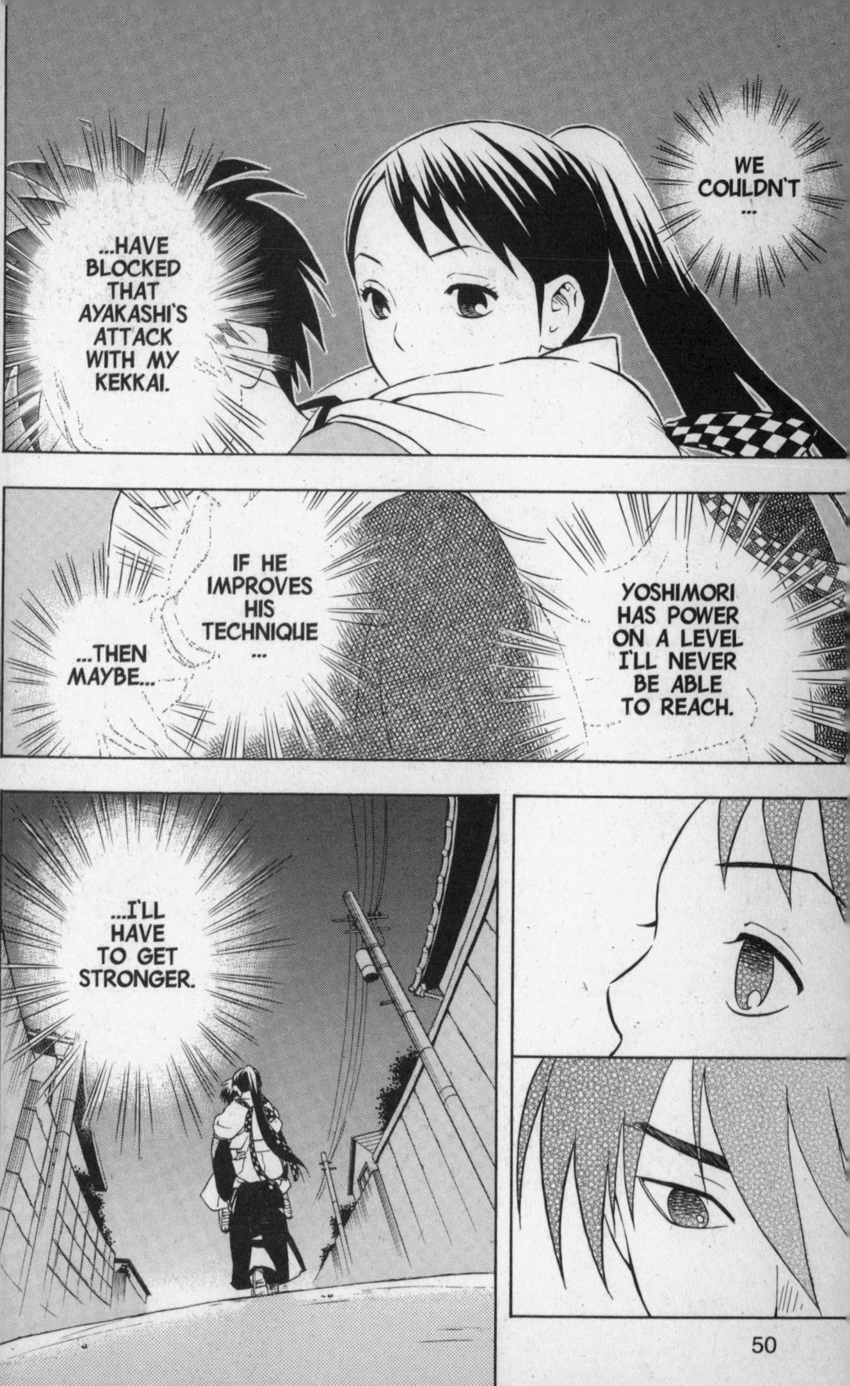
WE COULDN'T ...
...HAVE BLOCKED THAT AYAKASHI'S ATTACK WITH MY KEKKAI.
YOSHIMORI HAS POWER ON A LEVEL I'LL NEVER BE ABLE TO REACH.
IF HE IMPROVES HIS TECHNIQUE ...
...THEN MAYBE...
...I'LL HAVE TO GET STRONGER.

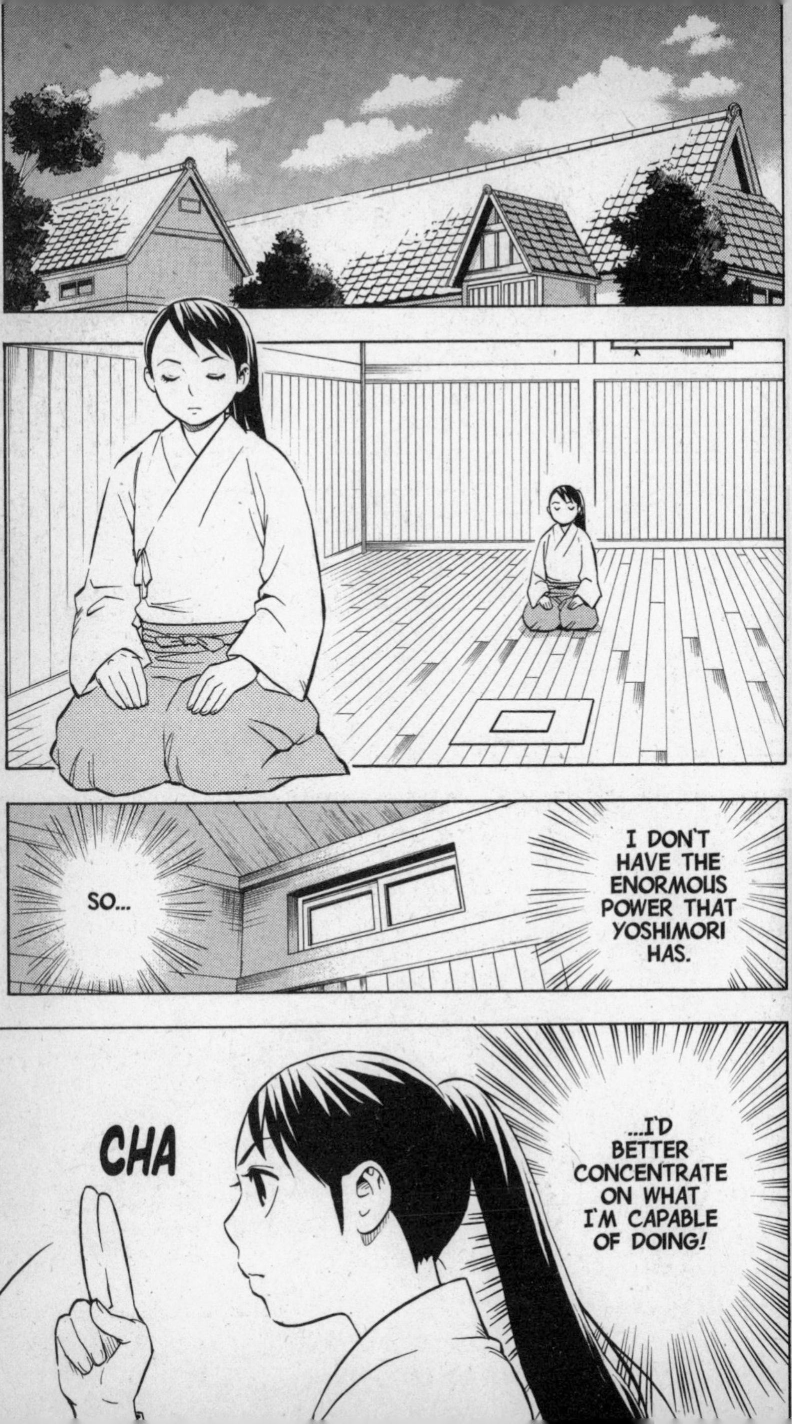
I DON'T HAVE THE ENORMOUS POWER THAT YOSHIMORI HAS.
SO...
...I'D BETTER CONCENTRATE ON WHAT I'M CAPABLE OF DOING!
CHA

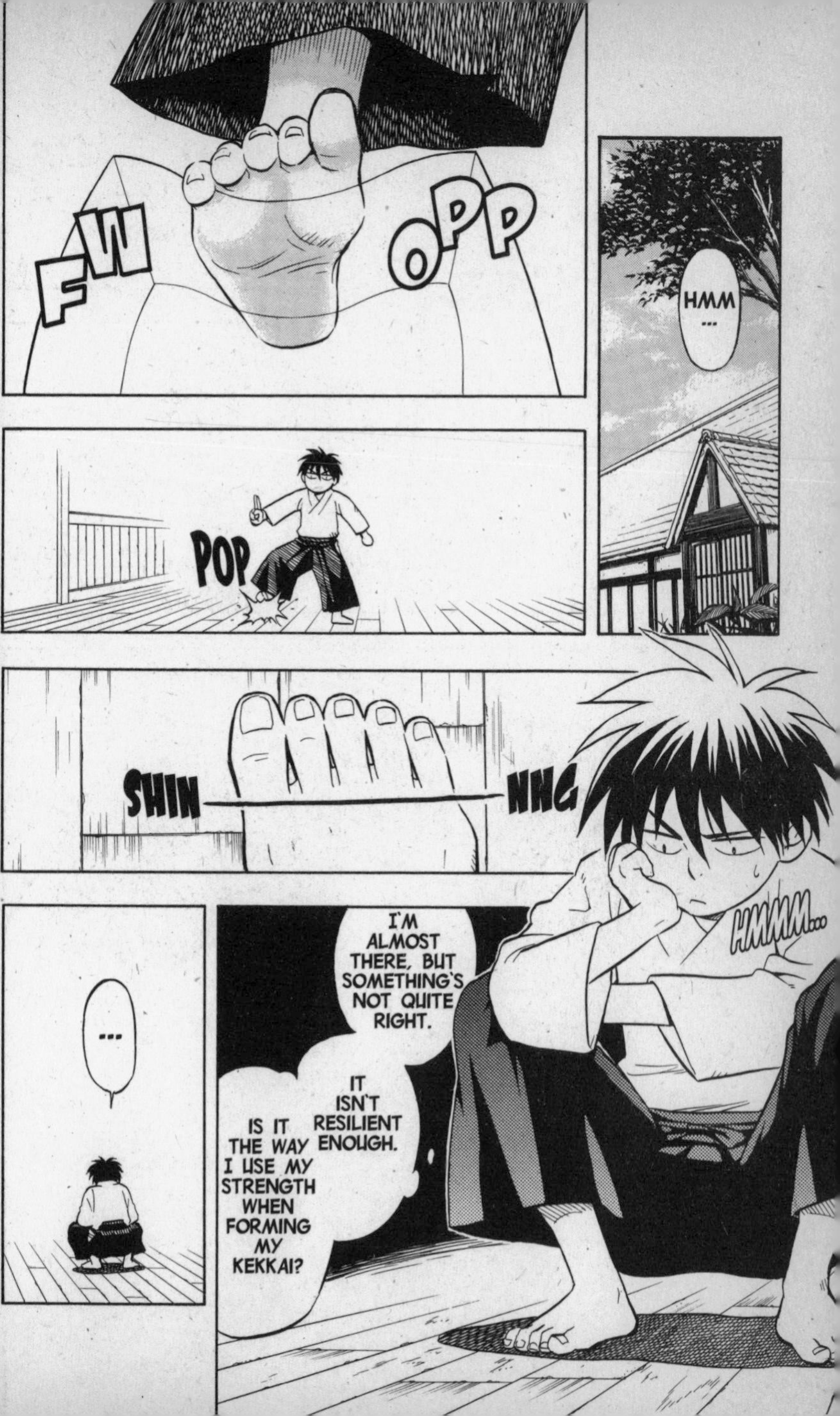
HMM...
FWOPP
POP
SHIN—NHG
HMMM...
I'M ALMOST THERE, BUT SOMETHING'S NOT QUITE RIGHT.
IT ISN'T RESILIENT ENOUGH.
IS IT THE WAY I USE MY STRENGTH WHEN FORMING MY KEKKAI?
...

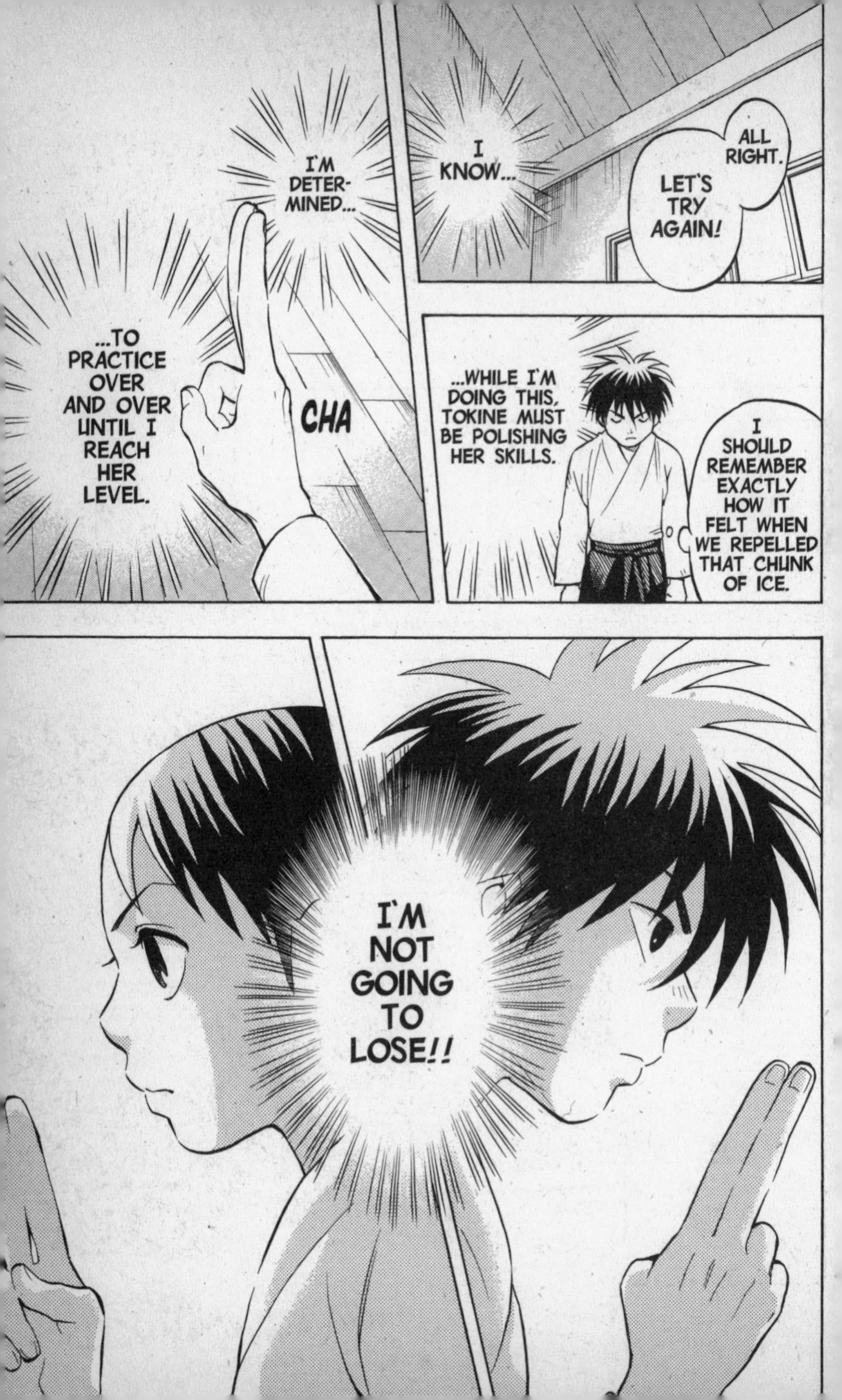
ALL RIGHT.
LET'S TRY AGAIN!
I KNOW...
I SHOULD REMEMBER EXACTLY HOW IT FELT WHEN WE REPELLED THAT CHUNK OF ICE.
...WHILE I'M DOING THIS, TOKINE MUST BE POLISHING HER SKILLS.
I'M DETERMINED...
CHA
...TO PRACTICE OVER AND OVER UNTIL I REACH HER LEVEL.
I'M NOT GOING TO LOSE!!

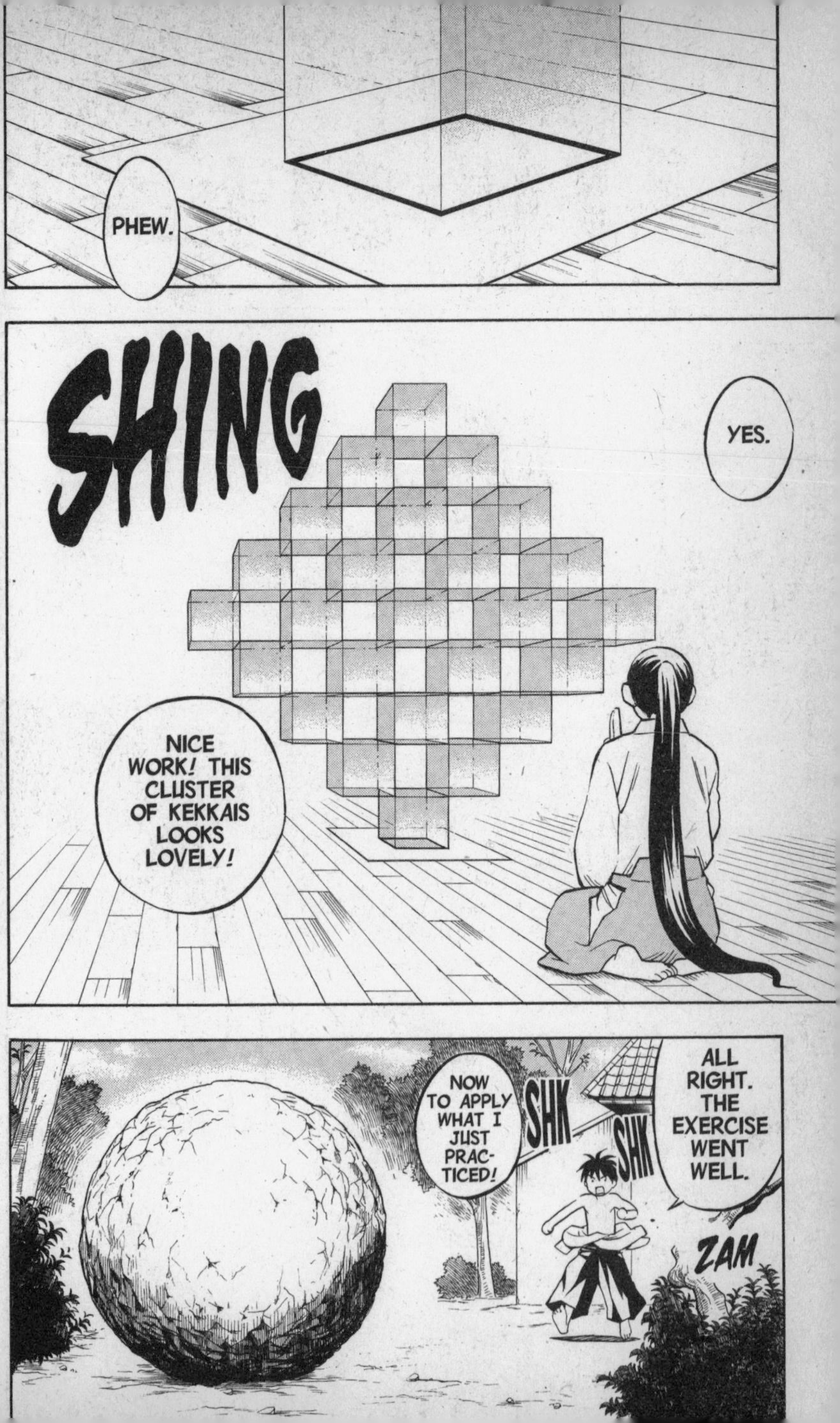
PHEW.
YES.
SHING
NICE WORK! THIS CLUSTER OF KEKKAIS LOOKS LOVELY!
ALL RIGHT. THE EXERCISE WENT WELL.
ZAM
SHK
SHK
NOW TO APPLY WHAT I JUST PRAC-TICED!

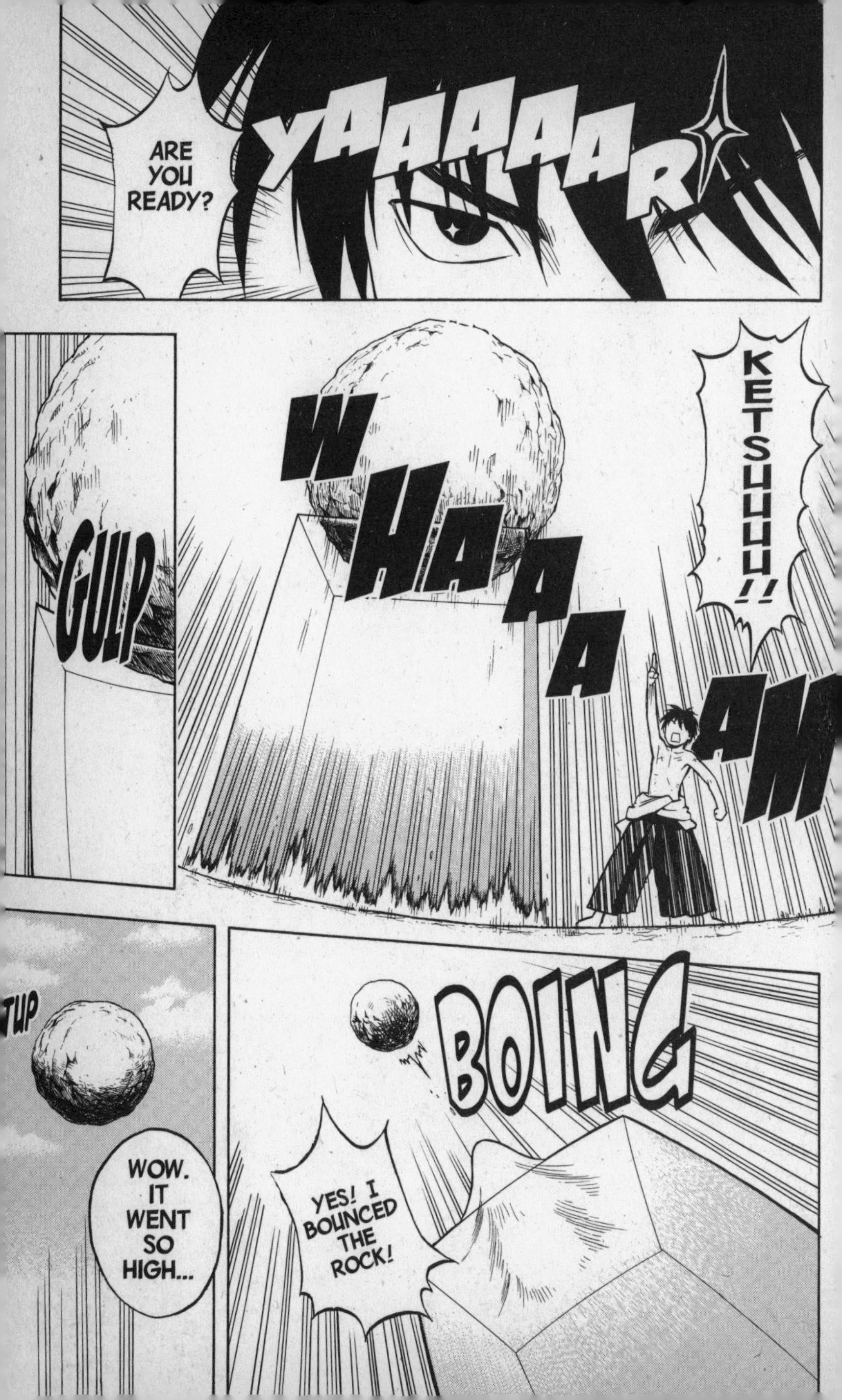
YAAAAAR
ARE YOU READY?
KETSUUUU!!
WHAAAAM
GULP
BOING
YES! I BOUNCED THE ROCK!
TUP
WOW. IT WENT SO HIGH...

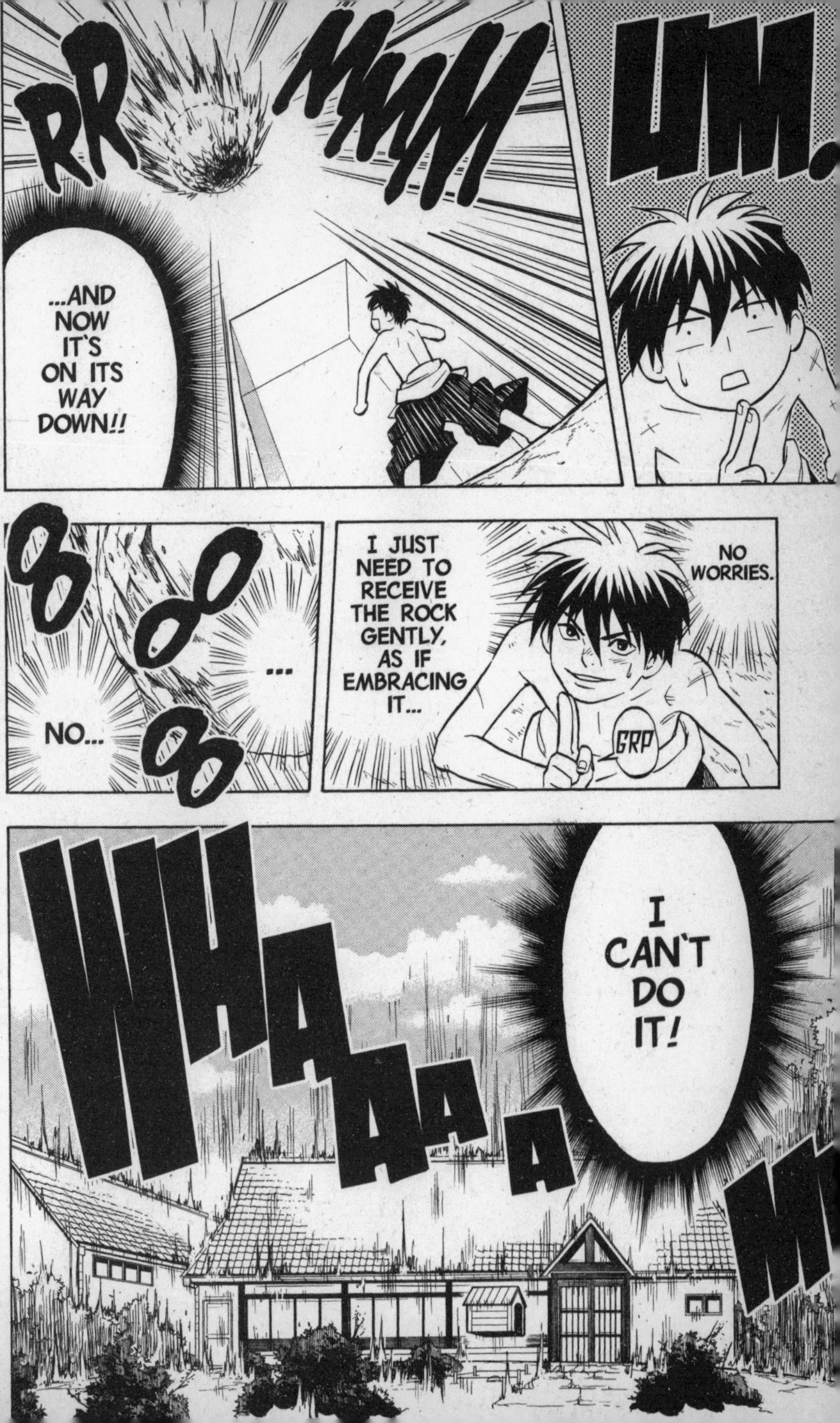
UM..
RR
MMMM
...AND NOW IT'S ON ITS WAY DOWN!!
NO WORRIES.
I JUST NEED TO RECEIVE THE ROCK GENTLY, AS IF EMBRACING IT...
GRP
...
NO...
I CAN'T DO IT!
WHAAAAAM

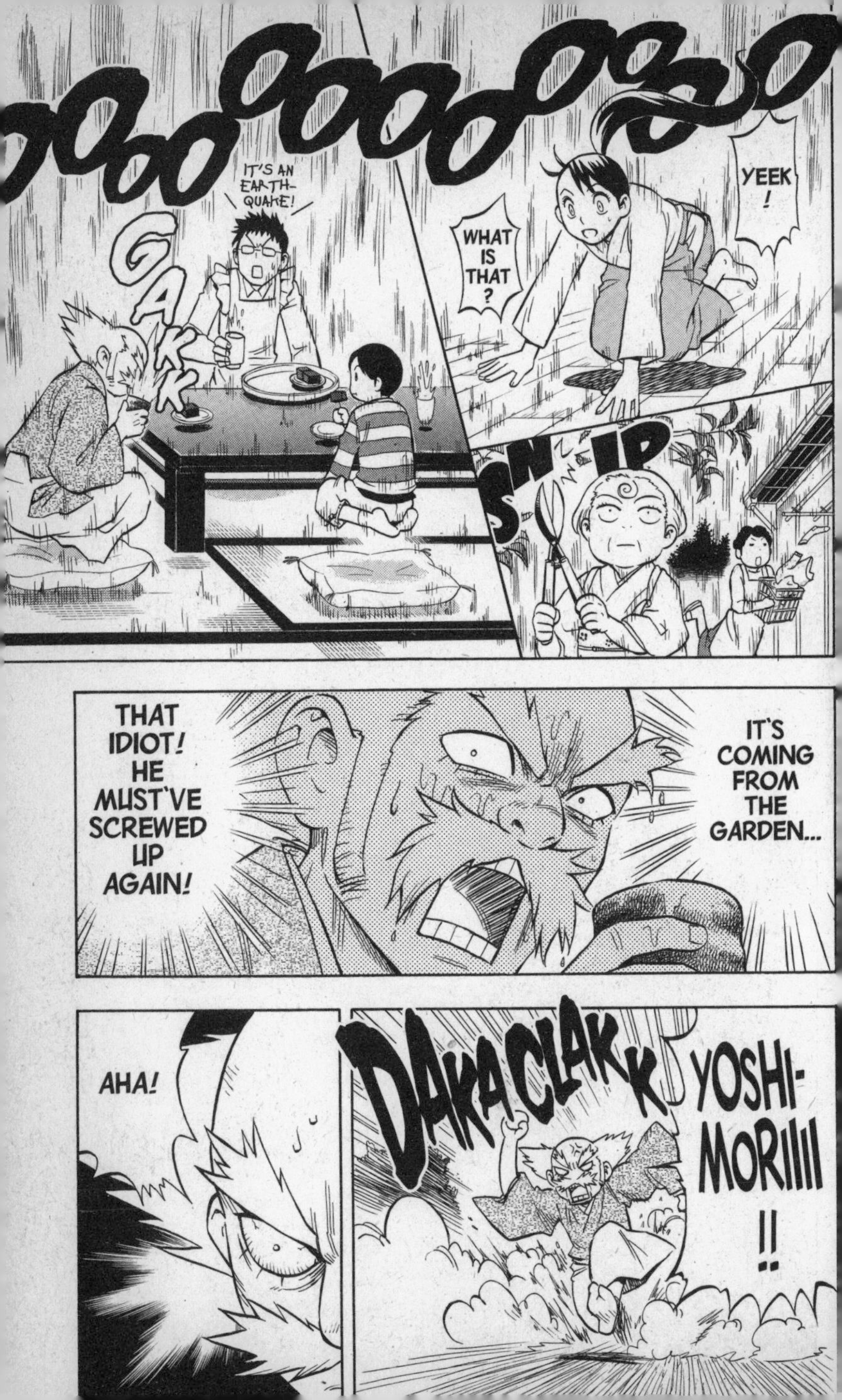
OOOOOOOOOOOOO
YEEK!
WHAT IS THAT?
IT'S AN EARTH-QUAKE!
GAKK
SNIP
IT'S COMING FROM THE GARDEN...
THAT IDIOT! HE MUST'VE SCREWED UP AGAIN!
AHA!
DAKACLAKK
YOSHI-MORIIIII!!

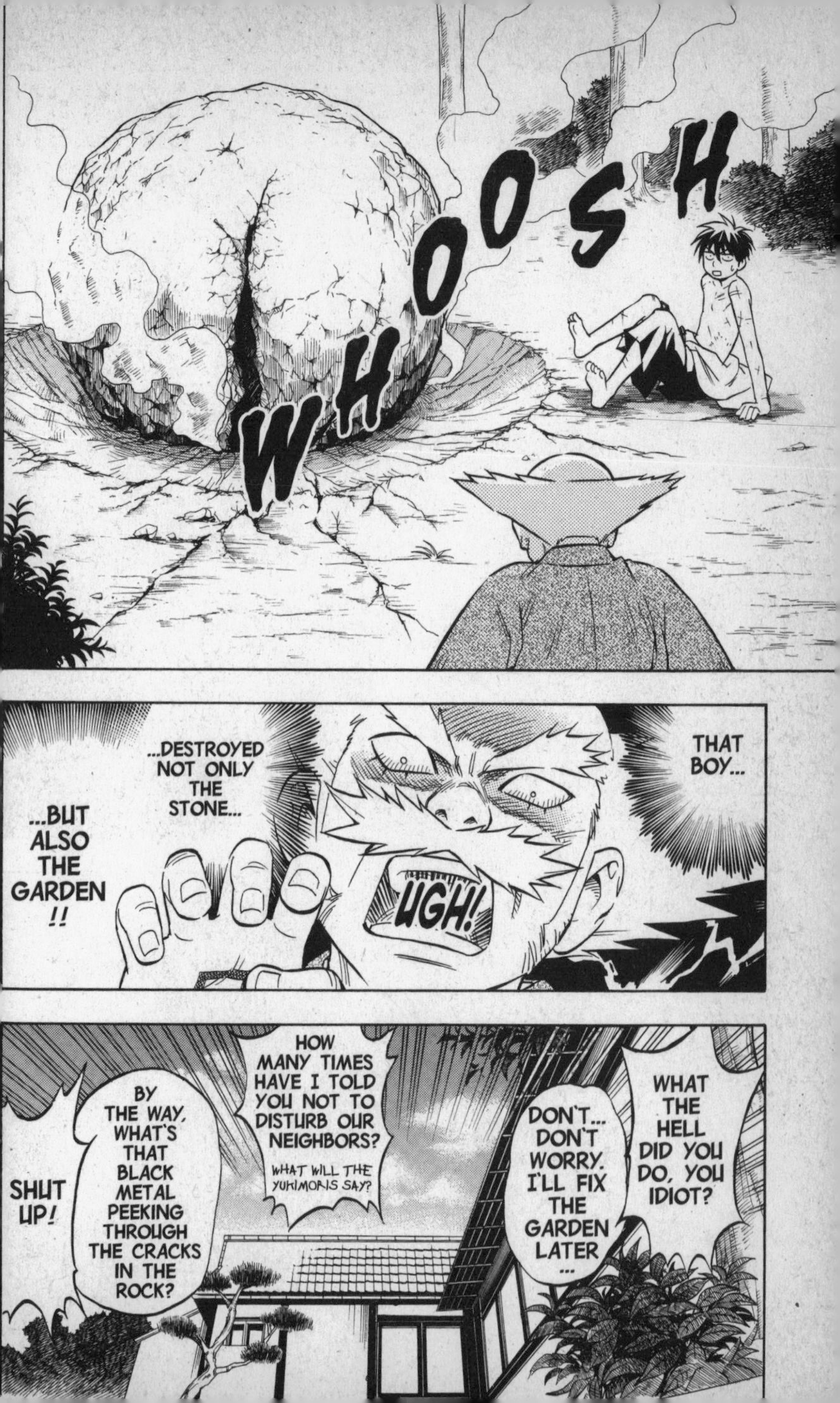
WHOOSH
THAT BOY...
UGH!
...DESTROYED NOT ONLY THE STONE...
...BUT ALSO THE GARDEN!!
WHAT THE HELL DID YOU DO, YOU IDIOT?
DON'T... DON'T WORRY. I'LL FIX THE GARDEN LATER...
HOW MANY TIMES HAVE I TOLD YOU NOT TO DISTURB OUR NEIGHBORS?
WHAT WILL THE YUKIMORIS SAY?
BY THE WAY, WHAT'S THAT BLACK METAL PEEKING THROUGH THE CRACKS IN THE ROCK?
SHUT UP!

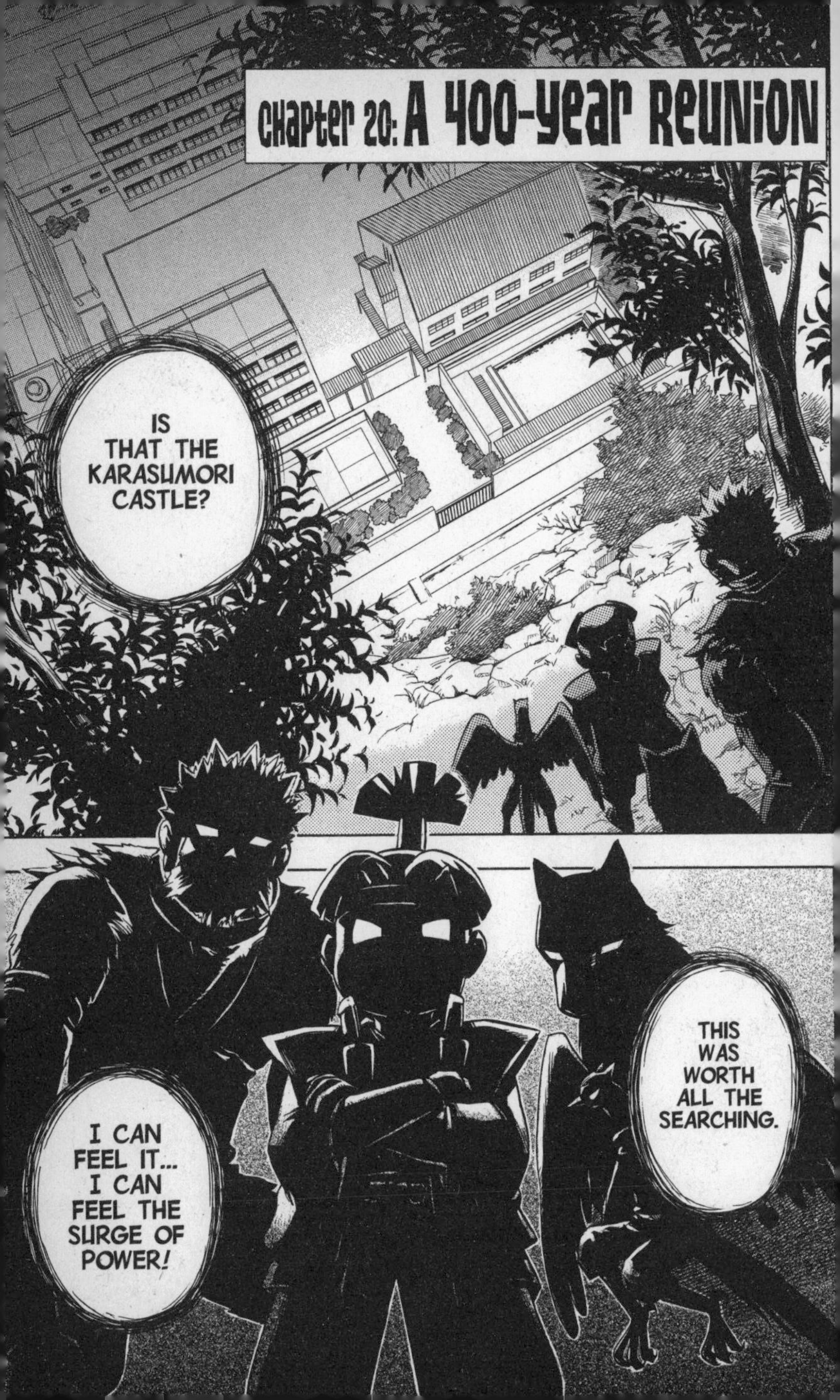
Chapter 20: A 400-year Reunion
IS THAT THE KARASUMORI CASTLE?
THIS WAS WORTH ALL THE SEARCHING.
I CAN FEEL IT... I CAN FEEL THE SURGE OF POWER!

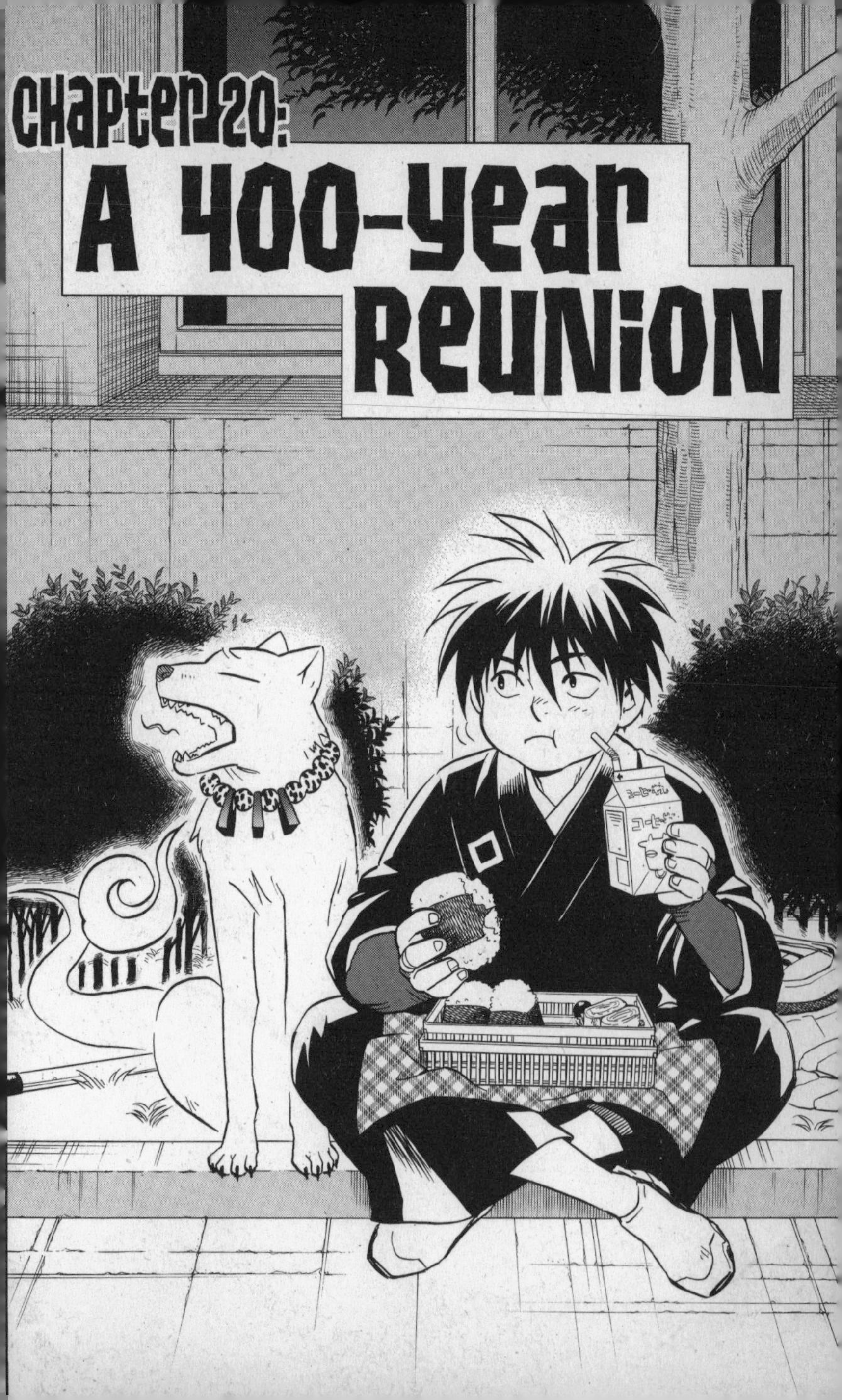
Chapter 20:
A 400-year Reunion

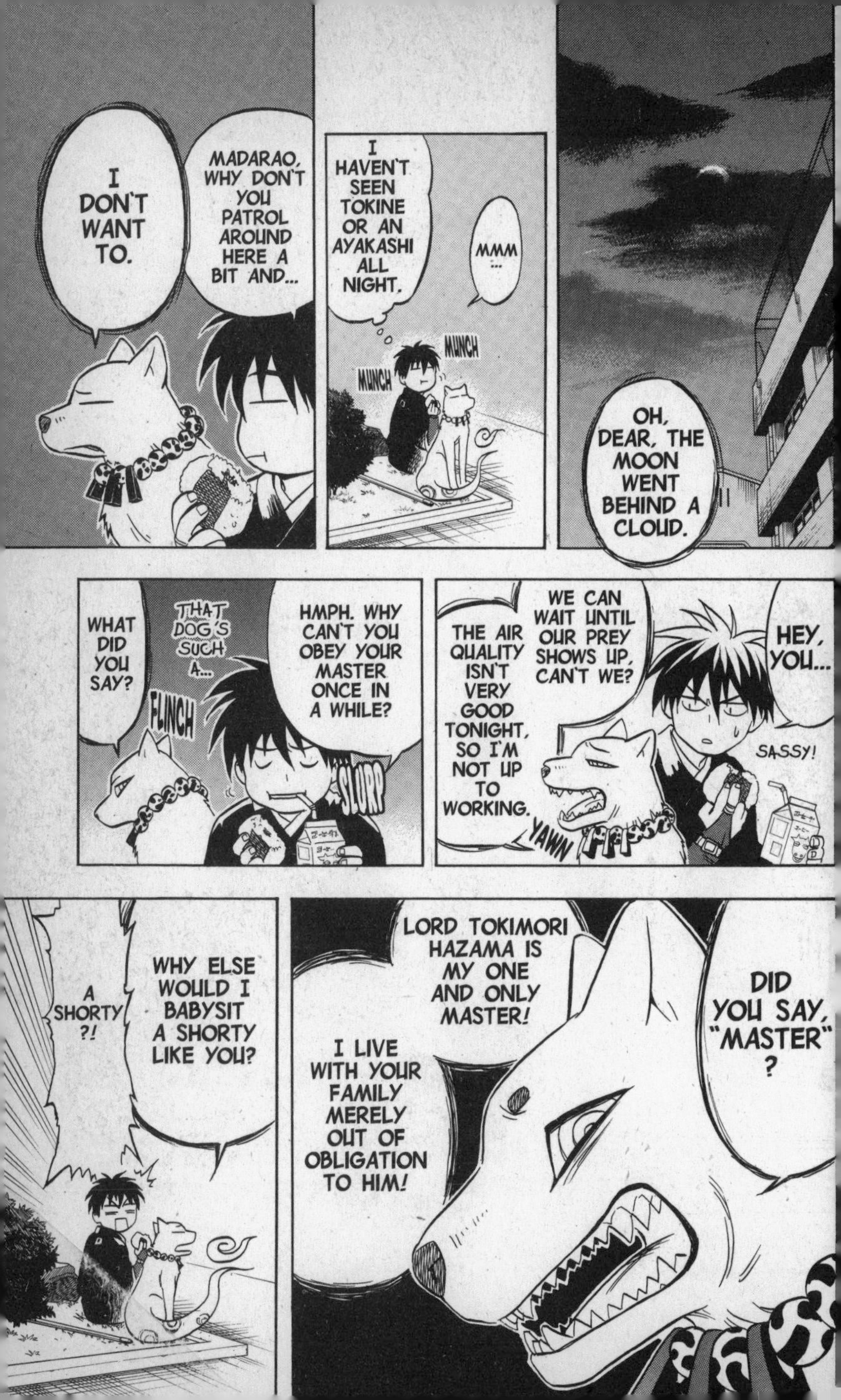

OH, DEAR, THE MOON WENT BEHIND A CLOUD.
MMM...
I HAVEN'T SEEN TOKINE OR AN AYAKASHI ALL NIGHT.
MUNCH
MUNCH
MADARAO, WHY DON'T YOU PATROL AROUND HERE A BIT AND...
I DON'T WANT TO.
HEY, YOU...
WE CAN WAIT UNTIL OUR PREY SHOWS UP, CAN'T WE?
THE AIR QUALITY ISN'T VERY GOOD TONIGHT, SO I'M NOT UP TO WORKING.
SASSY!
YAWN
HMPH. WHY CAN'T YOU OBEY YOUR MASTER ONCE IN A WHILE?
THAT DOG'S SUCH A...
WHAT DID YOU SAY?
FLINCH
SLURP
DID YOU SAY, "MASTER"?
LORD TOKIMORI HAZAMA IS MY ONE AND ONLY MASTER!
I LIVE WITH YOUR FAMILY MERELY OUT OF OBLIGATION TO HIM!
WHY ELSE WOULD I BABYSIT A SHORTY LIKE YOU?
A SHORTY?!

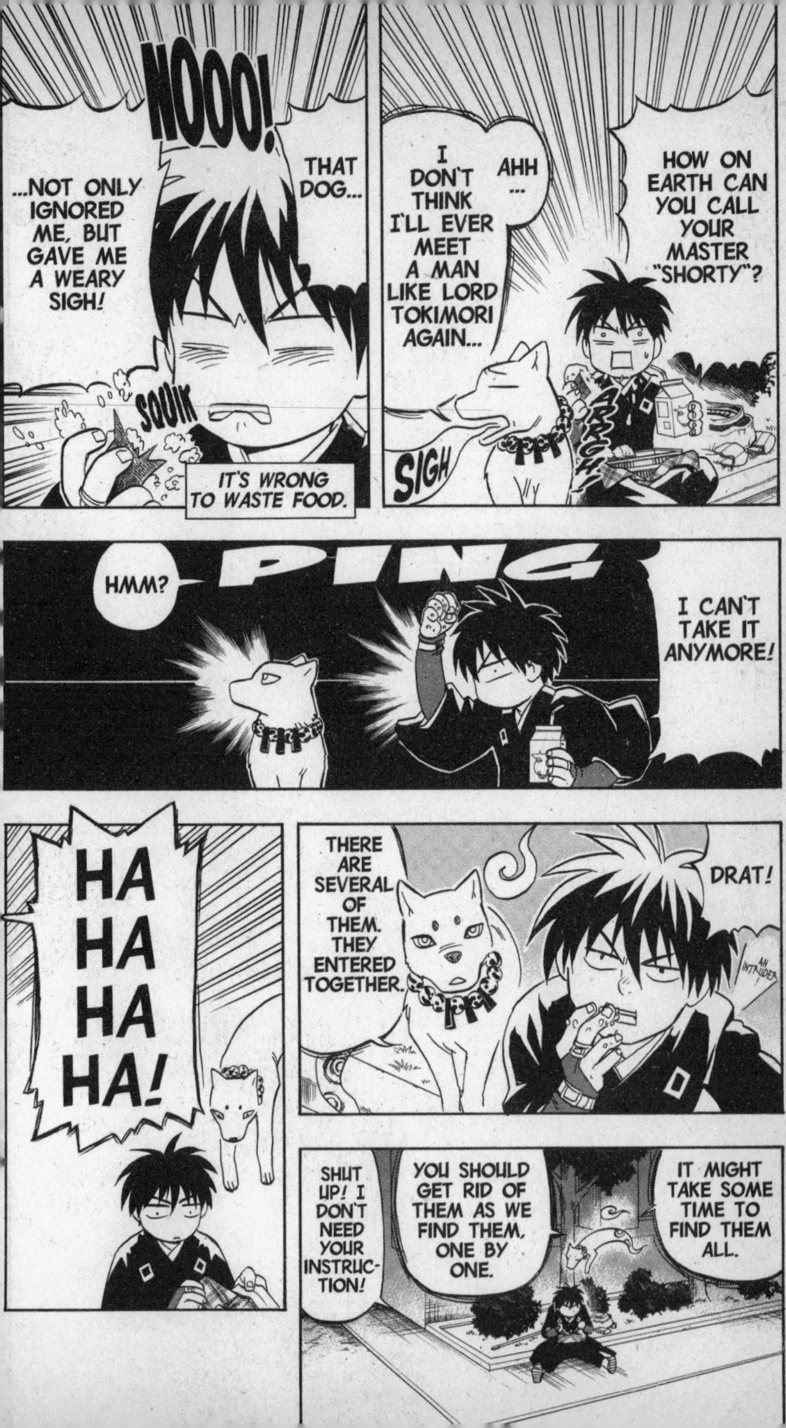
HOW ON EARTH CAN YOU CALL YOUR MASTER "SHORTY"?
AHH ...
I DON'T THINK I'LL EVER MEET A MAN LIKE LORD TOKIMORI AGAIN...
ARRGH!
SIGH
NOOO!
THAT DOG...
...NOT ONLY IGNORED ME, BUT GAVE ME A WEARY SIGH!
SQUIK
IT'S WRONG TO WASTE FOOD.
I CAN'T TAKE IT ANYMORE!
PING
HMM?
DRAT!
AN INTRUDER!
THERE ARE SEVERAL OF THEM. THEY ENTERED TOGETHER.
IT MIGHT TAKE SOME TIME TO FIND THEM ALL.
YOU SHOULD GET RID OF THEM AS WE FIND THEM, ONE BY ONE.
SHUT UP! I DON'T NEED YOUR INSTRUCTION!
HA HA HA HA HA!

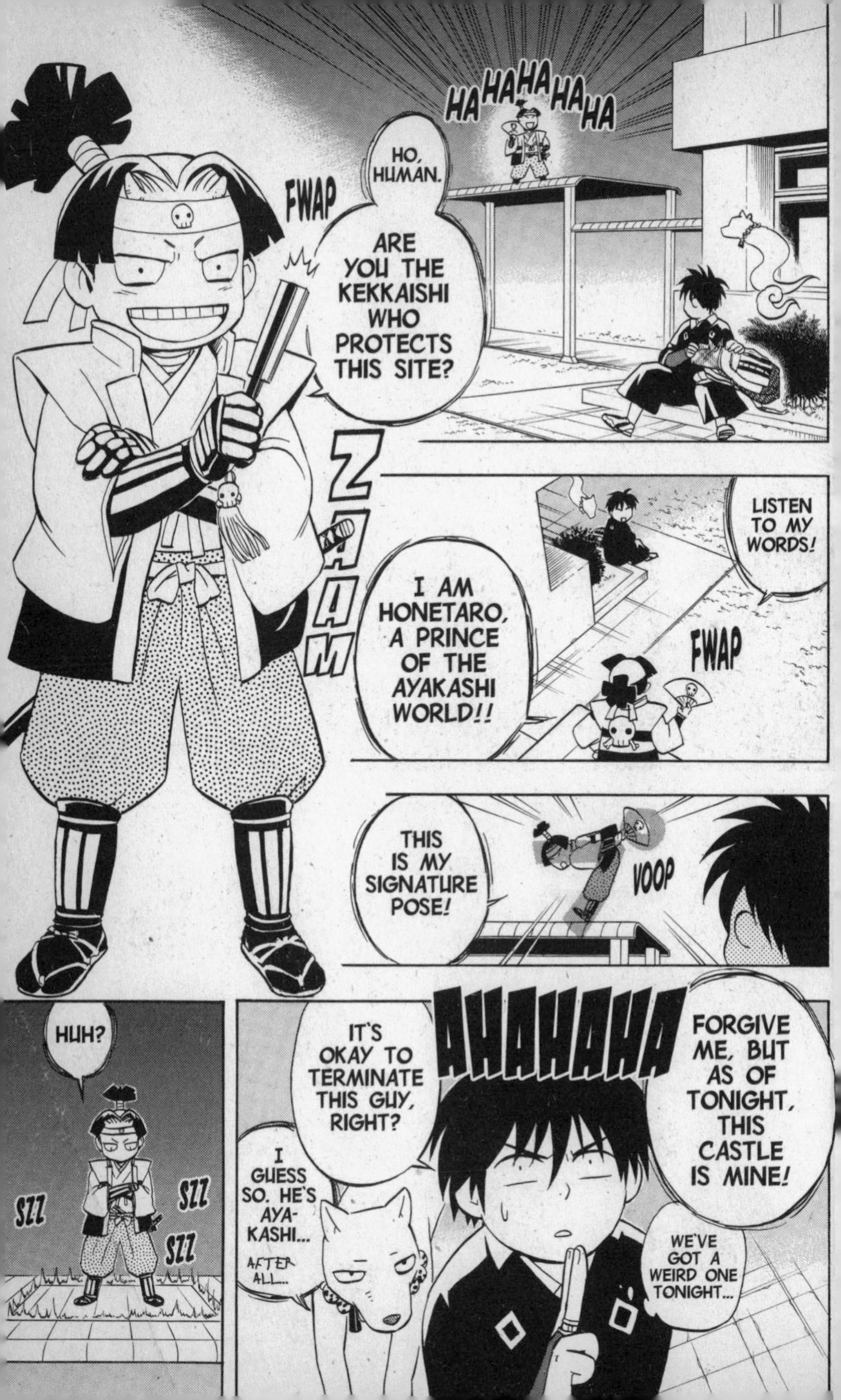
HA HA HA HA HA HA
HO, HUMAN.
ARE YOU THE KEKKAISHI WHO PROTECTS THIS SITE?
LISTEN TO MY WORDS!
I AM HONETARO, A PRINCE OF THE AYAKASHI WORLD!!
FWAP
THIS IS MY SIGNATURE POSE!
VOOP
FWAP
ZAAAM
AHAHAHA
FORGIVE ME, BUT AS OF TONIGHT, THIS CASTLE IS MINE!
WE'VE GOT A WEIRD ONE TONIGHT...
IT'S OKAY TO TERMINATE THIS GUY, RIGHT?
I GUESS SO. HE'S AYA-KASHI...
AFTER ALL...
HUH?
SZZ
SZZ
SZZ

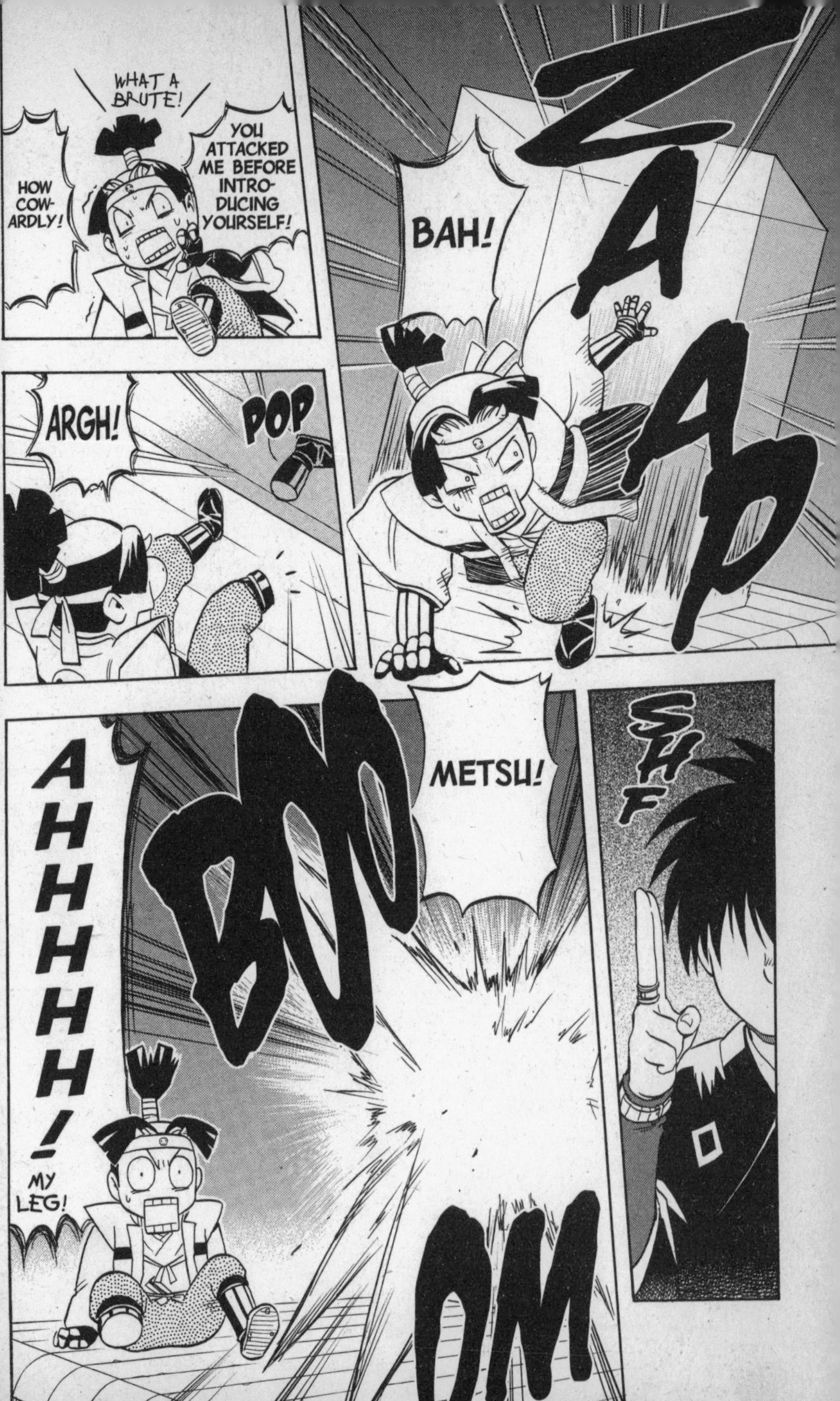
BAH!
ZAAP
WHAT A BRUTE!
YOU ATTACKED ME BEFORE INTRODUCING YOURSELF!
HOW COWARDLY!
ARGH!
POP
SHF
METSU!
BOOM
AHHHHH!
MY LEG!

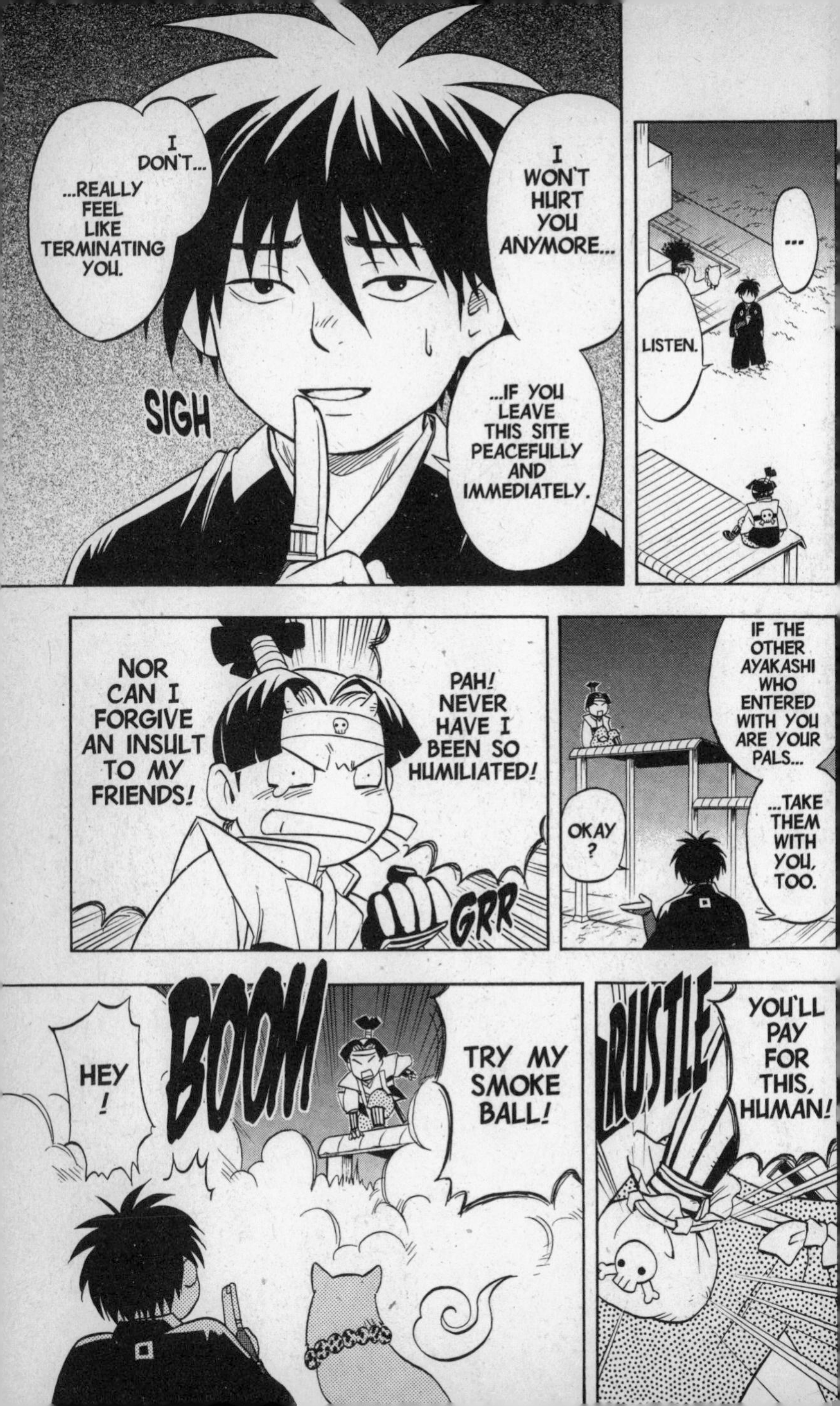
...
LISTEN.
I WON'T HURT YOU ANYMORE...
...IF YOU LEAVE THIS SITE PEACEFULLY AND IMMEDIATELY.
I DON'T... ...REALLY FEEL LIKE TERMINATING YOU.
SIGH
IF THE OTHER AYAKASHI WHO ENTERED WITH YOU ARE YOUR PALS...
...TAKE THEM WITH YOU, TOO.
OKAY?
PAH! NEVER HAVE I BEEN SO HUMILIATED!
NOR CAN I FORGIVE AN INSULT TO MY FRIENDS!
GRR
RUSTLE
YOU'LL PAY FOR THIS, HUMAN!
TRY MY SMOKE BALL!
BOOM
HEY!

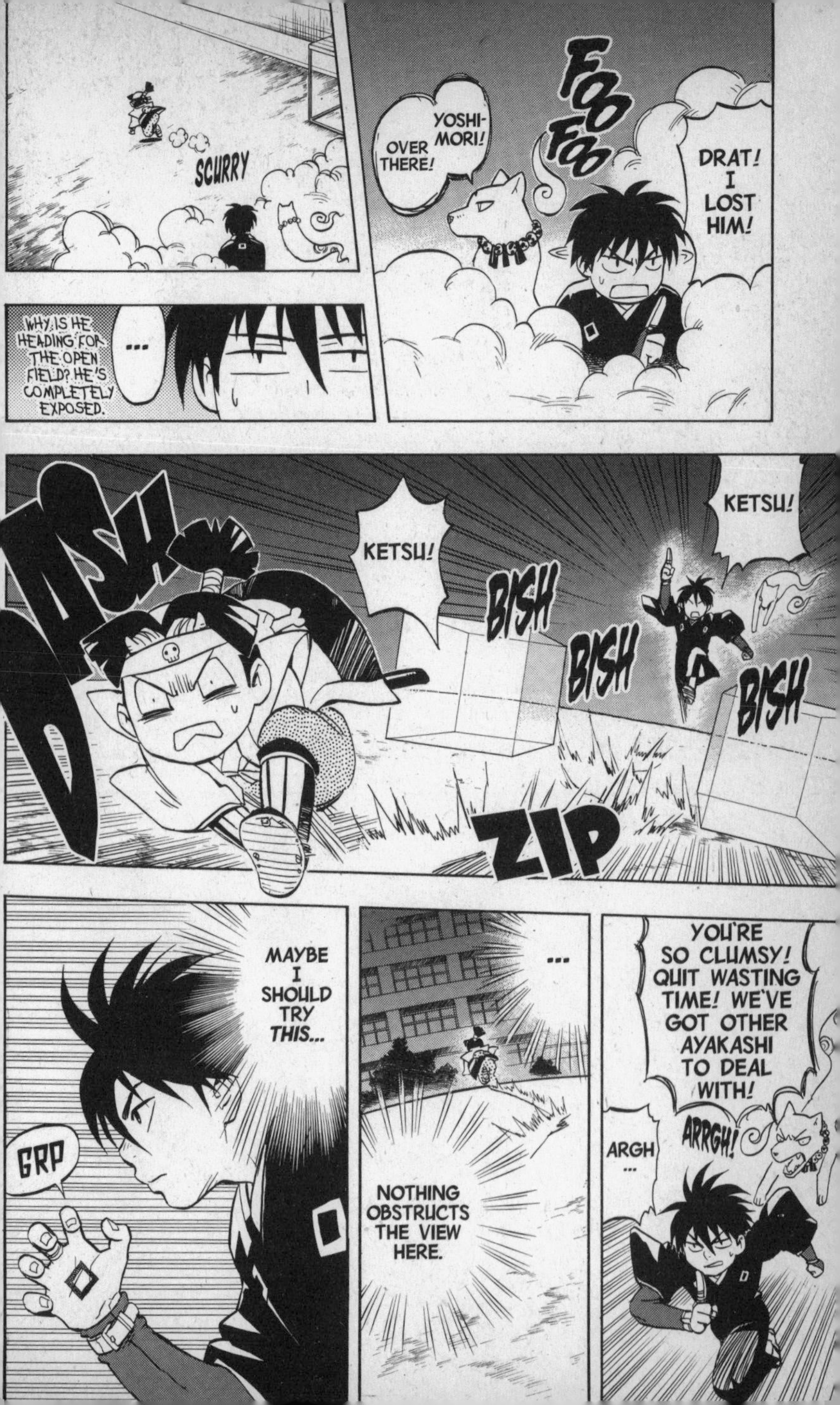
DRAT! I LOST HIM!
FOO FOO
YOSHI-MORI! OVER THERE!
SCURRY
...
WHY IS HE HEADING FOR THE OPEN FIELD? HE'S COMPLETELY EXPOSED.
KETSU!
BISH
BISH
KETSU!
BISH
DASH
ZIP
YOU'RE SO CLUMSY! QUIT WASTING TIME! WE'VE GOT OTHER AYAKASHI TO DEAL WITH!
ARRGH!
ARGH...
...
NOTHING OBSTRUCTS THE VIEW HERE.
MAYBE I SHOULD TRY THIS...
GRP

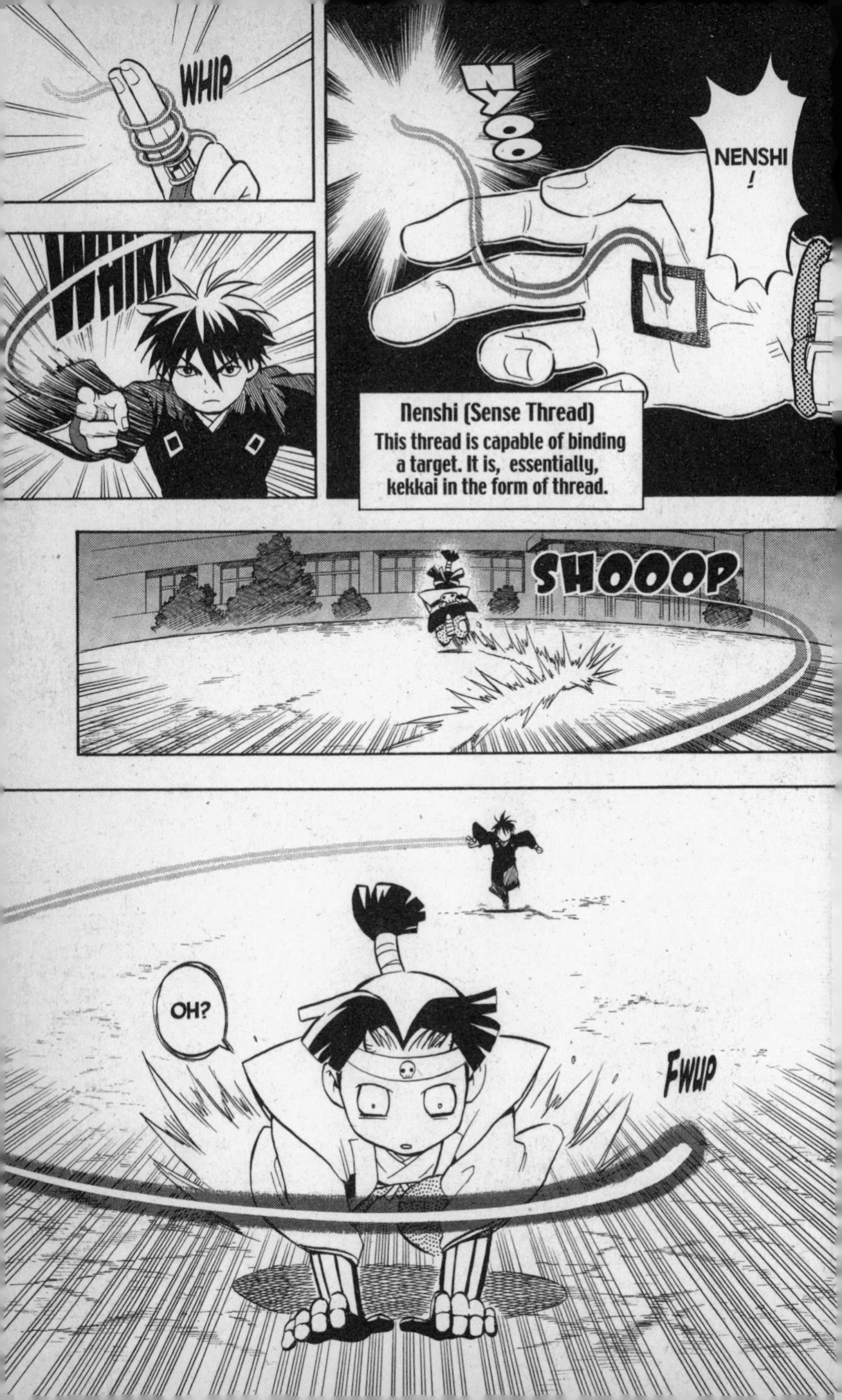

NYOO
NENSHI!
Nenshi (Sense Thread)
This thread is capable of binding a target. It is, essentially, kekkai in the form of thread.
WHIP
WHIKK
SHOOOP
OH?
FWUP

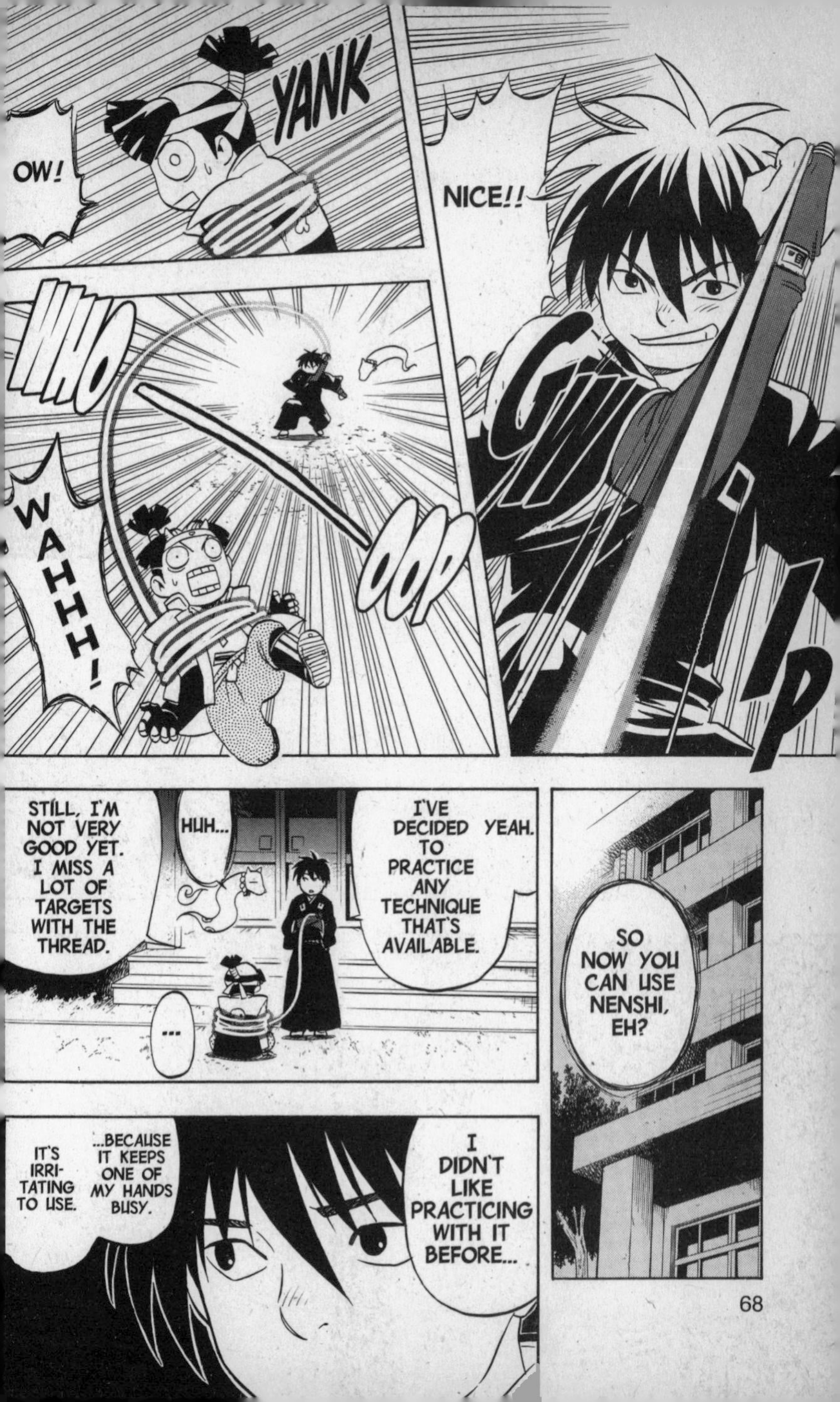
NICE!!
YANK
OW!
WHOOOP
WAHHH!
SO NOW YOU CAN USE NENSHI, EH?
I'VE DECIDED TO PRACTICE ANY TECHNIQUE THAT'S AVAILABLE.
YEAH.
HUH...
STILL, I'M NOT VERY GOOD YET. I MISS A LOT OF TARGETS WITH THE THREAD.
...
I DIDN'T LIKE PRACTICING WITH IT BEFORE...
...BECAUSE IT KEEPS ONE OF MY HANDS BUSY.
IT'S IRRI-TATING TO USE.

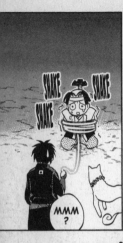

PLUS, I'VE HEARD THAT THE NENSHI IS USED FOR TORTURE.
WELL...
THAT'S BECAUSE IT'S PERFECT FOR BINDING AN OPPONENT.
SHAKE
SHAKE
SHAKE
MMM?
...
I FEEL BAD, FIGHTING THIS AYAKASHI.
IT'S LIKE PICKING ON A 90-POUND WEAKLING.
WAAH
CHOKE
SOB
SNIF
SHUDDER
WHAT'S THAT SMELL?
IT CAN'T BE...
WHY DON'T YOU CALL YOUR FRIENDS?
TELL THEM TO LEAVE HERE WITH YOU.
SNIF
SNIF
I...
...I CAN'T DO THAT.

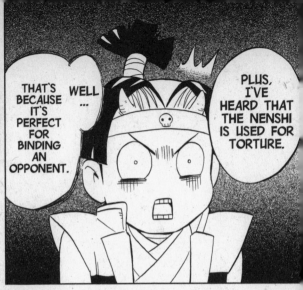

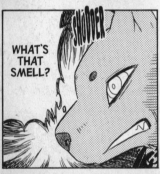

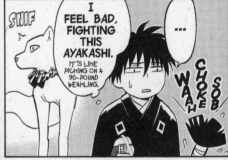

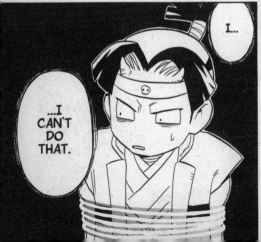

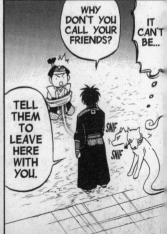

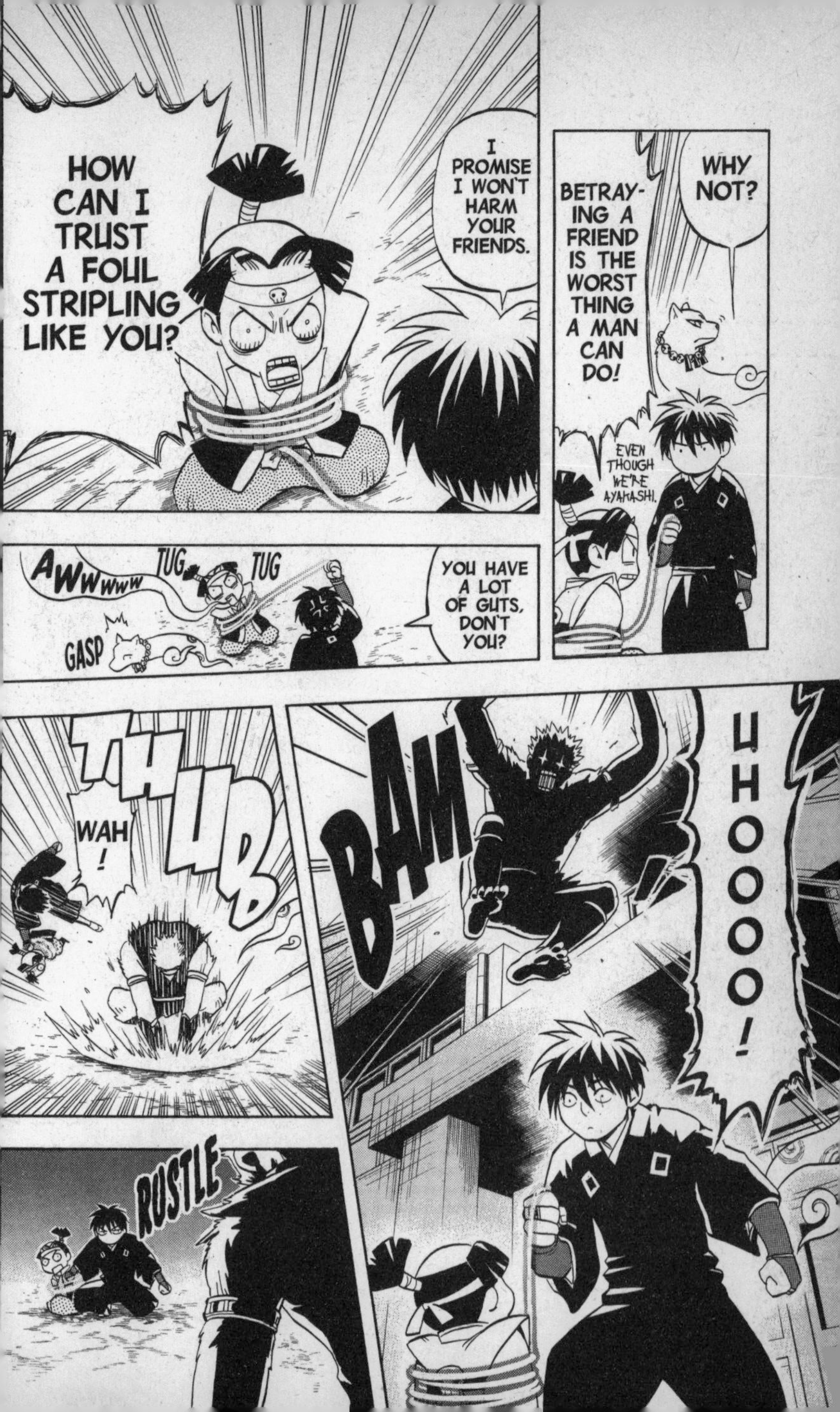
WHY NOT?
BETRAYING A FRIEND IS THE WORST THING A MAN CAN DO!
EVEN THOUGH WE'RE AYAKASHI.
I PROMISE I WON'T HARM YOUR FRIENDS.
HOW CAN I TRUST A FOUL STRIPLING LIKE YOU?
YOU HAVE A LOT OF GUTS, DON'T YOU?
TUG TUG
AWWWWW
GASP
UHOOOOO!
BAM
THUB
WAH!
RUSTLE

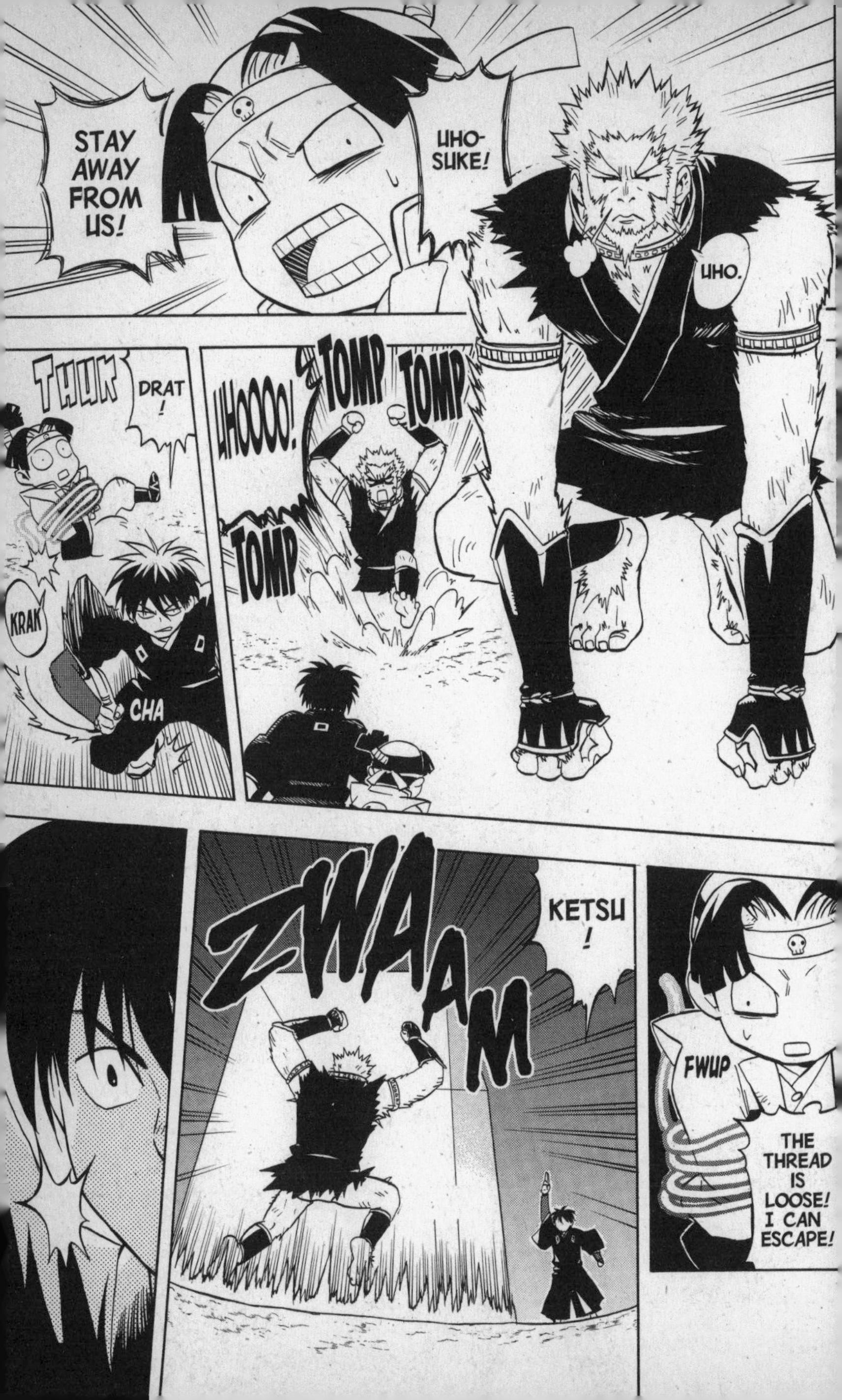

UHO-SUKE!
STAY AWAY FROM US!
UHO.
TOMP
TOMP
UHOOOO!
TOMP
DRAT!
THUK
KRAK
CHA
FWUP
THE THREAD IS LOOSE! I CAN ESCAPE!
KETSU!
ZWAAAM

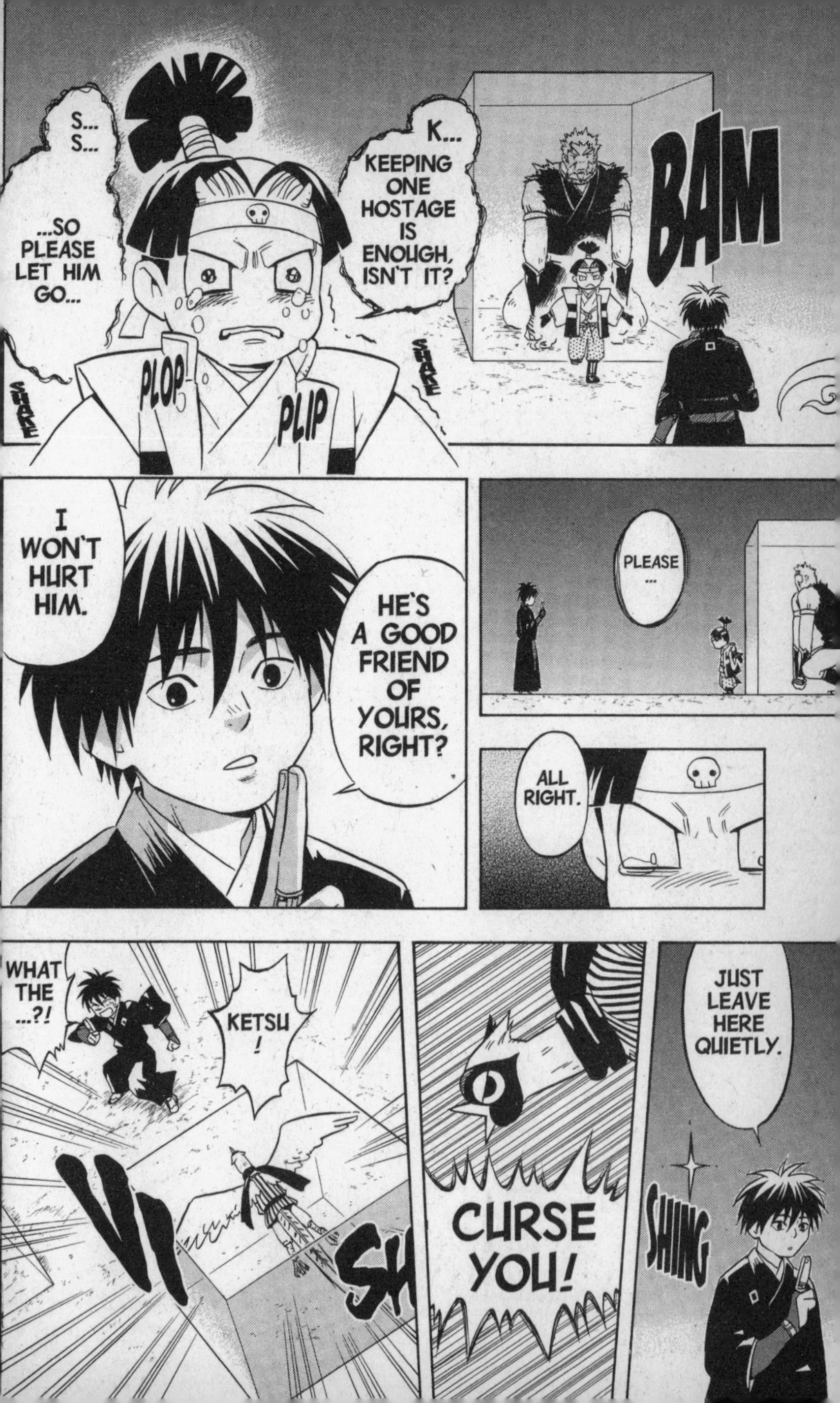
BAM
K... KEEPING ONE HOSTAGE IS ENOUGH, ISN'T IT?
S... S...
...SO PLEASE LET HIM GO...
SHAKE
PLOP
PLIP
SHAKE
PLEASE...
ALL RIGHT.
HE'S A GOOD FRIEND OF YOURS, RIGHT?
I WON'T HURT HIM.
JUST LEAVE HERE QUIETLY.
SHING
CURSE YOU!
SH
KETSU!
WHAT THE ...?!

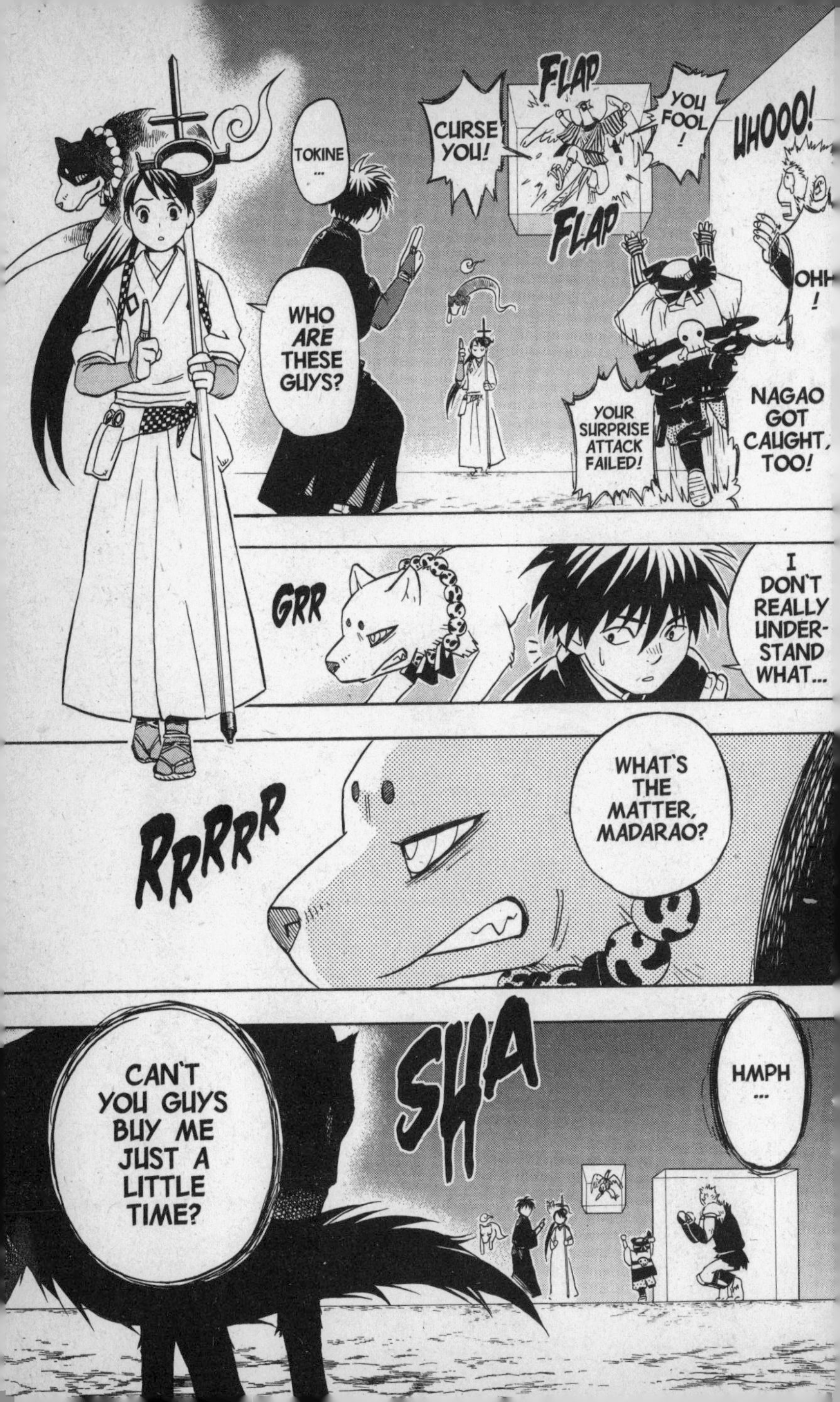
UHOOO!
YOU FOOL!
FLAP
CURSE YOU!
FLAP
TOKINE...
OHH!
NAGAO GOT CAUGHT, TOO!
YOUR SURPRISE ATTACK FAILED!
WHO *ARE* THESE GUYS?
I DON'T REALLY UNDER-STAND WHAT...
GRR
WHAT'S THE MATTER, MADARAO?
RRRRR
HMPH...
SHA
CAN'T YOU GUYS BUY ME JUST A LITTLE TIME?

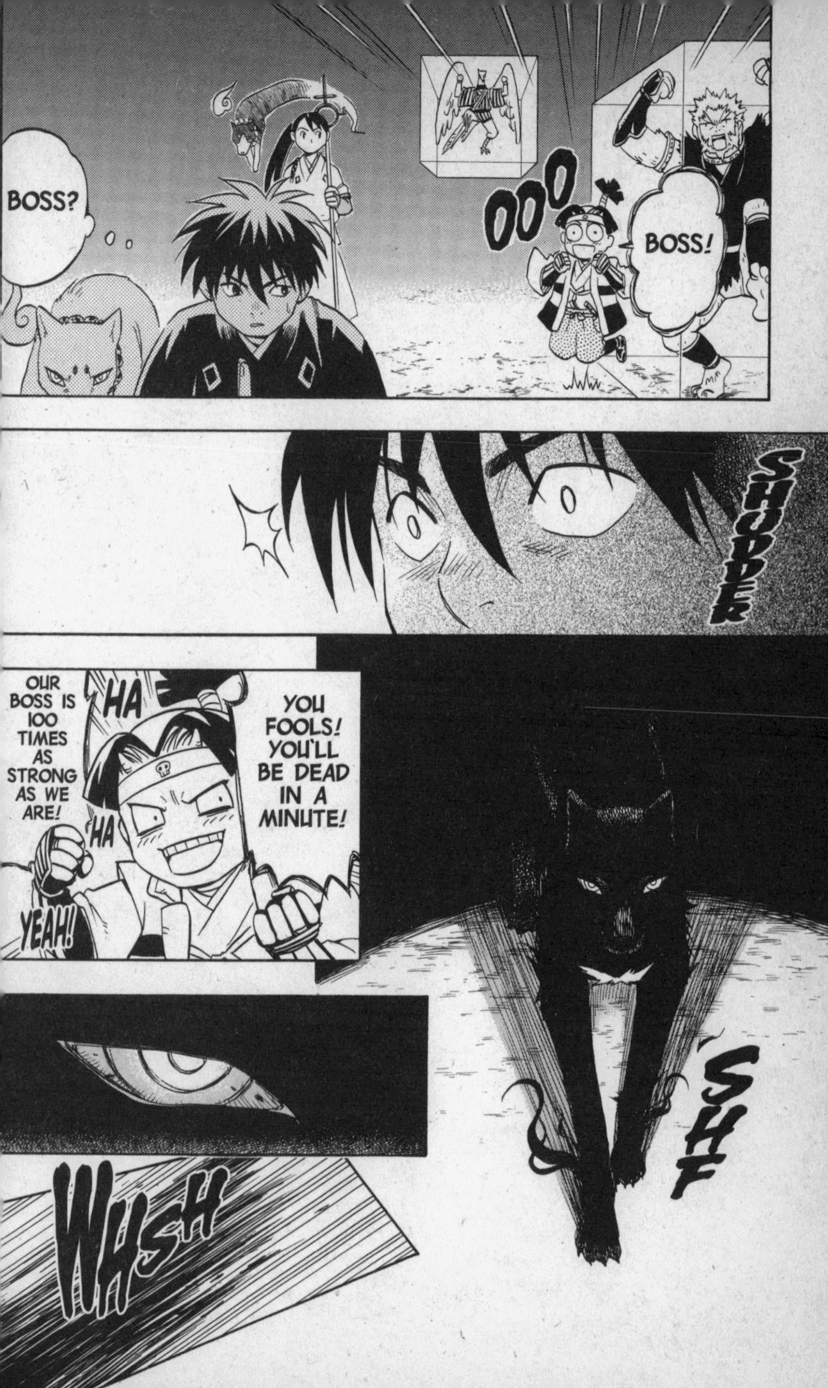
BOSS!
OOO
BOSS?
SHUDDER
SHF
YOU FOOLS! YOU'LL BE DEAD IN A MINUTE!
OUR BOSS IS 100 TIMES AS STRONG AS WE ARE!
HA
HA
YEAH!
WHSH

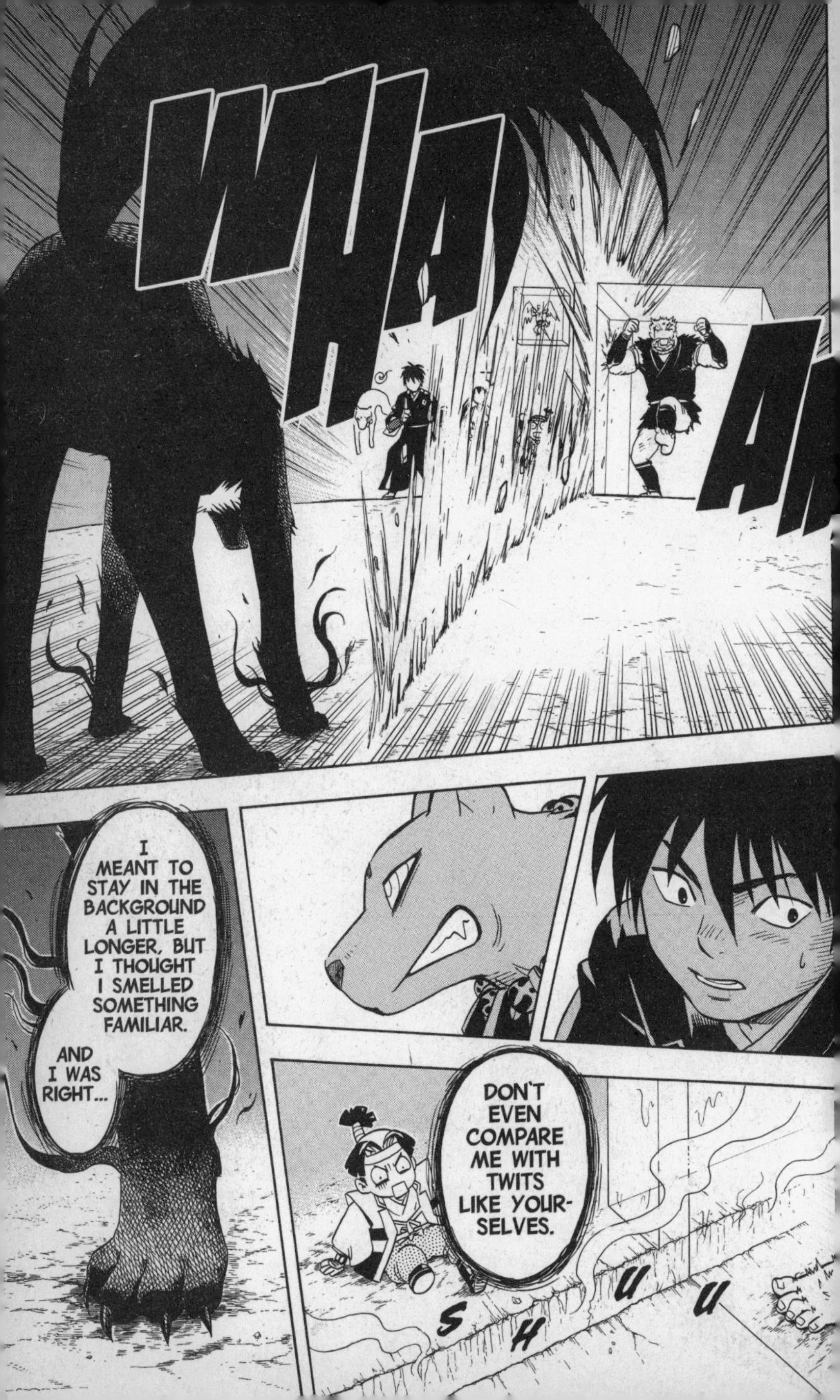
WHAAAH
I MEANT TO STAY IN THE BACKGROUND A LITTLE LONGER, BUT I THOUGHT I SMELLED SOMETHING FAMILIAR.
AND I WAS RIGHT...
DON'T EVEN COMPARE ME WITH TWITS LIKE YOUR-SELVES.
SHUUU

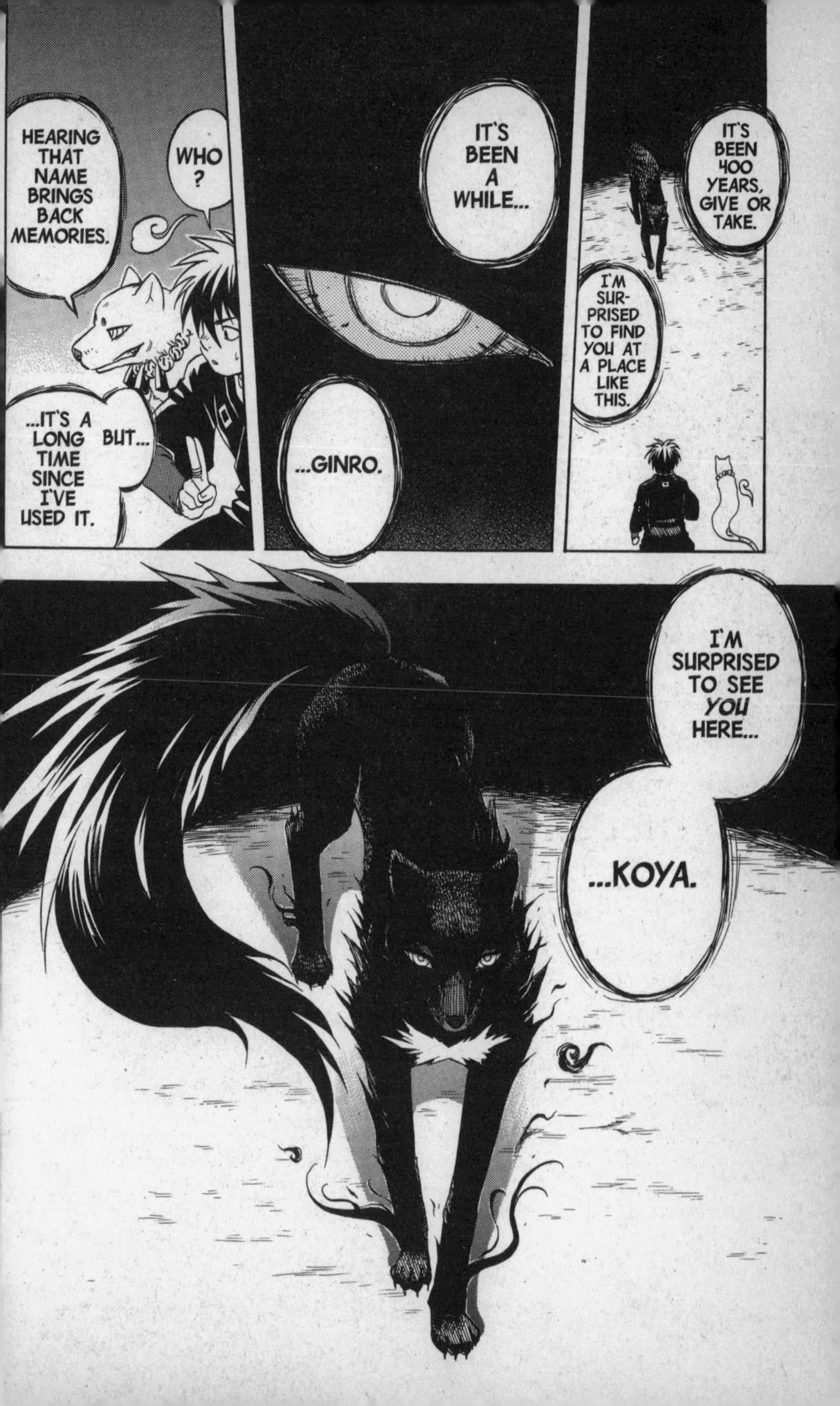
IT'S BEEN 400 YEARS, GIVE OR TAKE.
I'M SURPRISED TO FIND YOU AT A PLACE LIKE THIS.
IT'S BEEN A WHILE...
...GINRO.
WHO?
HEARING THAT NAME BRINGS BACK MEMORIES.
BUT...
...IT'S A LONG TIME SINCE I'VE USED IT.
I'M SURPRISED TO SEE *YOU* HERE...
...KOYA.

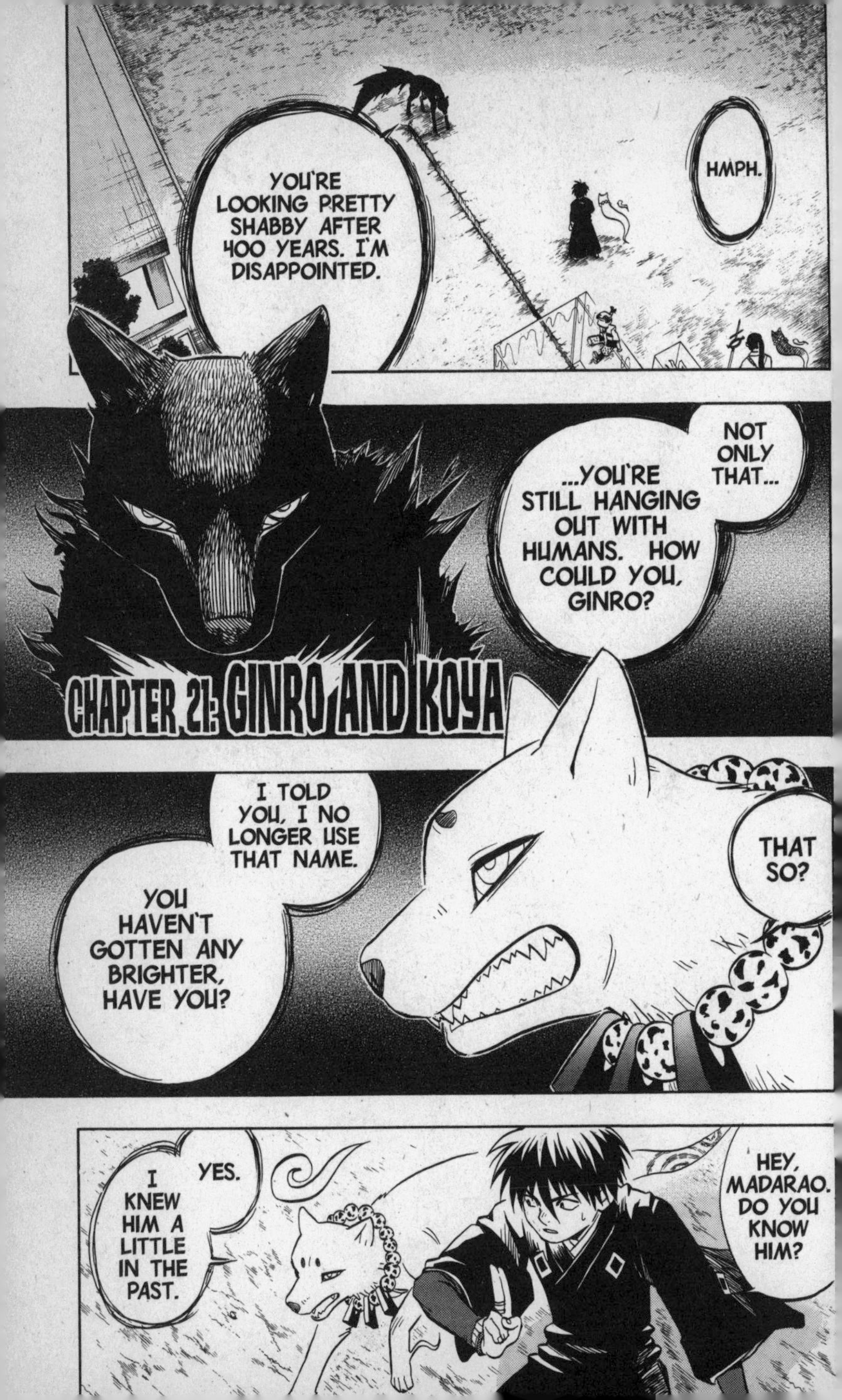
HMPH.
YOU'RE LOOKING PRETTY SHABBY AFTER 400 YEARS. I'M DISAPPOINTED.
NOT ONLY THAT...
...YOU'RE STILL HANGING OUT WITH HUMANS. HOW COULD YOU, GINRO?
CHAPTER 21: GINRO AND KOYA
I TOLD YOU, I NO LONGER USE THAT NAME.
THAT SO?
YOU HAVEN'T GOTTEN ANY BRIGHTER, HAVE YOU?
HEY, MADARAO. DO YOU KNOW HIM?
YES.
I KNEW HIM A LITTLE IN THE PAST.

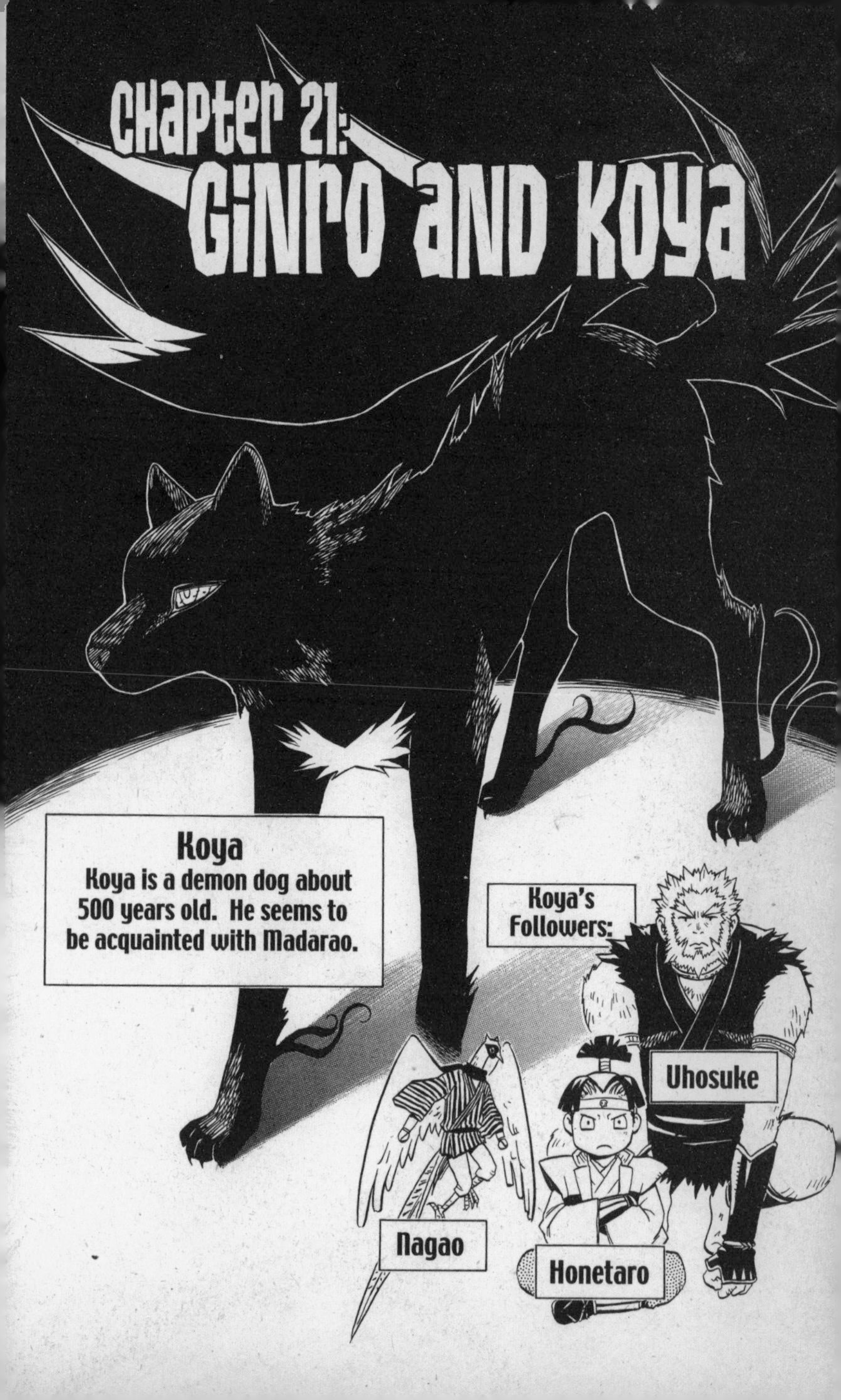
Chapter 21:
Ginro and Koya
Koya
Koya is a demon dog about 500 years old. He seems to be acquainted with Madarao.
Koya's Followers:
Uhosuke
Nagao
Honetaro

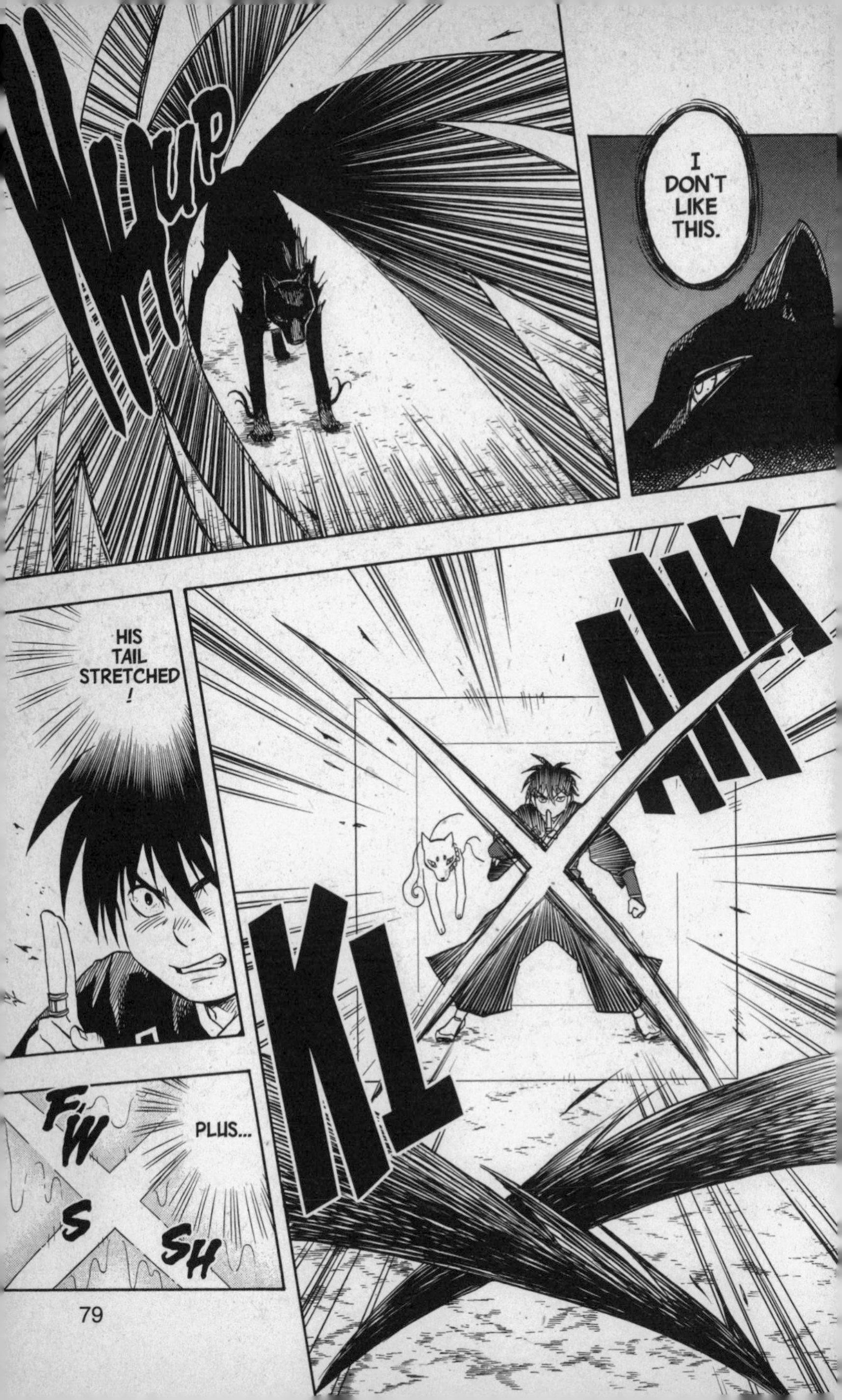
I DON'T LIKE THIS.
WHUP
KLANK
HIS TAIL STRETCHED!
PLUS...
FWSSH

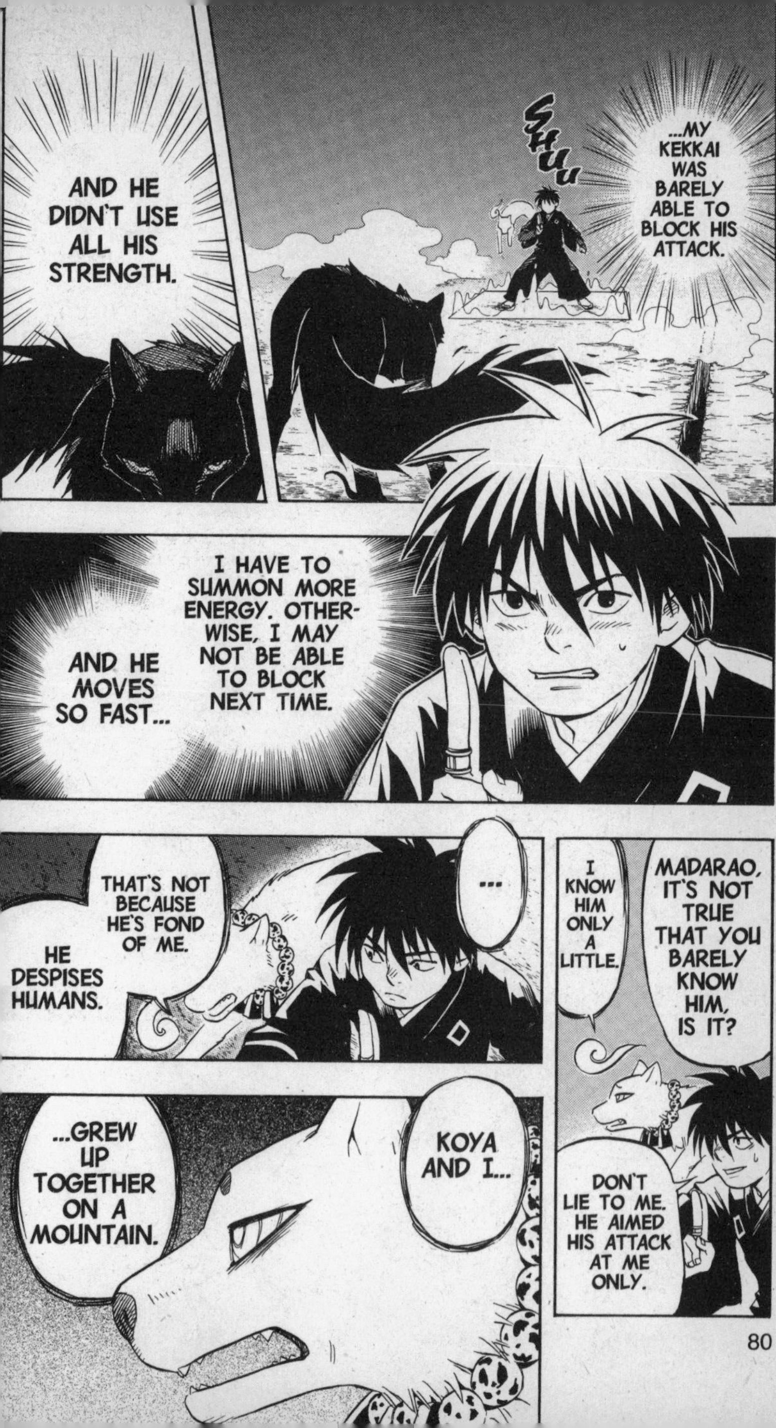
SHUU
...MY KEKKAI WAS BARELY ABLE TO BLOCK HIS ATTACK.
AND HE DIDN'T USE ALL HIS STRENGTH.
I HAVE TO SUMMON MORE ENERGY. OTHER-WISE, I MAY NOT BE ABLE TO BLOCK NEXT TIME.
AND HE MOVES SO FAST...
MADARAO, IT'S NOT TRUE THAT YOU BARELY KNOW HIM, IS IT?
I KNOW HIM ONLY A LITTLE.
DON'T LIE TO ME. HE AIMED HIS ATTACK AT ME ONLY.
...
THAT'S NOT BECAUSE HE'S FOND OF ME.
HE DESPISES HUMANS.
KOYA AND I...
...GREW UP TOGETHER ON A MOUNTAIN.

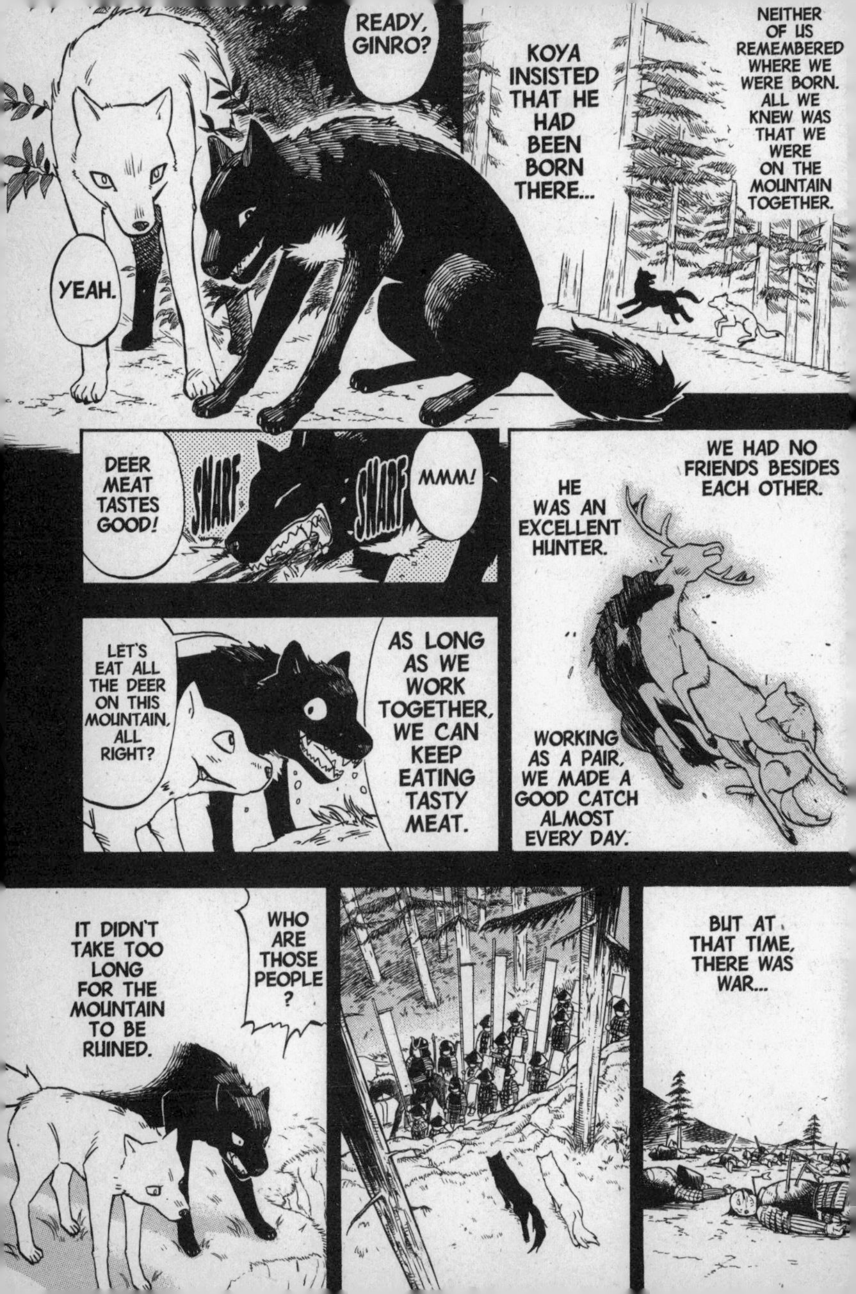
NEITHER OF US REMEMBERED WHERE WE WERE BORN. ALL WE KNEW WAS THAT WE WERE ON THE MOUNTAIN TOGETHER.
KOYA INSISTED THAT HE HAD BEEN BORN THERE...
READY, GINRO?
YEAH.
WE HAD NO FRIENDS BESIDES EACH OTHER.
HE WAS AN EXCELLENT HUNTER.
WORKING AS A PAIR, WE MADE A GOOD CATCH ALMOST EVERY DAY.
MMM!
SNARF
SNARF
DEER MEAT TASTES GOOD!
AS LONG AS WE WORK TOGETHER, WE CAN KEEP EATING TASTY MEAT.
LET'S EAT ALL THE DEER ON THIS MOUNTAIN, ALL RIGHT?
BUT AT THAT TIME, THERE WAS WAR...
WHO ARE THOSE PEOPLE?
IT DIDN'T TAKE TOO LONG FOR THE MOUNTAIN TO BE RUINED.

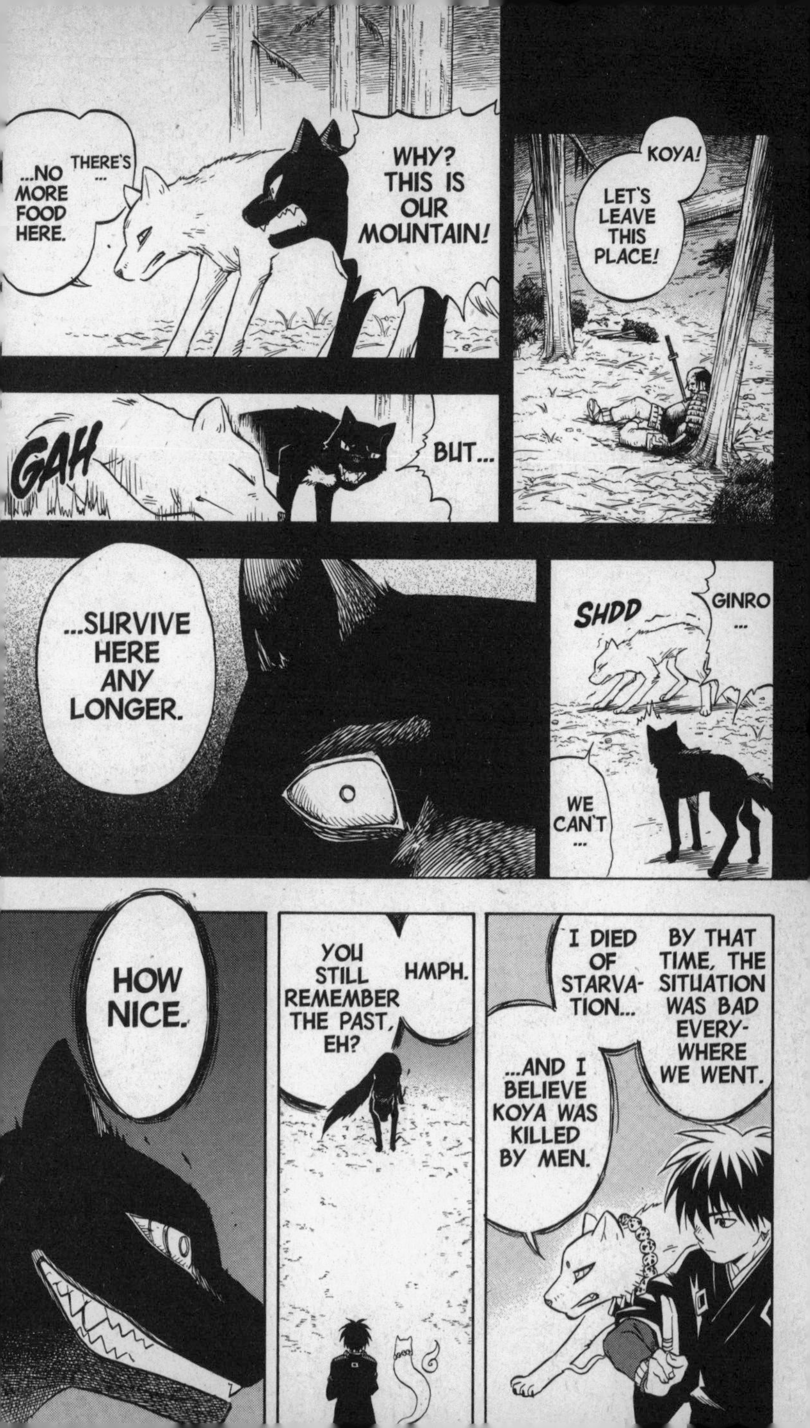
KOYA!
LET'S LEAVE THIS PLACE!
WHY? THIS IS OUR MOUNTAIN!
THERE'S ...
...NO MORE FOOD HERE.
BUT...
GAH
GINRO ...
SHDD
WE CAN'T ...
...SURVIVE HERE ANY LONGER.
BY THAT TIME, THE SITUATION WAS BAD EVERY-WHERE WE WENT.
I DIED OF STARVA-TION...
...AND I BELIEVE KOYA WAS KILLED BY MEN.
HMPH.
YOU STILL REMEMBER THE PAST, EH?
HOW NICE.

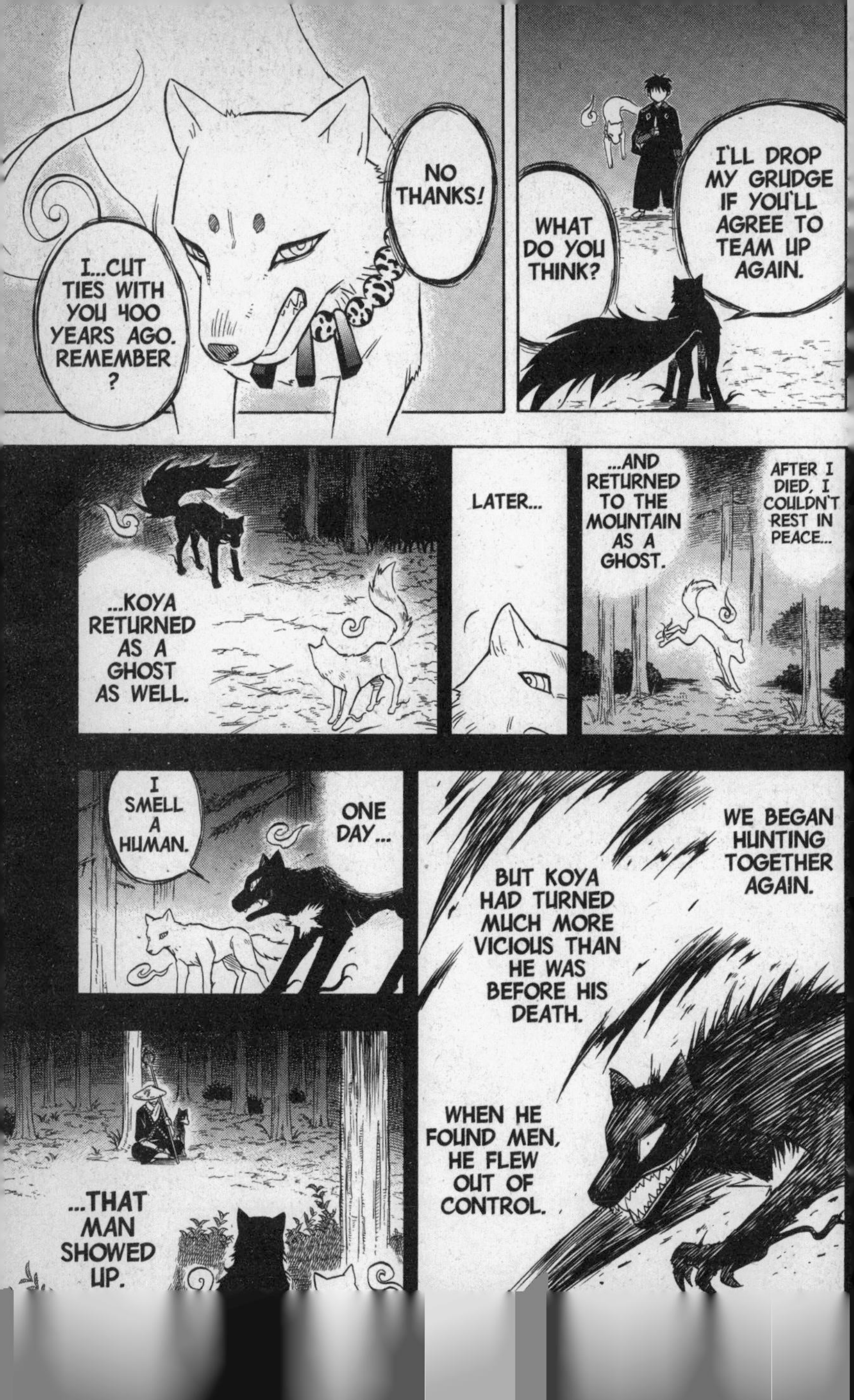
I'LL DROP MY GRUDGE IF YOU'LL AGREE TO TEAM UP AGAIN.
WHAT DO YOU THINK?
NO THANKS!
I...CUT TIES WITH YOU 400 YEARS AGO. REMEMBER?
AFTER I DIED, I COULDN'T REST IN PEACE...
...AND RETURNED TO THE MOUNTAIN AS A GHOST.
LATER...
...KOYA RETURNED AS A GHOST AS WELL.
WE BEGAN HUNTING TOGETHER AGAIN.
BUT KOYA HAD TURNED MUCH MORE VICIOUS THAN HE WAS BEFORE HIS DEATH.
WHEN HE FOUND MEN, HE FLEW OUT OF CONTROL.
ONE DAY...
I SMELL A HUMAN.
...THAT MAN SHOWED UP.

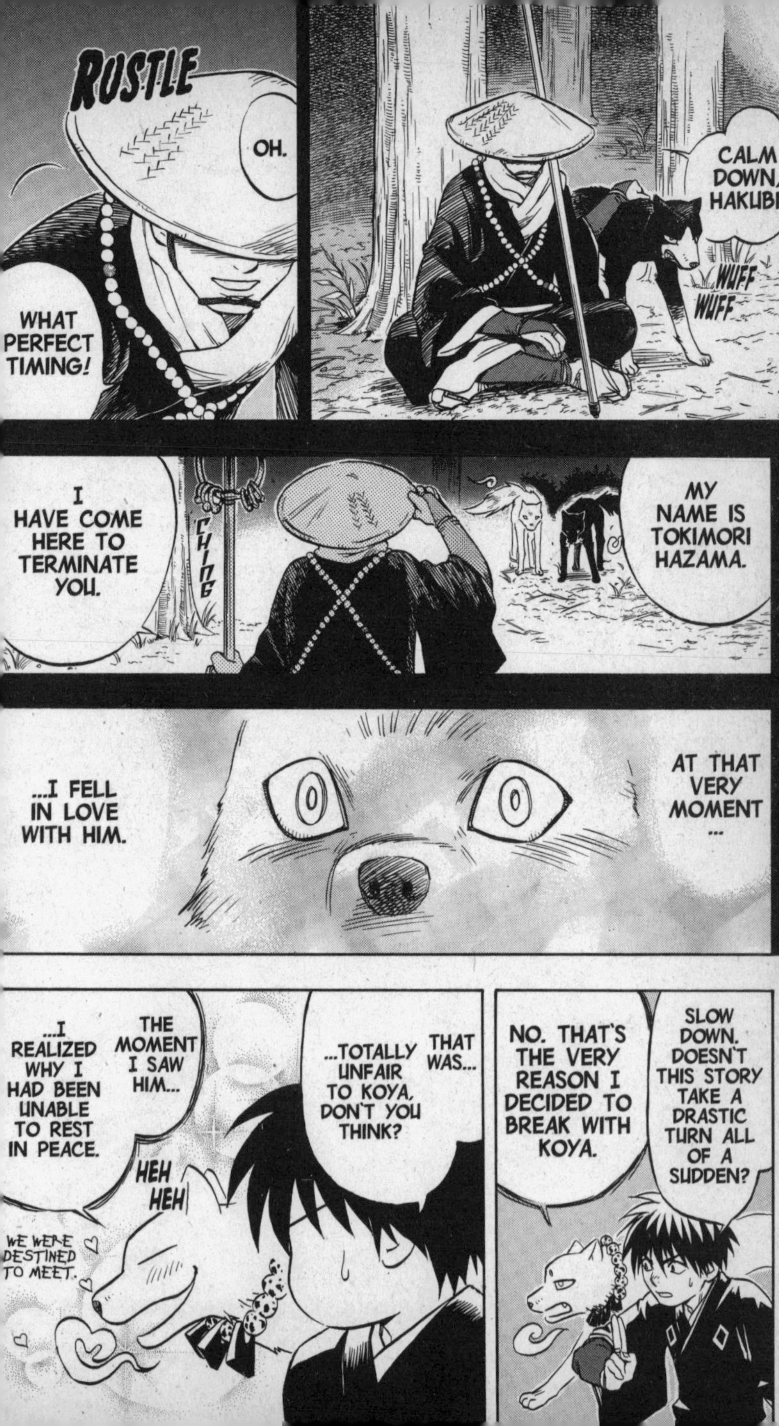
CALM DOWN, HAKUBI.
WUFF WUFF
RUSTLE
OH.
WHAT PERFECT TIMING!
MY NAME IS TOKIMORI HAZAMA.
CHING
I HAVE COME HERE TO TERMINATE YOU.
AT THAT VERY MOMENT...
...I FELL IN LOVE WITH HIM.
SLOW DOWN. DOESN'T THIS STORY TAKE A DRASTIC TURN ALL OF A SUDDEN?
NO. THAT'S THE VERY REASON I DECIDED TO BREAK WITH KOYA.
THAT WAS...
...TOTALLY UNFAIR TO KOYA, DON'T YOU THINK?
THE MOMENT I SAW HIM...
...I REALIZED WHY I HAD BEEN UNABLE TO REST IN PEACE.
HEH HEH
WE WERE DESTINED TO MEET.

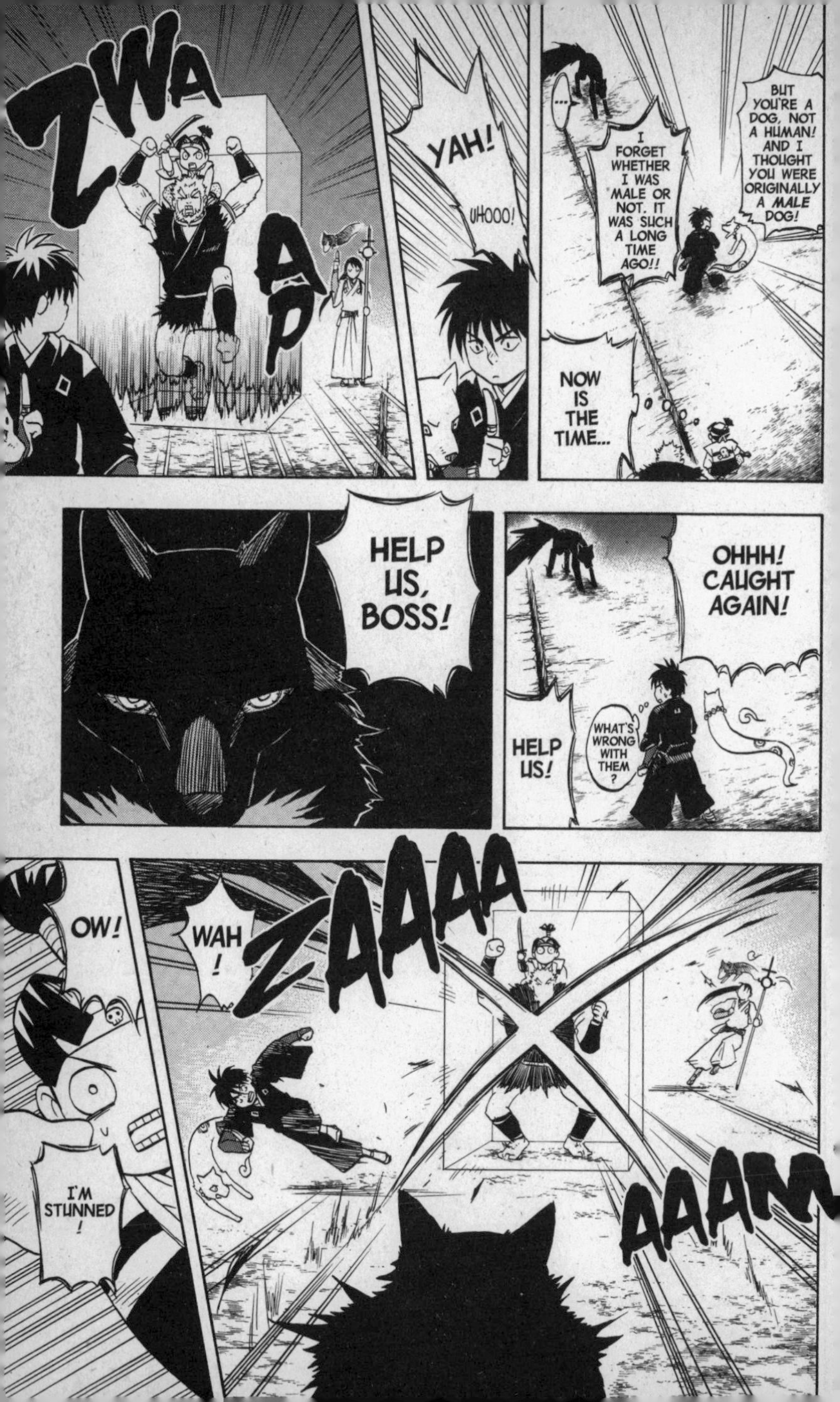
BUT YOU'RE A DOG, NOT A HUMAN! AND I THOUGHT YOU WERE ORIGINALLY A MALE DOG!
...
I FORGET WHETHER I WAS MALE OR NOT. IT WAS SUCH A LONG TIME AGO!!
NOW IS THE TIME...
YAH!
UHOOO!
ZWAAP
OHHH! CAUGHT AGAIN!
WHAT'S WRONG WITH THEM?
HELP US!
HELP US, BOSS!
ZAAAA
AAAM
WAH!
OW!
I'M STUNNED!

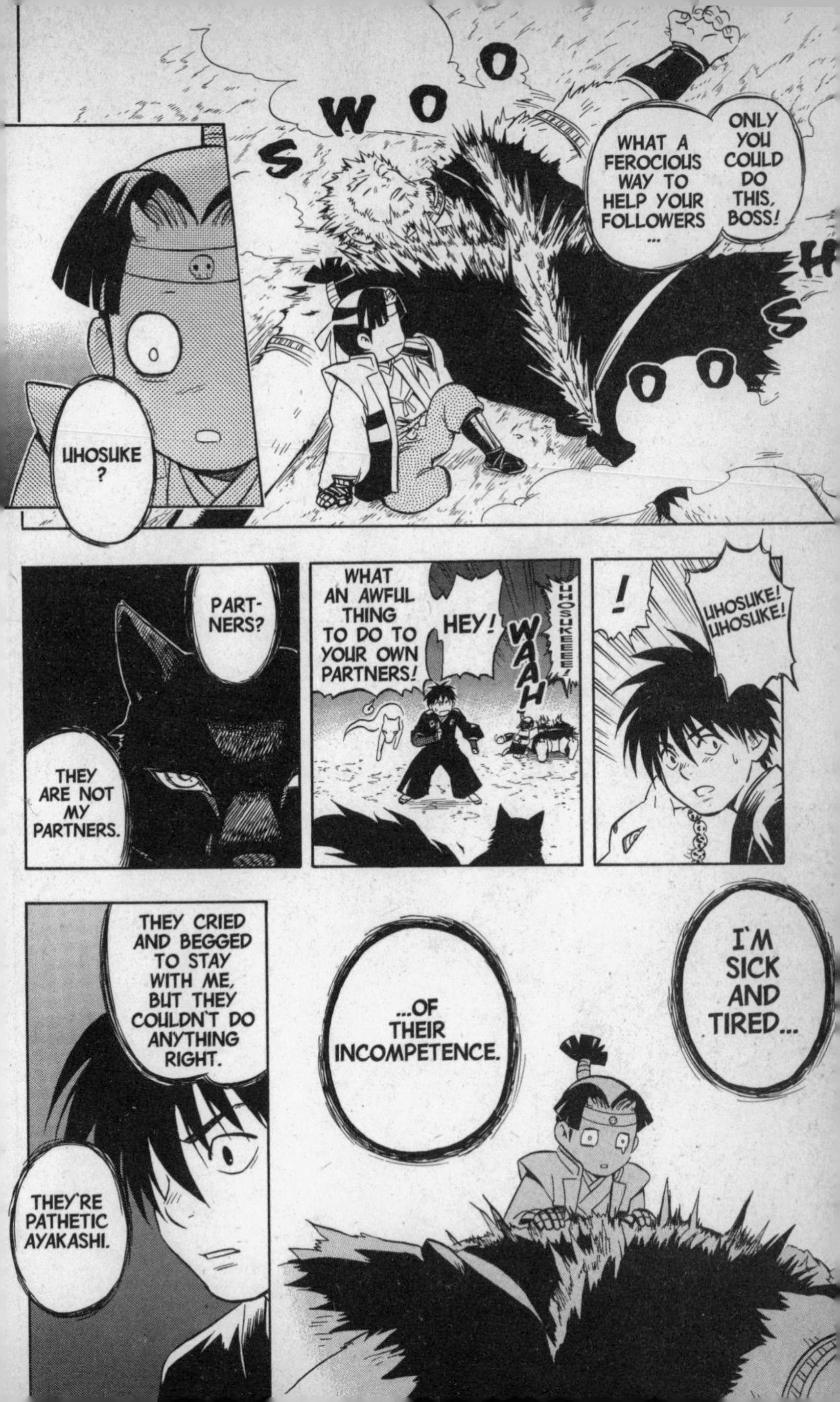
SWOOSH
ONLY YOU COULD DO THIS, BOSS!
WHAT A FEROCIOUS WAY TO HELP YOUR FOLLOWERS ...
UHOSUKE ?
!
UHOSUKE! UHOSUKE!
UHOSUKEEE!
WAAH
HEY!
WHAT AN AWFUL THING TO DO TO YOUR OWN PARTNERS!
PART-NERS?
THEY ARE NOT MY PARTNERS.
I'M SICK AND TIRED...
...OF THEIR INCOMPETENCE.
THEY CRIED AND BEGGED TO STAY WITH ME, BUT THEY COULDN'T DO ANYTHING RIGHT.
THEY'RE PATHETIC AYAKASHI.

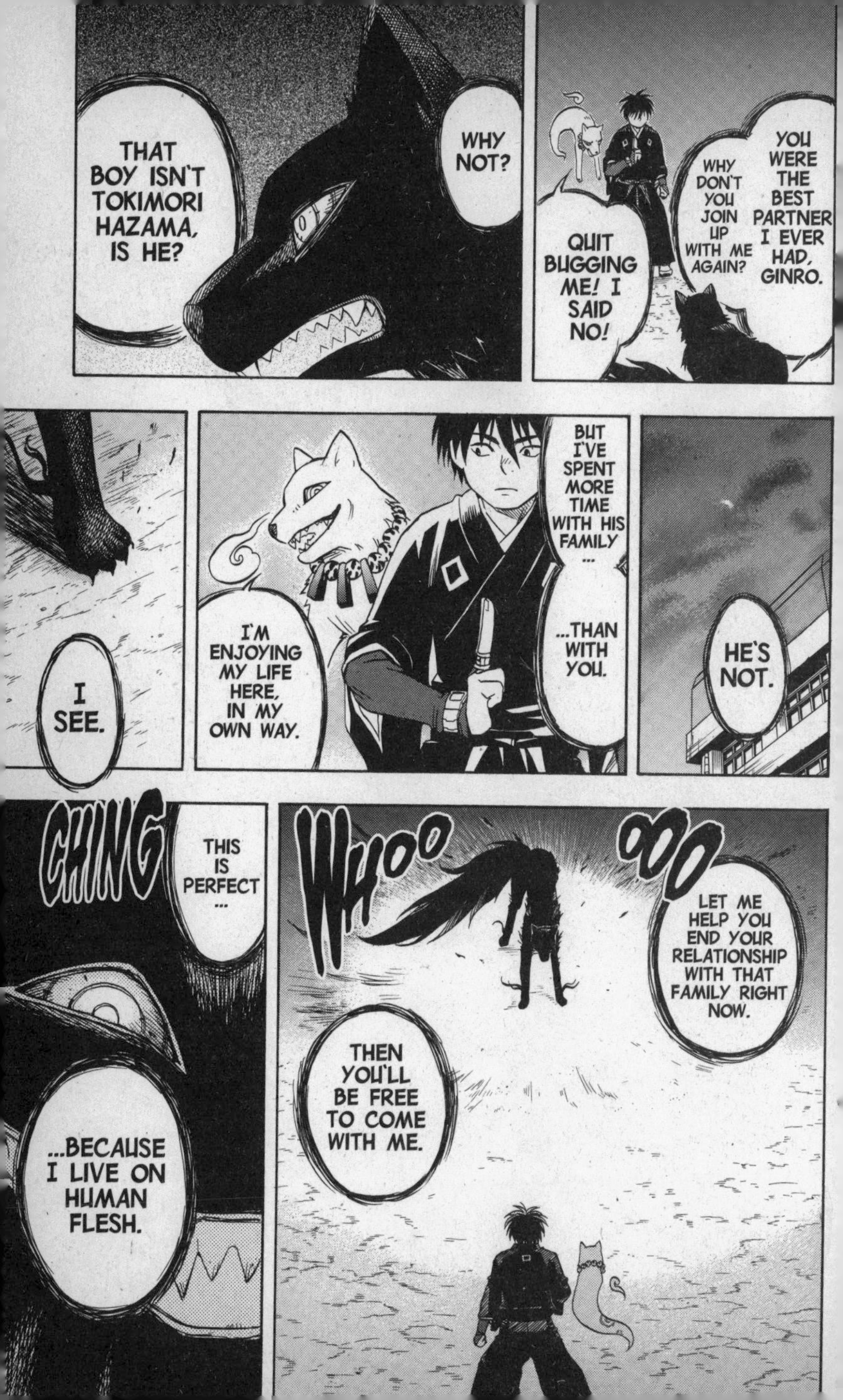
YOU WERE THE BEST PARTNER I EVER HAD, GINRO.
WHY DON'T YOU JOIN UP WITH ME AGAIN?
QUIT BUGGING ME! I SAID NO!
WHY NOT?
THAT BOY ISN'T TOKIMORI HAZAMA, IS HE?
HE'S NOT.
BUT I'VE SPENT MORE TIME WITH HIS FAMILY ...
...THAN WITH YOU.
I'M ENJOYING MY LIFE HERE, IN MY OWN WAY.
I SEE.
WHOOOOO
LET ME HELP YOU END YOUR RELATIONSHIP WITH THAT FAMILY RIGHT NOW.
THEN YOU'LL BE FREE TO COME WITH ME.
CHING
THIS IS PERFECT ...
...BECAUSE I LIVE ON HUMAN FLESH.

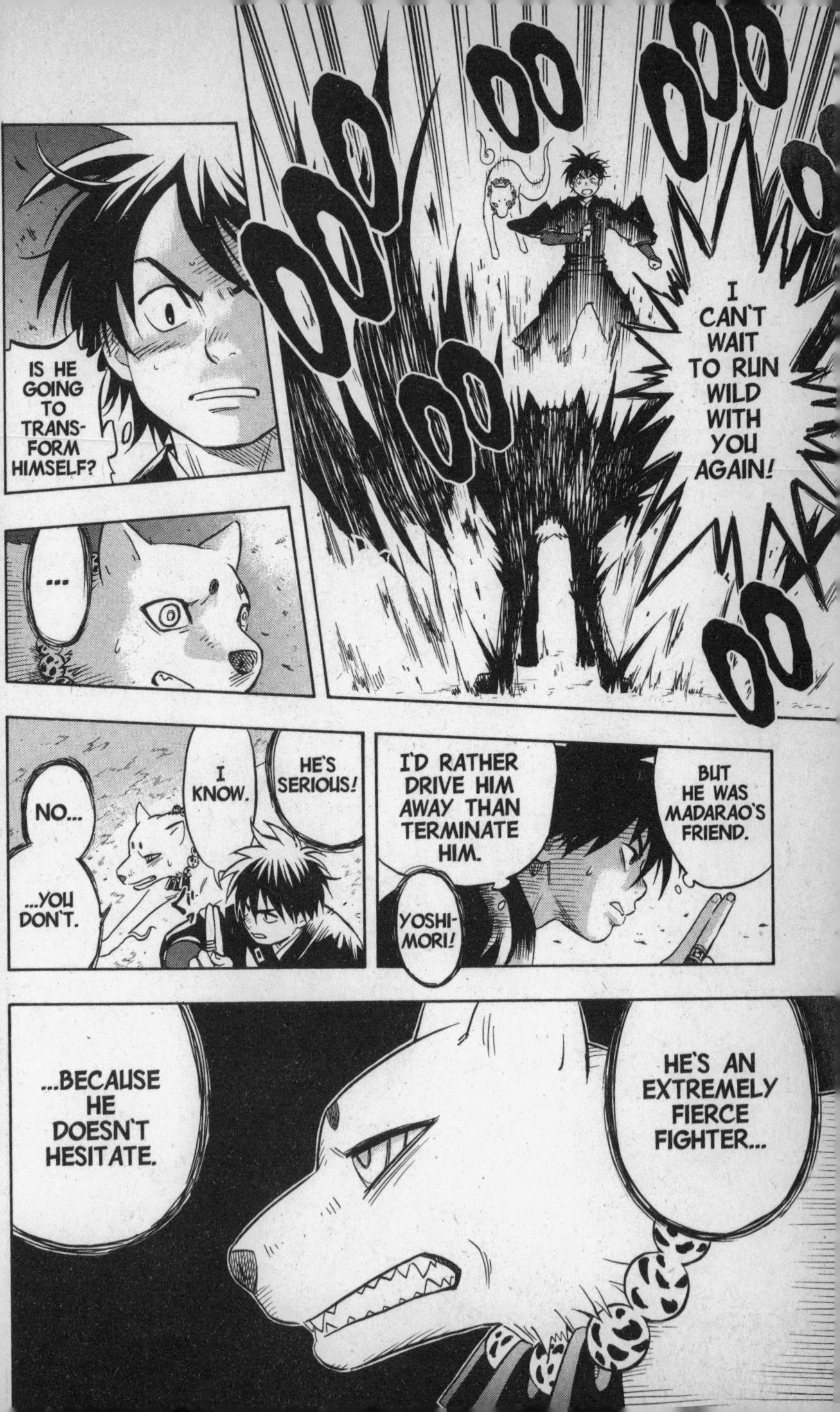
I CAN'T WAIT TO RUN WILD WITH YOU AGAIN!
IS HE GOING TO TRANS-FORM HIMSELF?
...
BUT HE WAS MADARAO'S FRIEND.
I'D RATHER DRIVE HIM AWAY THAN TERMINATE HIM.
YOSHI-MORI!
HE'S SERIOUS!
I KNOW.
NO...
...YOU DON'T.
HE'S AN EXTREMELY FIERCE FIGHTER...
...BECAUSE HE DOESN'T HESITATE.

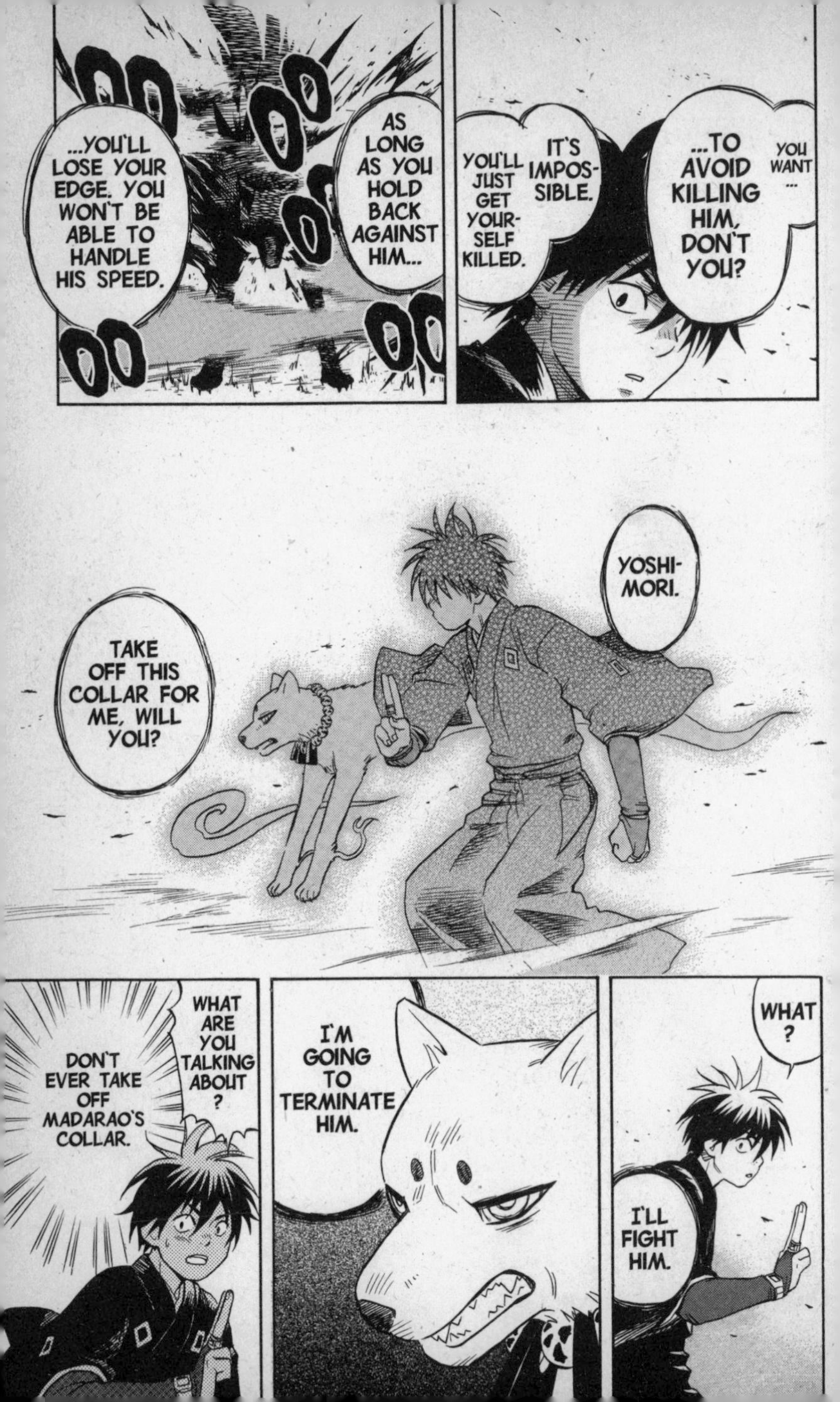
YOU WANT ...
...TO AVOID KILLING HIM, DON'T YOU?
IT'S IMPOSSIBLE.
YOU'LL JUST GET YOURSELF KILLED.
AS LONG AS YOU HOLD BACK AGAINST HIM...
...YOU'LL LOSE YOUR EDGE. YOU WON'T BE ABLE TO HANDLE HIS SPEED.
YOSHIMORI.
TAKE OFF THIS COLLAR FOR ME, WILL YOU?
WHAT?
I'LL FIGHT HIM.
I'M GOING TO TERMINATE HIM.
WHAT ARE YOU TALKING ABOUT?
DON'T EVER TAKE OFF MADARAO'S COLLAR.

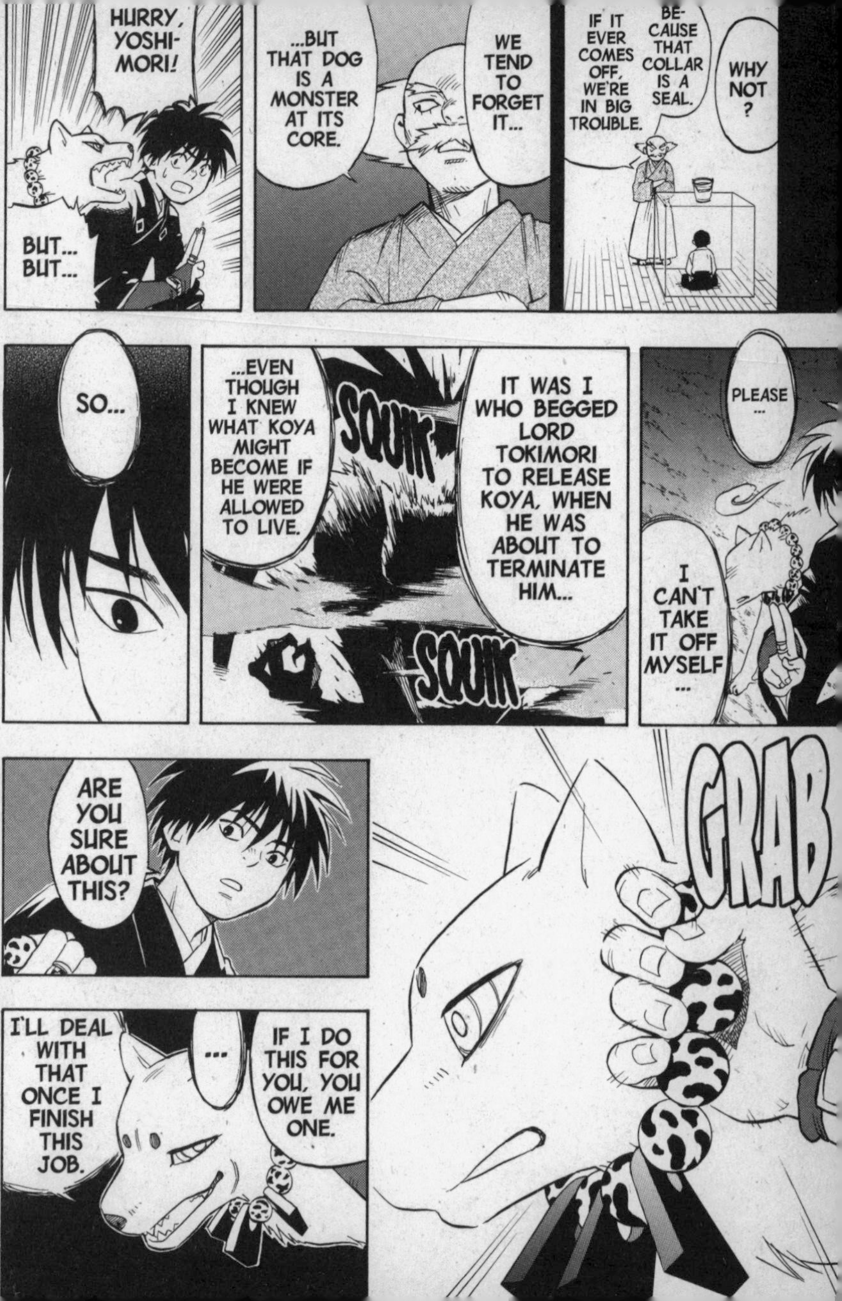

WHY NOT?
BECAUSE THAT COLLAR IS A SEAL.
IF IT EVER COMES OFF, WE'RE IN BIG TROUBLE.
WE TEND TO FORGET IT...
...BUT THAT DOG IS A MONSTER AT ITS CORE.
HURRY, YOSHIMORI!
BUT... BUT...
PLEASE...
I CAN'T TAKE IT OFF MYSELF...
IT WAS I WHO BEGGED LORD TOKIMORI TO RELEASE KOYA, WHEN HE WAS ABOUT TO TERMINATE HIM...
SQUIK
...EVEN THOUGH I KNEW WHAT KOYA MIGHT BECOME IF HE WERE ALLOWED TO LIVE.
SQUIK
SO...
GRAB
ARE YOU SURE ABOUT THIS?
IF I DO THIS FOR YOU, YOU OWE ME ONE.
...
I'LL DEAL WITH THAT ONCE I FINISH THIS JOB.

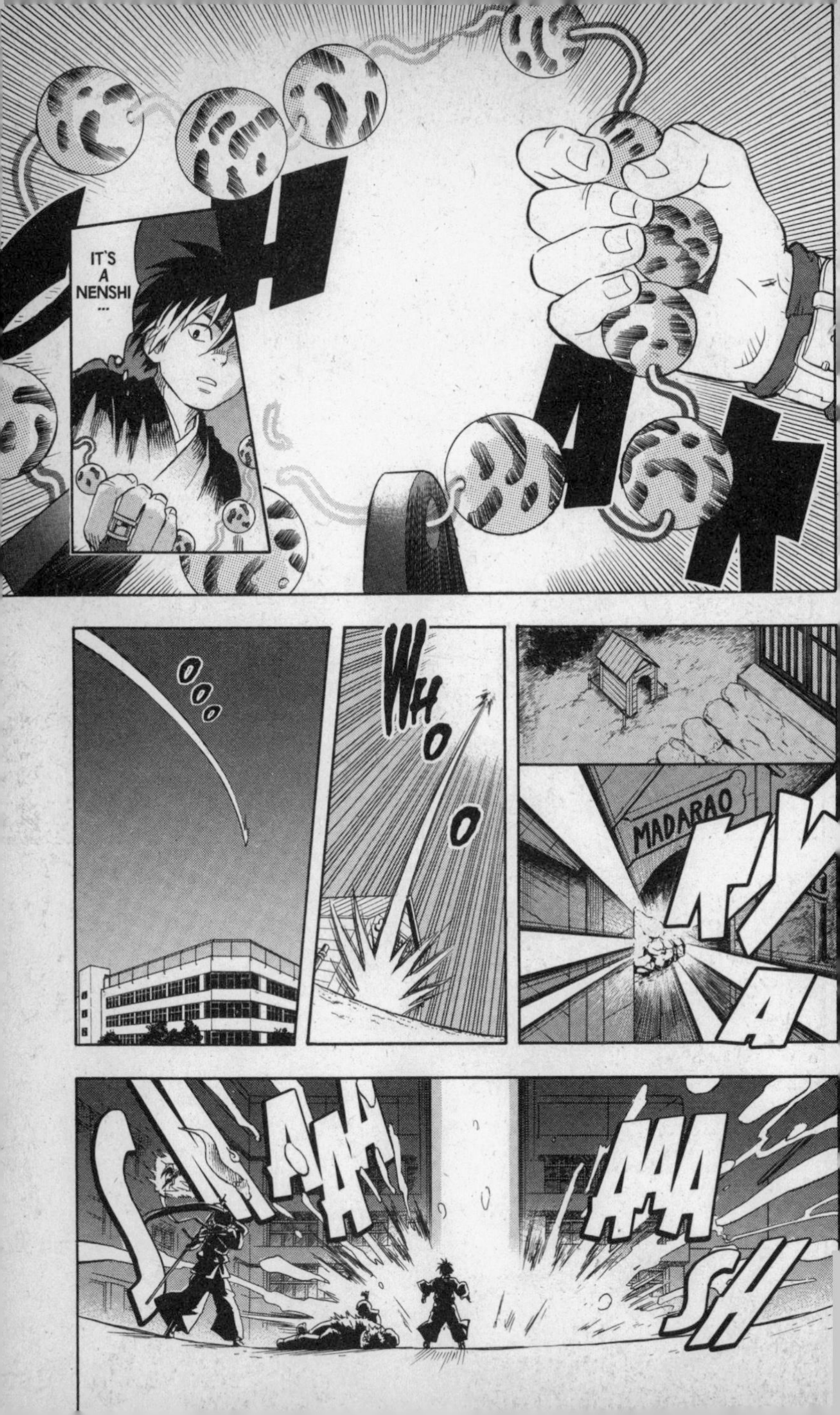
IT'S A NENSHI ...
CH
AK
MADARAO
KY
A
WHO
O
OOO
AAH
AAA
SH

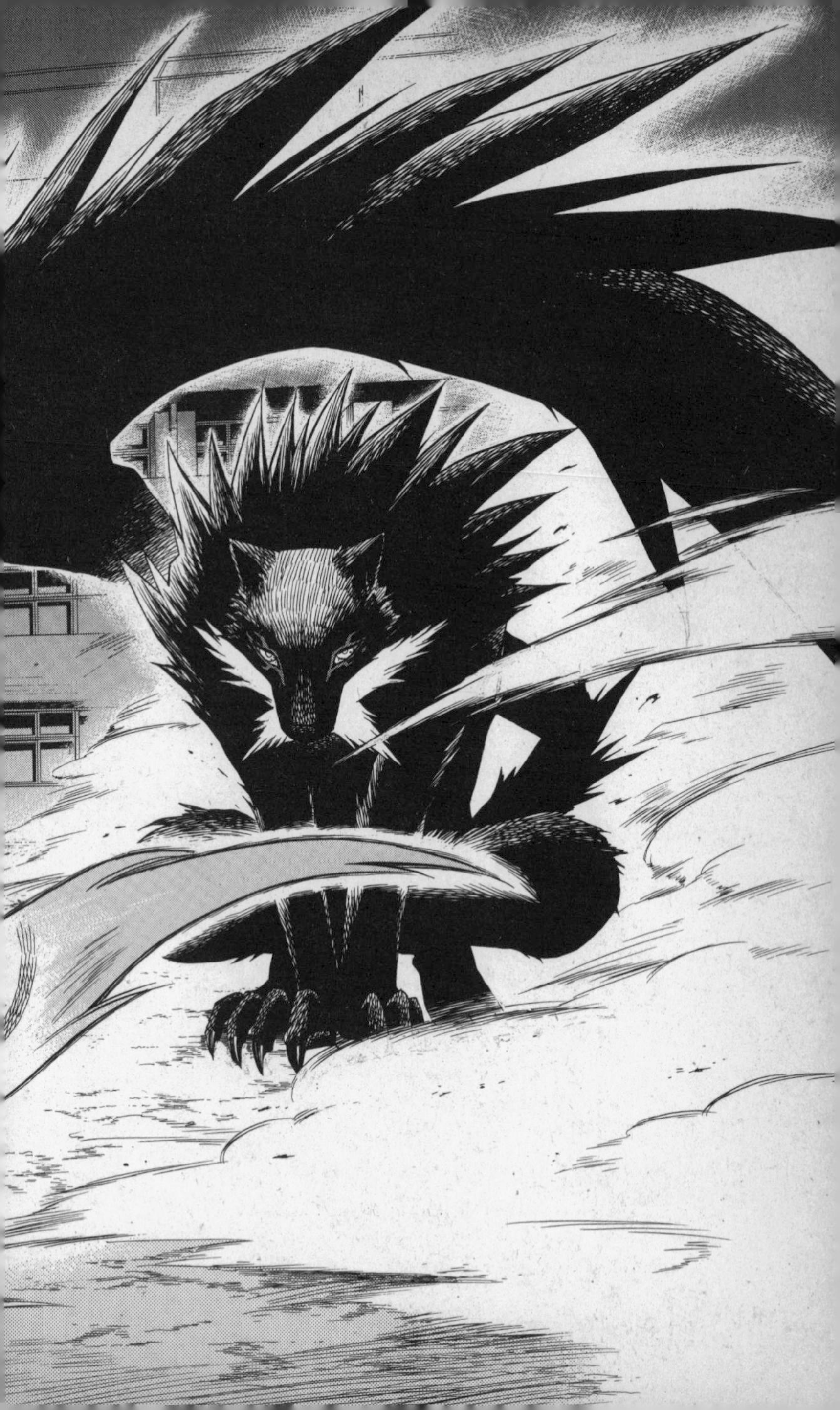

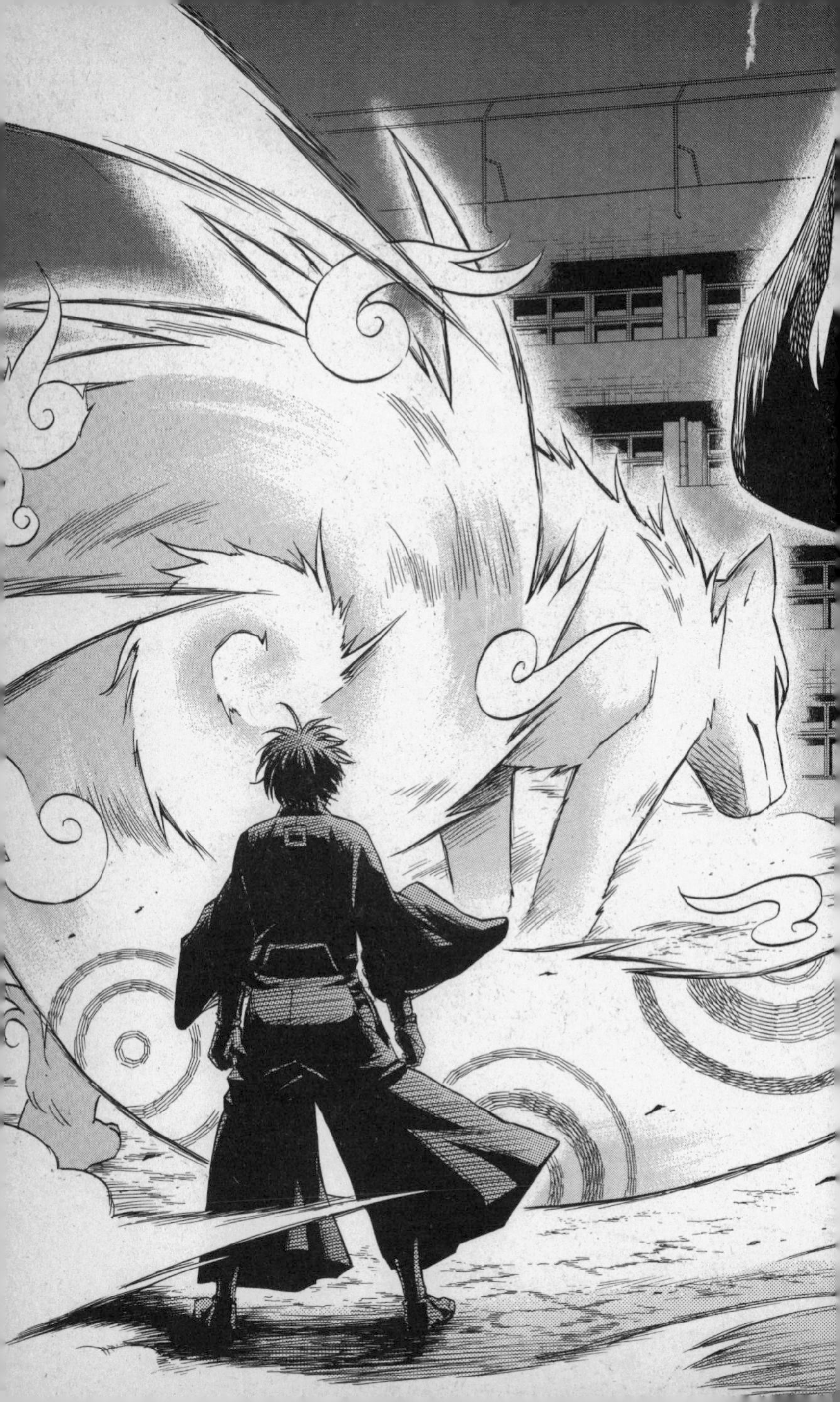

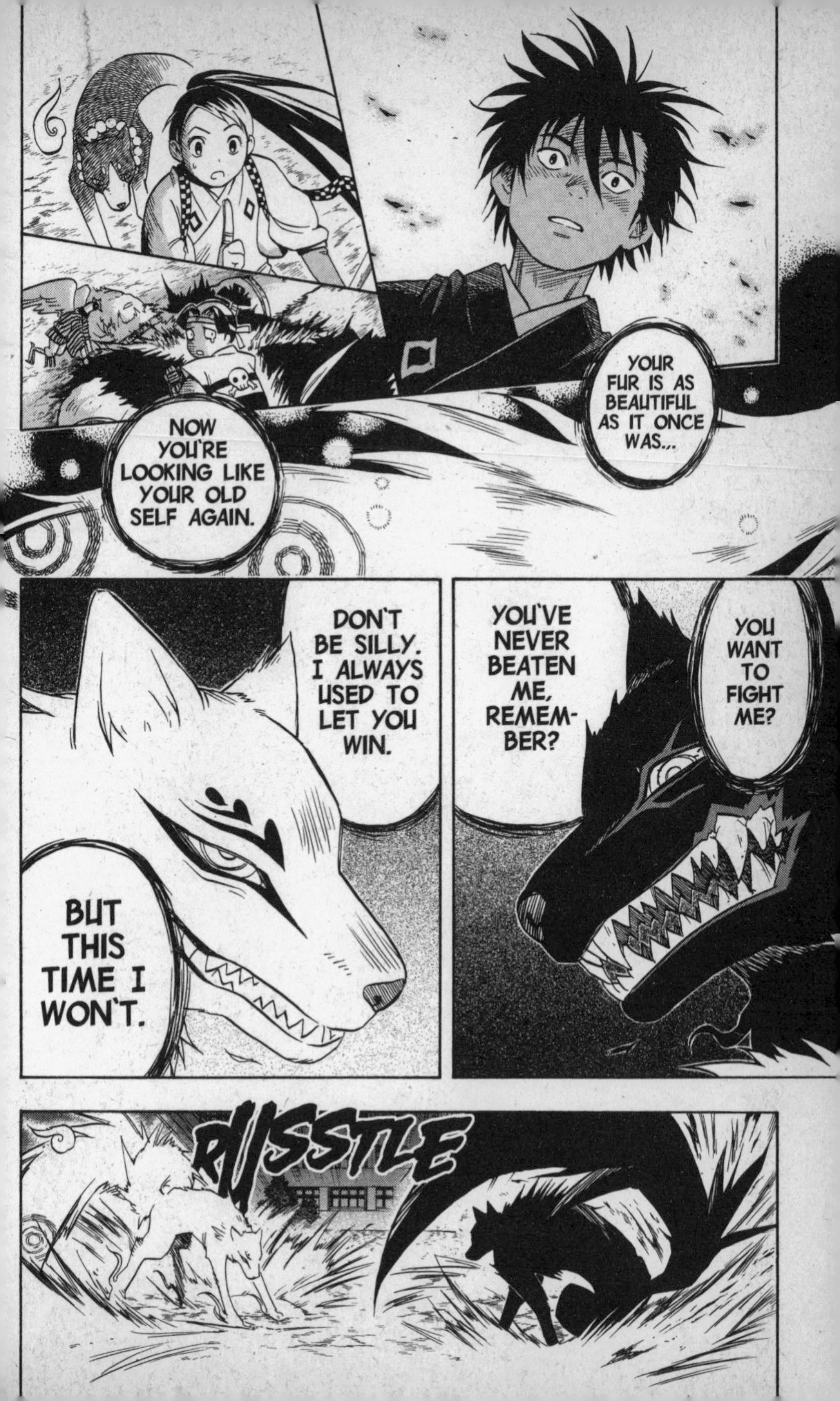
YOUR FUR IS AS BEAUTIFUL AS IT ONCE WAS...
NOW YOU'RE LOOKING LIKE YOUR OLD SELF AGAIN.
YOU WANT TO FIGHT ME?
YOU'VE NEVER BEATEN ME, REMEMBER?
DON'T BE SILLY. I ALWAYS USED TO LET YOU WIN.
BUT THIS TIME I WON'T.
RUSSTLE

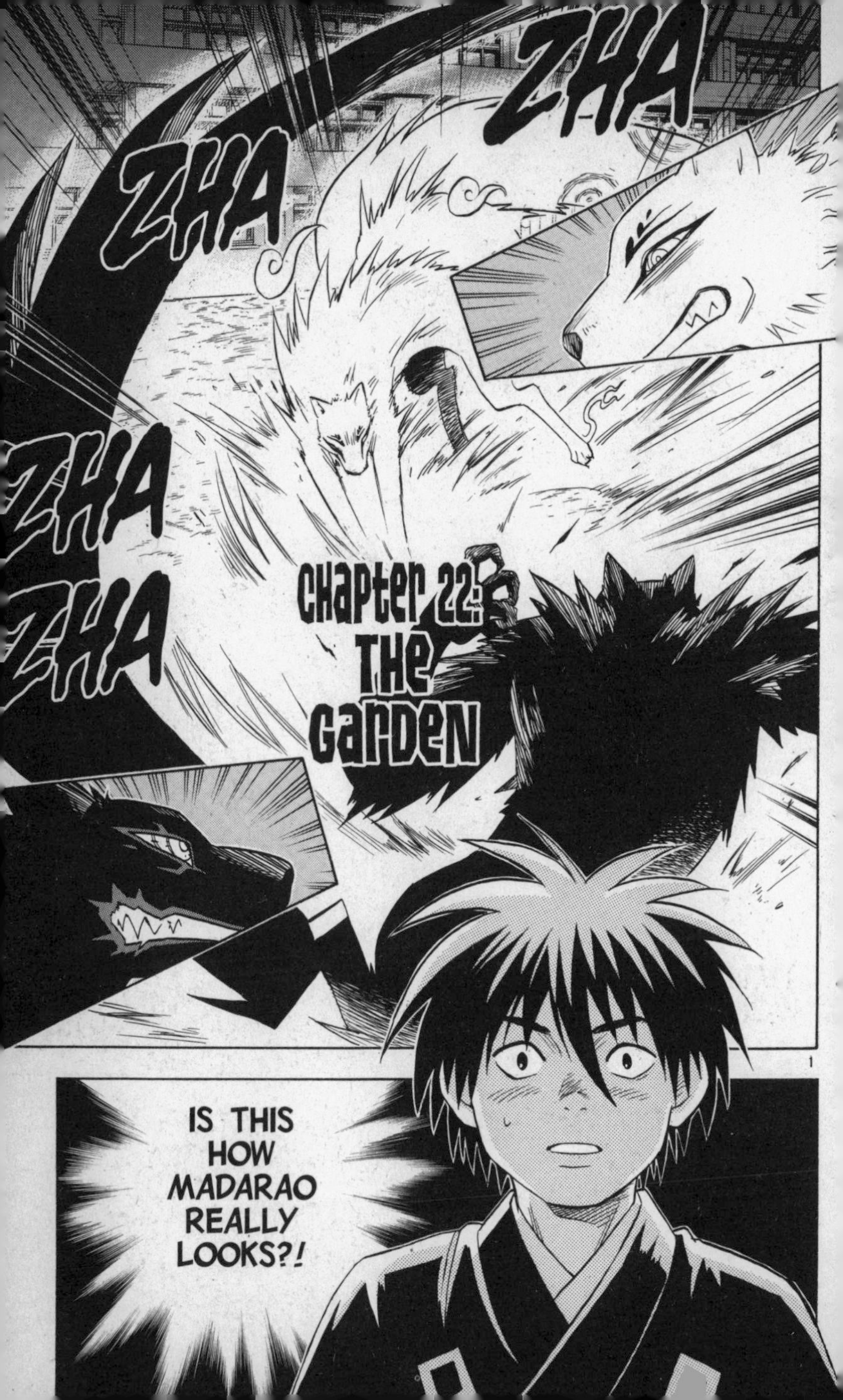
ZHA
ZHA
ZHA
ZHA
CHAPTER 22: THE GARDEN
IS THIS HOW MADARAO REALLY LOOKS?!

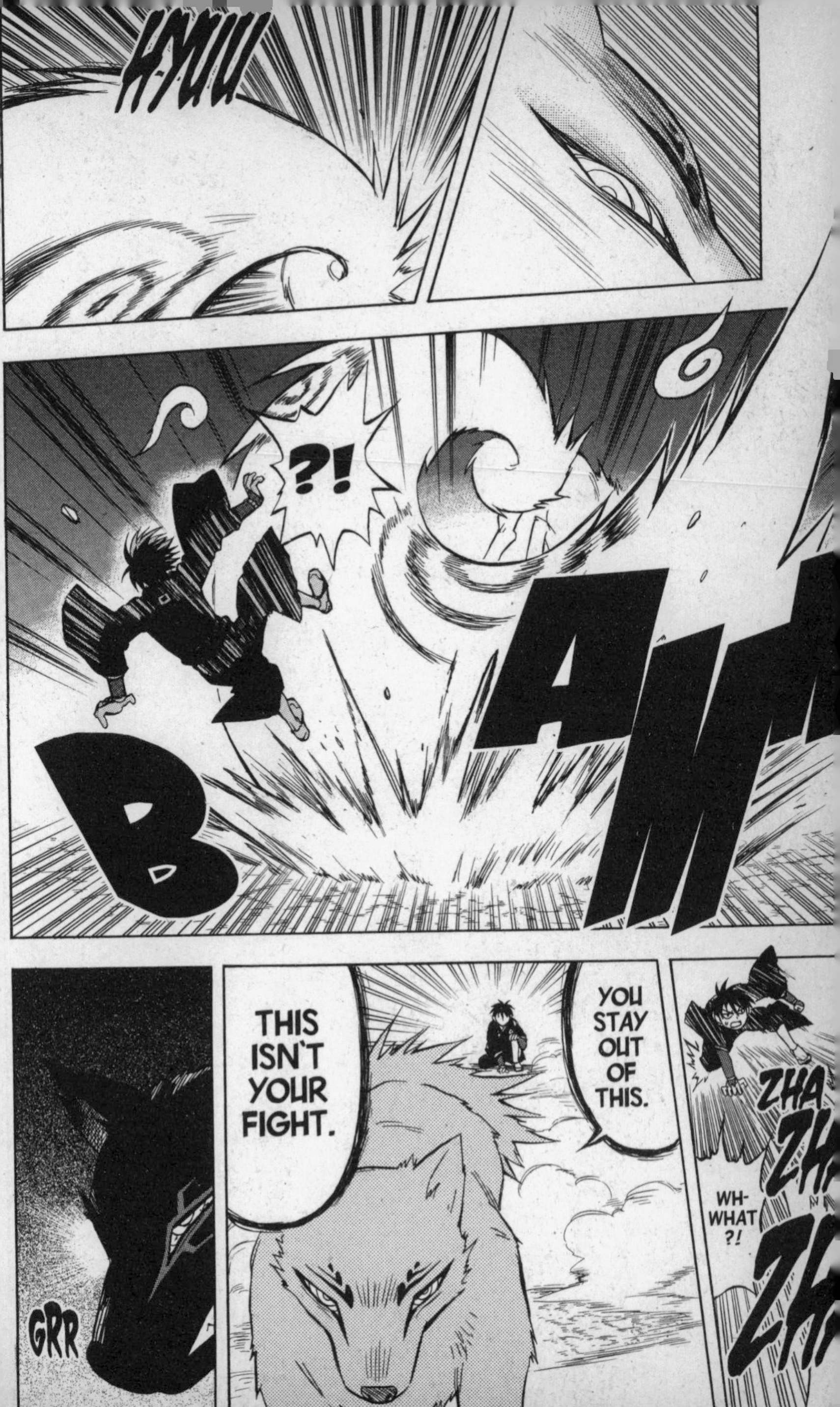
HYUU
?!
BAM
ZHA ZHA ZHA
WH-WHAT?!
YOU STAY OUT OF THIS.
THIS ISN'T YOUR FIGHT.
GRR

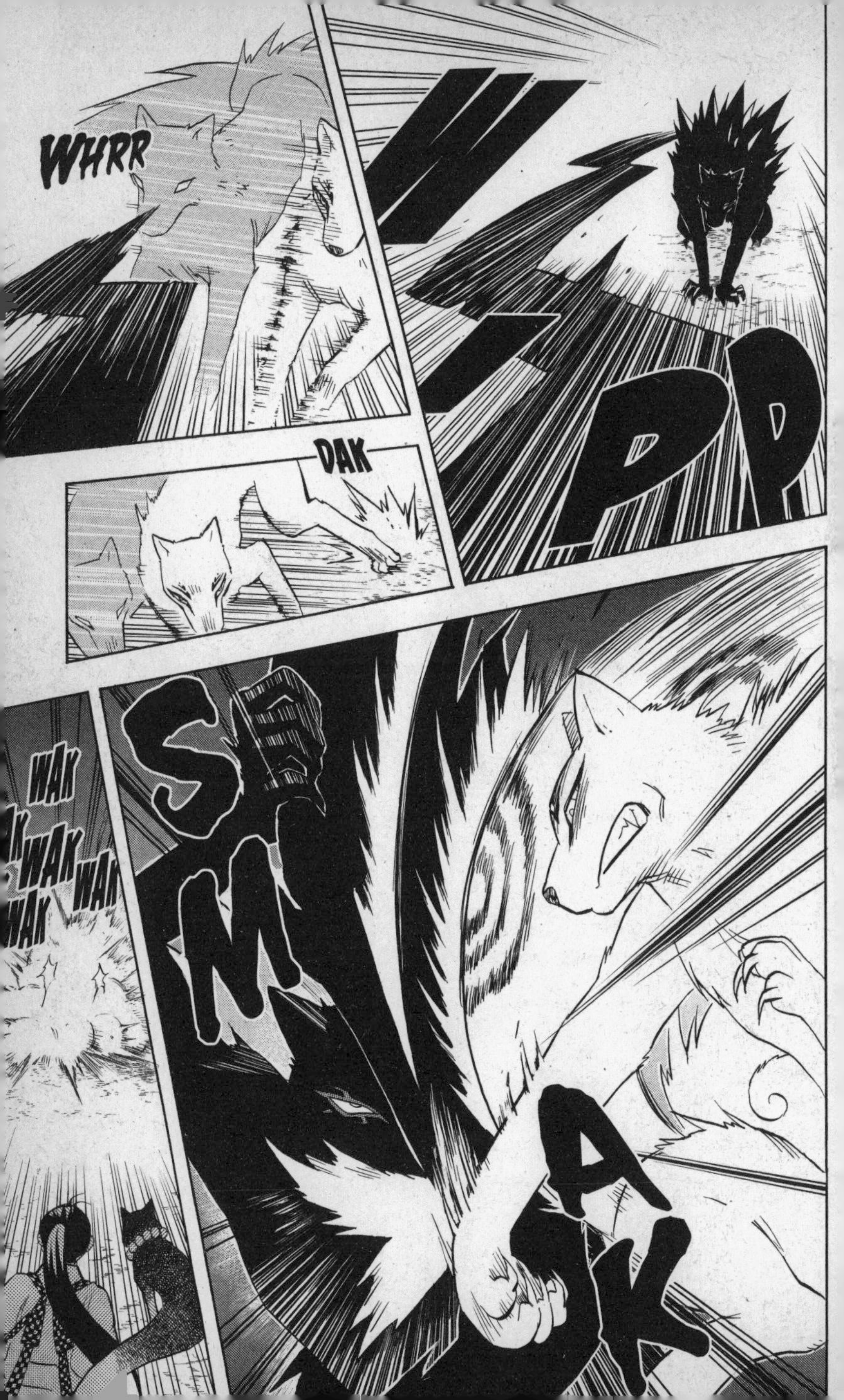
WHRR
DAK
WAK
WAK
WAK
WAK
WAK

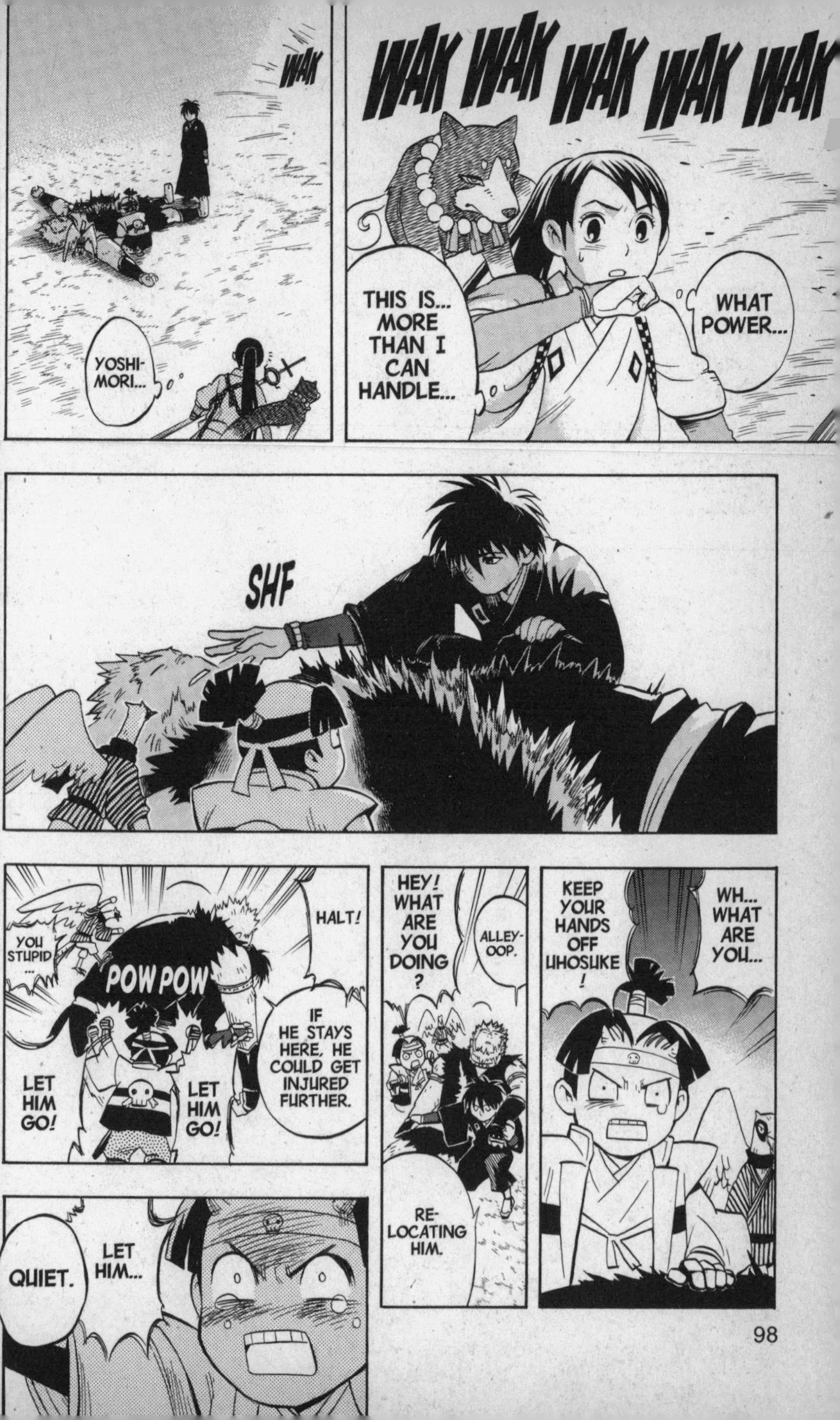
WAK WAK WAK WAK WAK
WHAT POWER...
THIS IS... MORE THAN I CAN HANDLE...
WAK
YOSHIMORI...
SHF
WH... WHAT ARE YOU...
KEEP YOUR HANDS OFF UHOSUKE!
HEY! WHAT ARE YOU DOING?
ALLEY-OOP.
RE-LOCATING HIM.
HALT!
IF HE STAYS HERE, HE COULD GET INJURED FURTHER.
LET HIM GO!
POW POW
YOU STUPID...
LET HIM GO!
LET HIM...
QUIET.

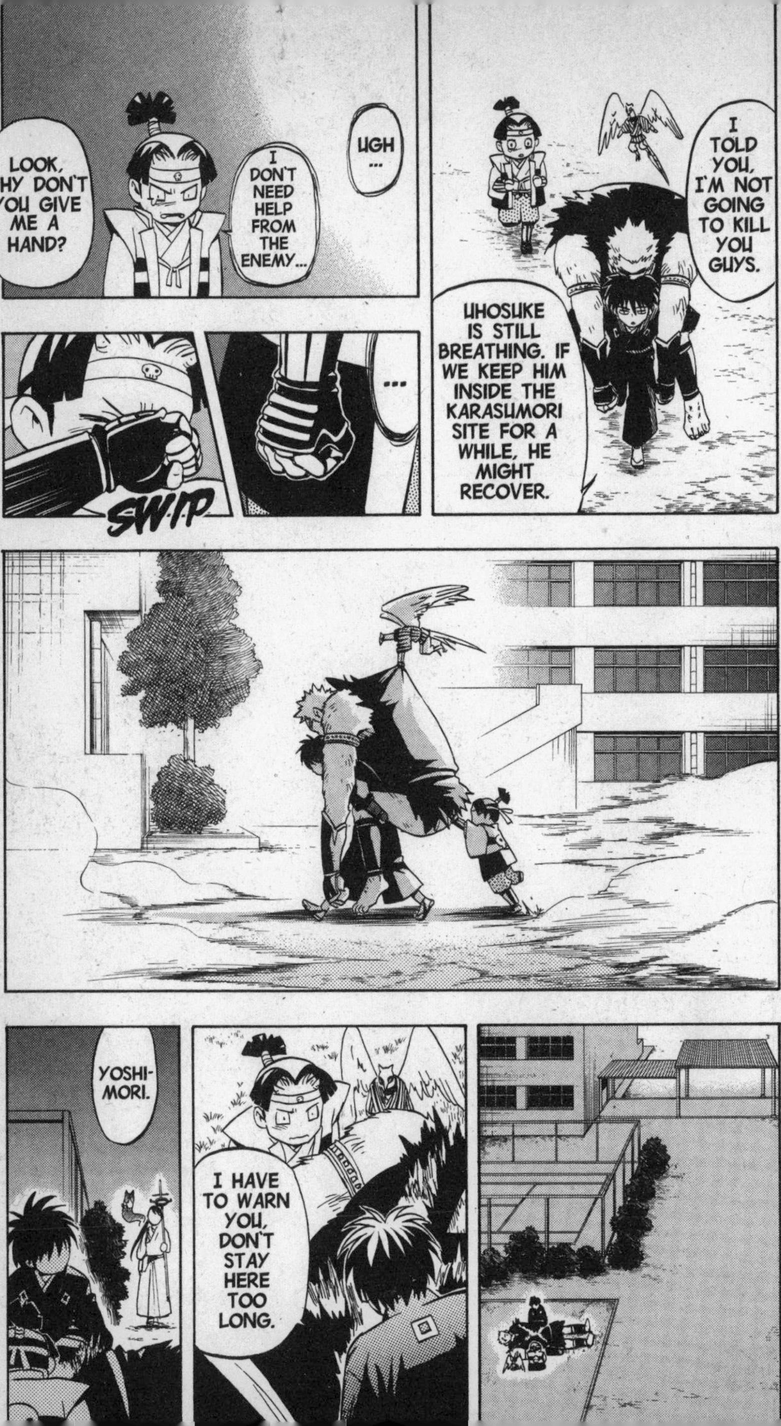

I TOLD YOU, I'M NOT GOING TO KILL YOU GUYS.
UHOSUKE IS STILL BREATHING. IF WE KEEP HIM INSIDE THE KARASUMORI SITE FOR A WHILE, HE MIGHT RECOVER.
UGH ...
I DON'T NEED HELP FROM THE ENEMY...
LOOK, WHY DON'T YOU GIVE ME A HAND?
...
SWIP
I HAVE TO WARN YOU, DON'T STAY HERE TOO LONG.
YOSHI-MORI.

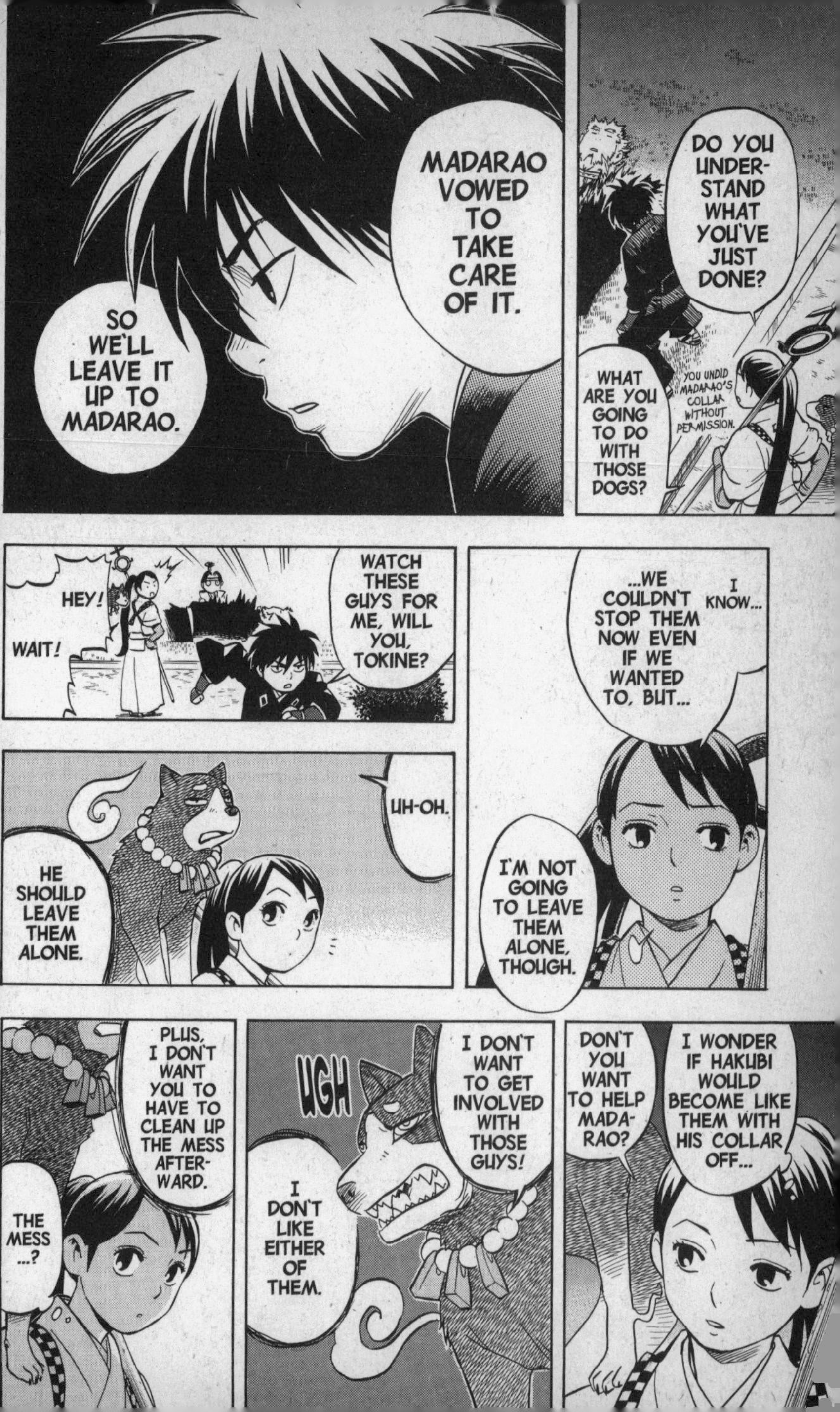
DO YOU UNDER-STAND WHAT YOU'VE JUST DONE?
YOU UNDID MADARAO'S COLLAR WITHOUT PERMISSION.
WHAT ARE YOU GOING TO DO WITH THOSE DOGS?
MADARAO VOWED TO TAKE CARE OF IT.
SO WE'LL LEAVE IT UP TO MADARAO.
I KNOW...
...WE COULDN'T STOP THEM NOW EVEN IF WE WANTED TO, BUT...
I'M NOT GOING TO LEAVE THEM ALONE, THOUGH.
WATCH THESE GUYS FOR ME, WILL YOU, TOKINE?
HEY!
WAIT!
UH-OH.
HE SHOULD LEAVE THEM ALONE.
I WONDER IF HAKUBI WOULD BECOME LIKE THEM WITH HIS COLLAR OFF...
DON'T YOU WANT TO HELP MADA-RAO?
I DON'T WANT TO GET INVOLVED WITH THOSE GUYS!
UGH
I DON'T LIKE EITHER OF THEM.
PLUS, I DON'T WANT YOU TO HAVE TO CLEAN UP THE MESS AFTER-WARD.
THE MESS ...?

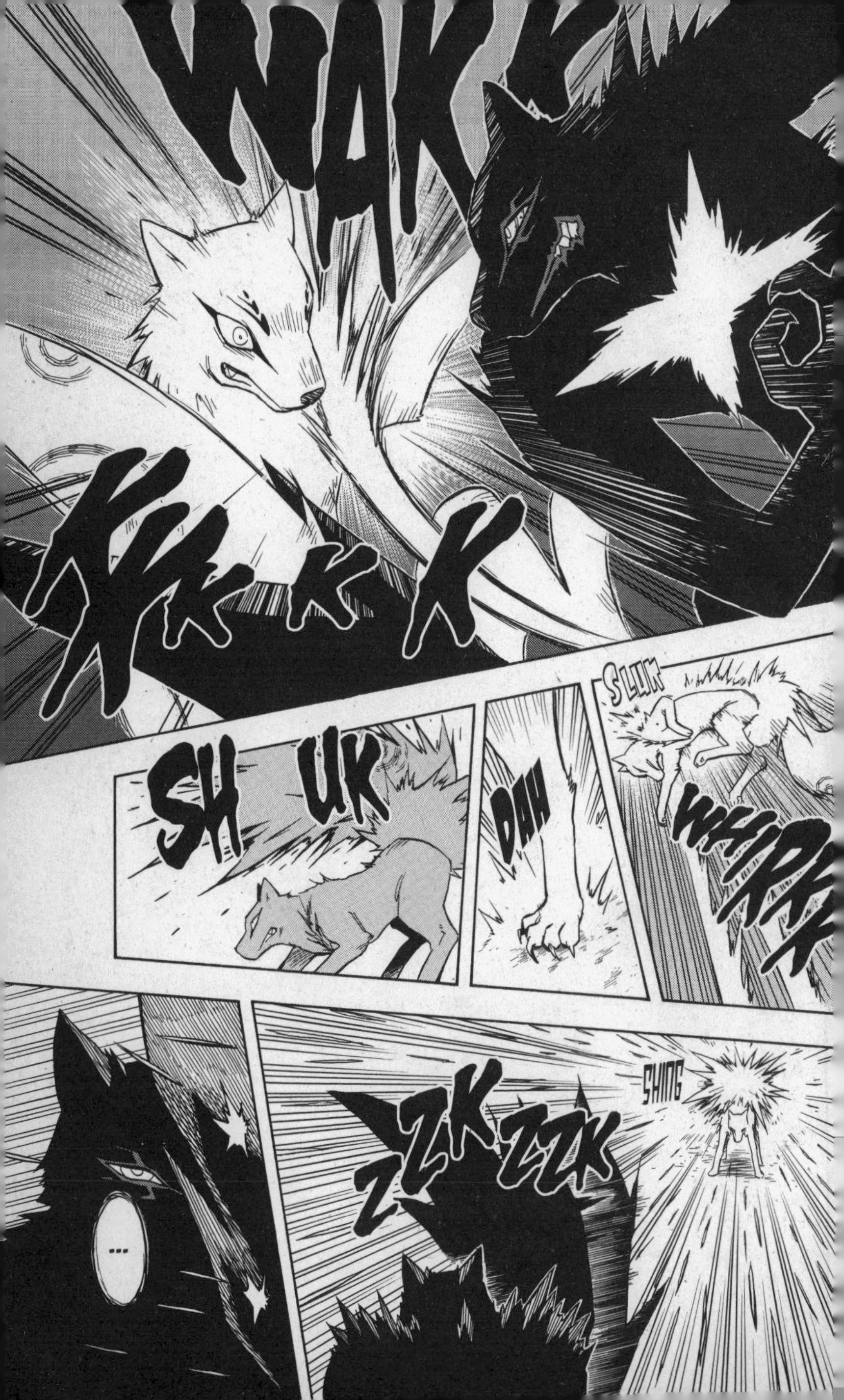
SLUR
DAH
SH UK
SHING
ZZK ZZK
...

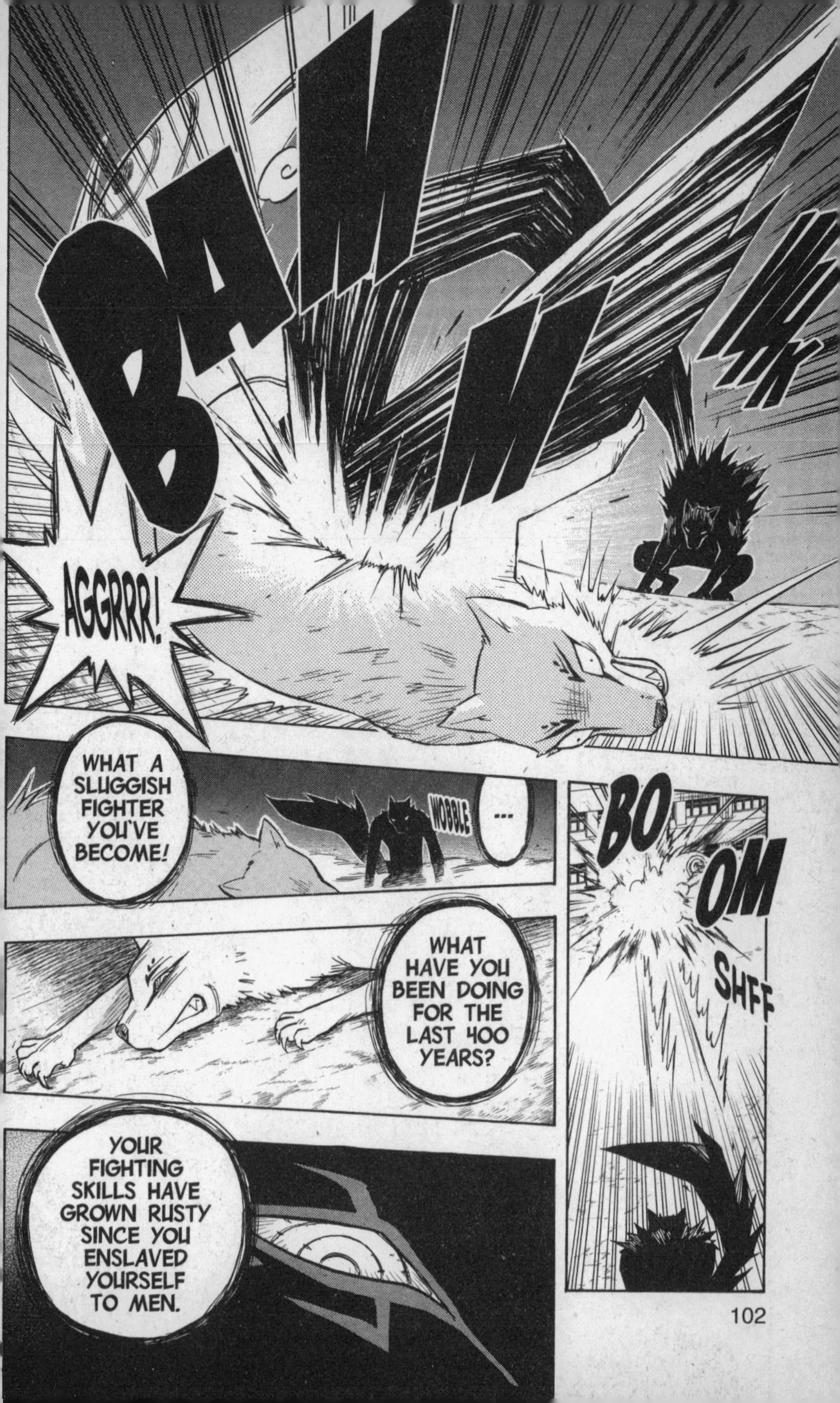
AGGRRR!
BO
OM
SHFF
...
WOBBLE
WHAT A SLUGGISH FIGHTER YOU'VE BECOME!
WHAT HAVE YOU BEEN DOING FOR THE LAST 400 YEARS?
YOUR FIGHTING SKILLS HAVE GROWN RUSTY SINCE YOU ENSLAVED YOURSELF TO MEN.

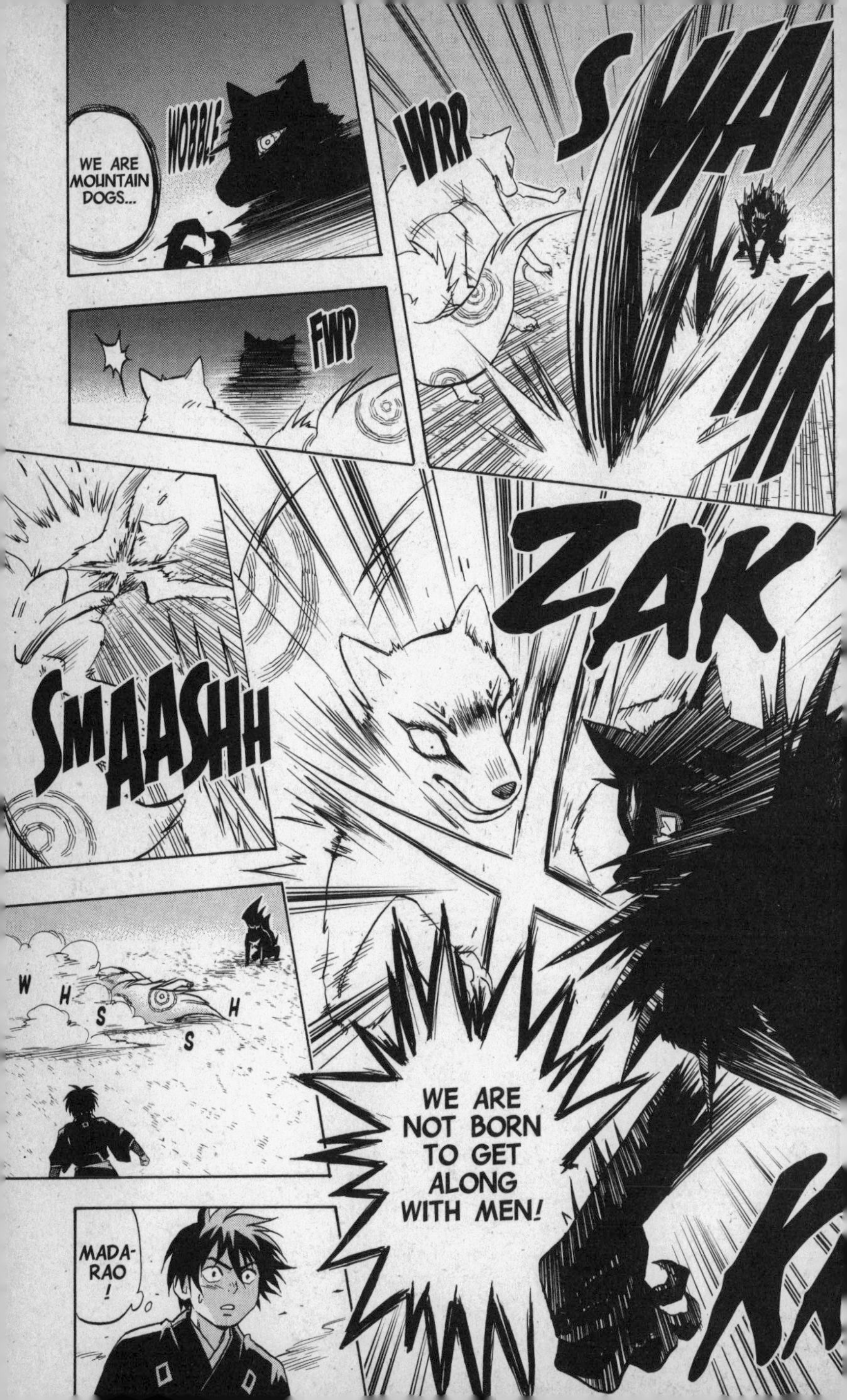
WRR
WOBBLE
WE ARE MOUNTAIN DOGS...
FWP
ZAK
WE ARE NOT BORN TO GET ALONG WITH MEN!
SMAASHH
WHSSH
MADA-RAO!

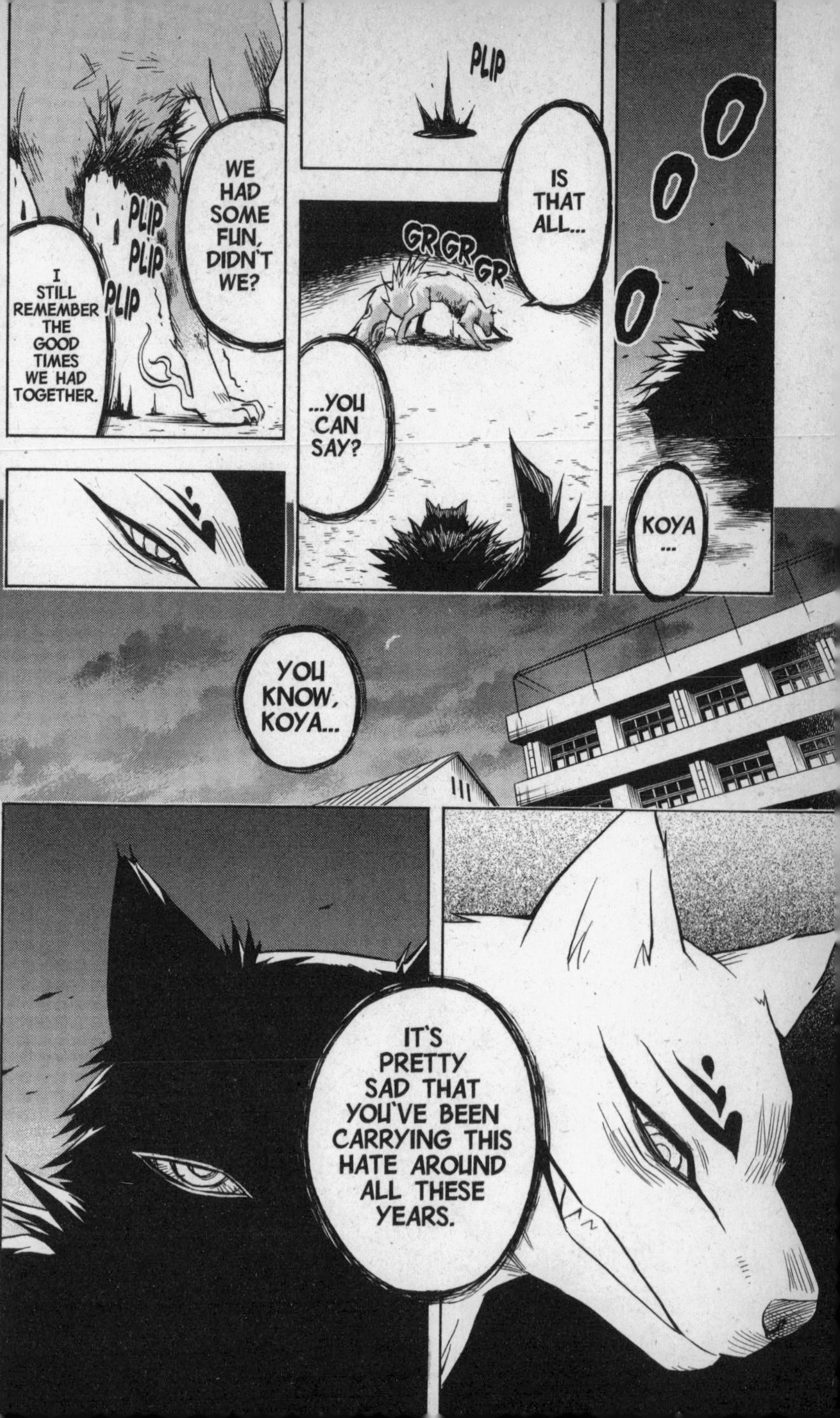
OOOO
KOYA...
PLIP
IS THAT ALL...
GR GR GR
...YOU CAN SAY?
WE HAD SOME FUN, DIDN'T WE?
PLIP PLIP PLIP
I STILL REMEMBER THE GOOD TIMES WE HAD TOGETHER.
YOU KNOW, KOYA...
IT'S PRETTY SAD THAT YOU'VE BEEN CARRYING THIS HATE AROUND ALL THESE YEARS.

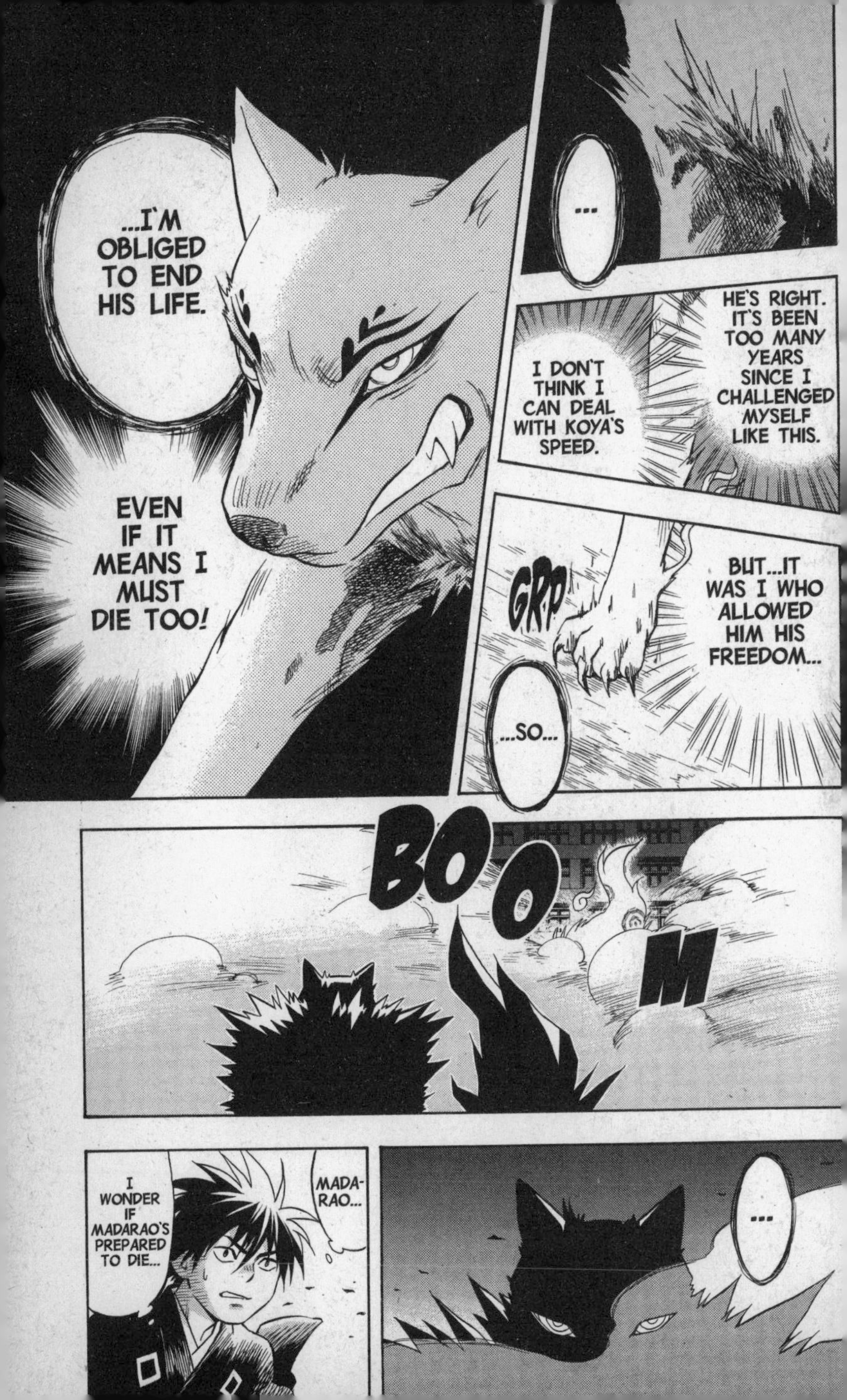

...
HE'S RIGHT. IT'S BEEN TOO MANY YEARS SINCE I CHALLENGED MYSELF LIKE THIS.
I DON'T THINK I CAN DEAL WITH KOYA'S SPEED.
BUT...IT WAS I WHO ALLOWED HIM HIS FREEDOM...
GRP
...SO...
...I'M OBLIGED TO END HIS LIFE.
EVEN IF IT MEANS I MUST DIE TOO!
BOOOM
...
MADA-RAO...
I WONDER IF MADARAO'S PREPARED TO DIE...

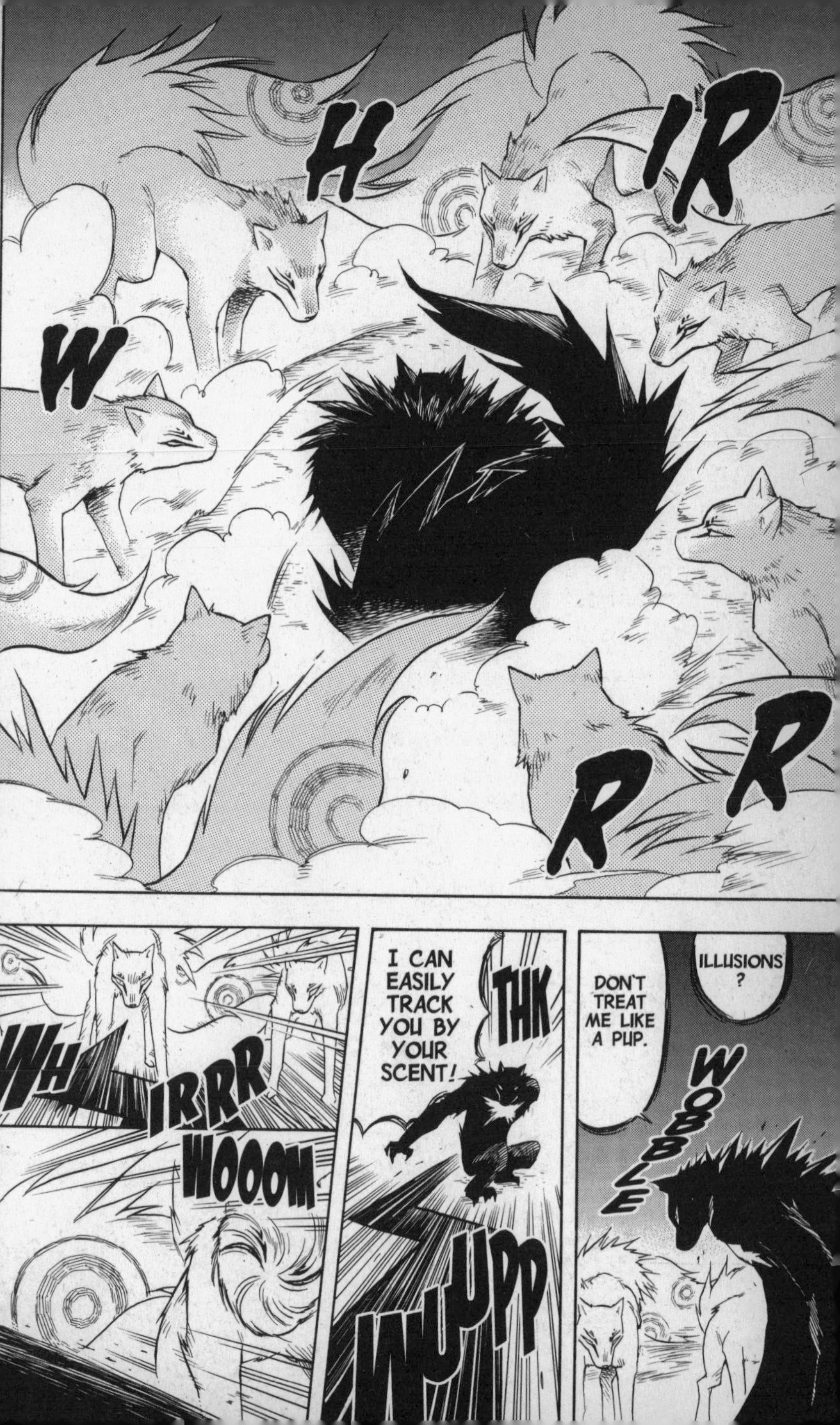
WHIRRR
ILLUSIONS?
DON'T TREAT ME LIKE A PUP.
WOBBLE
I CAN EASILY TRACK YOU BY YOUR SCENT!
THK
WHUPP
WHIRRR
WOOOM

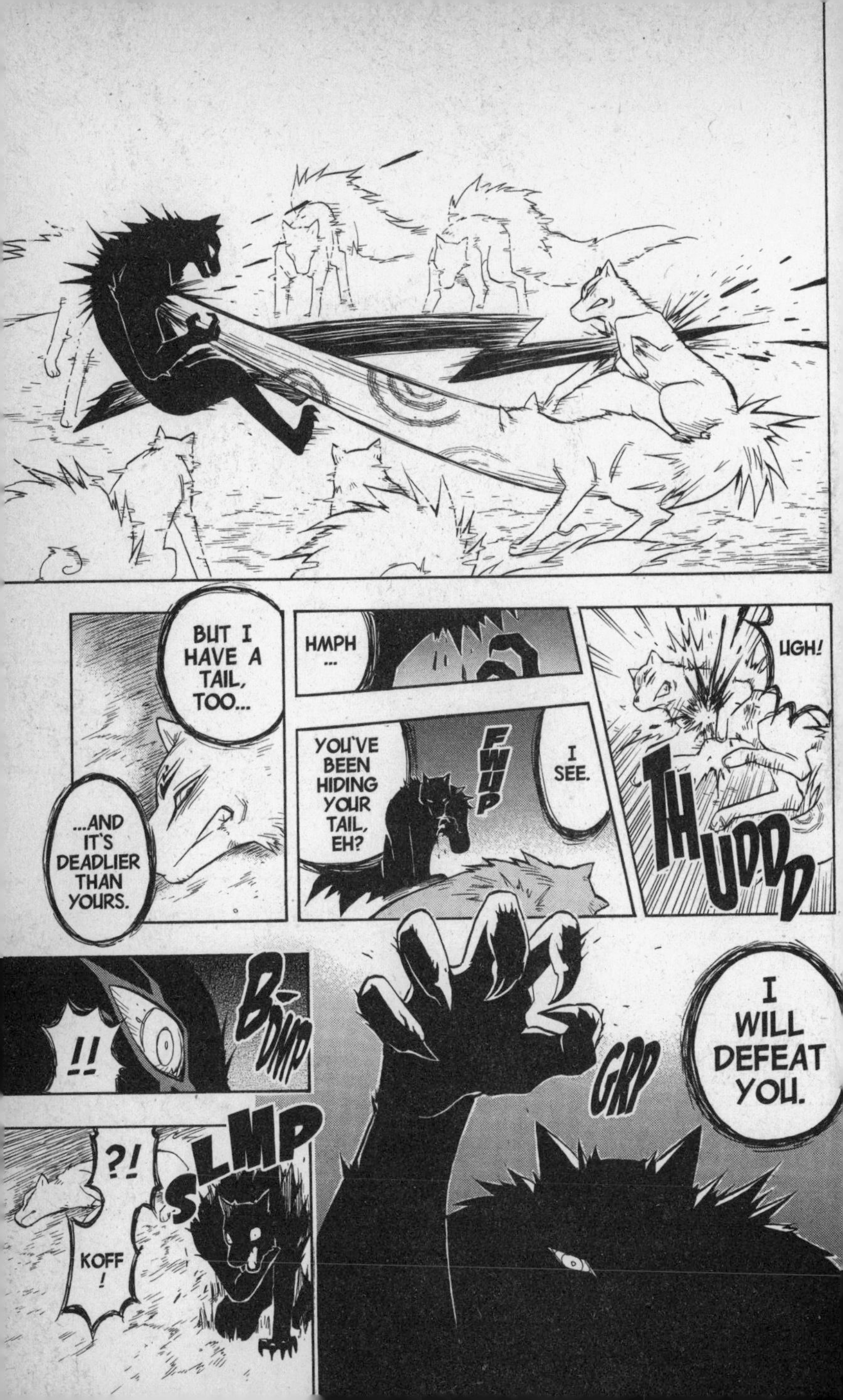
UGH!
THUDDD
HMPH...
I SEE.
FWUP
YOU'VE BEEN HIDING YOUR TAIL, EH?
BUT I HAVE A TAIL, TOO...
...AND IT'S DEADLIER THAN YOURS.
I WILL DEFEAT YOU.
GRP
!!
BDMP
?!
SLMP
KOFF!

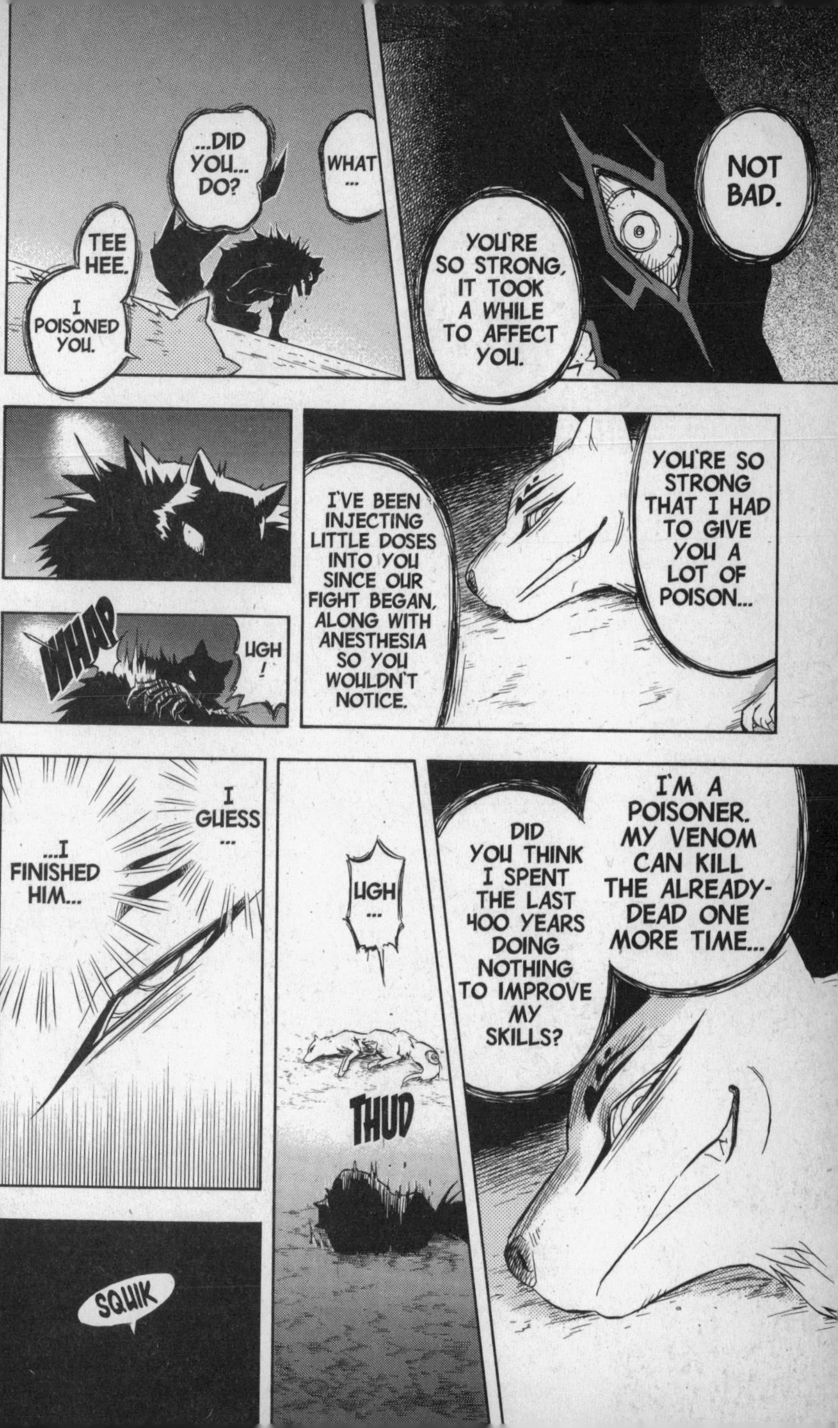
NOT BAD.
YOU'RE SO STRONG, IT TOOK A WHILE TO AFFECT YOU.
WHAT...
...DID YOU... DO?
TEE HEE.
I POISONED YOU.
YOU'RE SO STRONG THAT I HAD TO GIVE YOU A LOT OF POISON...
I'VE BEEN INJECTING LITTLE DOSES INTO YOU SINCE OUR FIGHT BEGAN, ALONG WITH ANESTHESIA SO YOU WOULDN'T NOTICE.
WHAP
UGH!
I'M A POISONER. MY VENOM CAN KILL THE ALREADY-DEAD ONE MORE TIME...
DID YOU THINK I SPENT THE LAST 400 YEARS DOING NOTHING TO IMPROVE MY SKILLS?
UGH...
THUD
I GUESS...
...I FINISHED HIM...
SQUIK

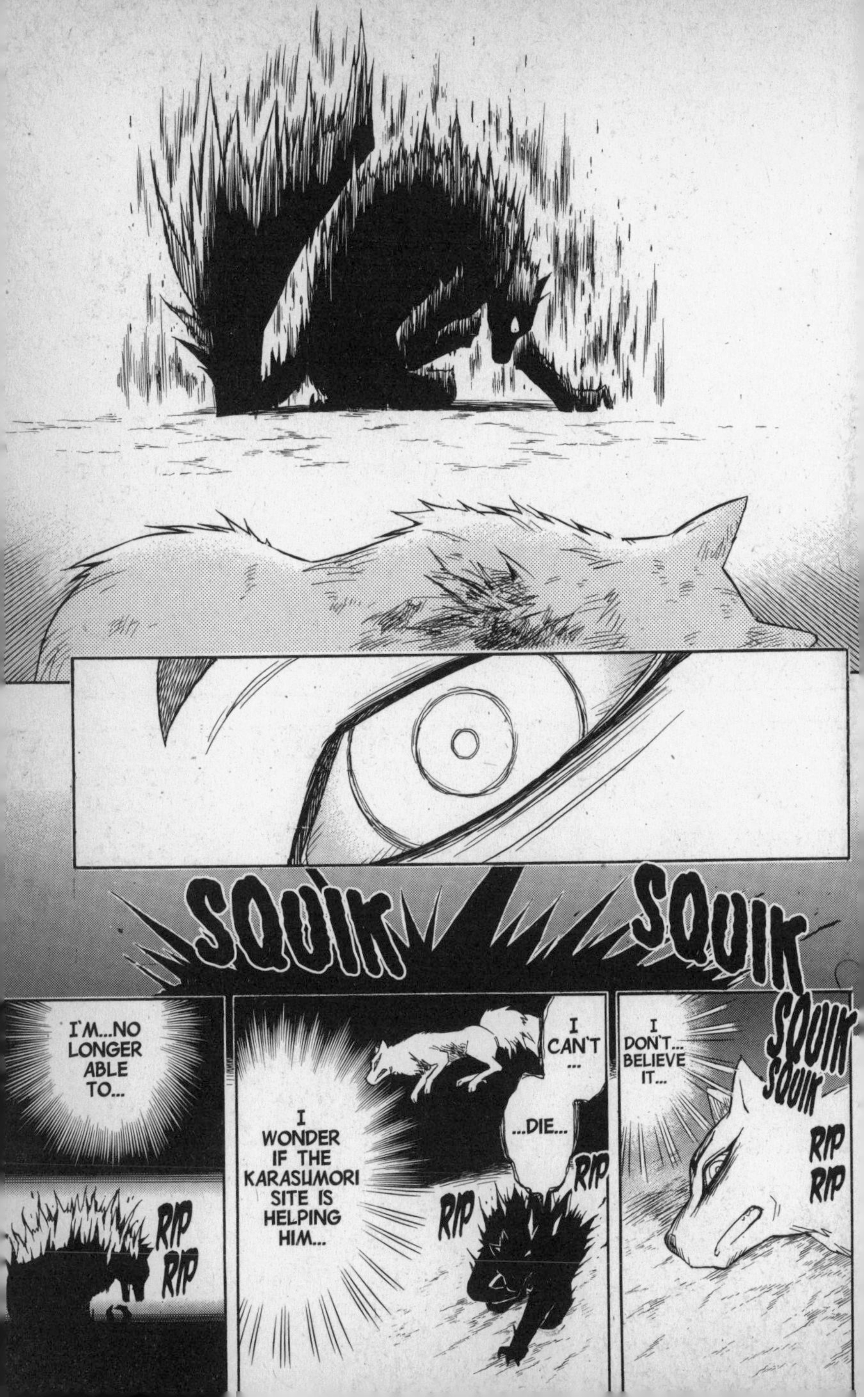
SQUIK
SQUIK
SQUIK
SQUIK
I DON'T... BELIEVE IT...
RIP RIP
I CAN'T ...
...DIE...
RIP
I WONDER IF THE KARASUMORI SITE IS HELPING HIM...
RIP
I'M...NO LONGER ABLE TO...
RIP RIP

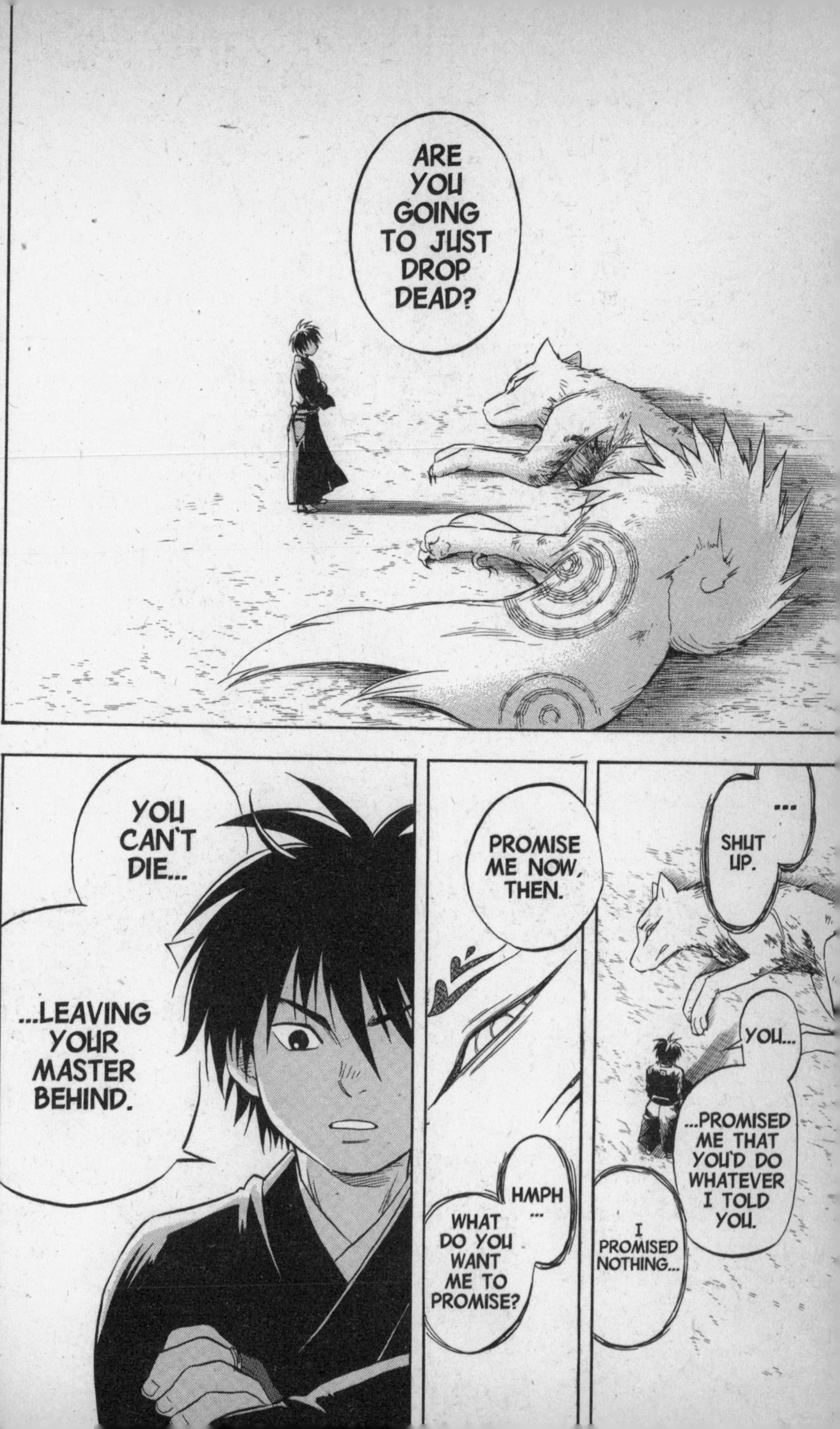
ARE YOU GOING TO JUST DROP DEAD?
... SHUT UP.
YOU...
...PROMISED ME THAT YOU'D DO WHATEVER I TOLD YOU.
I PROMISED NOTHING...
PROMISE ME NOW, THEN.
HMPH ...
WHAT DO YOU WANT ME TO PROMISE?
YOU CAN'T DIE...
...LEAVING YOUR MASTER BEHIND.

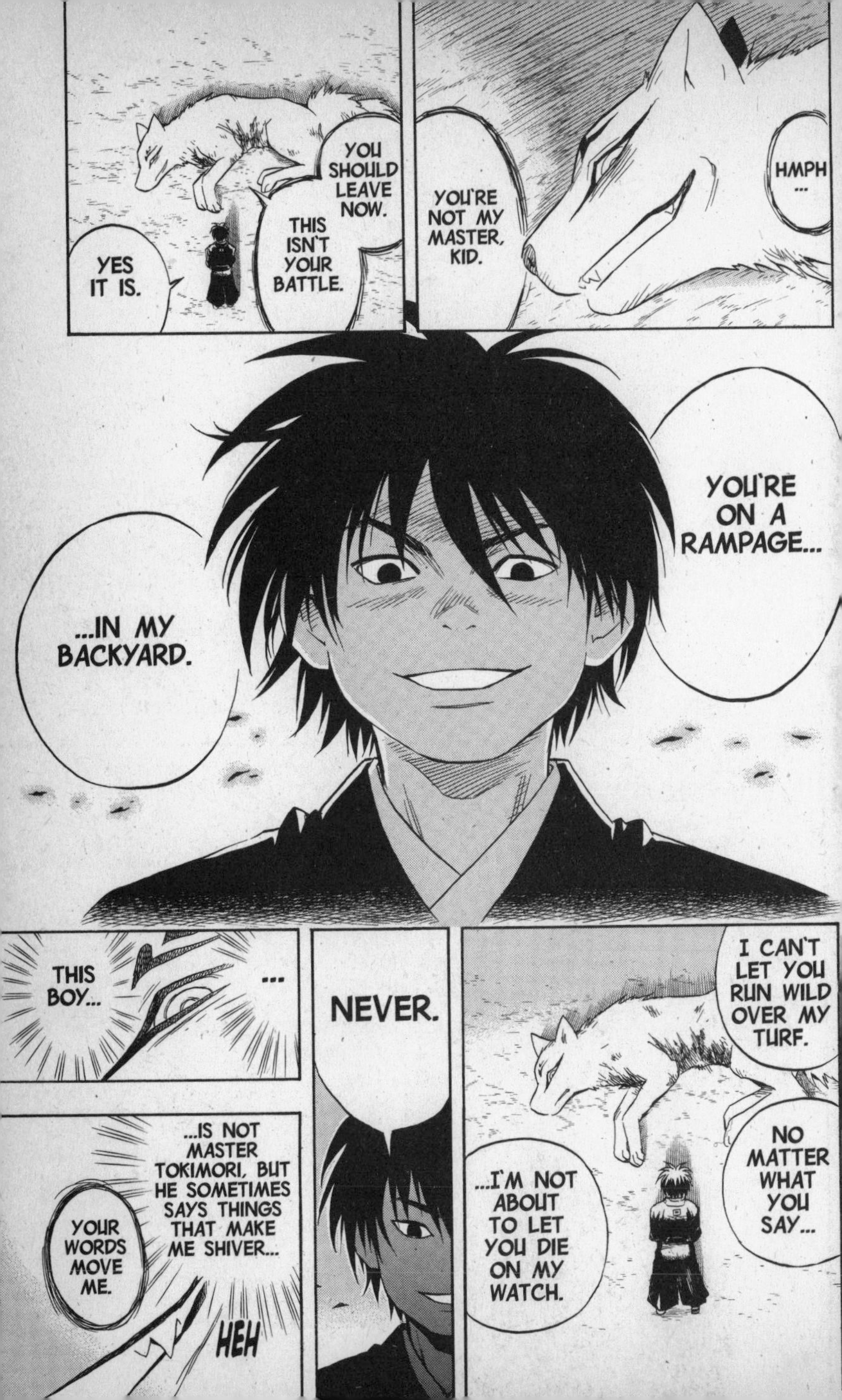
HMPH...
YOU'RE NOT MY MASTER, KID.
YOU SHOULD LEAVE NOW.
THIS ISN'T YOUR BATTLE.
YES IT IS.
YOU'RE ON A RAMPAGE...
...IN MY BACKYARD.
I CAN'T LET YOU RUN WILD OVER MY TURF.
NO MATTER WHAT YOU SAY...
...I'M NOT ABOUT TO LET YOU DIE ON MY WATCH.
NEVER.
...
THIS BOY...
...IS NOT MASTER TOKIMORI, BUT HE SOMETIMES SAYS THINGS THAT MAKE ME SHIVER...
YOUR WORDS MOVE ME.
HEH

I CAN'T DIE AND LEAVE THIS INSOLENT PUPPY BEHIND, CAN I?

VERY WELL...

ARGH...HOW DEMANDING MY NEW MASTER IS!

IT LOOKS LIKE I CAN'T DIE YET.

I'M SORRY, KOYA.

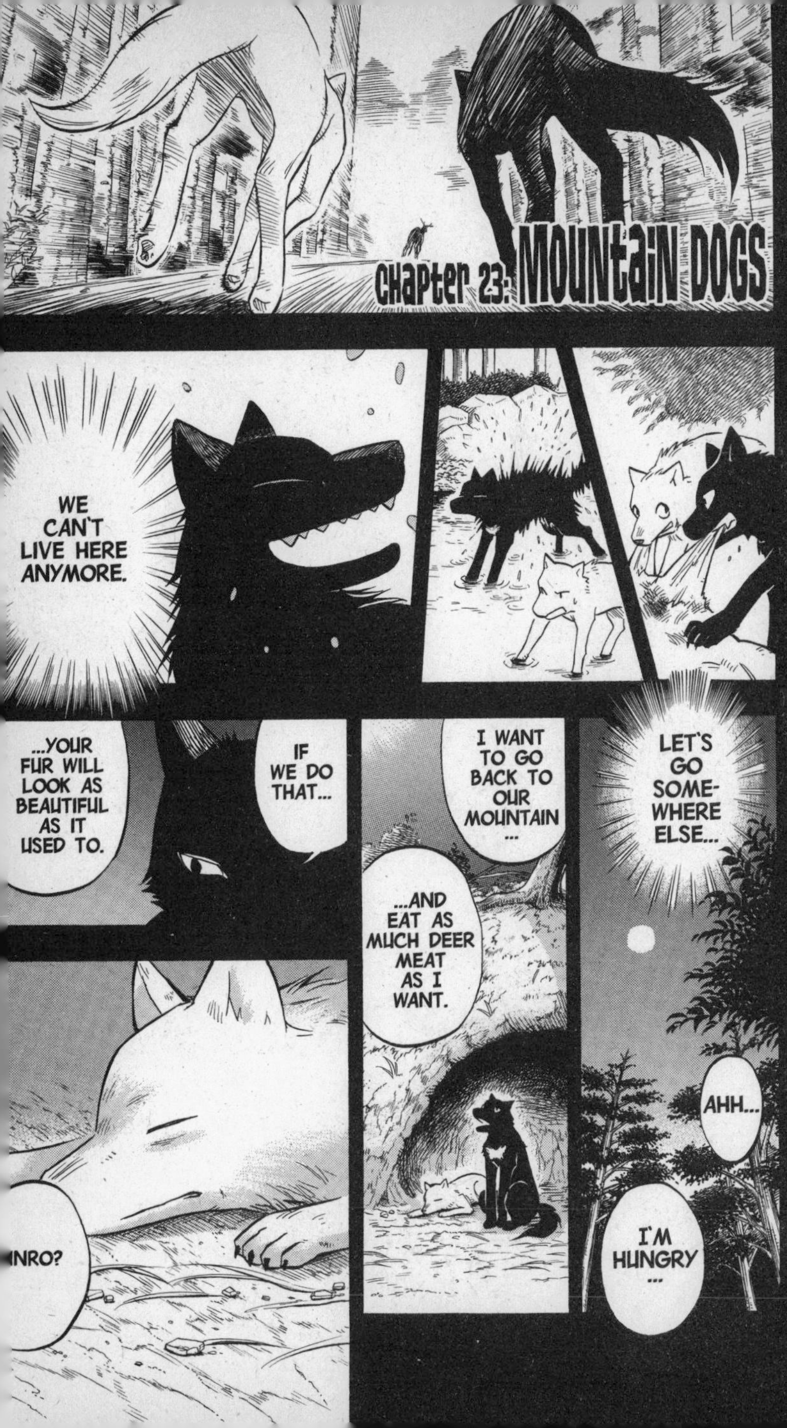
Chapter 23: Mountain Dogs
WE CAN'T LIVE HERE ANYMORE.
LET'S GO SOME-WHERE ELSE...
AHH...
I'M HUNGRY ...
I WANT TO GO BACK TO OUR MOUNTAIN ...
...AND EAT AS MUCH DEER MEAT AS I WANT.
IF WE DO THAT...
...YOUR FUR WILL LOOK AS BEAUTIFUL AS IT USED TO.
INRO?

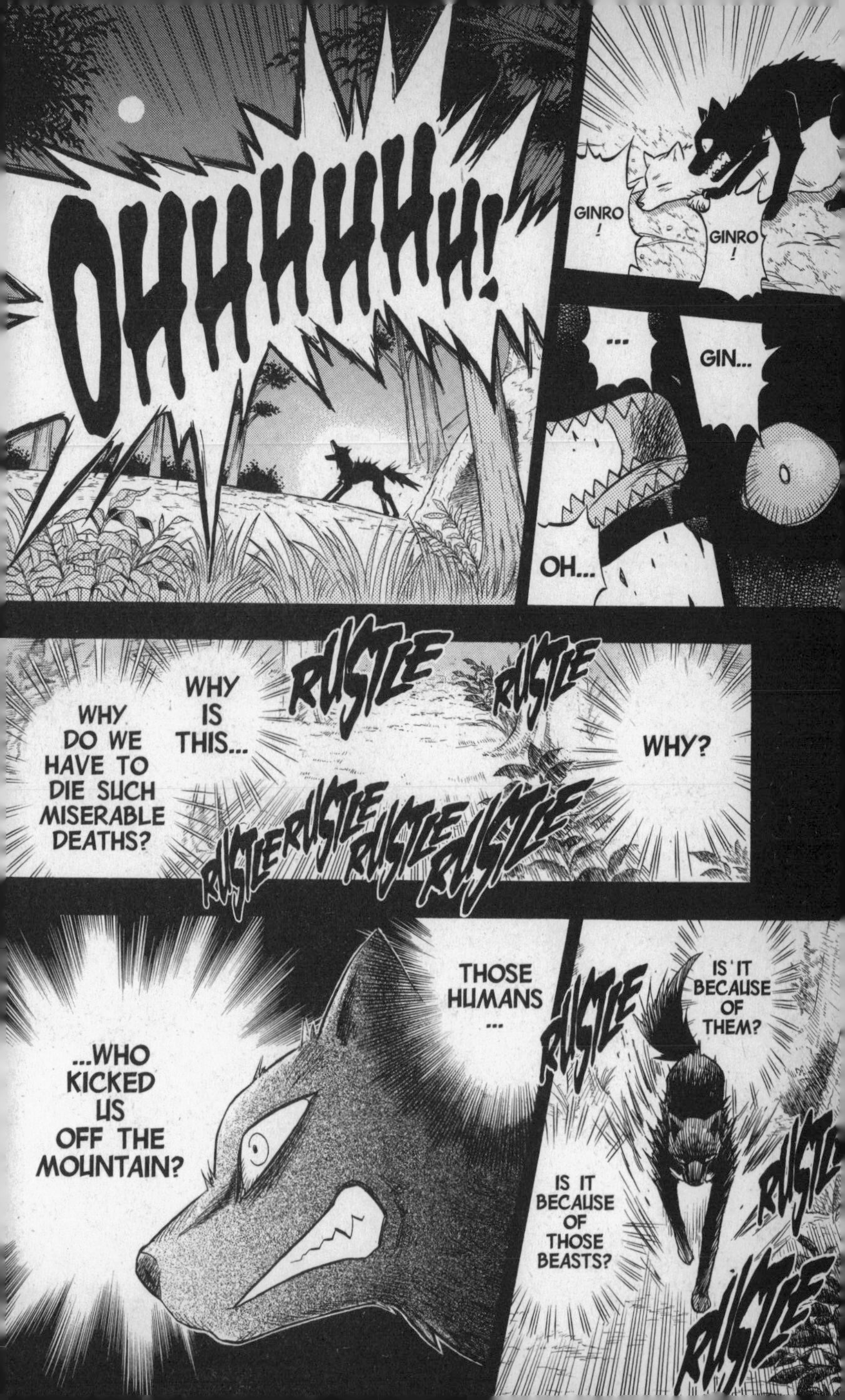
GINRO!
GINRO!
GIN...
...
OH...
OHHHHHHH!
WHY?
RUSTLE
RUSTLE
WHY IS THIS...
WHY DO WE HAVE TO DIE SUCH MISERABLE DEATHS?
RUSTLE RUSTLE RUSTLE RUSTLE
IS IT BECAUSE OF THEM?
RUSTLE
IS IT BECAUSE OF THOSE BEASTS?
RUSTLE
RUSTLE
THOSE HUMANS...
...WHO KICKED US OFF THE MOUNTAIN?

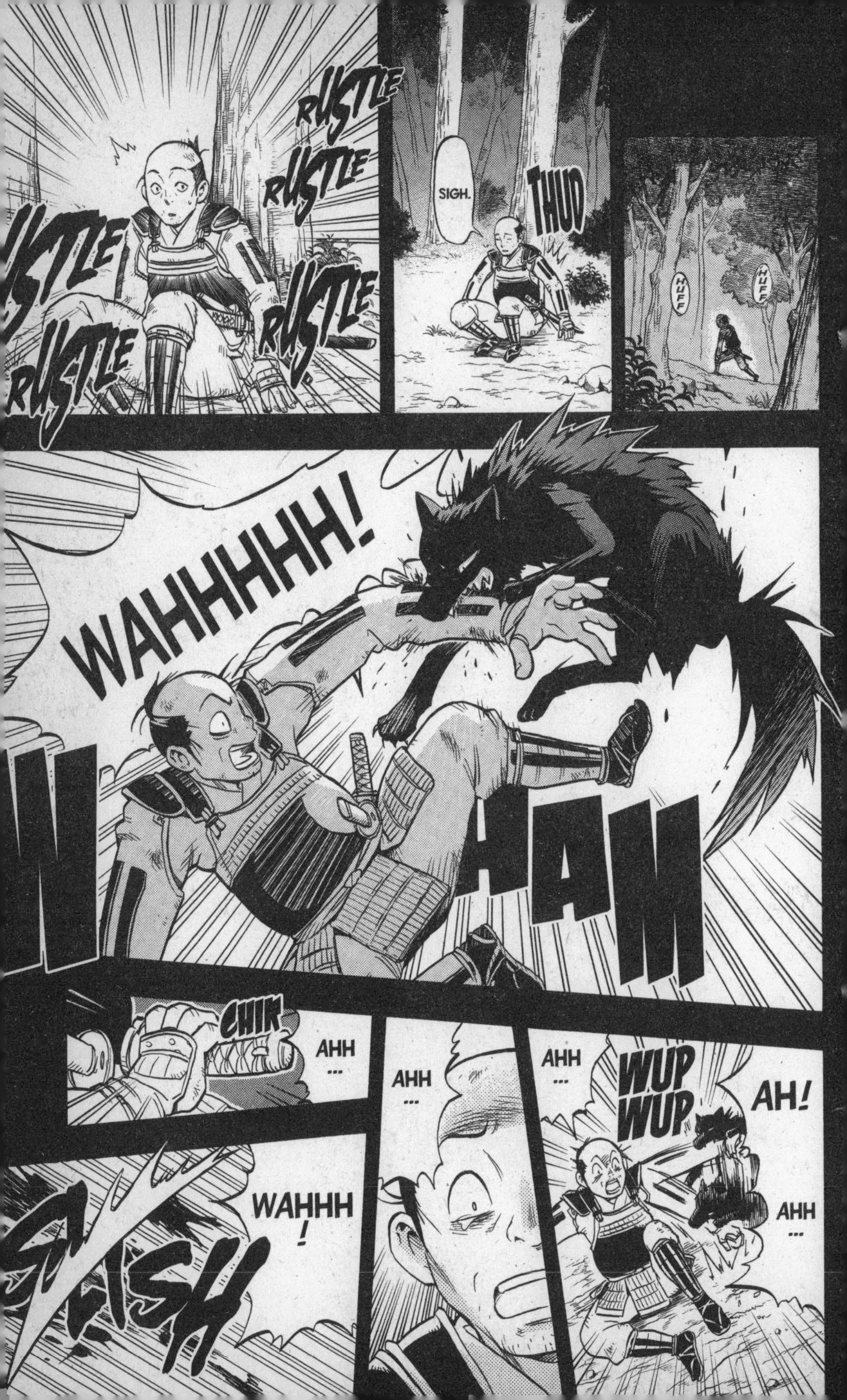

HUFF
HUFF
SIGH.
THUD
RUSTLE
RUSTLE
RUSTLE
RUSTLE
RUSTLE
WAHHHHH!
WHAM
AHH...
WUP WUP
AH!
AHH...
AHH...
CHIR
AHH...
WAHHH!
SWISH

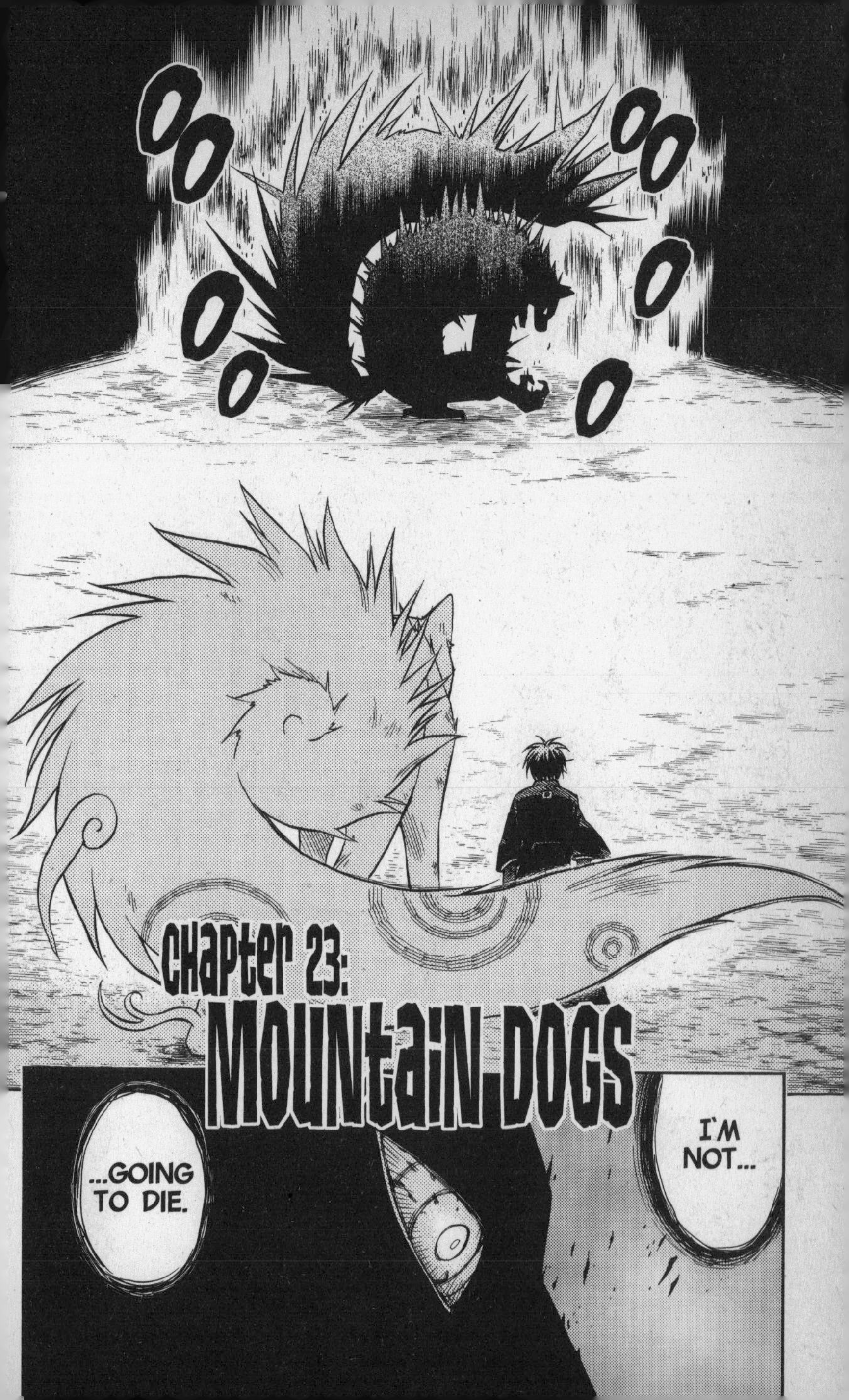
OOOOOO
OOOOOO
CHAPTER 23:
MOUNTAIN DOGS
I'M NOT...
...GOING TO DIE.

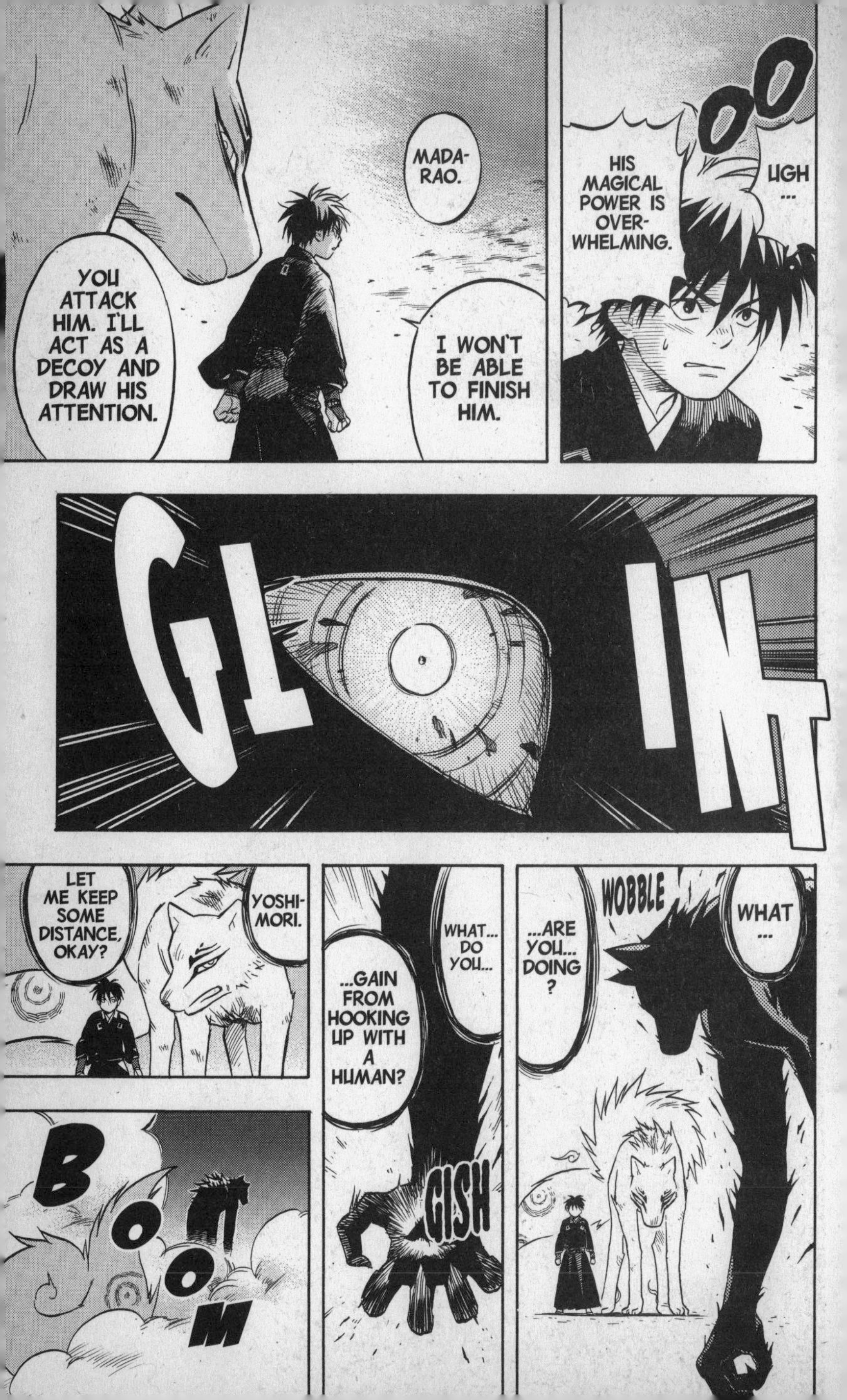
OO
UGH ...
HIS MAGICAL POWER IS OVER-WHELMING.
MADA-RAO.
I WON'T BE ABLE TO FINISH HIM.
YOU ATTACK HIM. I'LL ACT AS A DECOY AND DRAW HIS ATTENTION.
GLINT
WHAT ...
WOBBLE
...ARE YOU... DOING?
WHAT... DO YOU...
...GAIN FROM HOOKING UP WITH A HUMAN?
GISH
YOSHI-MORI.
LET ME KEEP SOME DISTANCE, OKAY?
BOOM

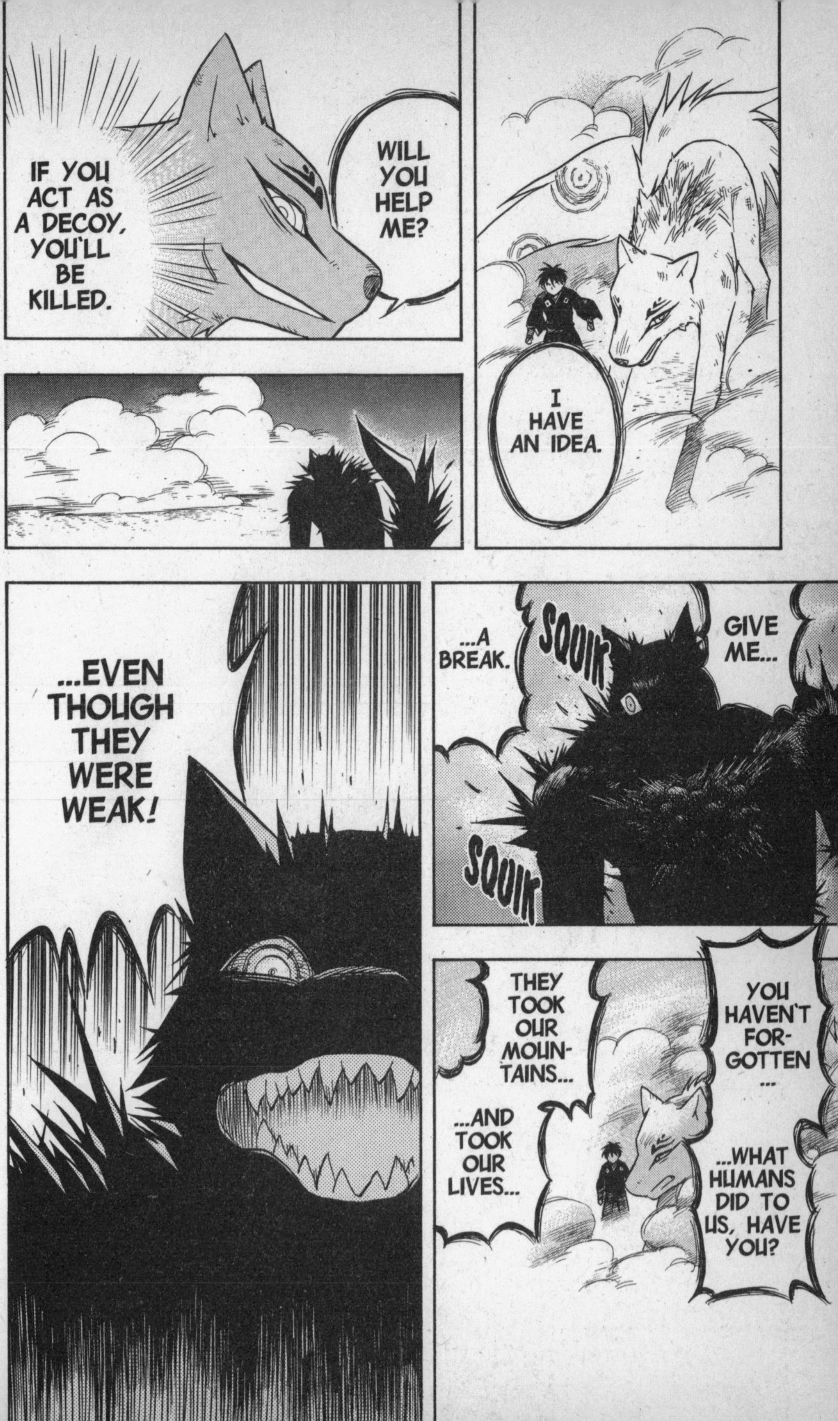
I HAVE AN IDEA.
WILL YOU HELP ME?
IF YOU ACT AS A DECOY, YOU'LL BE KILLED.
GIVE ME...
SQUIK
...A BREAK.
SQUIK
YOU HAVEN'T FORGOTTEN ...
...WHAT HUMANS DID TO US, HAVE YOU?
THEY TOOK OUR MOUNTAINS...
...AND TOOK OUR LIVES...
...EVEN THOUGH THEY WERE WEAK!

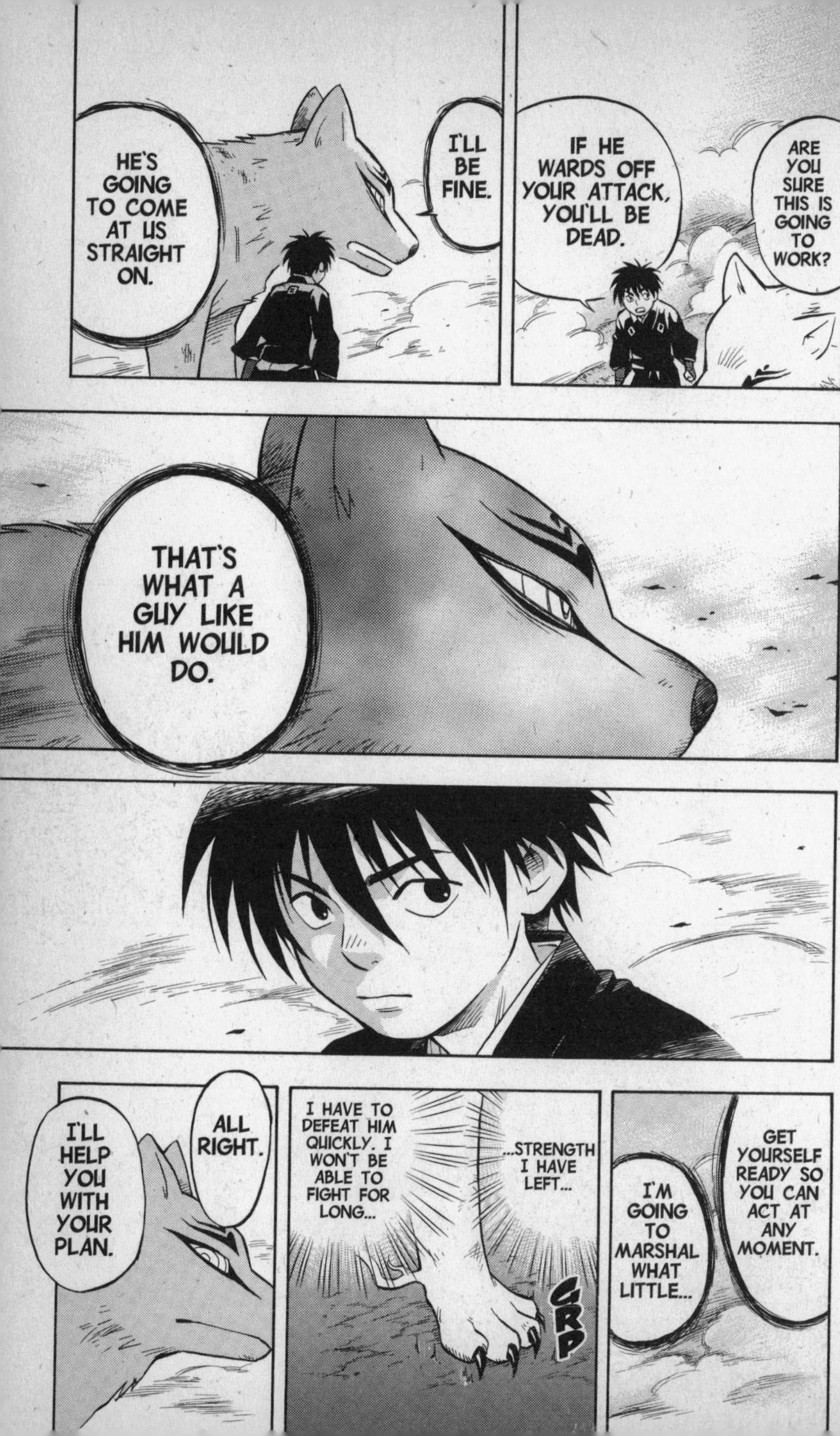
ARE YOU SURE THIS IS GOING TO WORK?
IF HE WARDS OFF YOUR ATTACK, YOU'LL BE DEAD.
I'LL BE FINE.
HE'S GOING TO COME AT US STRAIGHT ON.
THAT'S WHAT A GUY LIKE HIM WOULD DO.
GET YOURSELF READY SO YOU CAN ACT AT ANY MOMENT.
I'M GOING TO MARSHAL WHAT LITTLE...
...STRENGTH I HAVE LEFT...
I HAVE TO DEFEAT HIM QUICKLY. I WON'T BE ABLE TO FIGHT FOR LONG...
GRP
ALL RIGHT.
I'LL HELP YOU WITH YOUR PLAN.

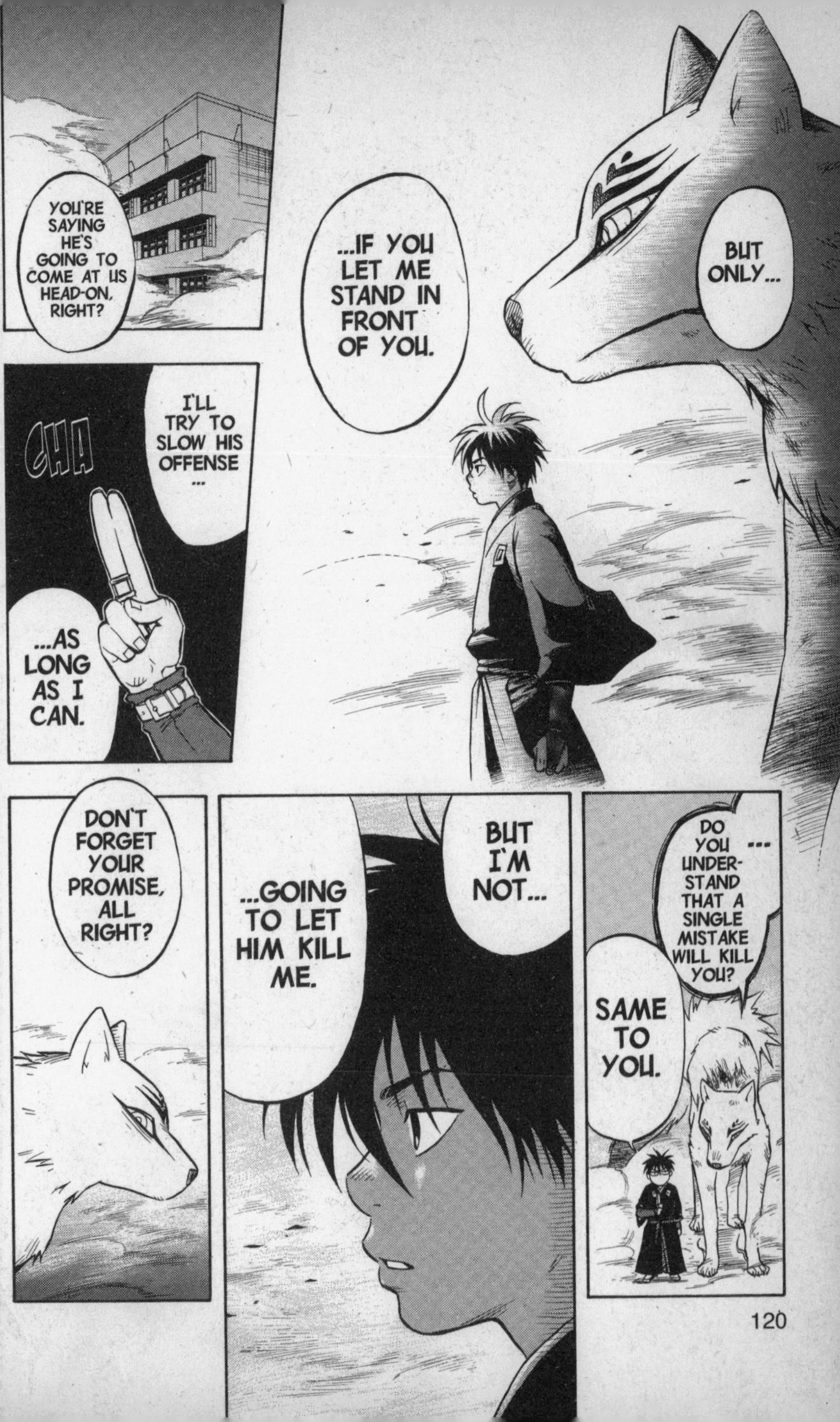
BUT ONLY...
...IF YOU LET ME STAND IN FRONT OF YOU.
YOU'RE SAYING HE'S GOING TO COME AT US HEAD-ON, RIGHT?
I'LL TRY TO SLOW HIS OFFENSE ...
CHA
...AS LONG AS I CAN.
DO YOU UNDERSTAND THAT A SINGLE MISTAKE WILL KILL YOU?
SAME TO YOU.
BUT I'M NOT...
...GOING TO LET HIM KILL ME.
DON'T FORGET YOUR PROMISE, ALL RIGHT?

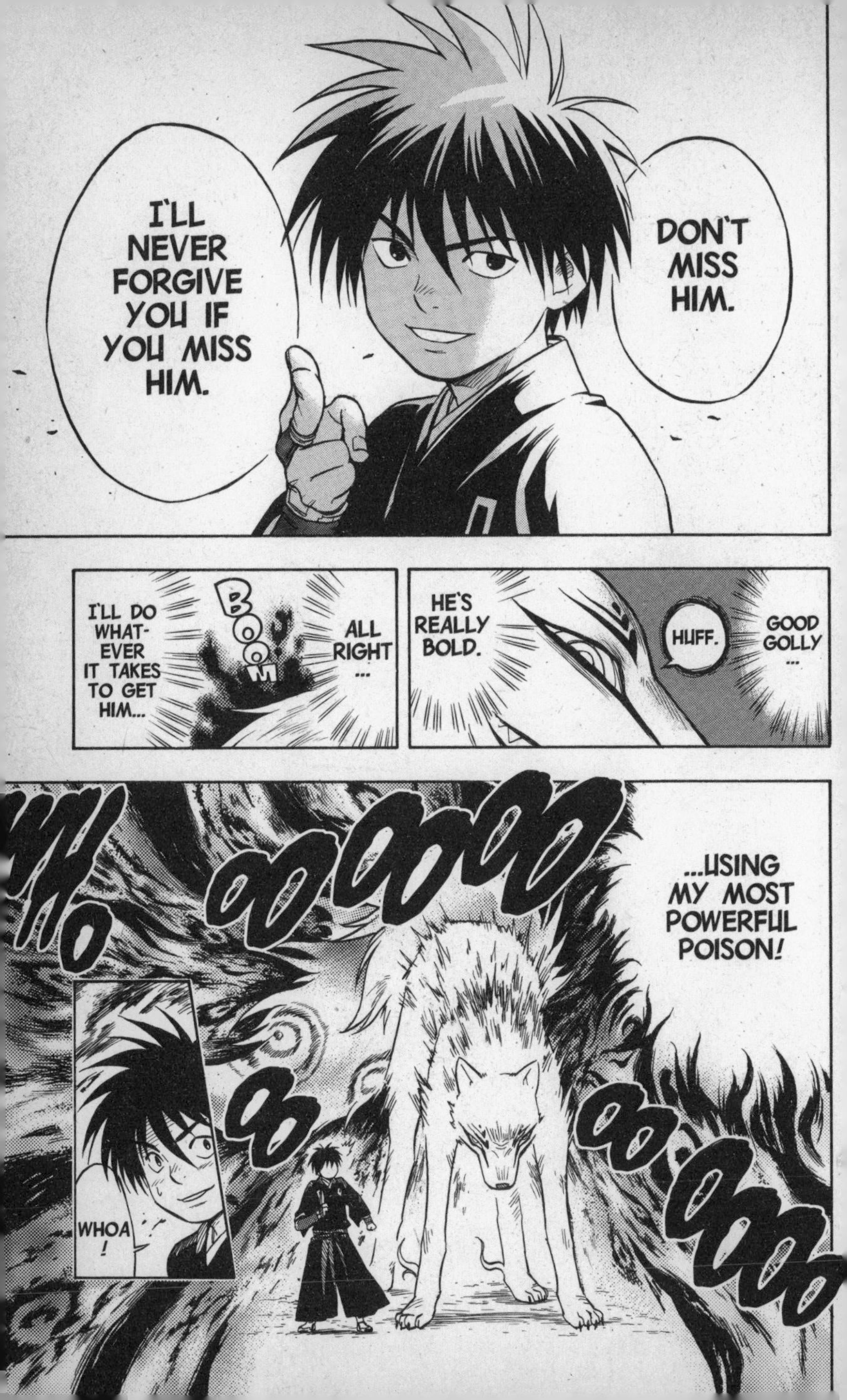
DON'T MISS HIM.
I'LL NEVER FORGIVE YOU IF YOU MISS HIM.
GOOD GOLLY ...
HUFF.
HE'S REALLY BOLD.
ALL RIGHT ...
BOOM
I'LL DO WHATEVER IT TAKES TO GET HIM...
...USING MY MOST POWERFUL POISON!
WHOOOOOOOOO
WHOA!

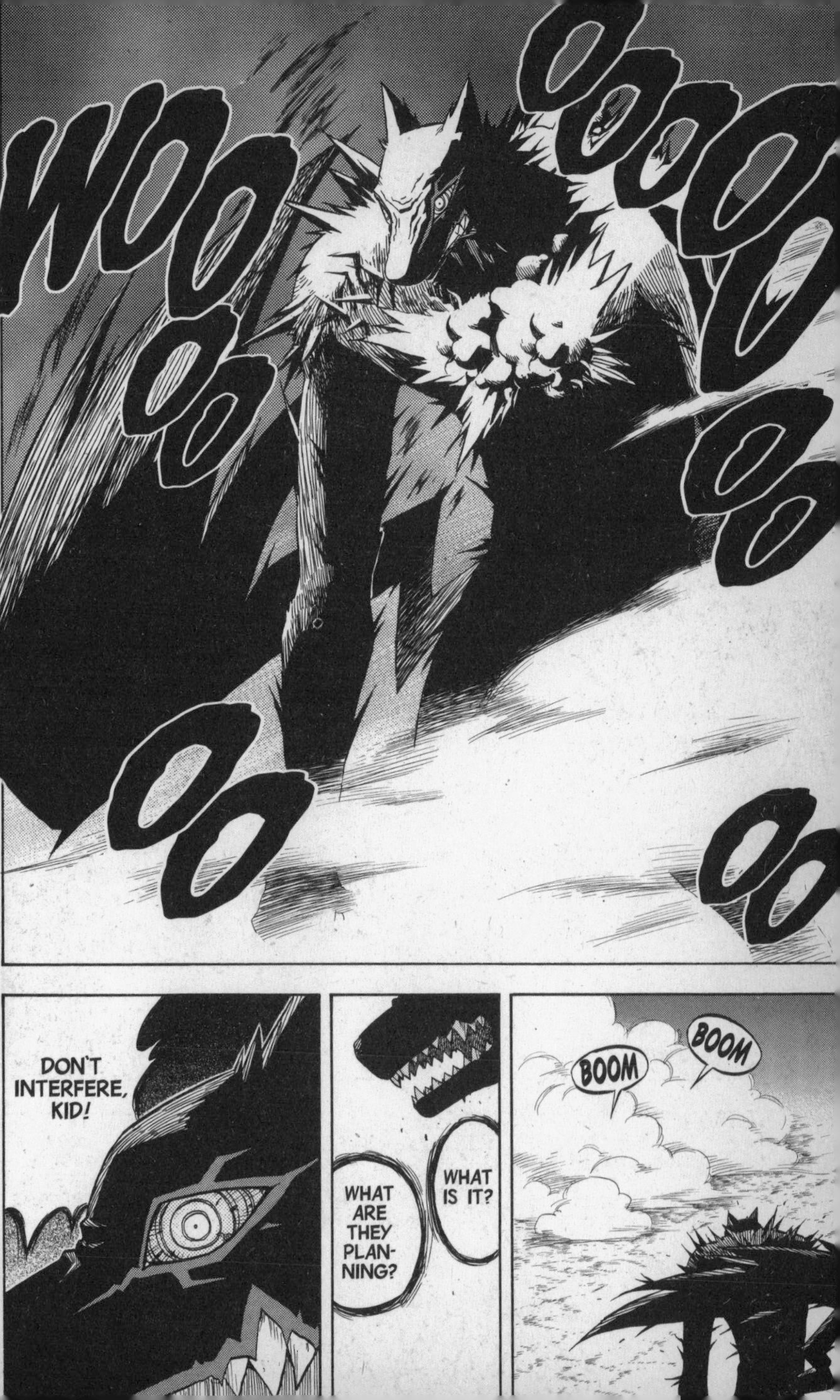
WOOOOOOOOOOOOOOOOOOOO
BOOM
BOOM
WHAT IS IT?
WHAT ARE THEY PLANNING?
DON'T INTERFERE, KID!

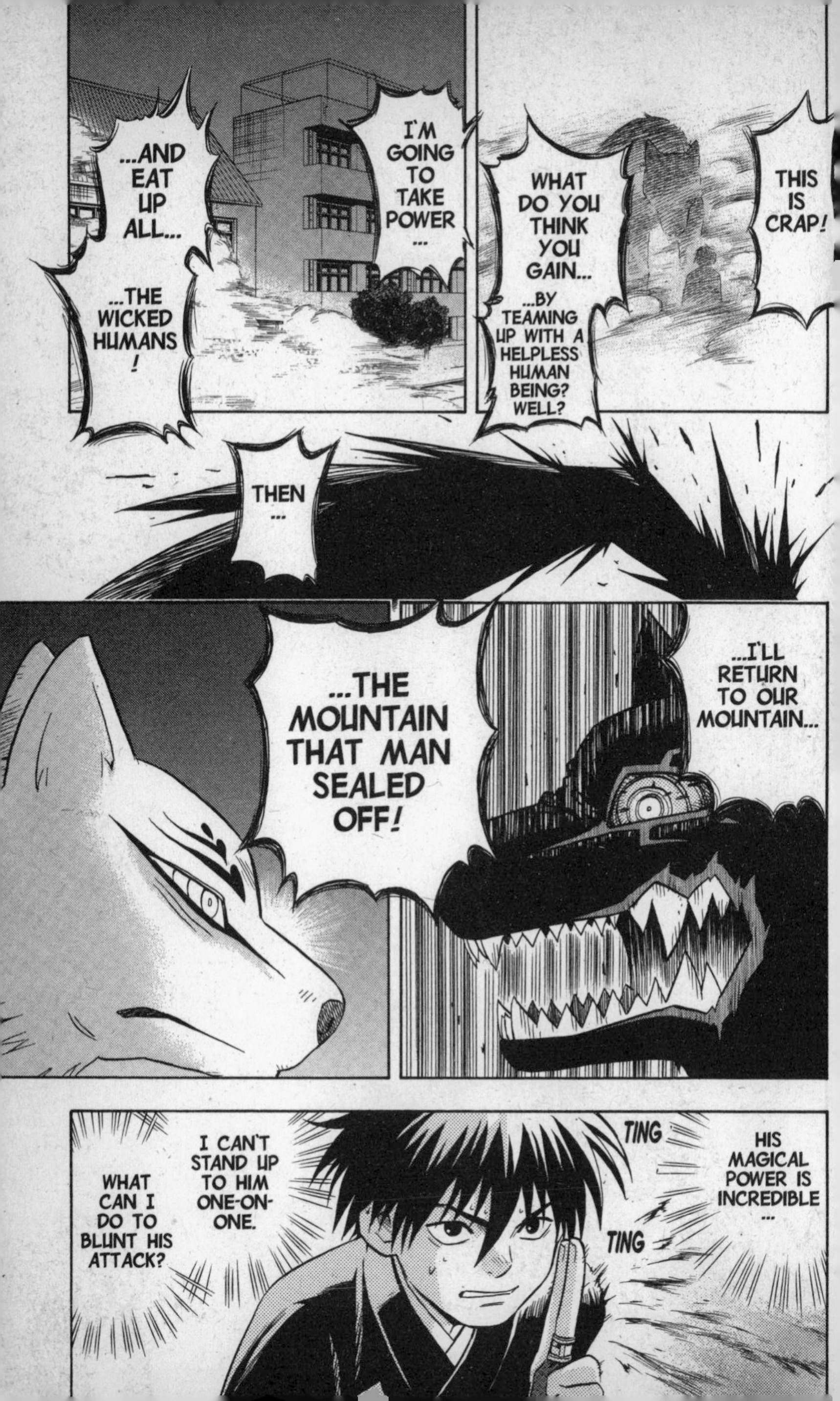
THIS IS CRAP!
WHAT DO YOU THINK YOU GAIN...
...BY TEAMING UP WITH A HELPLESS HUMAN BEING? WELL?
I'M GOING TO TAKE POWER ...
...AND EAT UP ALL...
...THE WICKED HUMANS!
THEN ...
...I'LL RETURN TO OUR MOUNTAIN...
...THE MOUNTAIN THAT MAN SEALED OFF!
HIS MAGICAL POWER IS INCREDIBLE ...
TING
TING
I CAN'T STAND UP TO HIM ONE-ON-ONE.
WHAT CAN I DO TO BLUNT HIS ATTACK?

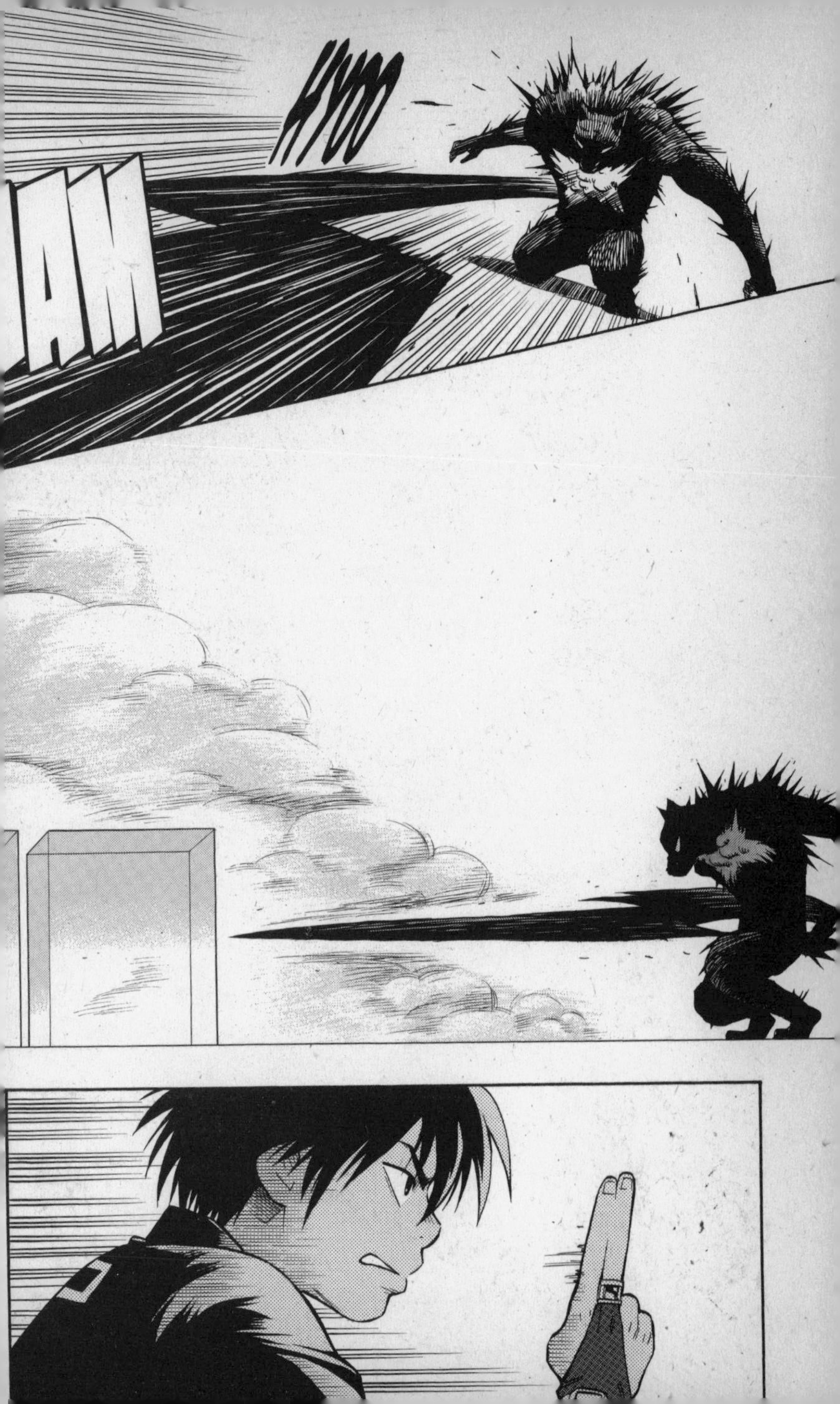
HYOO

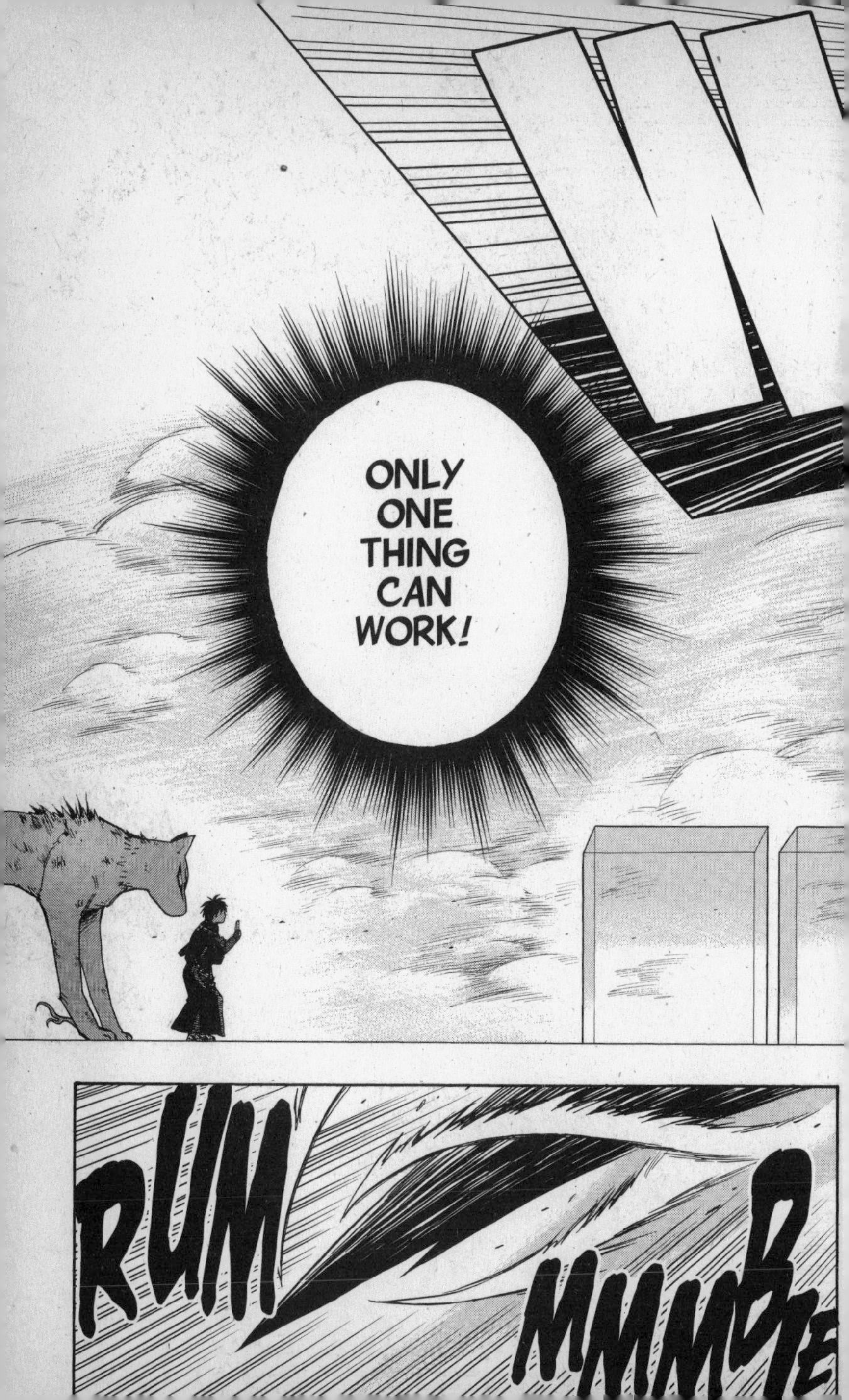
ONLY ONE THING CAN WORK!

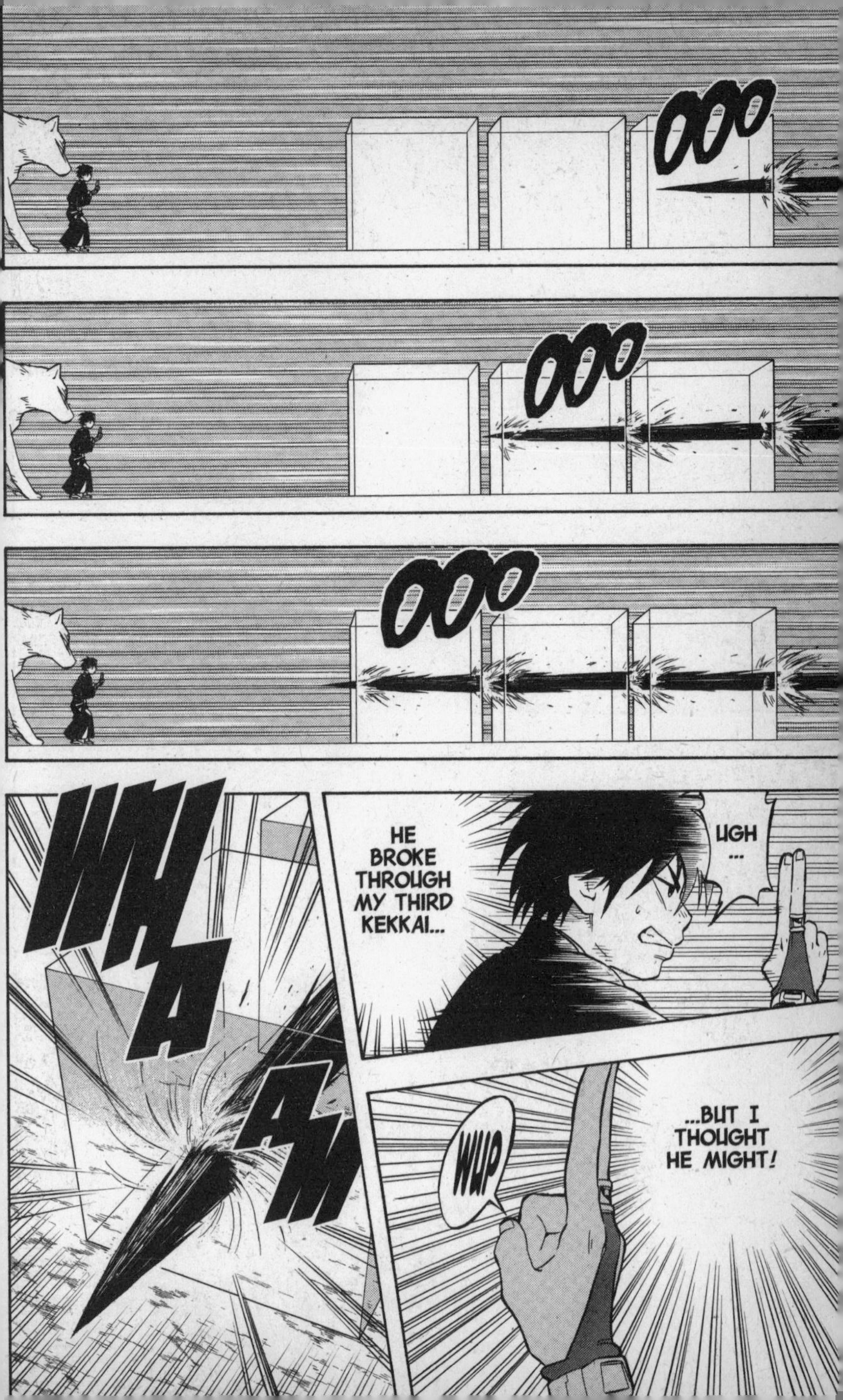
OOO
OOO
OOO
UGH ...
HE BROKE THROUGH MY THIRD KEKKAI...
...BUT I THOUGHT HE MIGHT!
WUP
WHAM

I'M NOT GOING TO LET YOU GO.

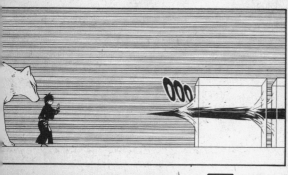

OOO

GKGIK

WHAM

GOOD! HIS TAIL'S SLOWED DOWN!

MADA-RAO!

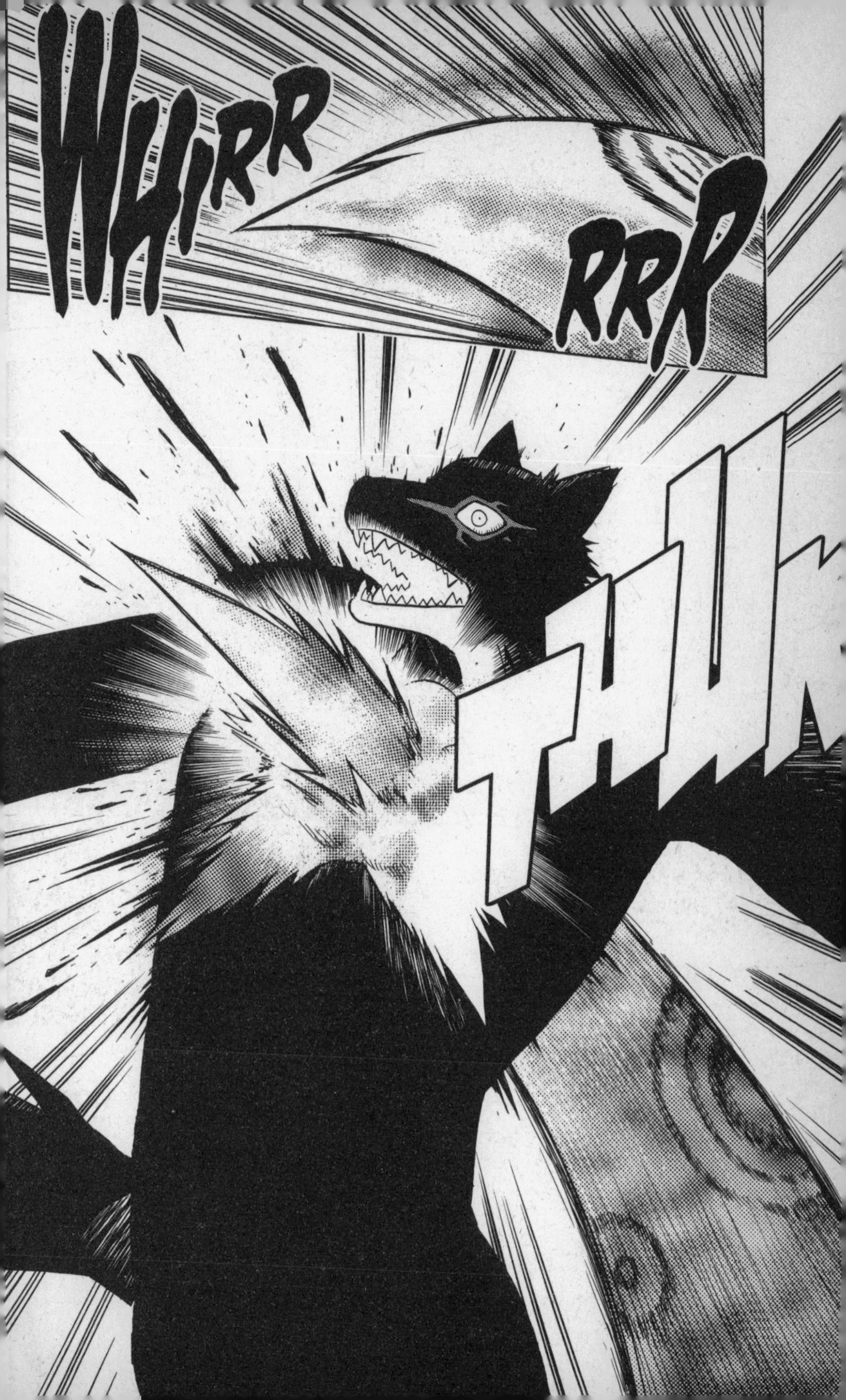
WHIRR
RRR
THUN

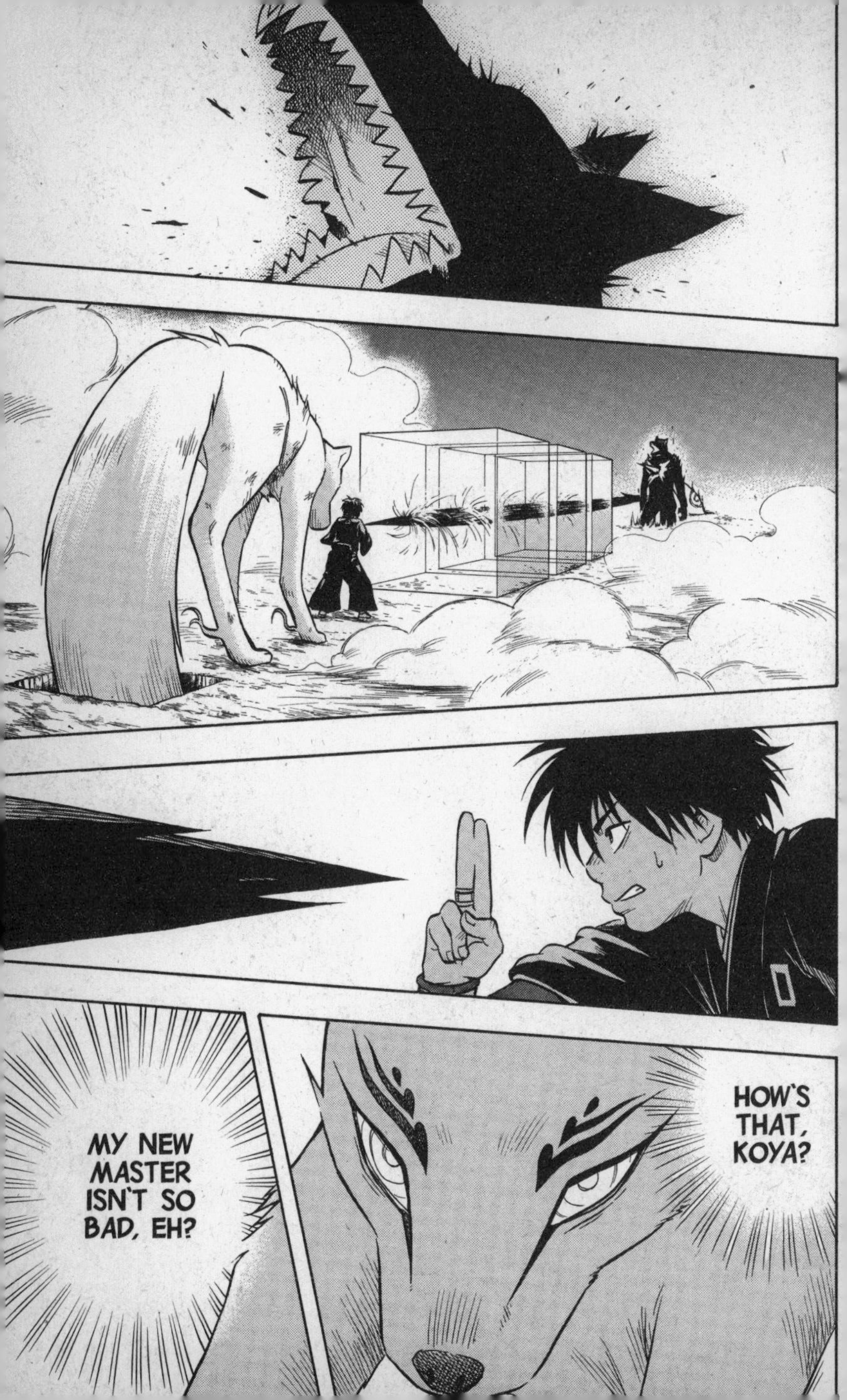
HOW'S THAT, KOYA?
MY NEW MASTER ISN'T SO BAD, EH?

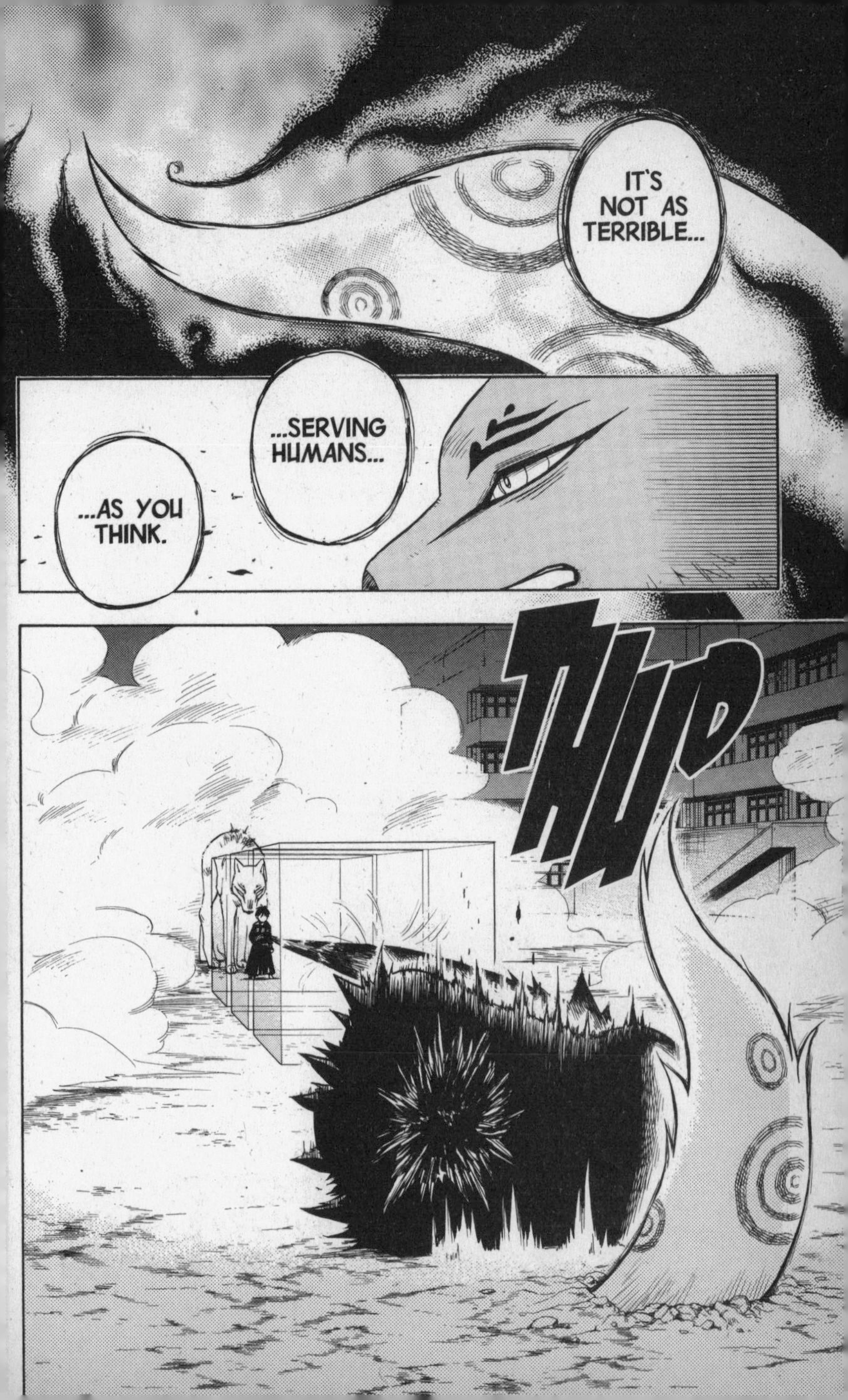
IT'S NOT AS TERRIBLE...
...SERVING HUMANS...
...AS YOU THINK.
THUD

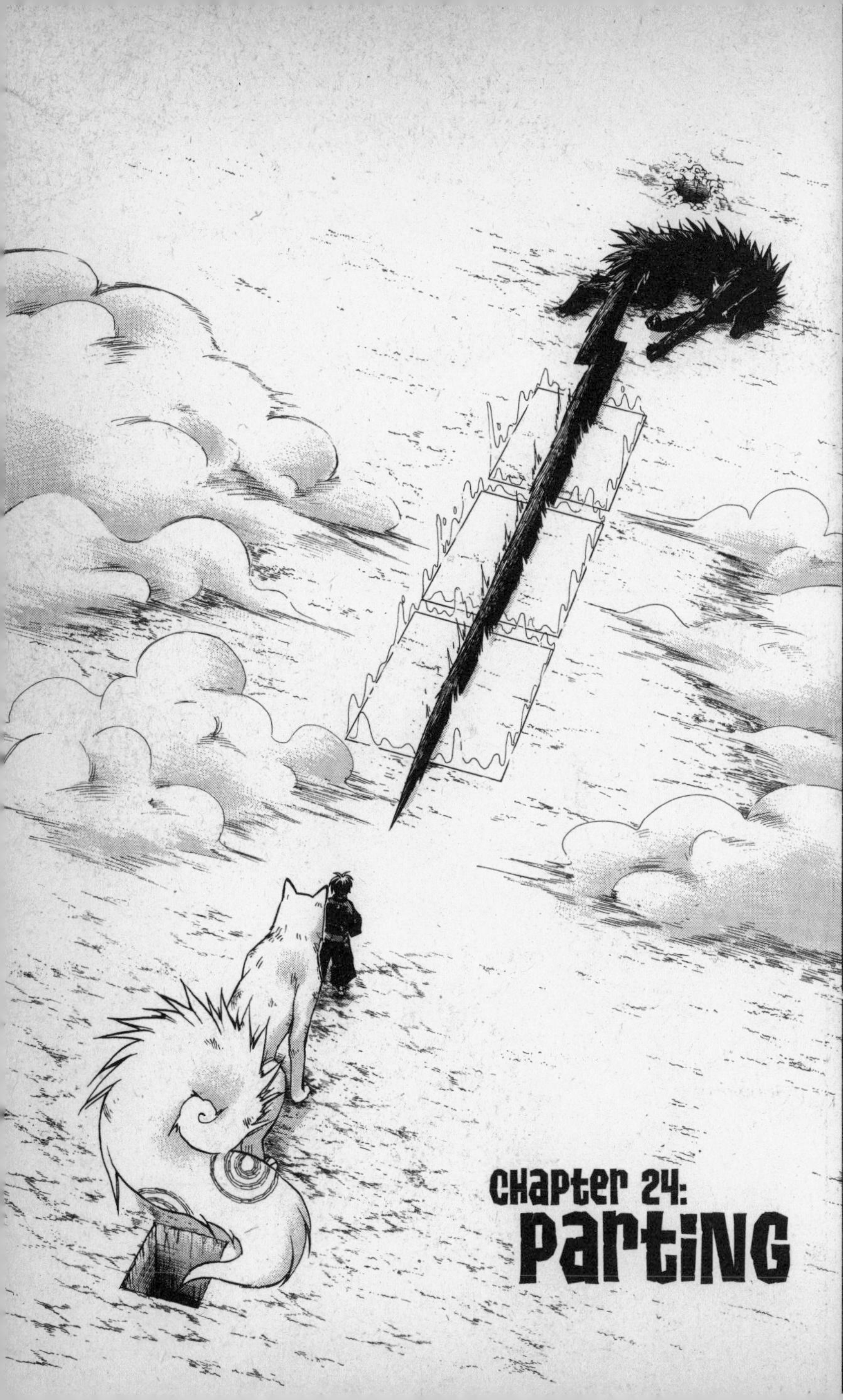
Chapter 24:
Parting

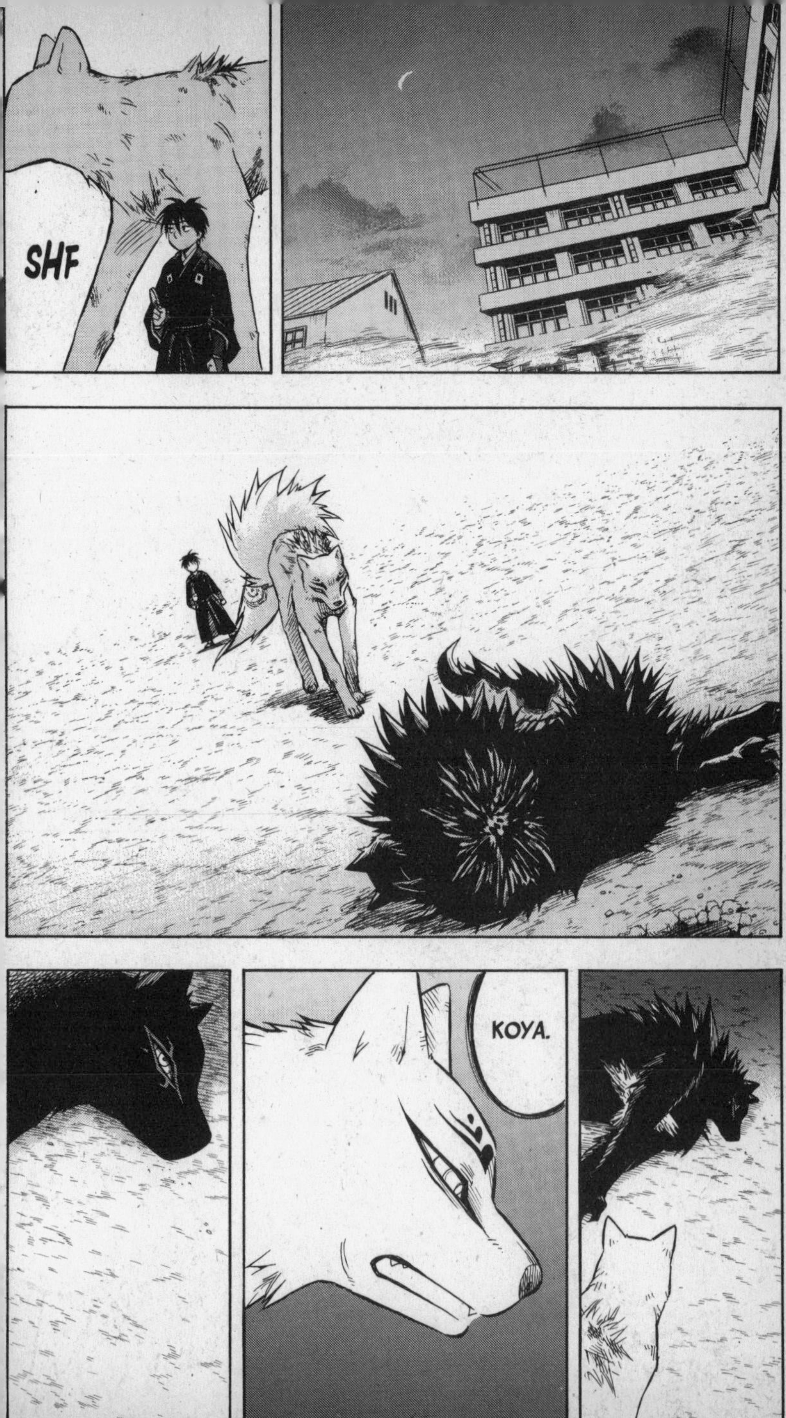
SHF
KOYA.

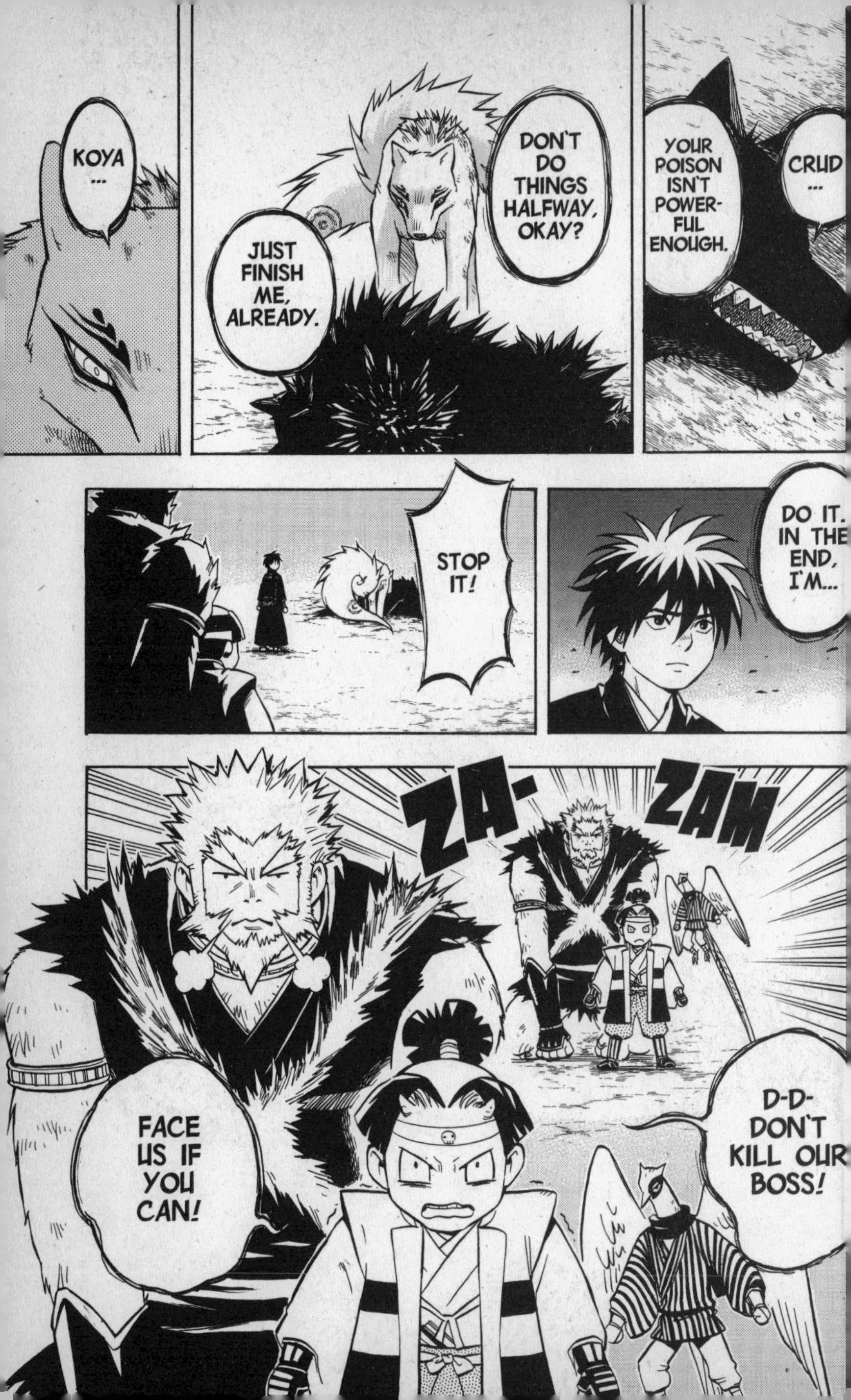
CRUD ...
YOUR POISON ISN'T POWER-FUL ENOUGH.
DON'T DO THINGS HALFWAY, OKAY?
JUST FINISH ME, ALREADY.
KOYA ...
DO IT. IN THE END, I'M...
STOP IT!
ZA-ZAM
D-D-DON'T KILL OUR BOSS!
FACE US IF YOU CAN!

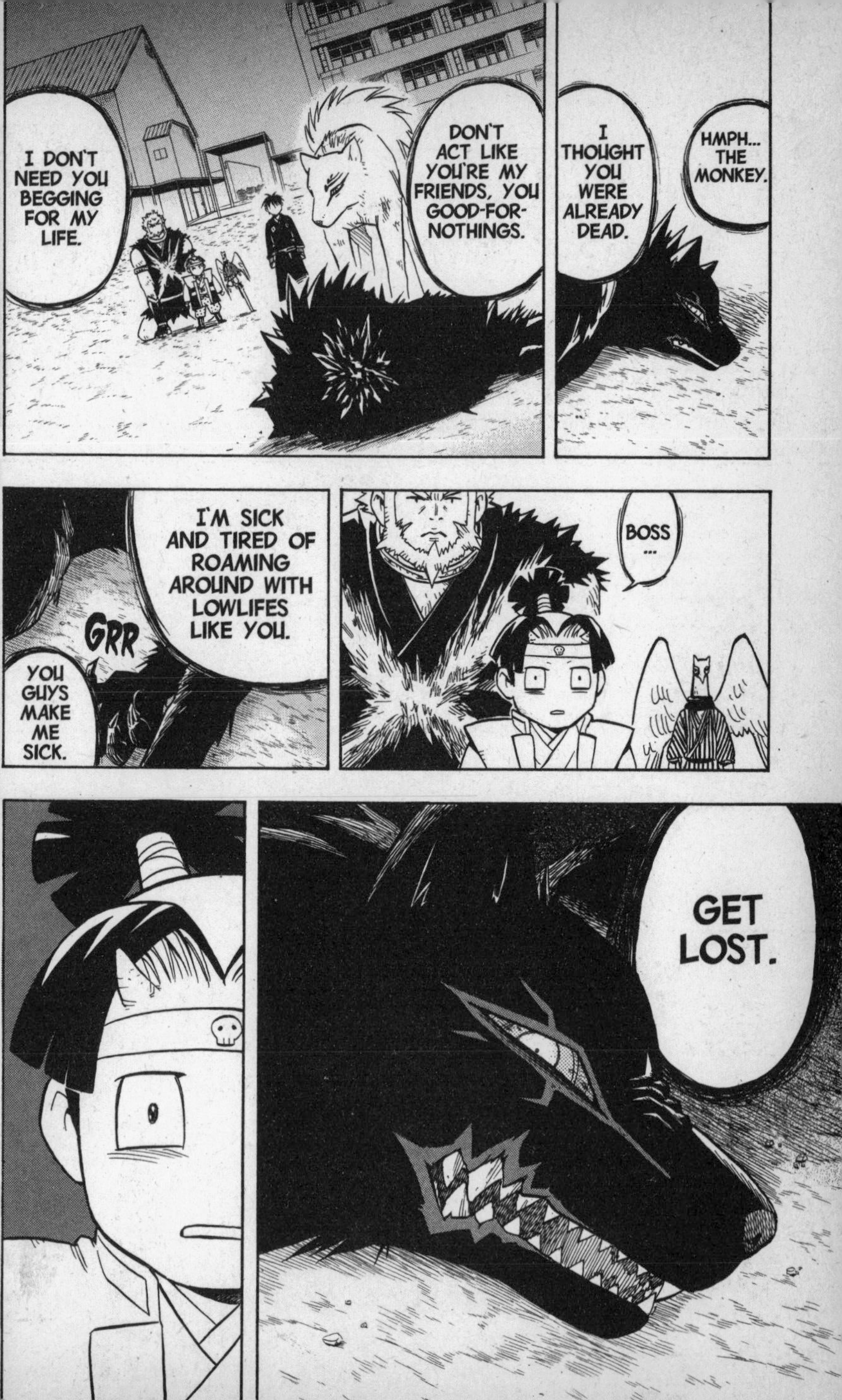
HMPH... THE MONKEY.
I THOUGHT YOU WERE ALREADY DEAD.
DON'T ACT LIKE YOU'RE MY FRIENDS, YOU GOOD-FOR-NOTHINGS.
I DON'T NEED YOU BEGGING FOR MY LIFE.
BOSS ...
I'M SICK AND TIRED OF ROAMING AROUND WITH LOWLIFES LIKE YOU.
GRR
YOU GUYS MAKE ME SICK.
GET LOST.

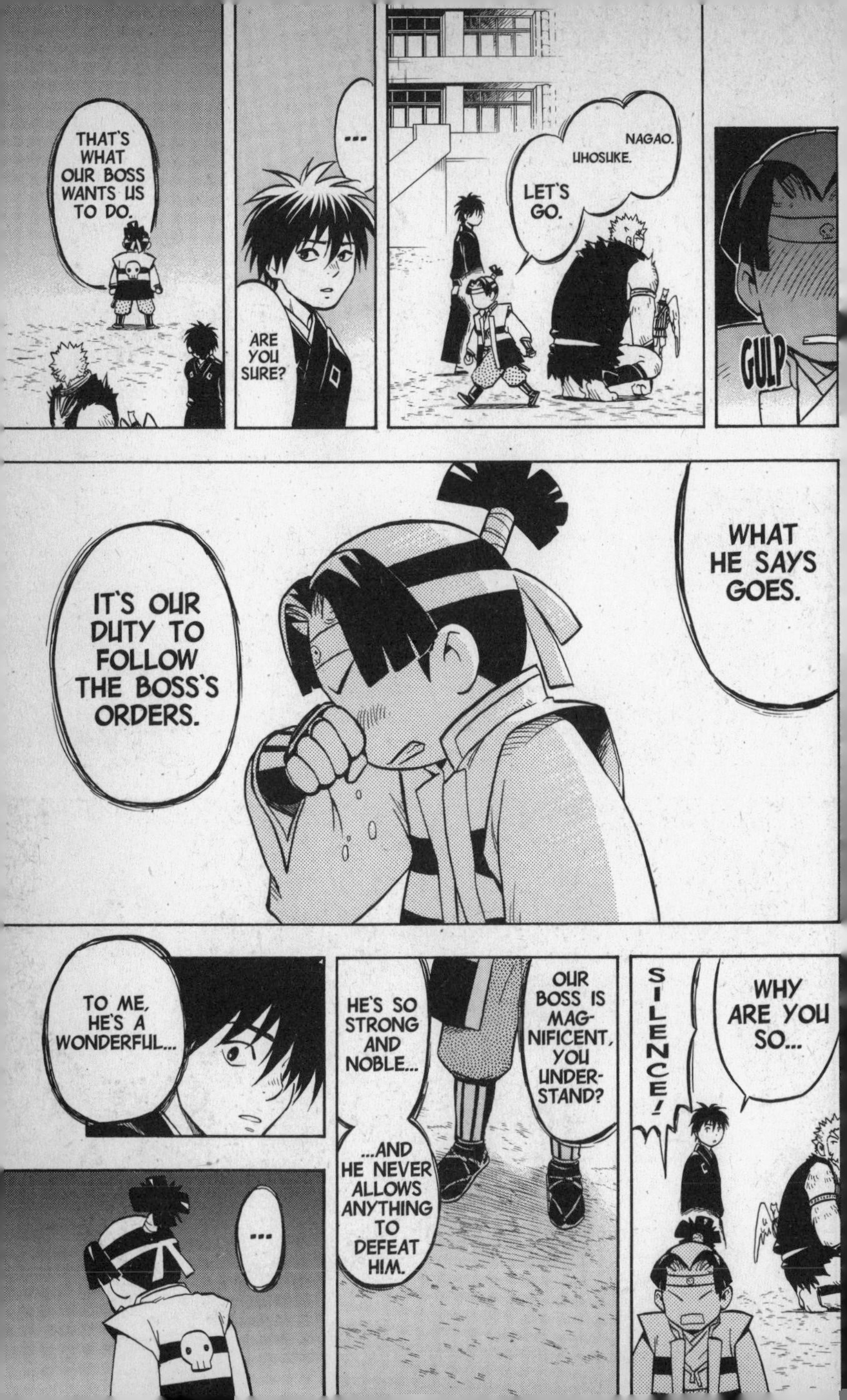
GULP
NAGAO.
UHOSUKE.
LET'S GO.
...
ARE YOU SURE?
THAT'S WHAT OUR BOSS WANTS US TO DO.
WHAT HE SAYS GOES.
IT'S OUR DUTY TO FOLLOW THE BOSS'S ORDERS.
WHY ARE YOU SO...
SILENCE!
OUR BOSS IS MAG-NIFICENT, YOU UNDER-STAND?
HE'S SO STRONG AND NOBLE...
...AND HE NEVER ALLOWS ANYTHING TO DEFEAT HIM.
TO ME, HE'S A WONDERFUL...
...

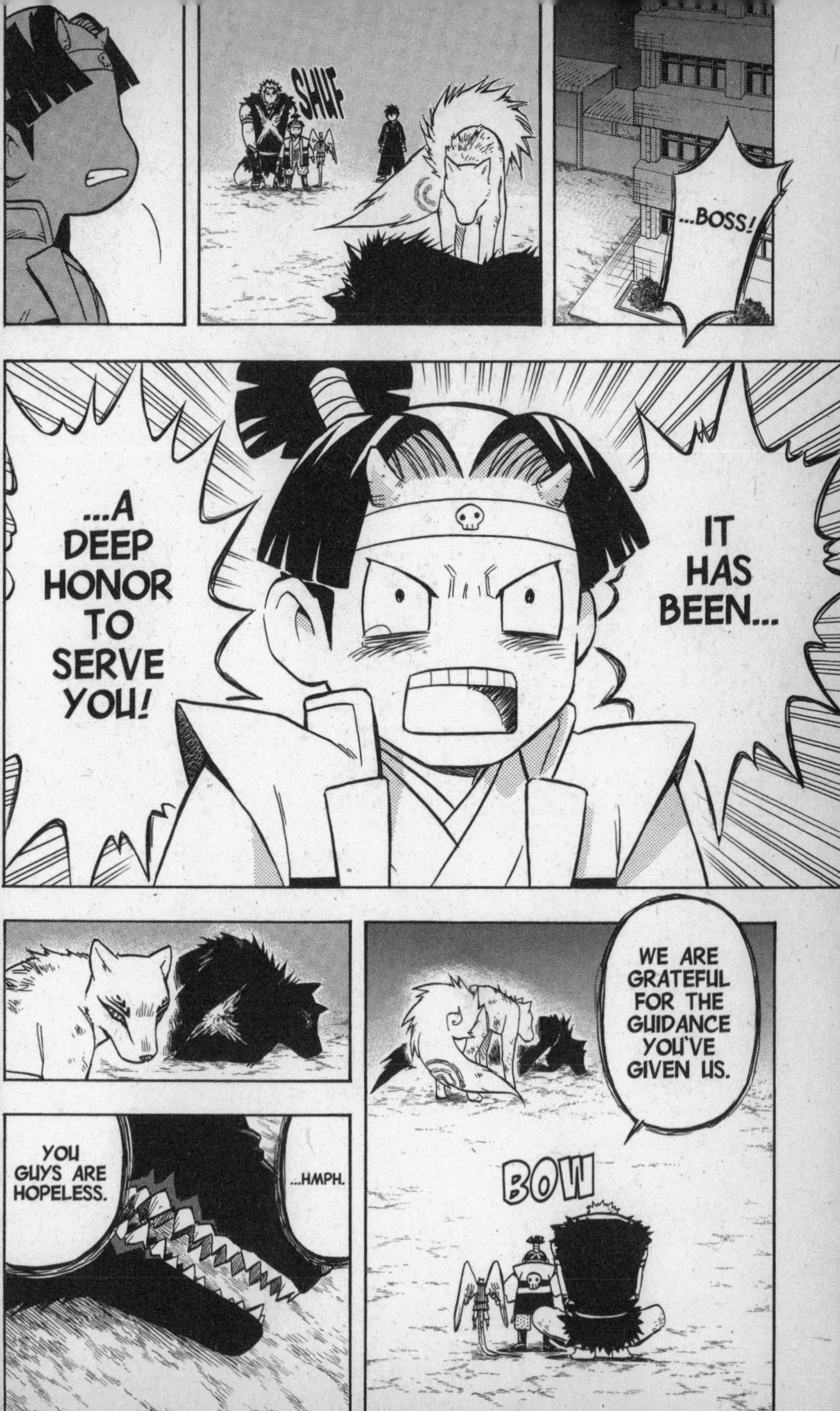
...BOSS!
SHUF
IT HAS BEEN...
...A DEEP HONOR TO SERVE YOU!
WE ARE GRATEFUL FOR THE GUIDANCE YOU'VE GIVEN US.
BOW
...HMPH.
YOU GUYS ARE HOPELESS.

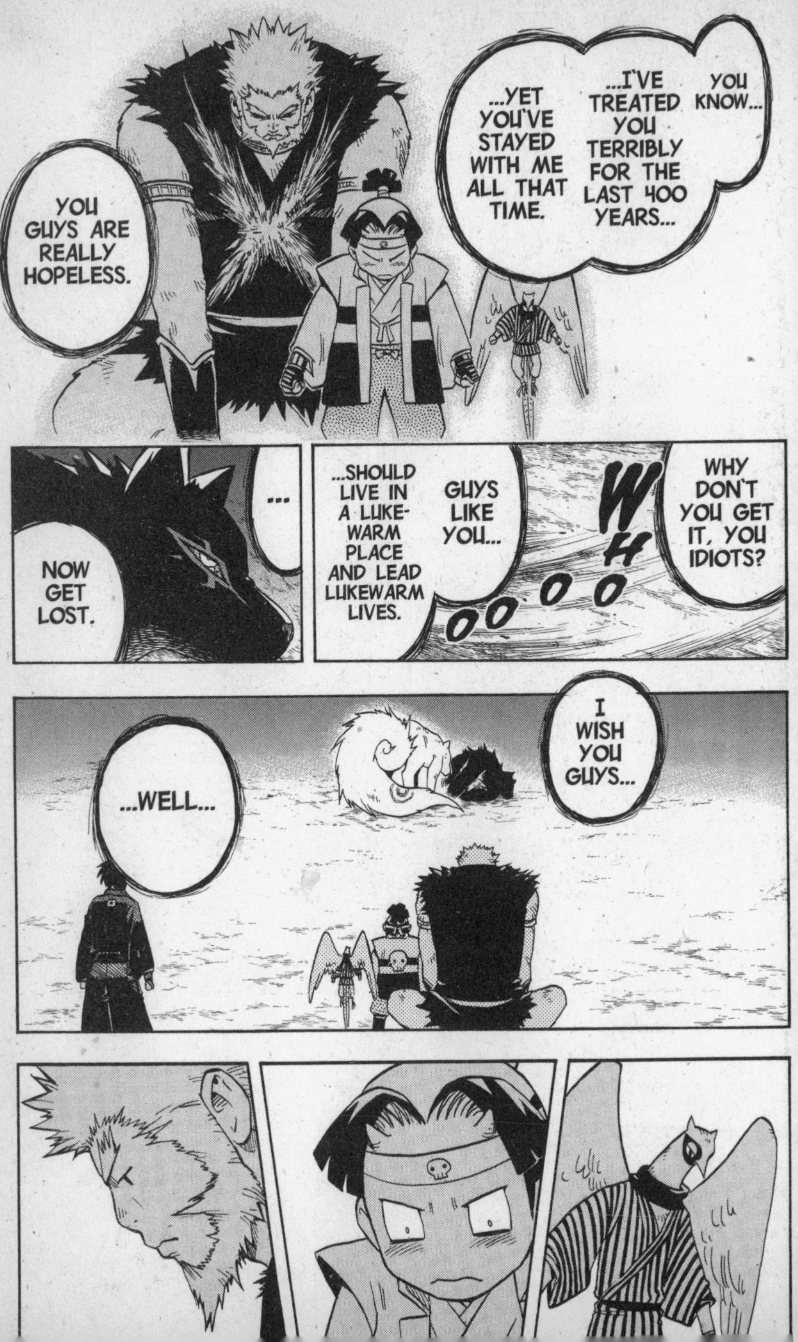
YOU KNOW...
...I'VE TREATED YOU TERRIBLY FOR THE LAST 400 YEARS...
...YET YOU'VE STAYED WITH ME ALL THAT TIME.
YOU GUYS ARE REALLY HOPELESS.
WHY DON'T YOU GET IT, YOU IDIOTS?
WHOOOOO
GUYS LIKE YOU...
...SHOULD LIVE IN A LUKE-WARM PLACE AND LEAD LUKEWARM LIVES.
...
NOW GET LOST.
I WISH YOU GUYS...
...WELL...

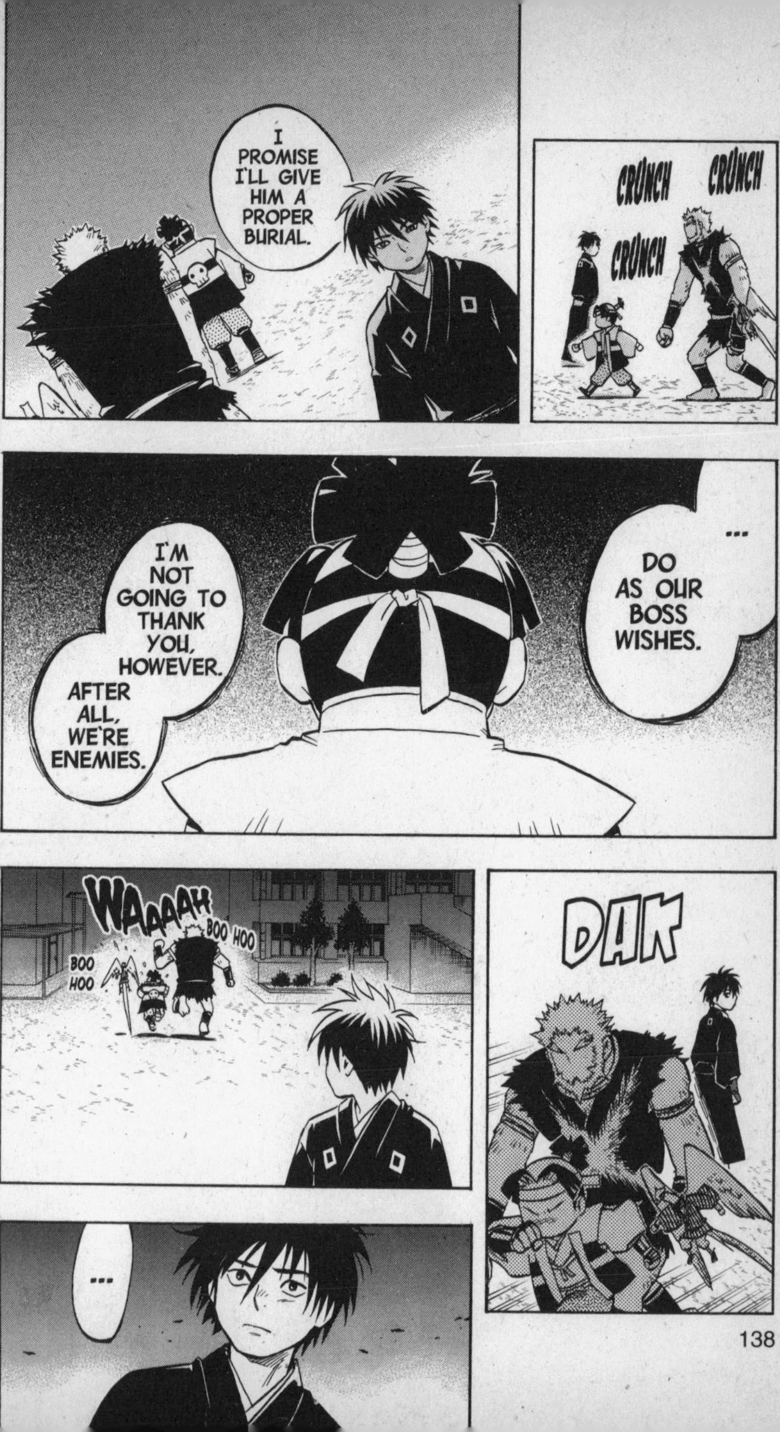

CRUNCH CRUNCH
CRUNCH
I PROMISE I'LL GIVE HIM A PROPER BURIAL.
... DO AS OUR BOSS WISHES.
I'M NOT GOING TO THANK YOU, HOWEVER. AFTER ALL, WE'RE ENEMIES.
DAK
WAAAAH
BOO HOO
BOO HOO
...

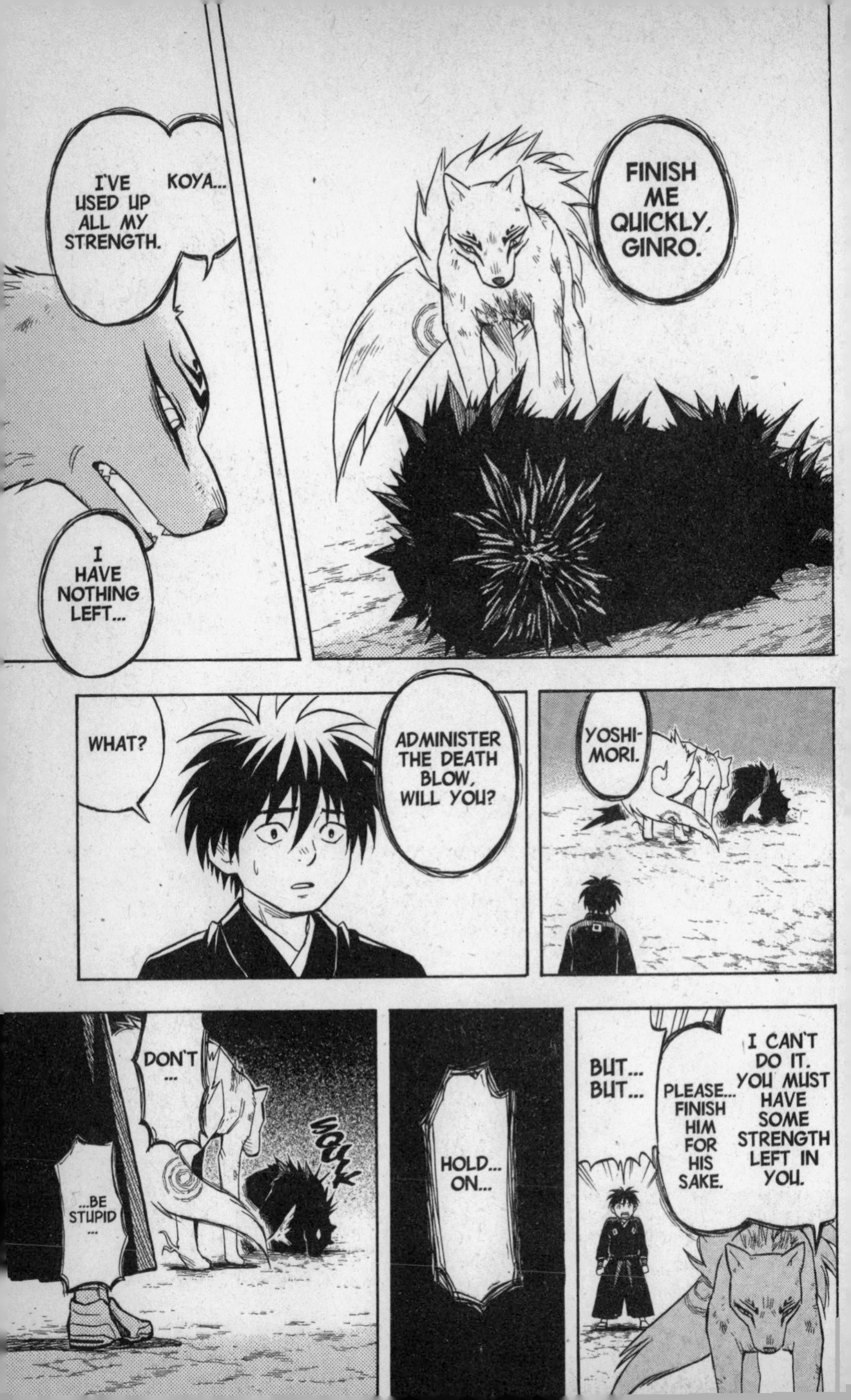
FINISH ME QUICKLY, GINRO.
KOYA...
I'VE USED UP ALL MY STRENGTH.
I HAVE NOTHING LEFT...
YOSHI-MORI.
ADMINISTER THE DEATH BLOW, WILL YOU?
WHAT?
I CAN'T DO IT. YOU MUST HAVE SOME STRENGTH LEFT IN YOU.
PLEASE... FINISH HIM FOR HIS SAKE.
BUT... BUT...
HOLD... ON...
SQUK
DON'T ...
...BE STUPID ...

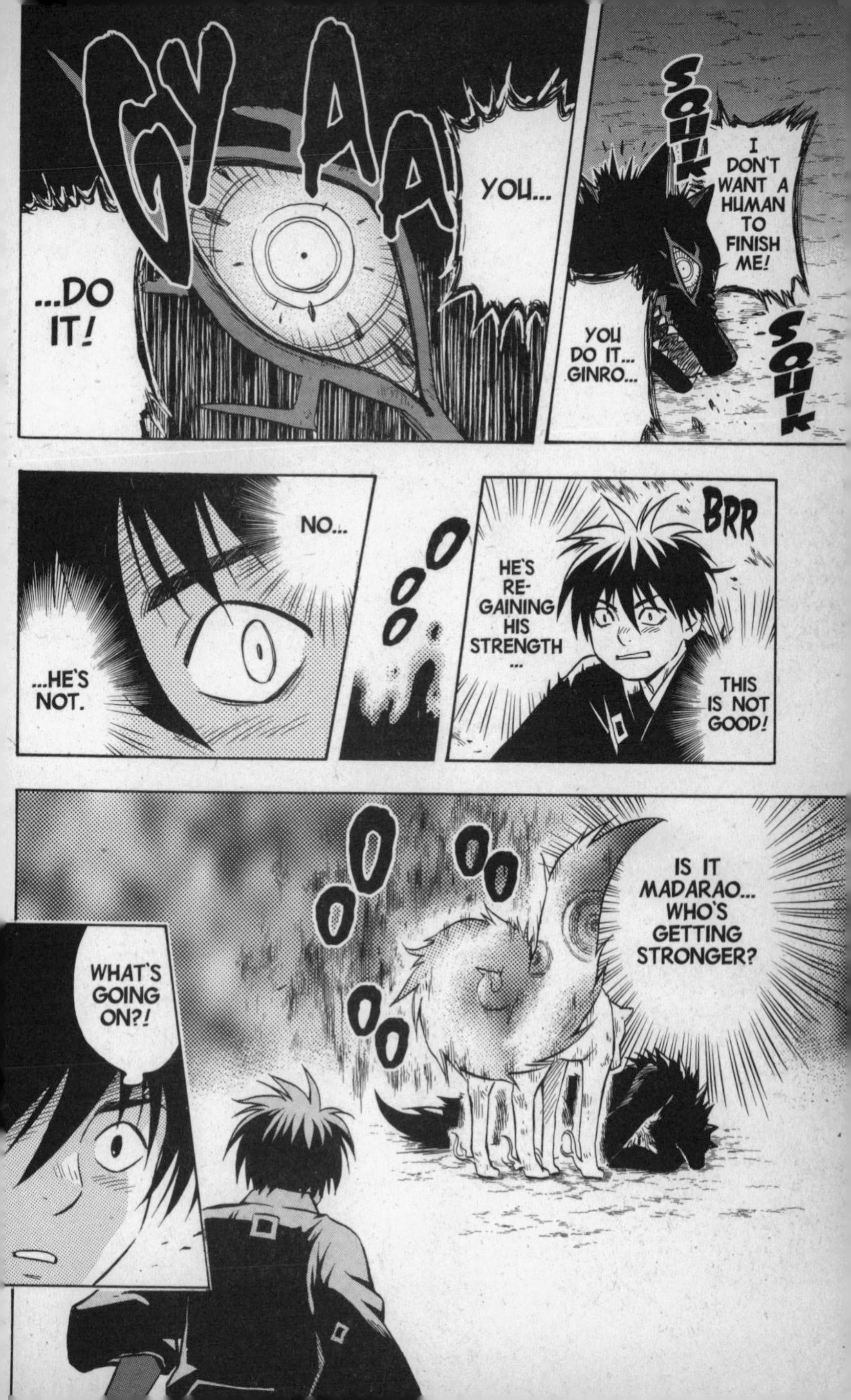
SQUIK
I DON'T WANT A HUMAN TO FINISH ME!
YOU DO IT... GINRO...
SQUIK
GYAA
YOU...
...DO IT!
BRR
HE'S RE-GAINING HIS STRENGTH...
THIS IS NOT GOOD!
OOOO
NO...
...HE'S NOT.
IS IT MADARAO... WHO'S GETTING STRONGER?
OOOOOOO
WHAT'S GOING ON?!

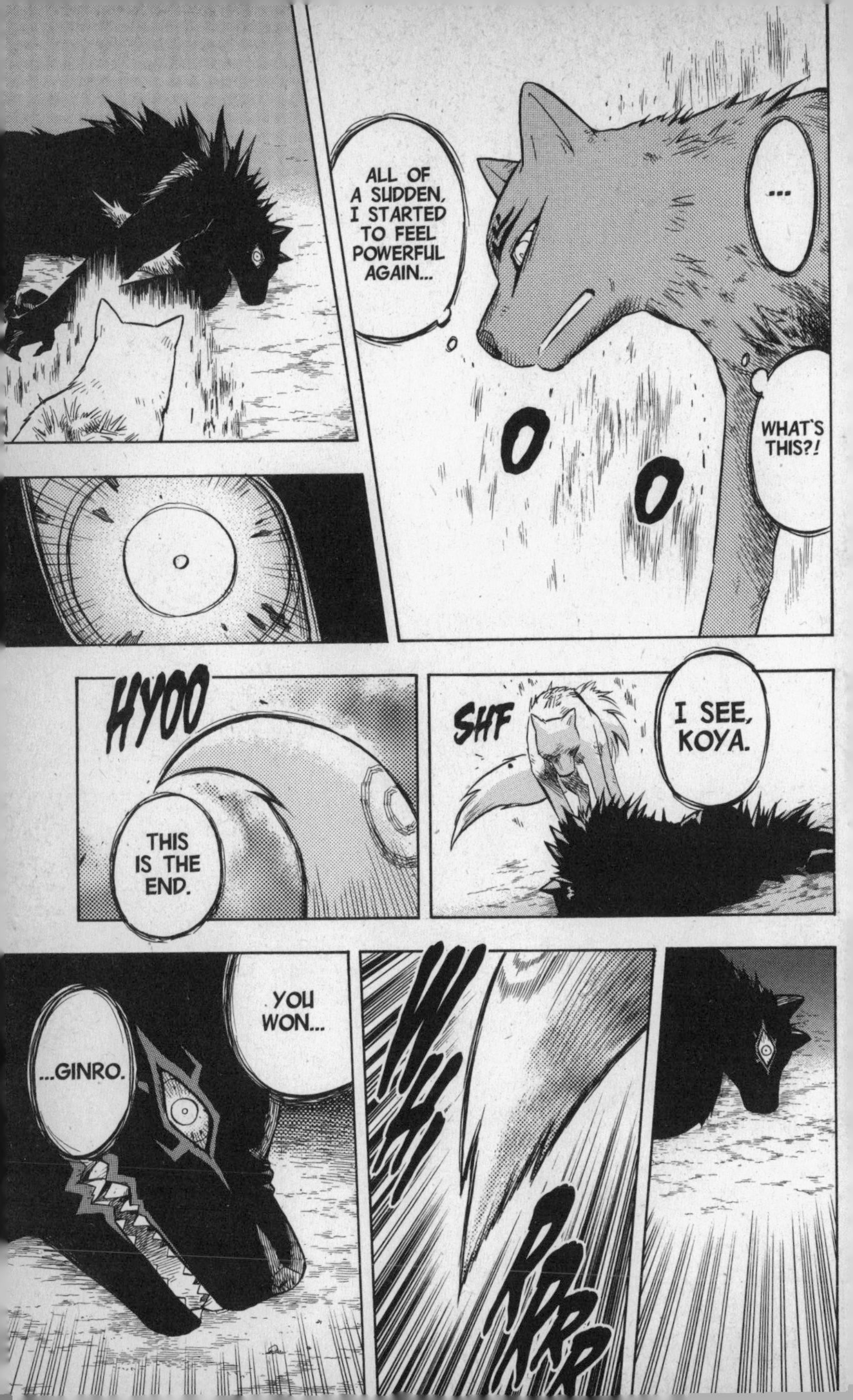
...
ALL OF A SUDDEN, I STARTED TO FEEL POWERFUL AGAIN...
WHAT'S THIS?!
I SEE, KOYA.
SHF
HYOO
THIS IS THE END.
YOU WON...
...GINRO.

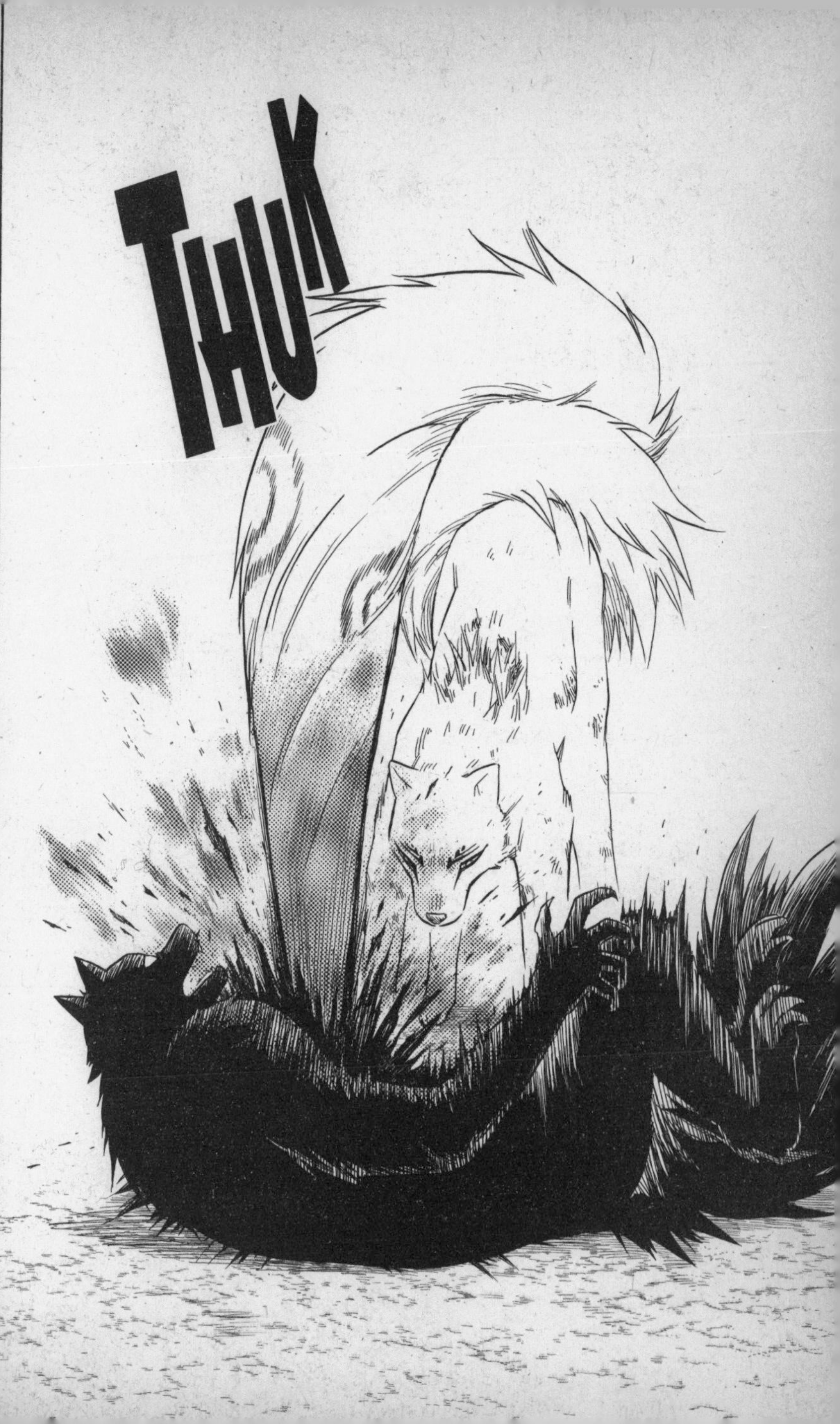
THUNK

I'M SORRY, KOYA...

I GAVE YOU A LOT OF ANESTHESIA.

YOU'LL BE UNCONSCIOUS SOON.

...BUT YOU'RE SO STRONG THAT IT'S TAKING TIME...

MY POISON IS SUPPOSED TO KILL VERY QUICKLY...

YES, YOU WERE...

WAS I STRONG?

HEY, GINRO.

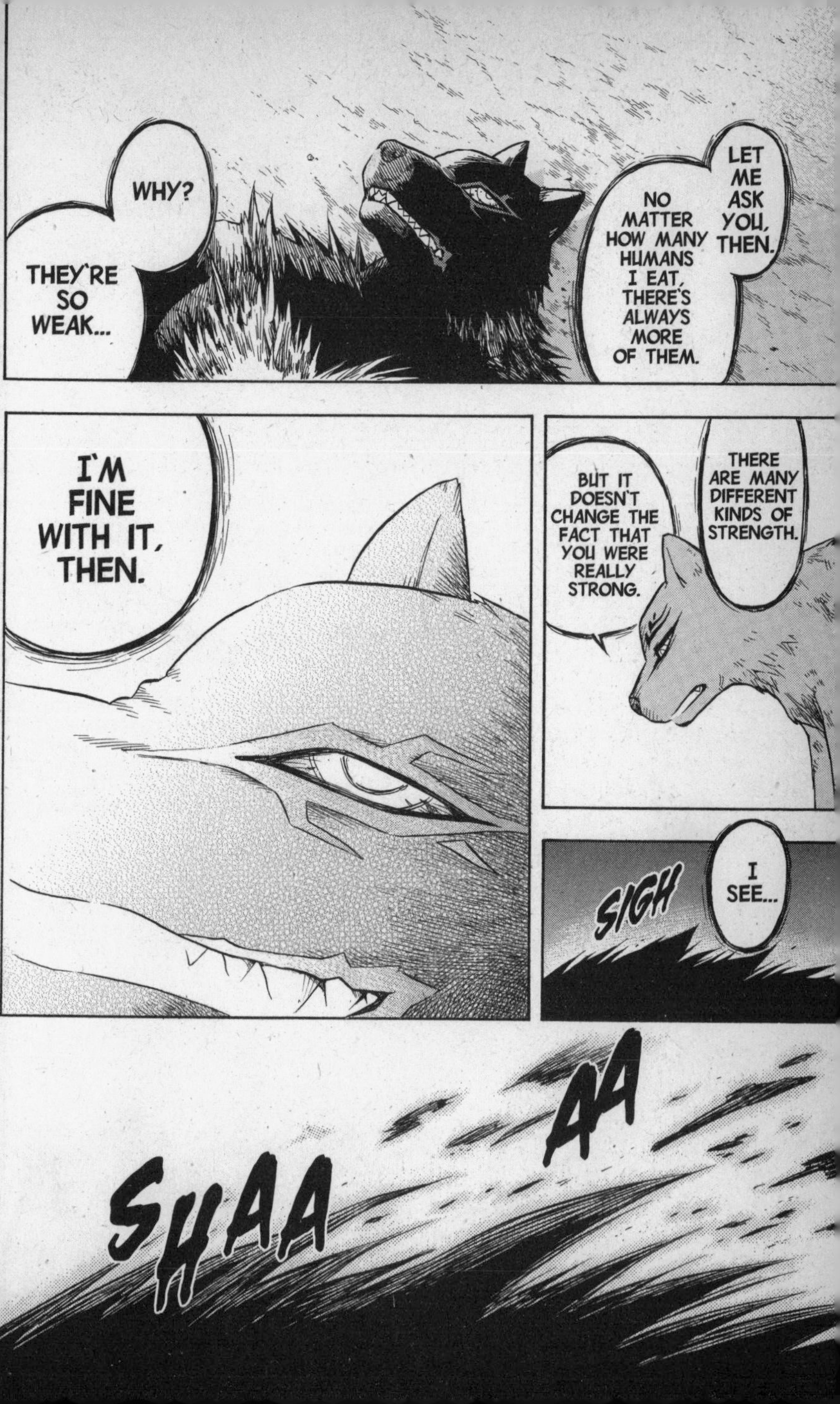
LET ME ASK YOU, THEN.
NO MATTER HOW MANY HUMANS I EAT, THERE'S ALWAYS MORE OF THEM.
WHY?
THEY'RE SO WEAK...
THERE ARE MANY DIFFERENT KINDS OF STRENGTH.
BUT IT DOESN'T CHANGE THE FACT THAT YOU WERE REALLY STRONG.
I SEE...
SIGH
I'M FINE WITH IT, THEN.
SHAA AA

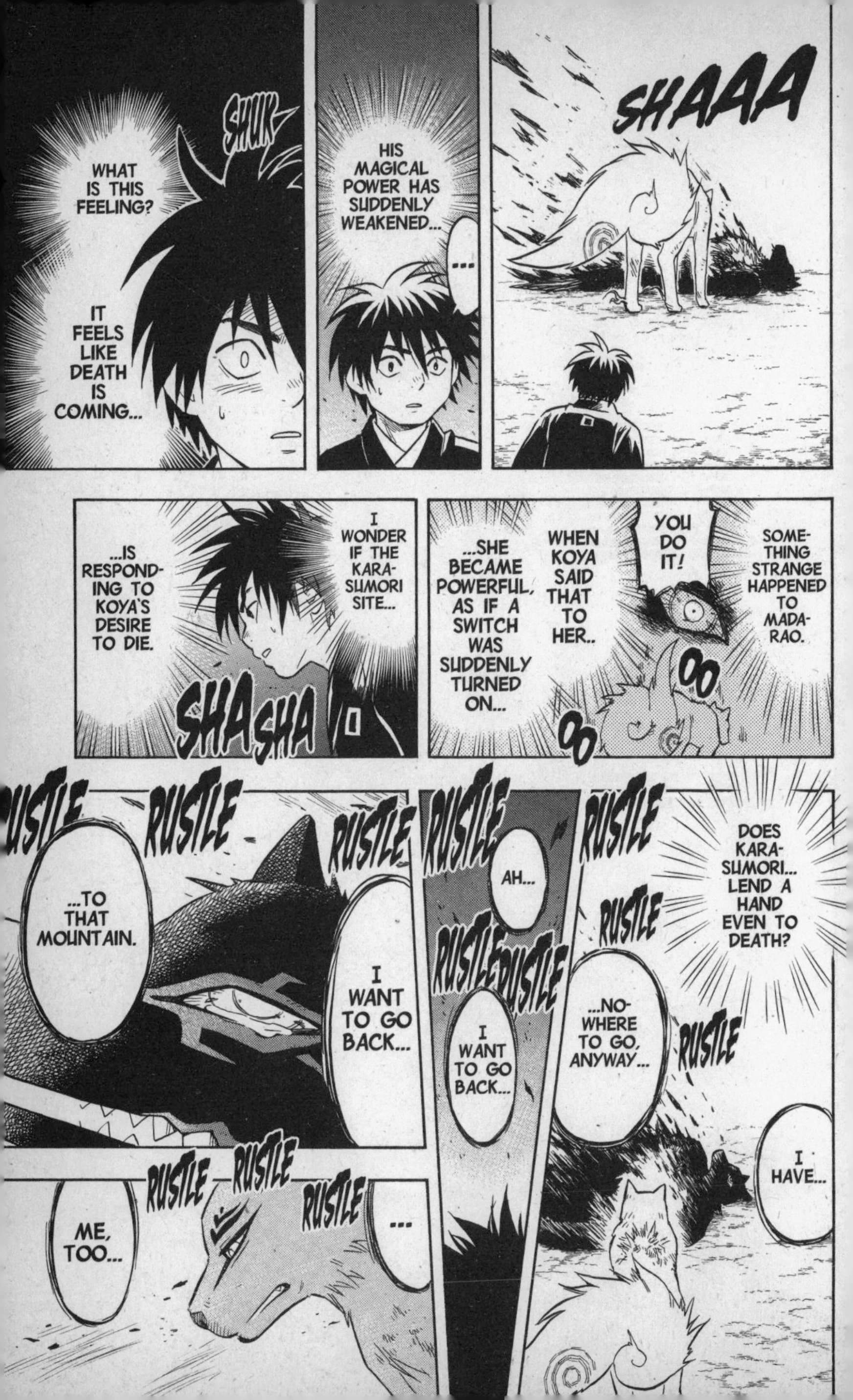
SHAAA
HIS MAGICAL POWER HAS SUDDENLY WEAKENED...
...
SHUK
WHAT IS THIS FEELING?
IT FEELS LIKE DEATH IS COMING...
SOME-THING STRANGE HAPPENED TO MADA-RAO.
YOU DO IT!
WHEN KOYA SAID THAT TO HER..
...SHE BECAME POWERFUL, AS IF A SWITCH WAS SUDDENLY TURNED ON...
OO
OO
I WONDER IF THE KARA-SUMORI SITE...
...IS RESPOND-ING TO KOYA'S DESIRE TO DIE.
SHASHA
DOES KARA-SUMORI... LEND A HAND EVEN TO DEATH?
RUSTLE
RUSTLE
RUSTLE
I HAVE...
...NO-WHERE TO GO, ANYWAY...
RUSTLE
AH...
RUSTLE RUSTLE
I WANT TO GO BACK...
RUSTLE
RUSTLE
RUSTLE
I WANT TO GO BACK...
...TO THAT MOUNTAIN.
RUSTLE
RUSTLE
RUSTLE
...
ME, TOO...

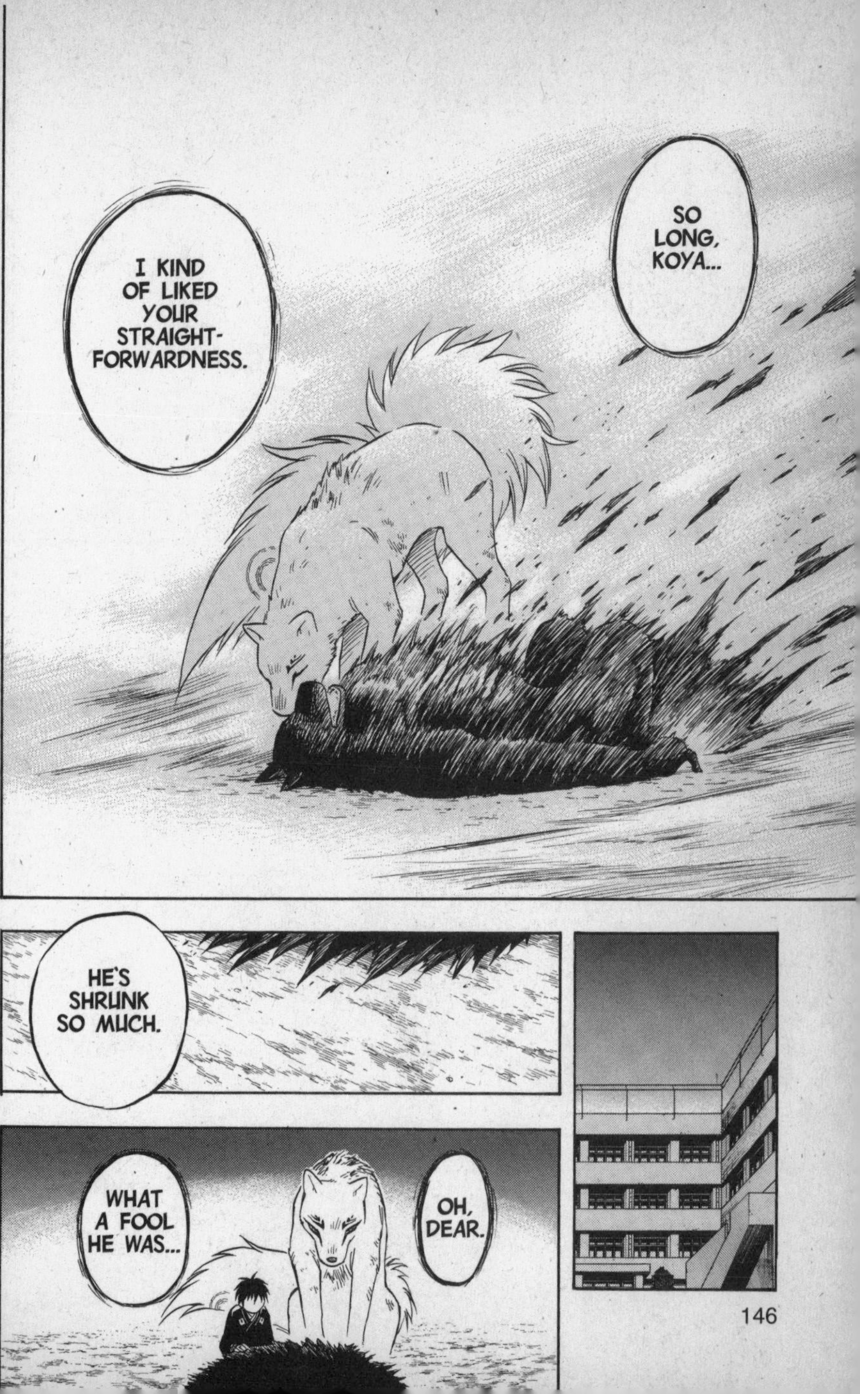
SO LONG, KOYA...
I KIND OF LIKED YOUR STRAIGHT-FORWARDNESS.
HE'S SHRUNK SO MUCH.
OH, DEAR.
WHAT A FOOL HE WAS...

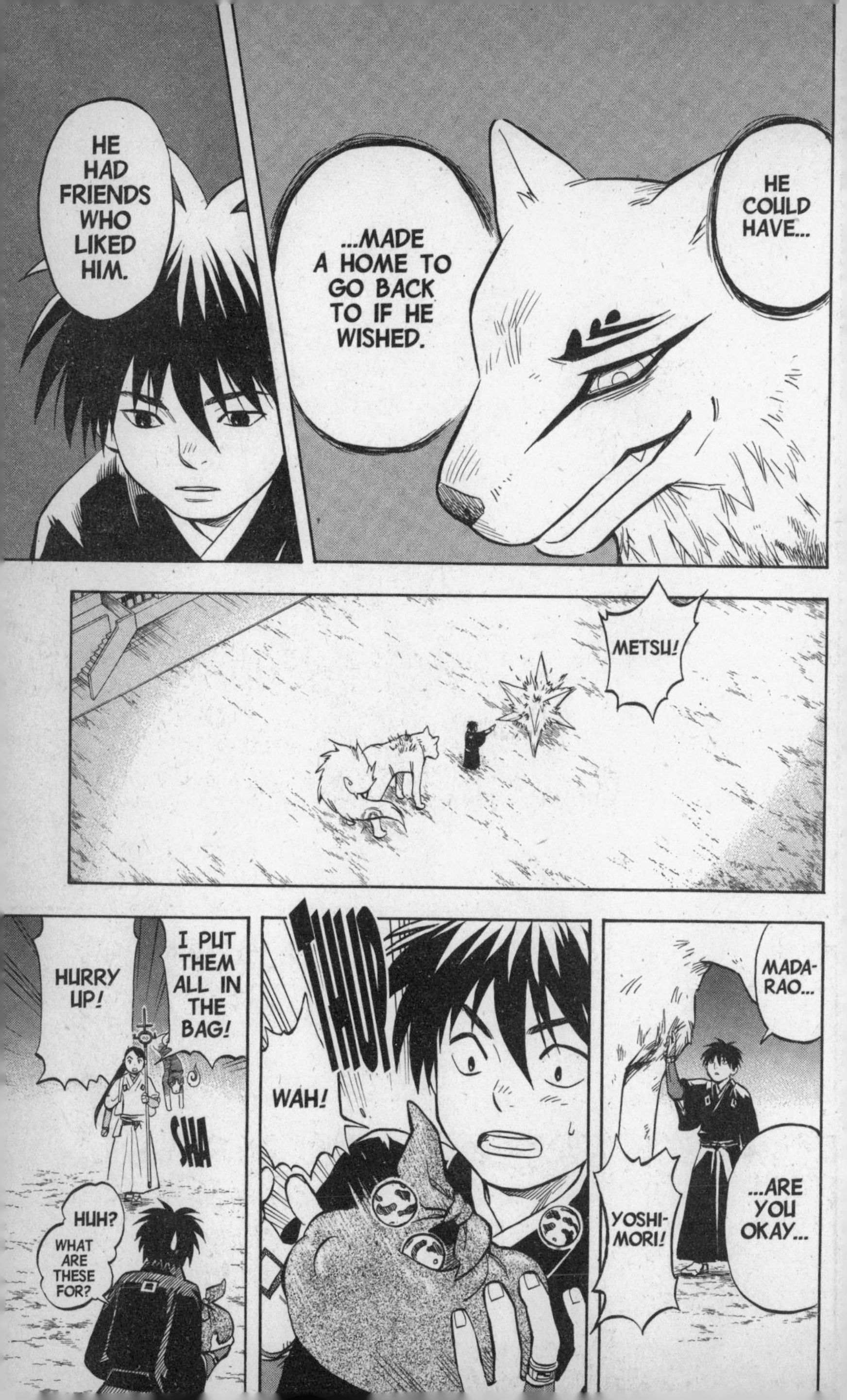
HE COULD HAVE...
...MADE A HOME TO GO BACK TO IF HE WISHED.
HE HAD FRIENDS WHO LIKED HIM.
METSU!
MADA-RAO...
...ARE YOU OKAY...
YOSHI-MORI!
THUD
WAH!
I PUT THEM ALL IN THE BAG!
HURRY UP!
SHA
HUH? WHAT ARE THESE FOR?

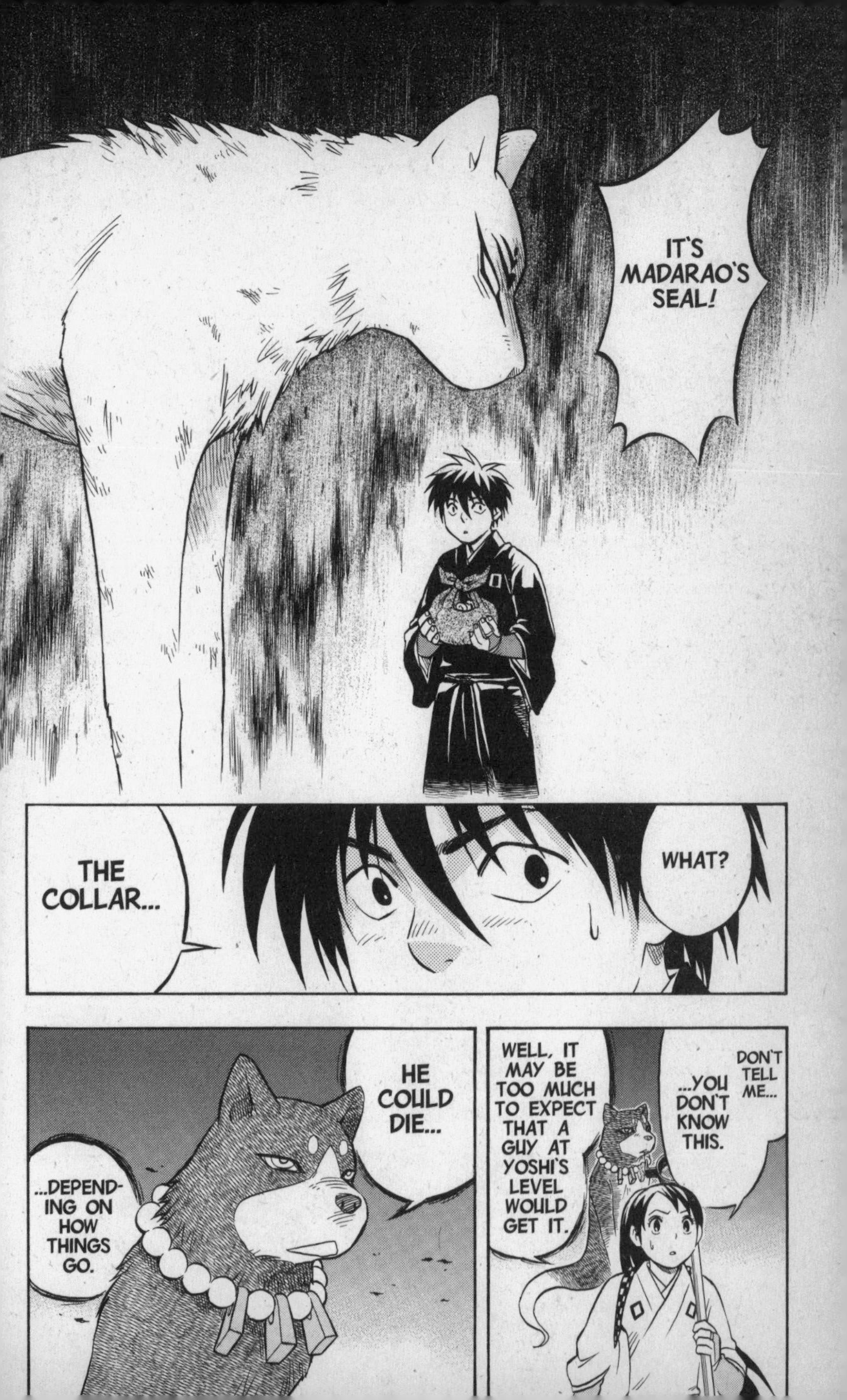
IT'S MADARAO'S SEAL!
WHAT?
THE COLLAR...
DON'T TELL ME...
...YOU DON'T KNOW THIS.
WELL, IT MAY BE TOO MUCH TO EXPECT THAT A GUY AT YOSHI'S LEVEL WOULD GET IT.
HE COULD DIE...
...DEPENDING ON HOW THINGS GO.

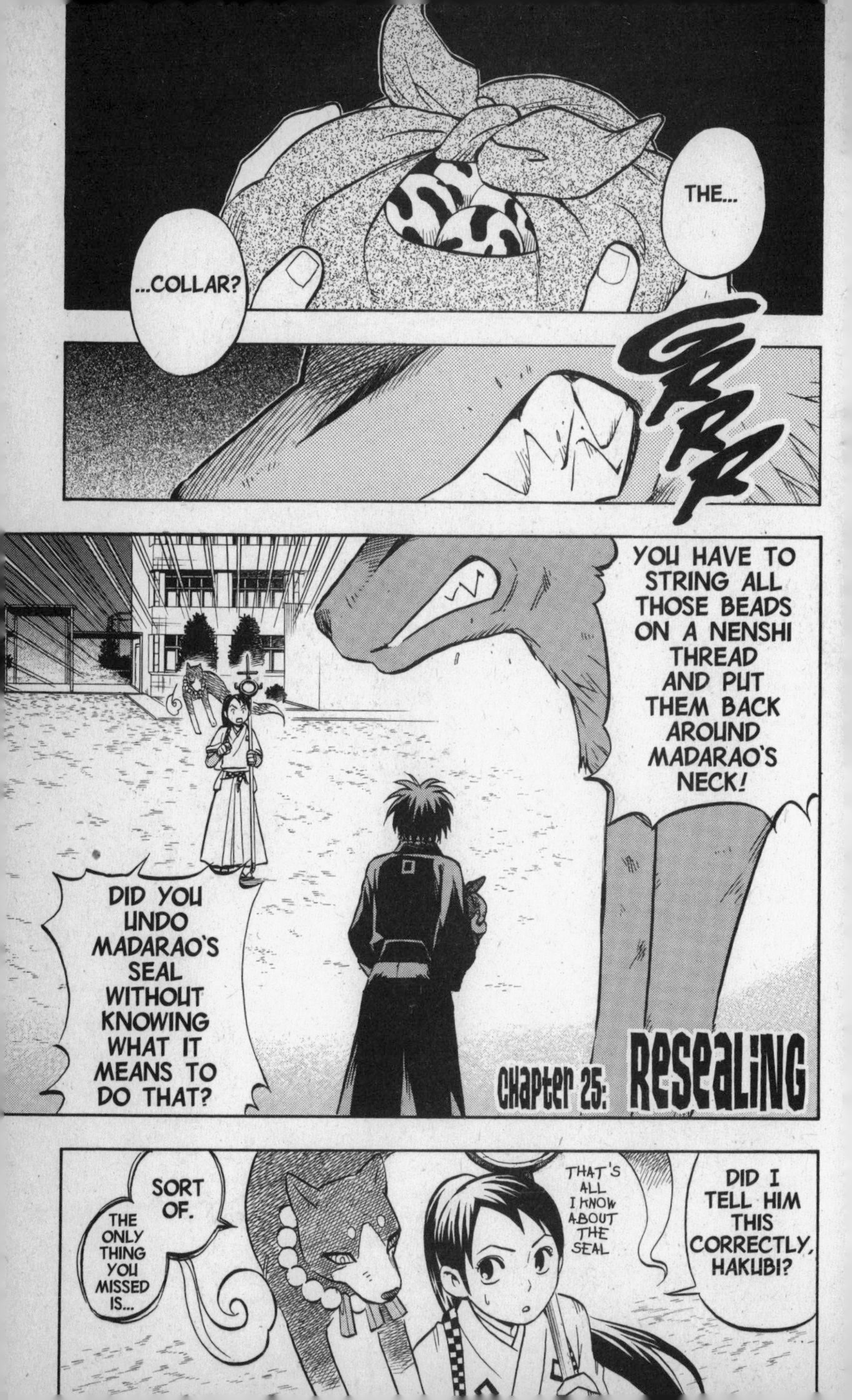
THE...
...COLLAR?
GRRR
YOU HAVE TO STRING ALL THOSE BEADS ON A NENSHI THREAD AND PUT THEM BACK AROUND MADARAO'S NECK!
DID YOU UNDO MADARAO'S SEAL WITHOUT KNOWING WHAT IT MEANS TO DO THAT?
Chapter 25: Resealing
DID I TELL HIM THIS CORRECTLY, HAKUBI?
THAT'S ALL I KNOW ABOUT THE SEAL
SORT OF.
THE ONLY THING YOU MISSED IS...

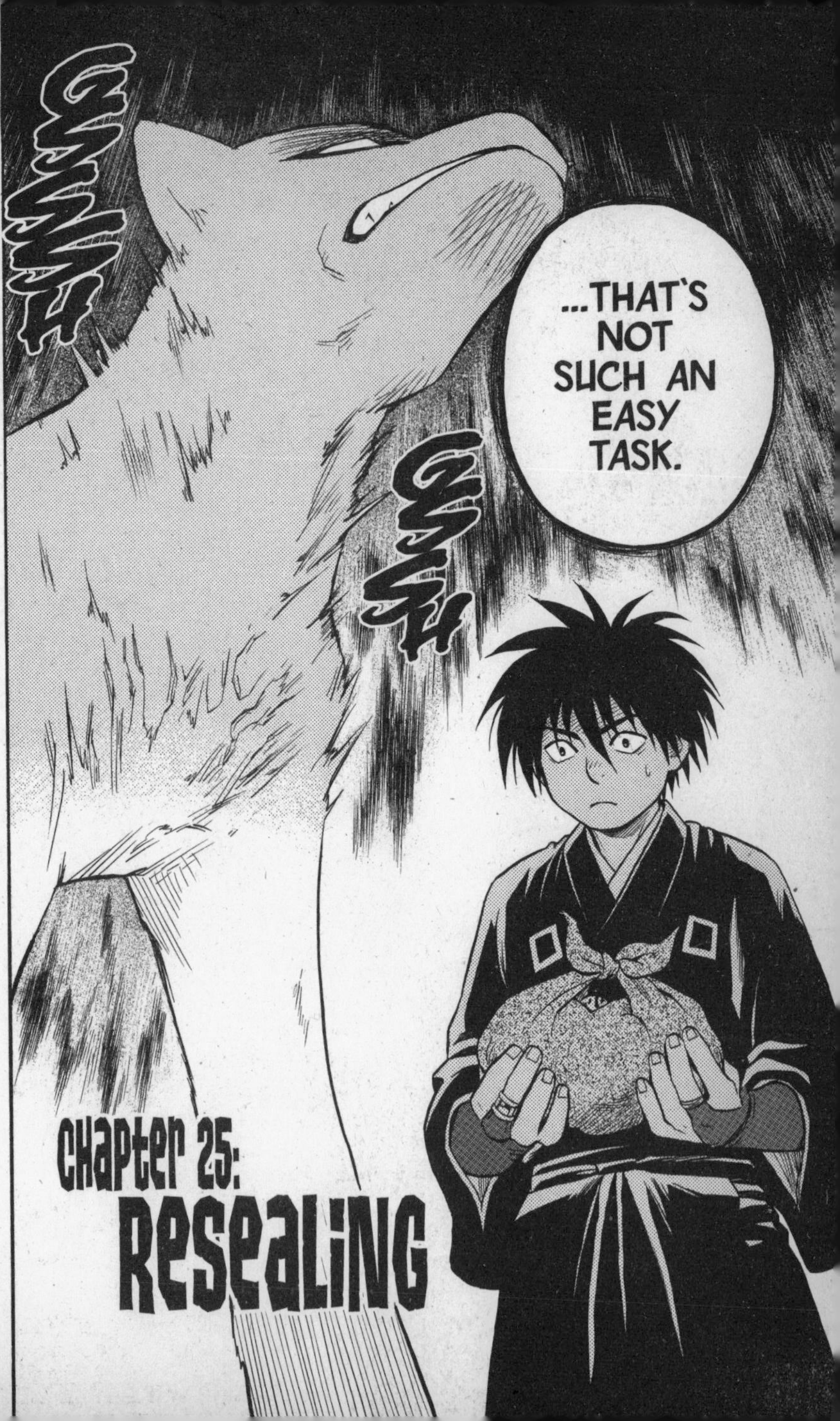
GSSSHH
...THAT'S NOT SUCH AN EASY TASK.
GSSH
Chapter 25:
Resealing

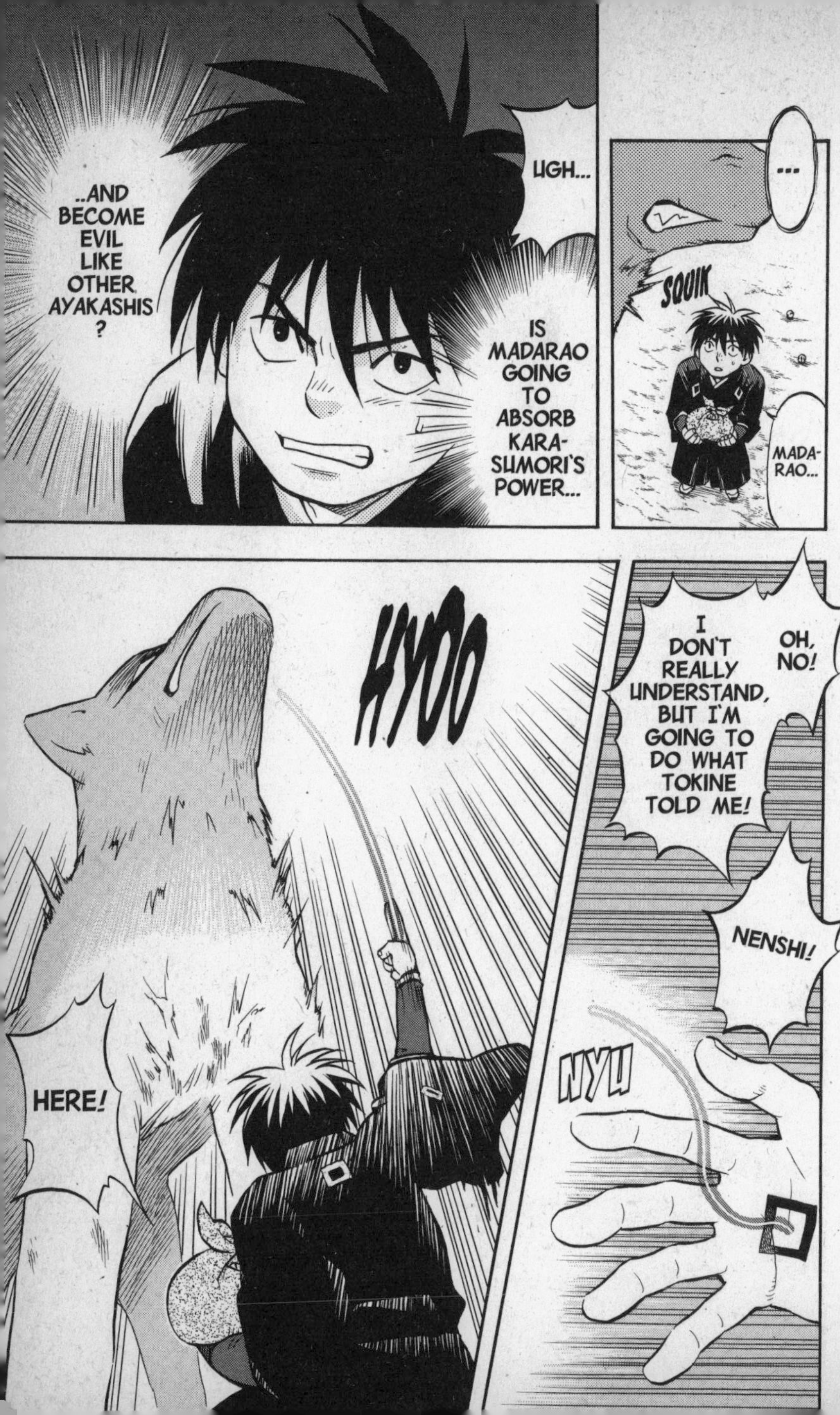
...
SQUIK
MADARAO...
UGH...
IS MADARAO GOING TO ABSORB KARASUMORI'S POWER...
..AND BECOME EVIL LIKE OTHER AYAKASHIS?
OH, NO!
I DON'T REALLY UNDERSTAND, BUT I'M GOING TO DO WHAT TOKINE TOLD ME!
NENSHI!
NYU
HYOO
HERE!

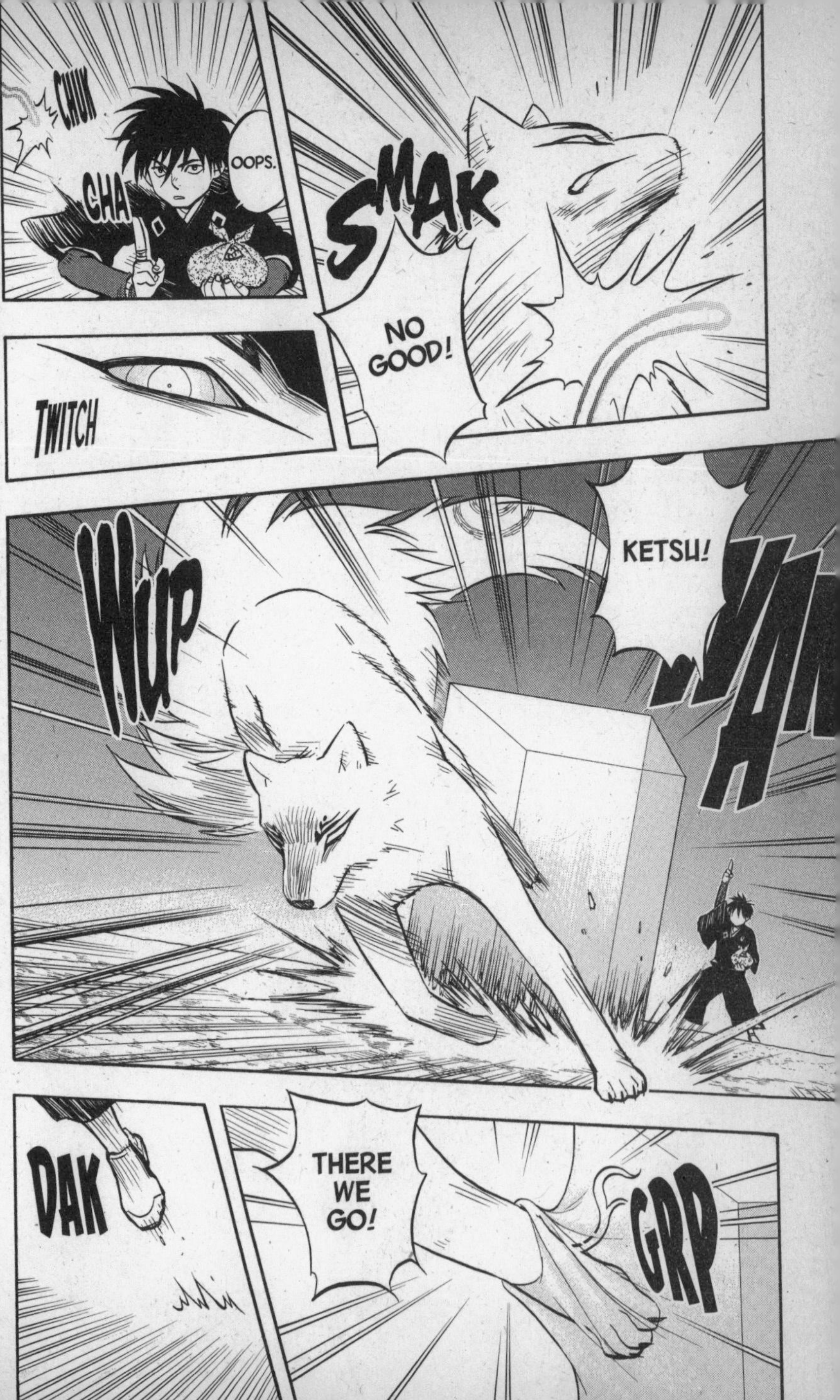
SMAK
NO GOOD!
CHUK
CHA
OOPS.
TWITCH
KETSU!
WUP
GRP
THERE WE GO!
DAK

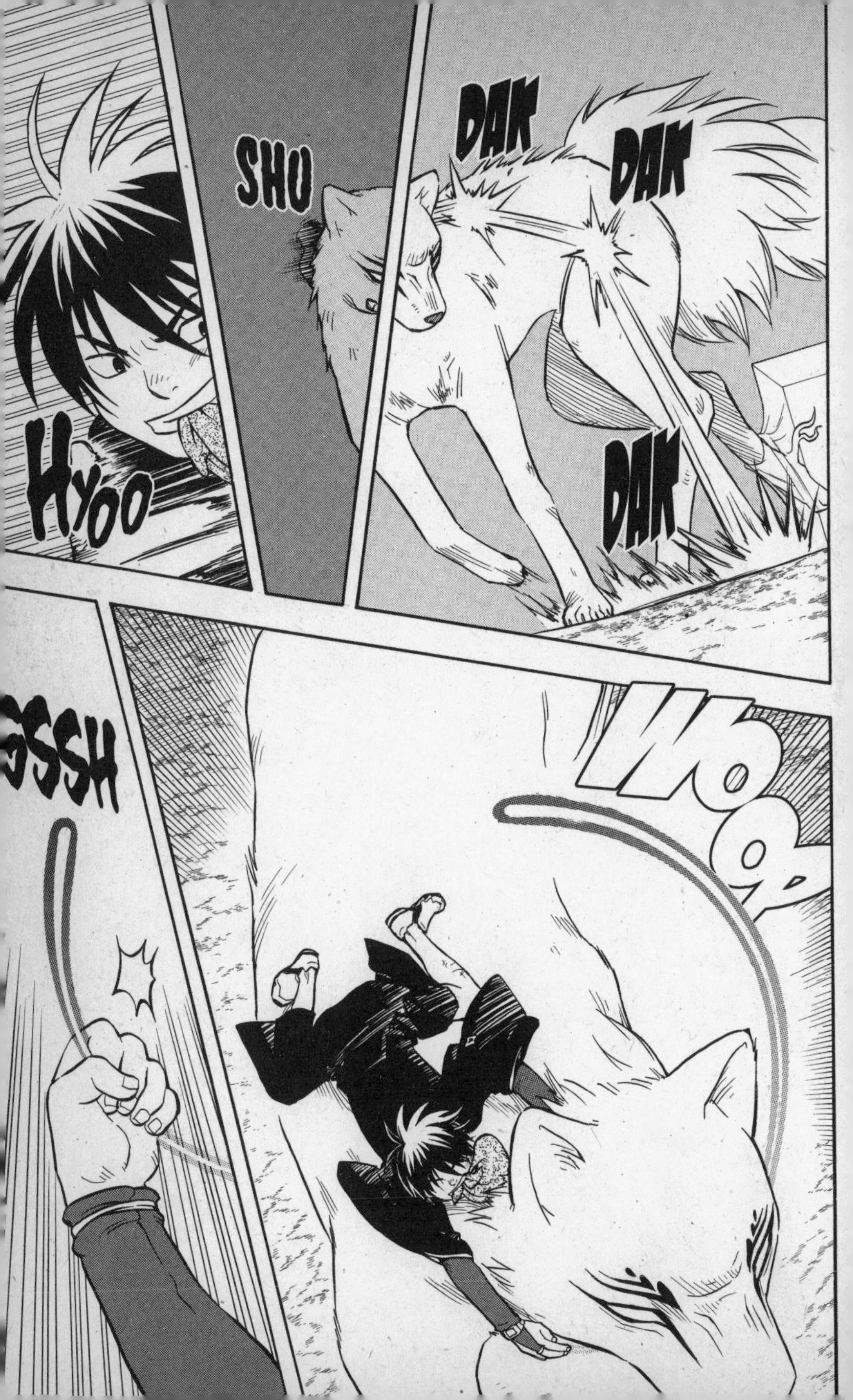
DAK
DAK
DAK
SHU
HYOO
SSH

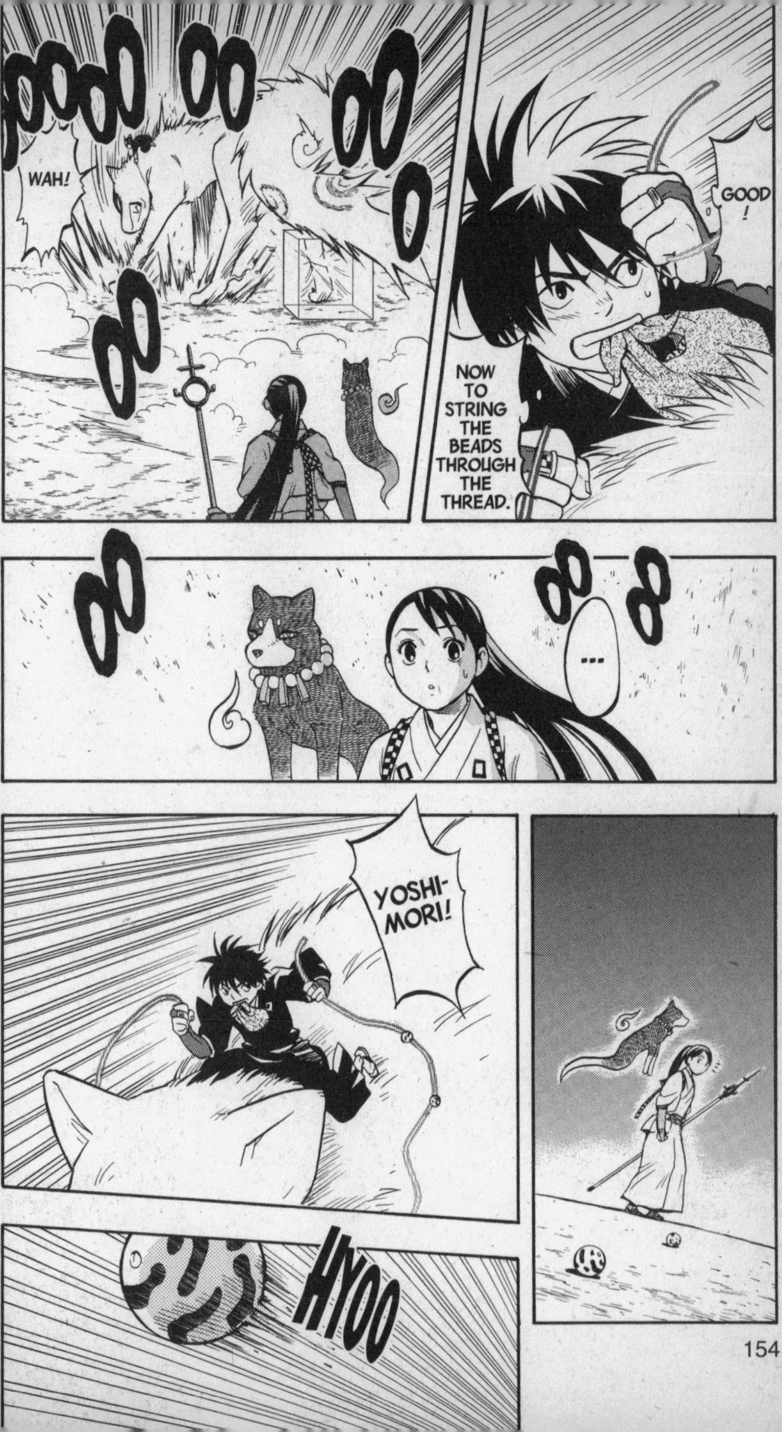
GOOD!
NOW TO STRING THE BEADS THROUGH THE THREAD.
WAH!
...
YOSHI-MORI!
HYOO

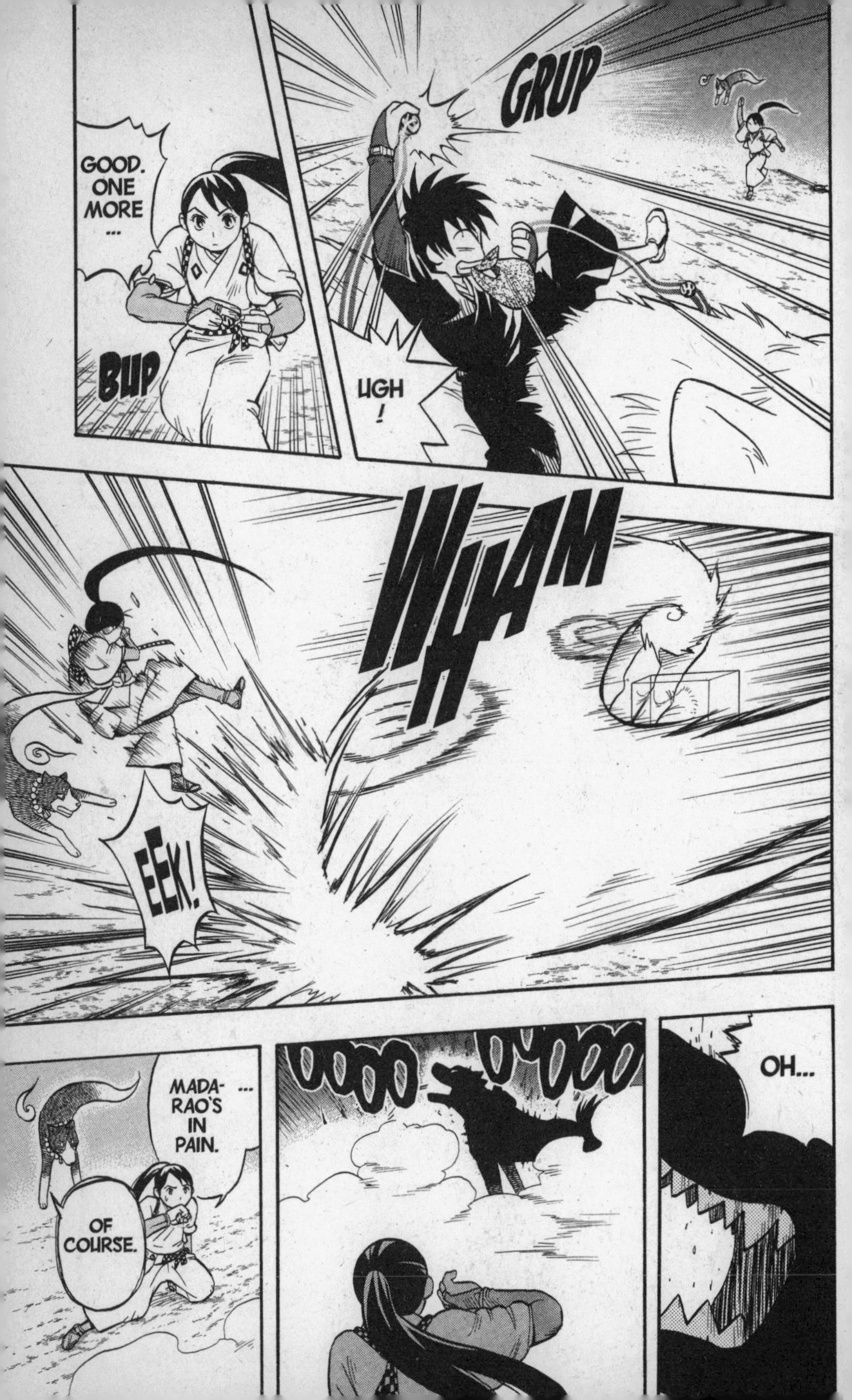
GRUP
UGH!
GOOD. ONE MORE ...
BUP
WHAM
EEK!
OH...
OOOO
OOOOO
... MADA-RAO'S IN PAIN.
OF COURSE.

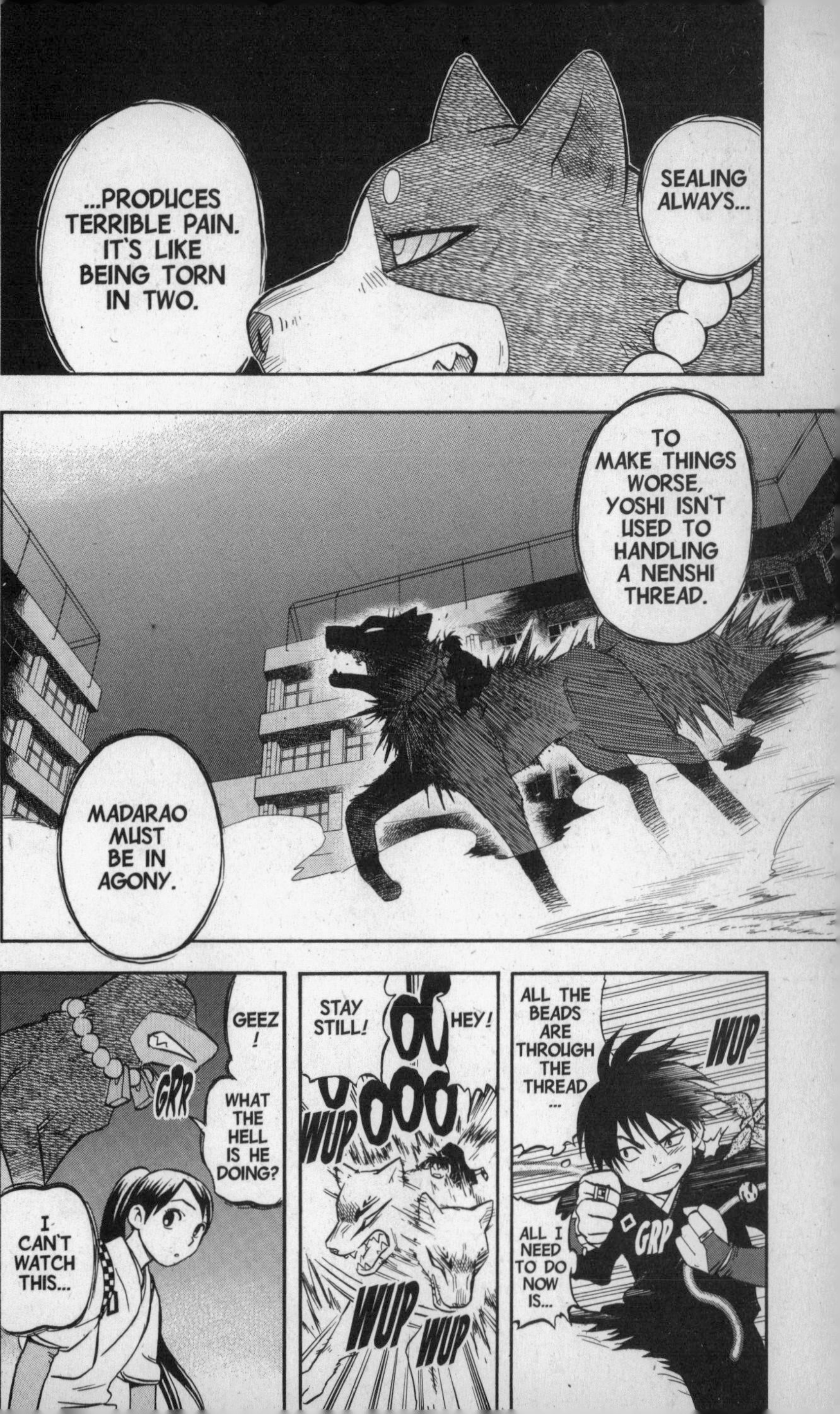
SEALING ALWAYS...
...PRODUCES TERRIBLE PAIN. IT'S LIKE BEING TORN IN TWO.
TO MAKE THINGS WORSE, YOSHI ISN'T USED TO HANDLING A NENSHI THREAD.
MADARAO MUST BE IN AGONY.
ALL THE BEADS ARE THROUGH THE THREAD...
WUP
ALL I NEED TO DO NOW IS...
GRP
HEY!
STAY STILL!
WUP
WUP
WUP
GEEZ!
GRR
WHAT THE HELL IS HE DOING?
I CAN'T WATCH THIS...

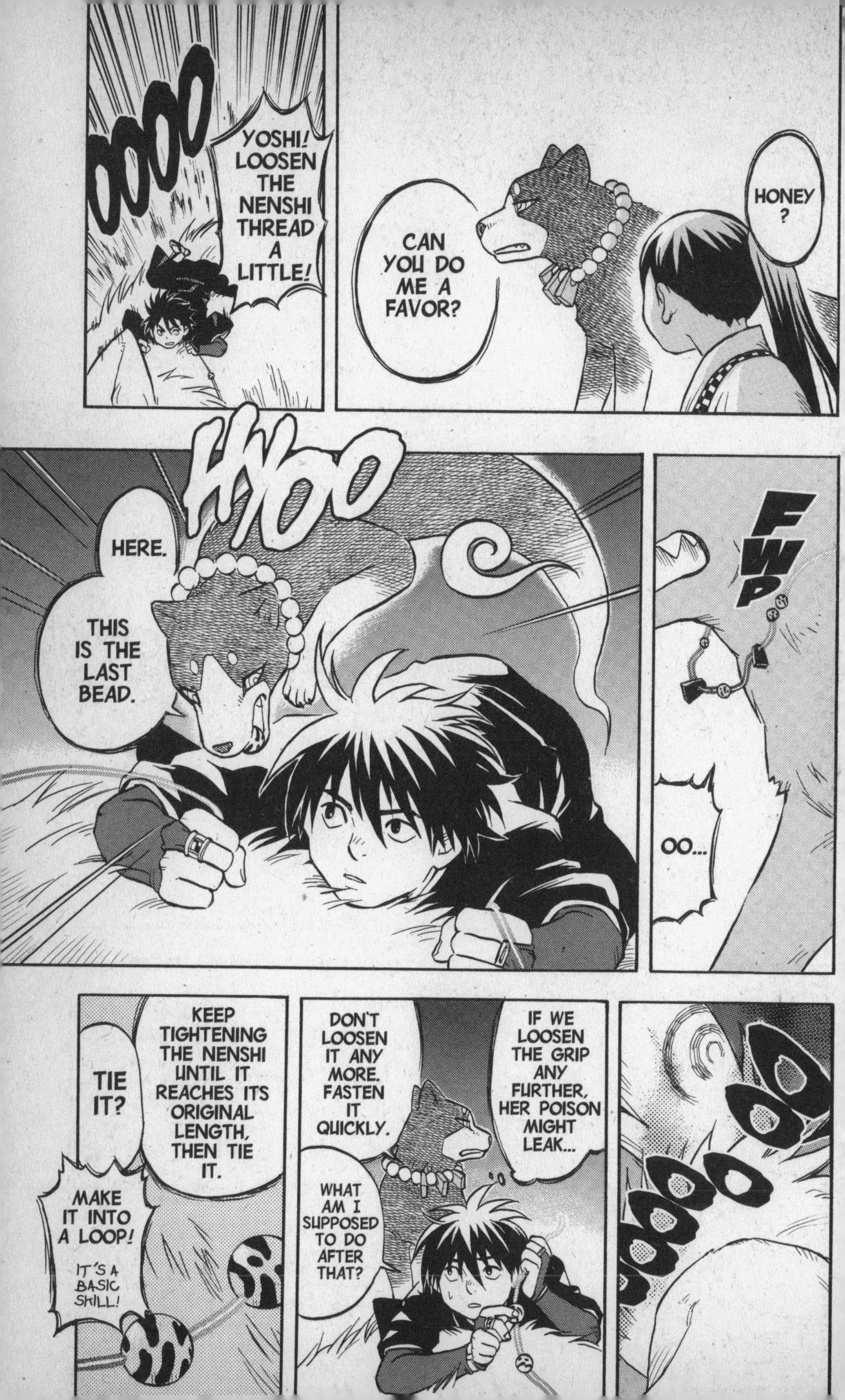
HONEY ?
CAN YOU DO ME A FAVOR?
YOSHI! LOOSEN THE NENSHI THREAD A LITTLE!
OOOO
FWP
OO...
HYOO
HERE.
THIS IS THE LAST BEAD.
OOOOOOOO
IF WE LOOSEN THE GRIP ANY FURTHER, HER POISON MIGHT LEAK...
DON'T LOOSEN IT ANY MORE. FASTEN IT QUICKLY.
WHAT AM I SUPPOSED TO DO AFTER THAT?
KEEP TIGHTENING THE NENSHI UNTIL IT REACHES ITS ORIGINAL LENGTH, THEN TIE IT.
TIE IT?
MAKE IT INTO A LOOP!
IT'S A BASIC SKILL!

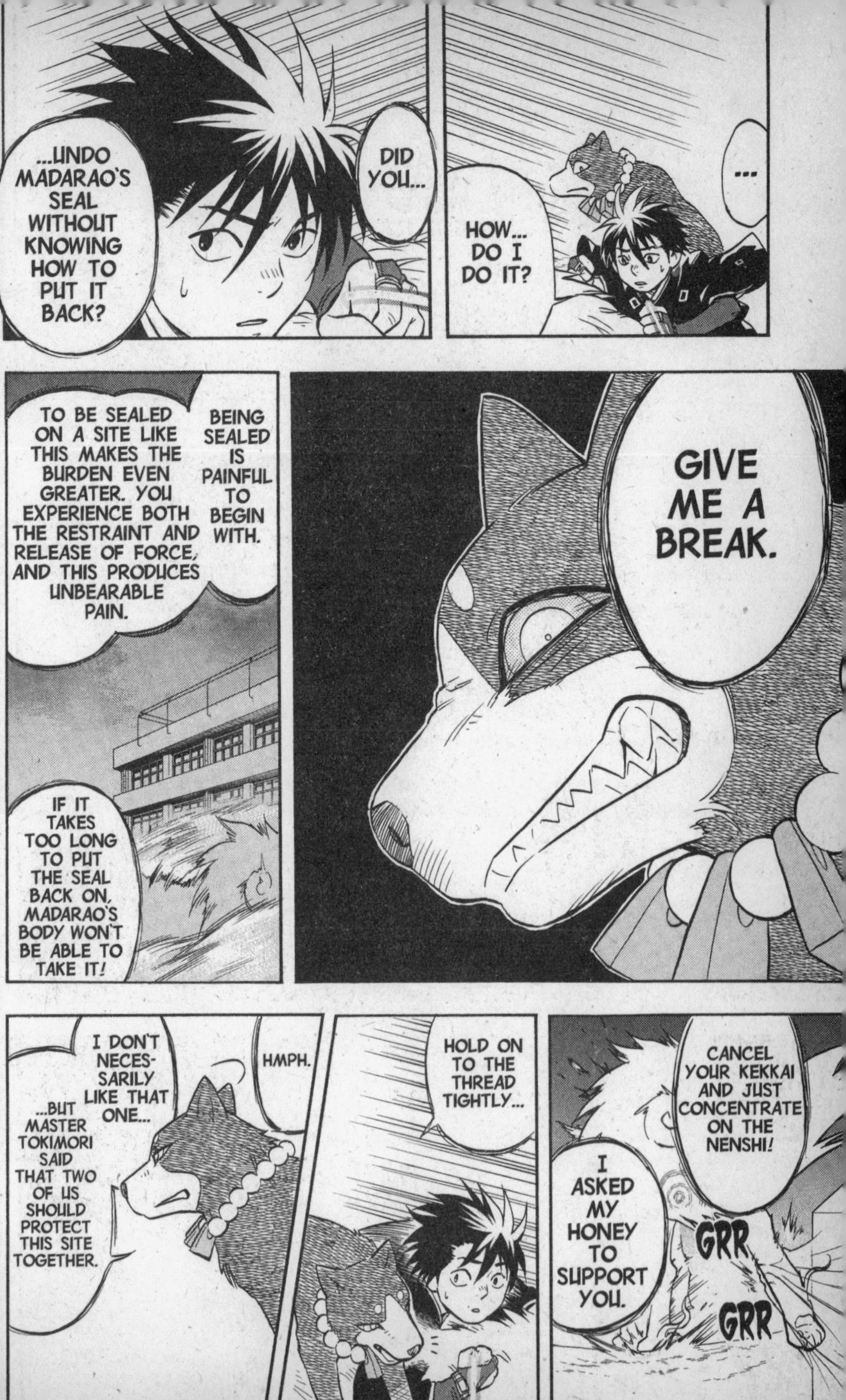
...
HOW... DO I DO IT?
DID YOU...
...UNDO MADARAO'S SEAL WITHOUT KNOWING HOW TO PUT IT BACK?
GIVE ME A BREAK.
BEING SEALED IS PAINFUL TO BEGIN WITH.
TO BE SEALED ON A SITE LIKE THIS MAKES THE BURDEN EVEN GREATER. YOU EXPERIENCE BOTH THE RESTRAINT AND RELEASE OF FORCE, AND THIS PRODUCES UNBEARABLE PAIN.
IF IT TAKES TOO LONG TO PUT THE SEAL BACK ON, MADARAO'S BODY WON'T BE ABLE TO TAKE IT!
CANCEL YOUR KEKKAI AND JUST CONCENTRATE ON THE NENSHI!
I ASKED MY HONEY TO SUPPORT YOU.
GRR
GRR
HOLD ON TO THE THREAD TIGHTLY...
HMPH.
I DON'T NECES-SARILY LIKE THAT ONE...
...BUT MASTER TOKIMORI SAID THAT TWO OF US SHOULD PROTECT THIS SITE TOGETHER.

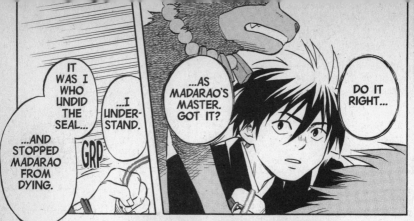

DO IT RIGHT...
...AS MADARAO'S MASTER. GOT IT?
...I UNDERSTAND.
GRP
IT WAS I WHO UNDID THE SEAL...
...AND STOPPED MADARAO FROM DYING.
I'LL PUT THE SEAL BACK NO MATTER WHAT.
THAT'S MY DUTY AS HER MASTER!
HMPH!
LISTEN, HONEY.
WHEN YOSHIMORI IS READY...
...TRY TO STOP MADARAO FROM MOVING FOR A WHILE.
IF YOU CAN'T DO THAT...
I'M SORRY, HAKUBI... SHE'S TOO STRONG FOR ME...

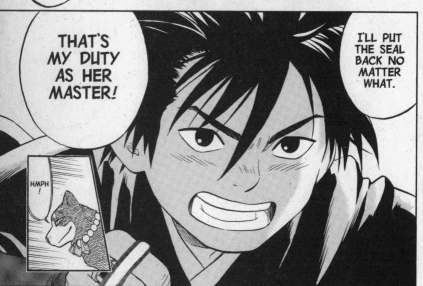

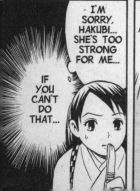

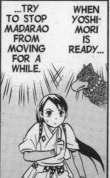

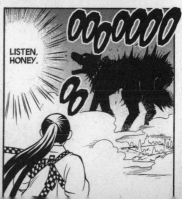

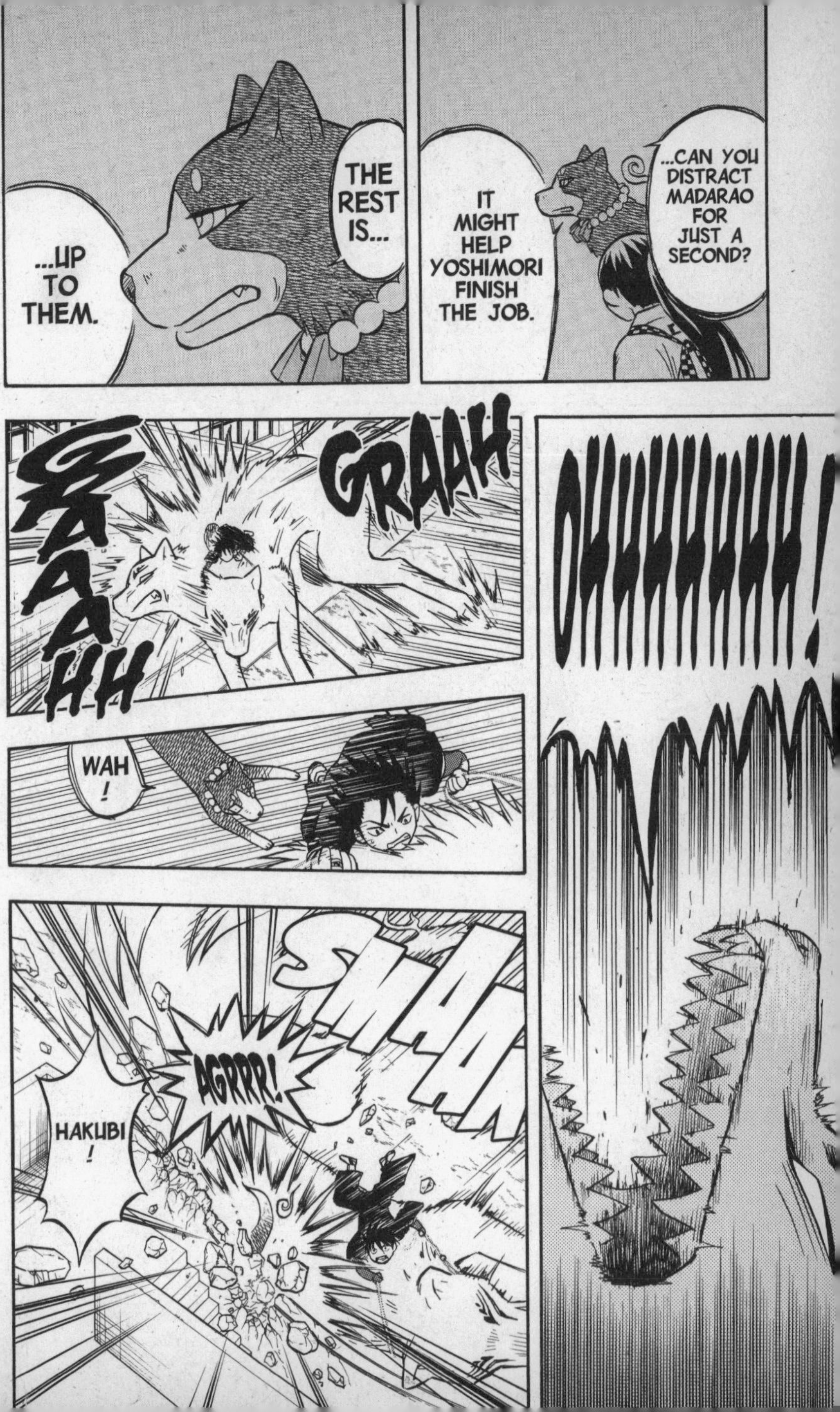
...CAN YOU DISTRACT MADARAO FOR JUST A SECOND?
IT MIGHT HELP YOSHIMORI FINISH THE JOB.
THE REST IS...
...UP TO THEM.
OHHHHHHH!
GRAAH
GRAAAHH
WAH!
SHAA
AGRRR!
HAKUBI!

I'M SORRY, HAKUBI...

I'M SORRY, MADARAO...

···

WHOOSH

LIGH...

MY...

YOU'RE SUFFERING BECAUSE OF MY INEXPERIENCE!

PI NG

NOW!

PAK

SHU

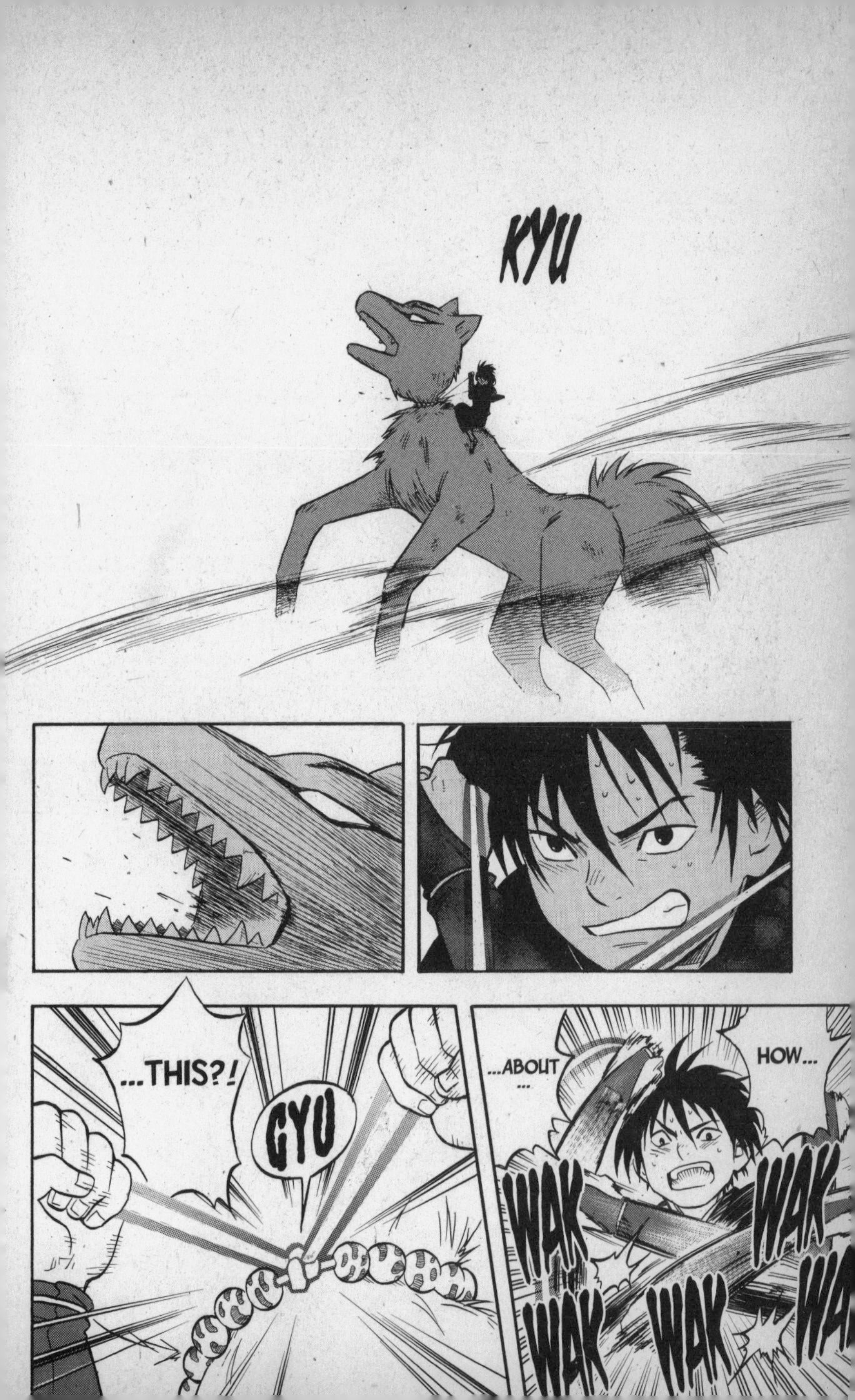
KYU
HOW...
...ABOUT ...
WAK
WAK
WAK
WAK
...THIS?!
GYU

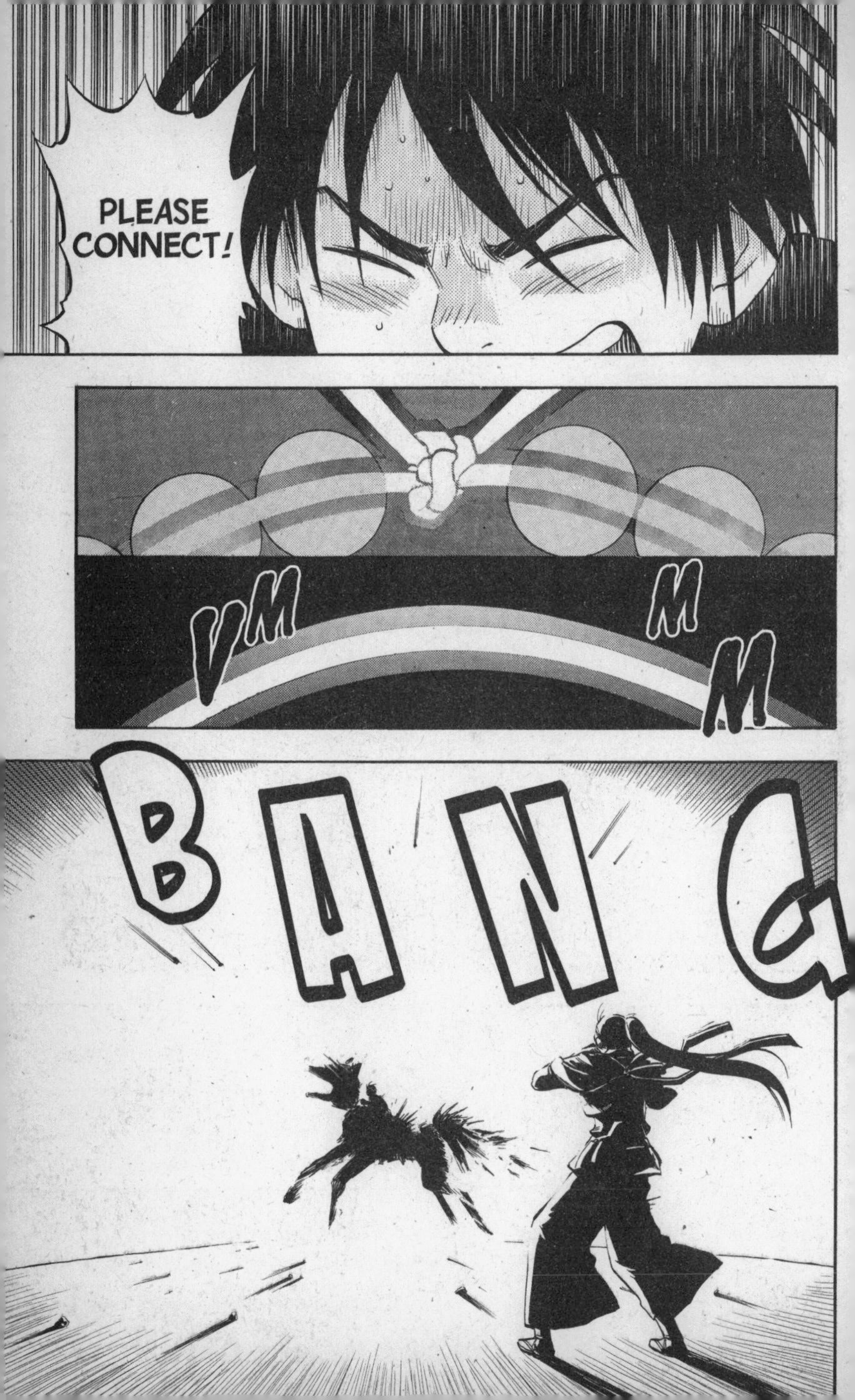
PLEASE CONNECT!
VM
M
M
BANG

SOME-
THING
SHOT
UP IN
THE
AIR...

TH UD WAH!

SHAA

MADA-
RAO!

I'M SORRY, MADARAO! ARE YOU ALL RIGHT?

BAH

OHHH!

BEFORE I DIE, I WANT TO EAT DEER MEAT ONCE AGAIN...

B...

PANT PANT

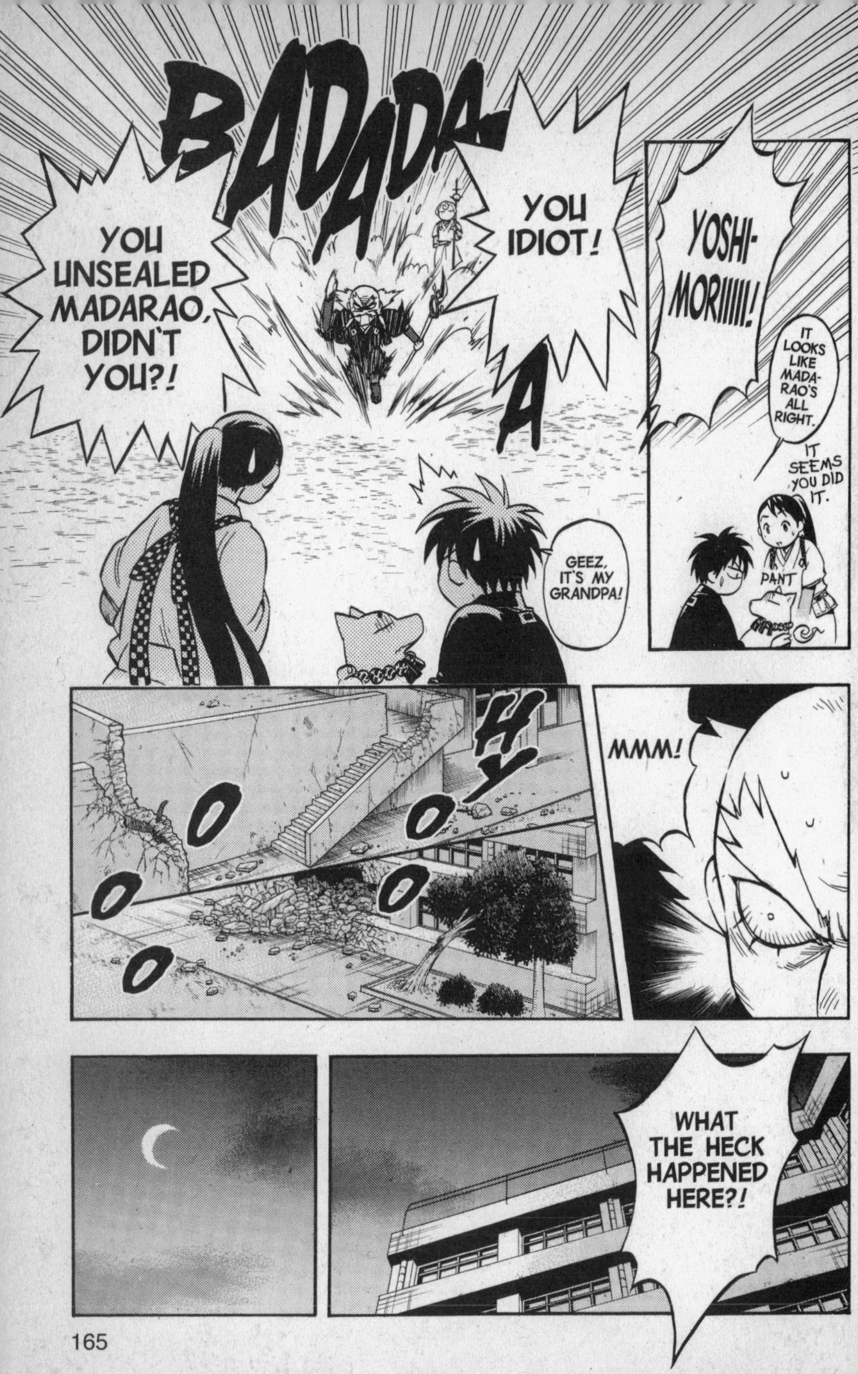
YOSHI-MORIIIII!
IT LOOKS LIKE MADARAO'S ALL RIGHT.
IT SEEMS YOU DID IT.
PANT
BADADA
A
YOU IDIOT!
YOU UNSEALED MADARAO, DIDN'T YOU?!
GEEZ, IT'S MY GRANDPA!
MMM!
HYOOOOO
WHAT THE HECK HAPPENED HERE?!

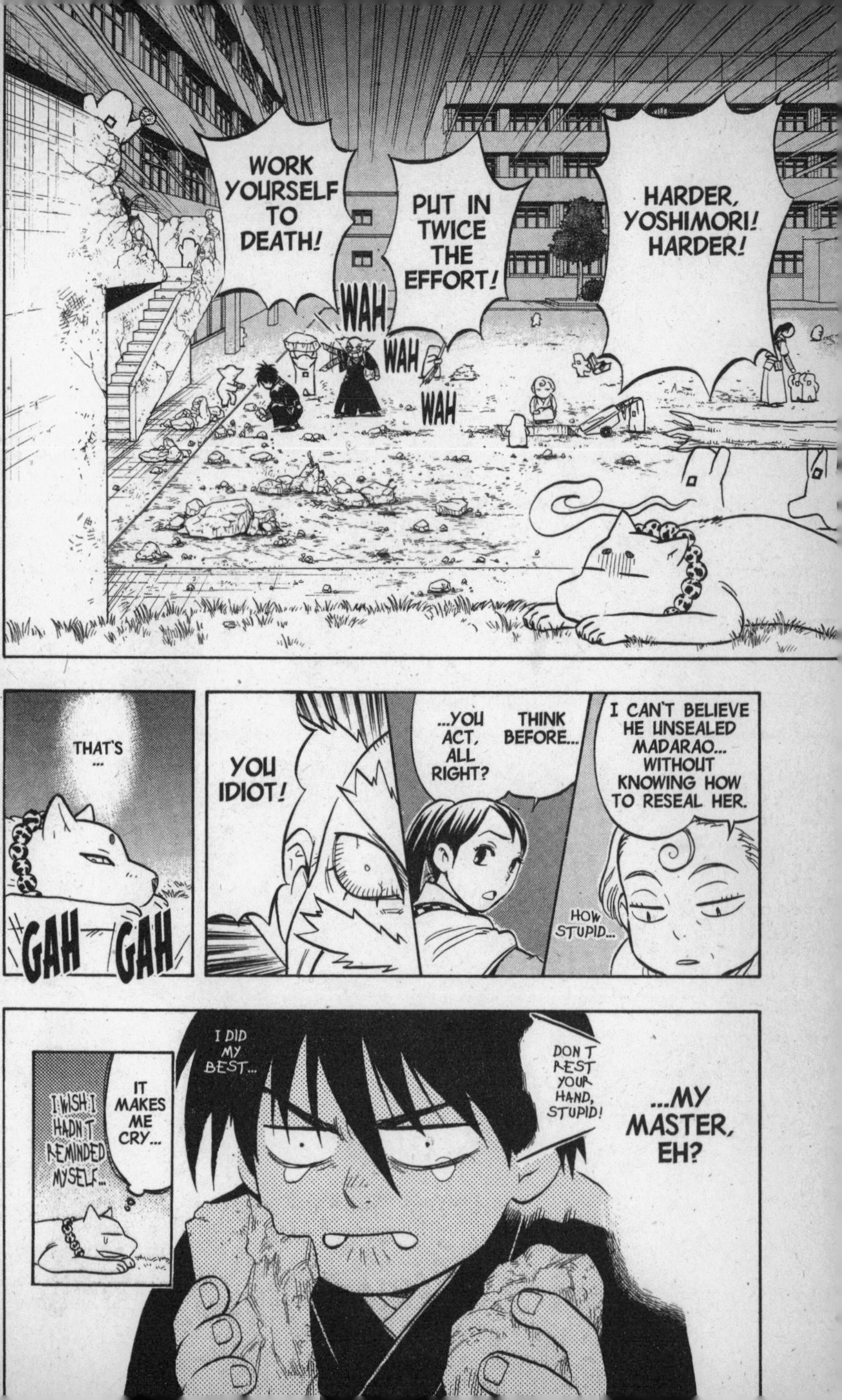
HARDER, YOSHIMORI! HARDER!
PUT IN TWICE THE EFFORT!
WORK YOURSELF TO DEATH!
WAH
WAH
WAH
I CAN'T BELIEVE HE UNSEALED MADARAO... WITHOUT KNOWING HOW TO RESEAL HER.
HOW STUPID...
THINK BEFORE...
...YOU ACT, ALL RIGHT?
YOU IDIOT!
THAT'S ...
GAH
GAH
...MY MASTER, EH?
DON'T REST YOUR HAND, STUPID!
I DID MY BEST...
IT MAKES ME CRY...
I WISH I HADN'T REMINDED MYSELF...

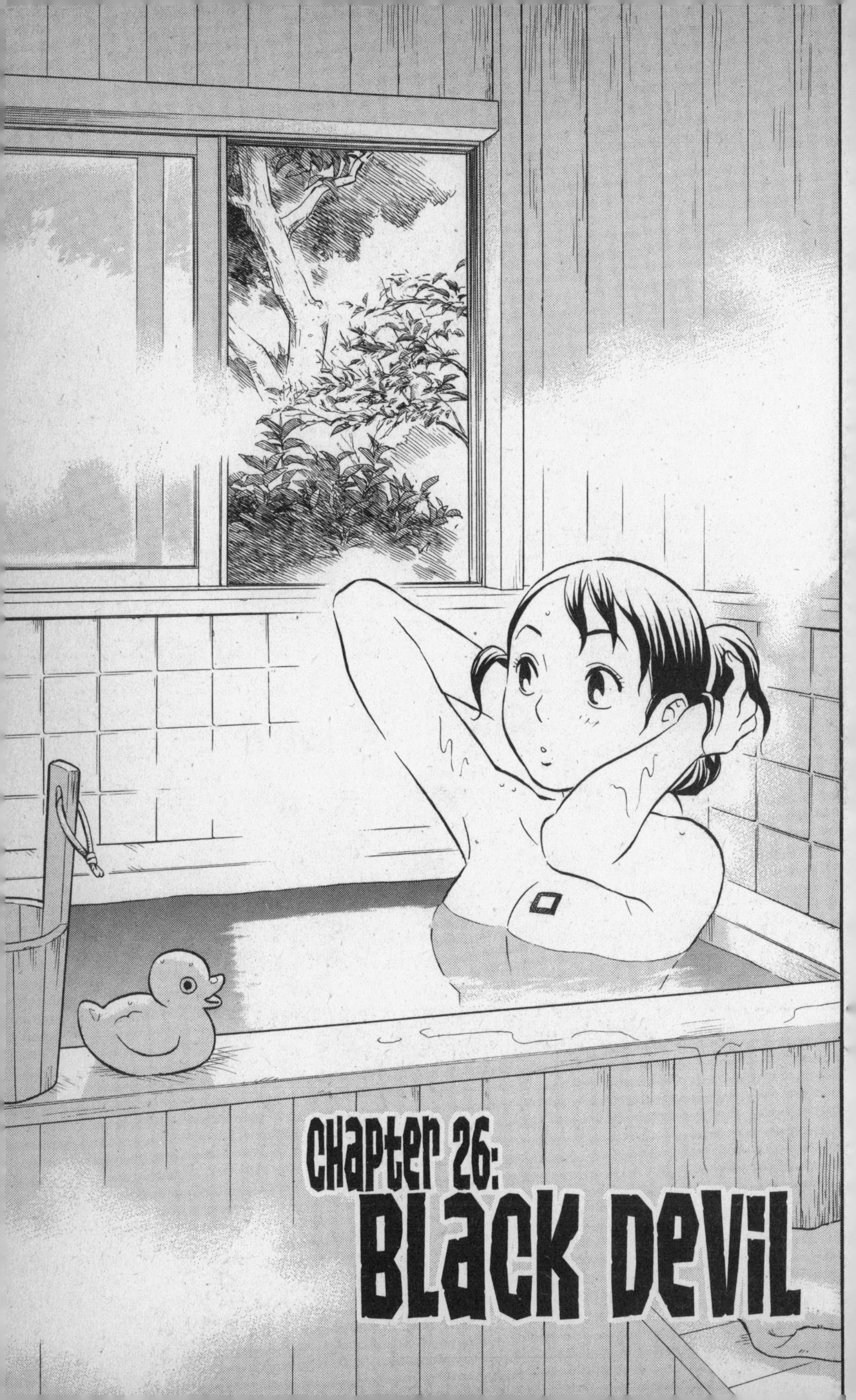
Chapter 26:
Black Devil

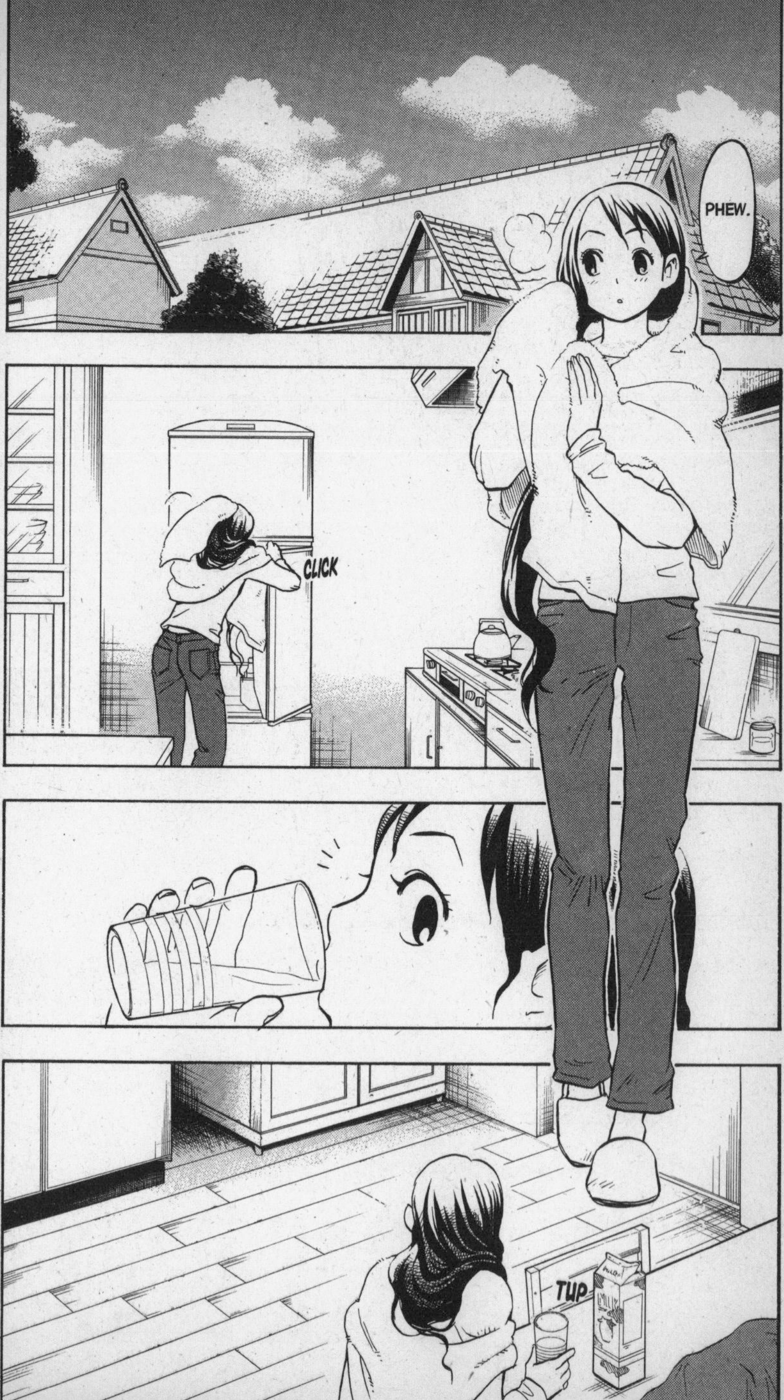
PHEW.
CLICK
TUP

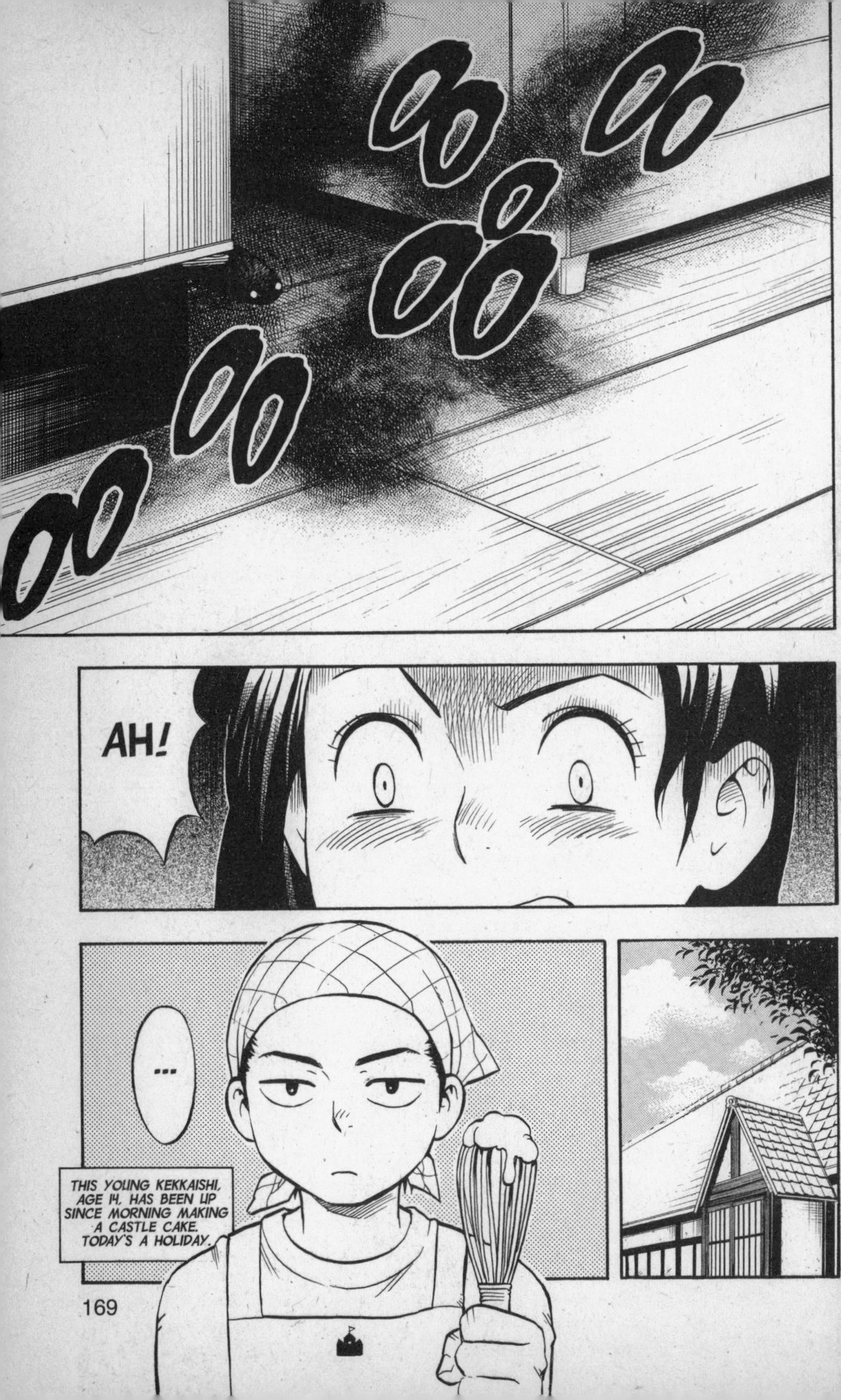
AH!
...
THIS YOUNG KEKKAISHI, AGE 14, HAS BEEN UP SINCE MORNING MAKING A CASTLE CAKE. TODAY'S A HOLIDAY.

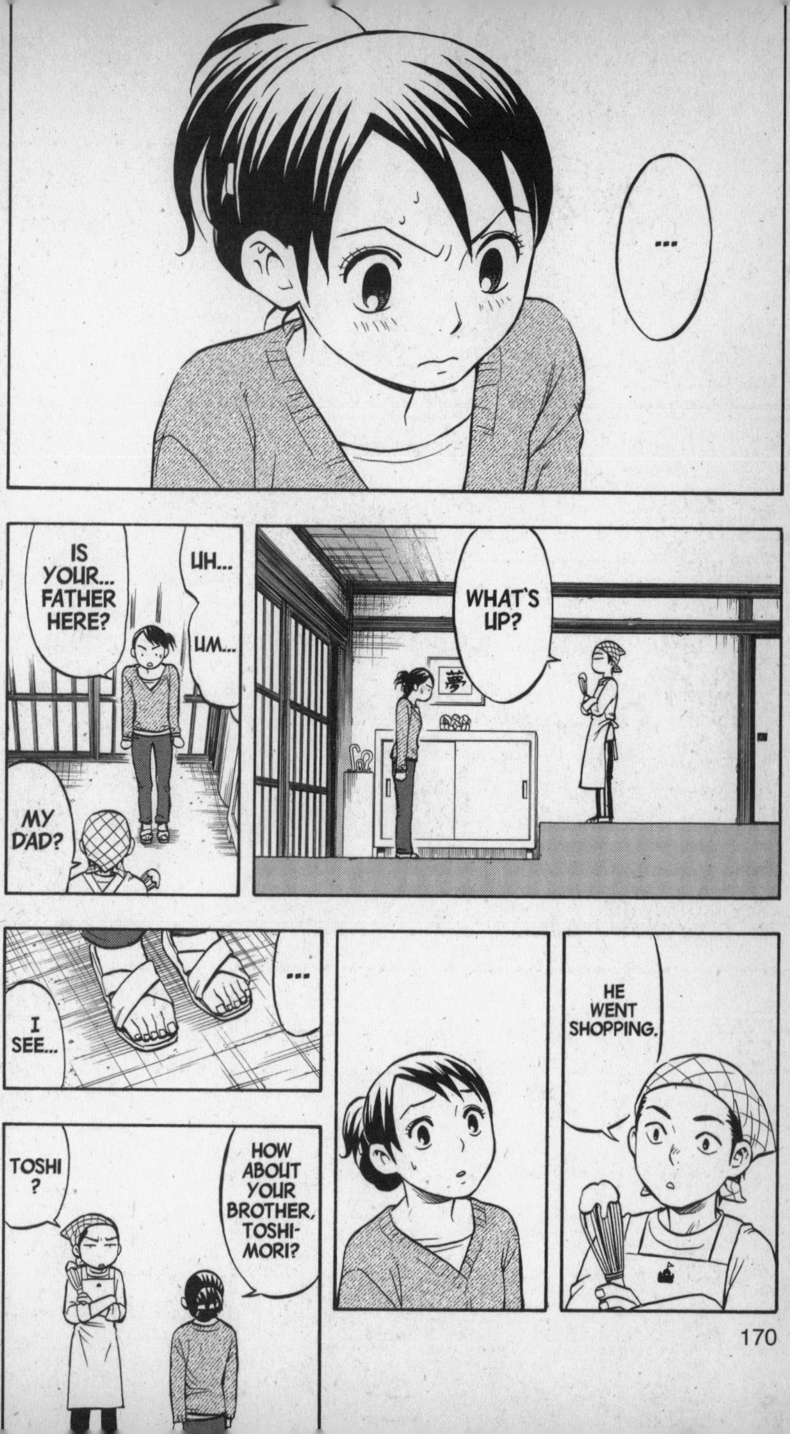
...
WHAT'S UP?
UH...
UM...
IS YOUR... FATHER HERE?
MY DAD?
HE WENT SHOPPING.
...
I SEE...
HOW ABOUT YOUR BROTHER, TOSHI-MORI?
TOSHI?

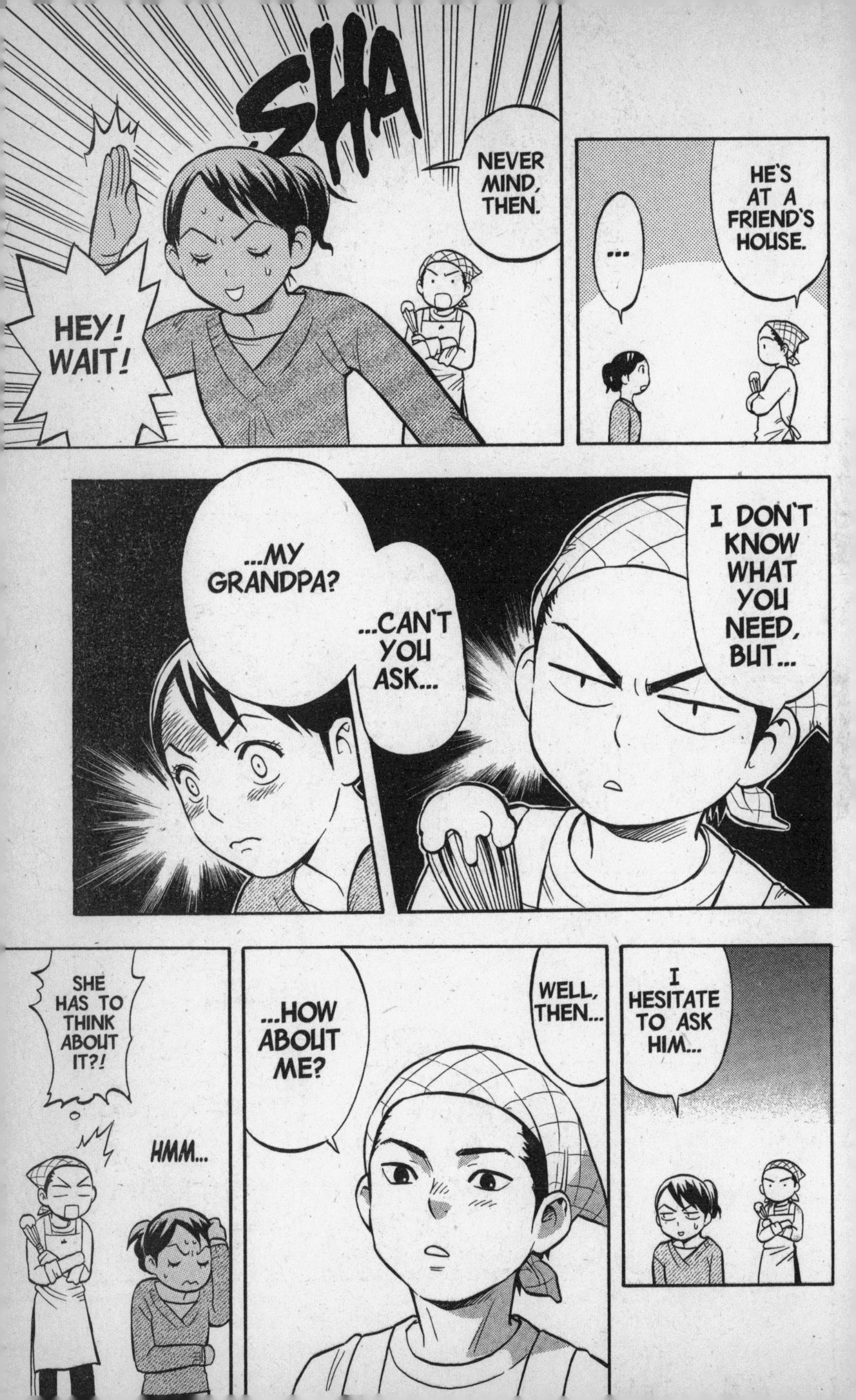
HE'S AT A FRIEND'S HOUSE.
...
NEVER MIND, THEN.
SHA
HEY! WAIT!
I DON'T KNOW WHAT YOU NEED, BUT...
...CAN'T YOU ASK...
...MY GRANDPA?
I HESITATE TO ASK HIM...
WELL, THEN...
...HOW ABOUT ME?
SHE HAS TO THINK ABOUT IT?!
HMM...

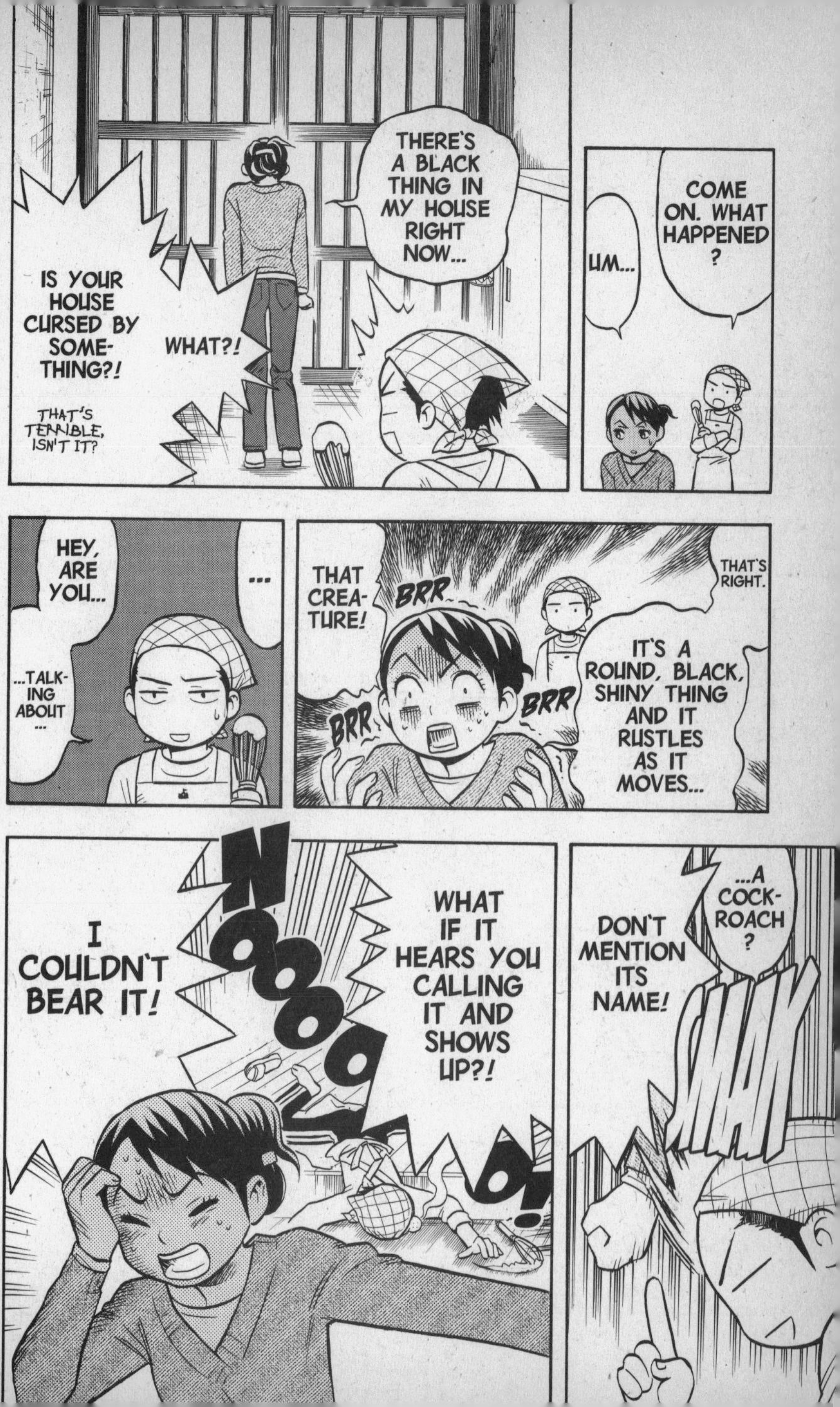
COME ON. WHAT HAPPENED?
UM...
THERE'S A BLACK THING IN MY HOUSE RIGHT NOW...
WHAT?!
IS YOUR HOUSE CURSED BY SOME-THING?!
THAT'S TERRIBLE, ISN'T IT?
THAT'S RIGHT.
IT'S A ROUND, BLACK, SHINY THING AND IT RUSTLES AS IT MOVES...
BRR
BRR
BRR
THAT CREA-TURE!
...
HEY, ARE YOU...
...TALK-ING ABOUT...
...A COCK-ROACH?
DON'T MENTION ITS NAME!
WHAT IF IT HEARS YOU CALLING IT AND SHOWS UP?!
NOOOOO!
I COULDN'T BEAR IT!

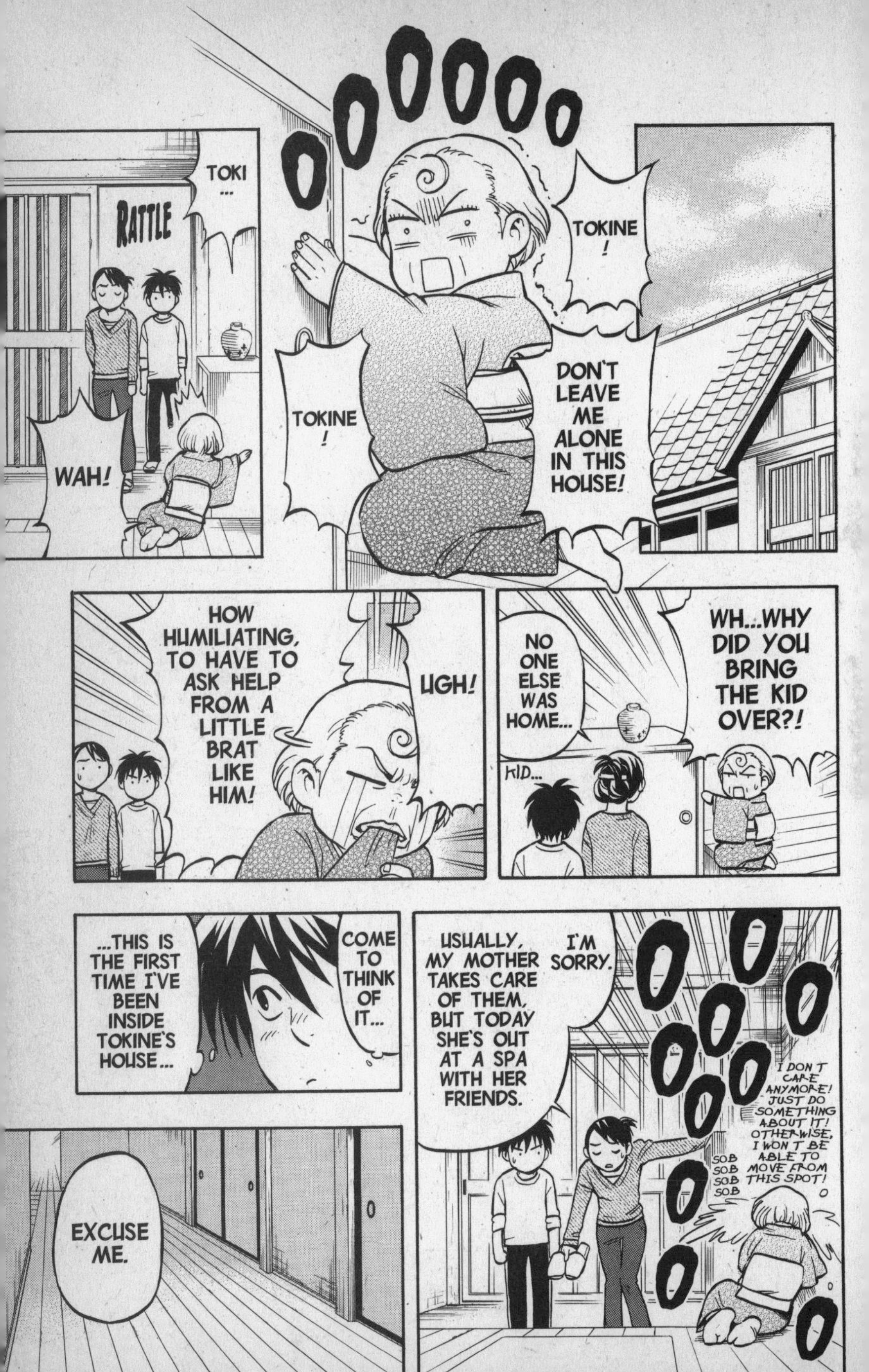
OOOOOO
TOKINE!
DON'T LEAVE ME ALONE IN THIS HOUSE!
TOKINE!
TOKI...
RATTLE
WAH!
WH...WHY DID YOU BRING THE KID OVER?!
NO ONE ELSE WAS HOME...
KID...
UGH!
HOW HUMILIATING, TO HAVE TO ASK HELP FROM A LITTLE BRAT LIKE HIM!
I'M SORRY.
USUALLY, MY MOTHER TAKES CARE OF THEM, BUT TODAY SHE'S OUT AT A SPA WITH HER FRIENDS.
I DONT CARE ANYMORE! JUST DO SOMETHING ABOUT IT! OTHERWISE, I WONT BE ABLE TO MOVE FROM THIS SPOT!
SOB SOB SOB SOB
COME TO THINK OF IT...
...THIS IS THE FIRST TIME I'VE BEEN INSIDE TOKINE'S HOUSE...
EXCUSE ME.

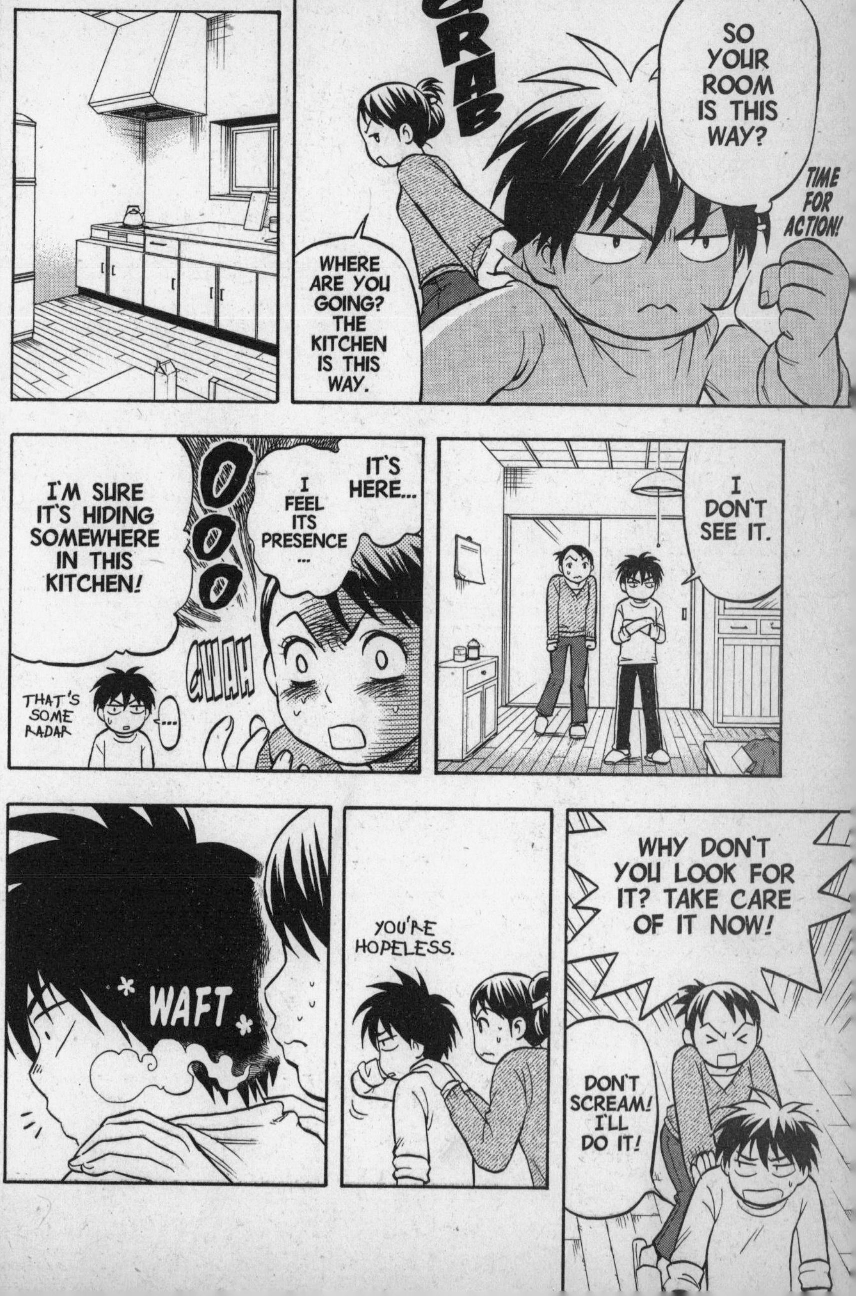
SO YOUR ROOM IS THIS WAY?
TIME FOR ACTION!
GRAB
WHERE ARE YOU GOING? THE KITCHEN IS THIS WAY.
I DON'T SEE IT.
IT'S HERE...
I FEEL ITS PRESENCE ...
I'M SURE IT'S HIDING SOMEWHERE IN THIS KITCHEN!
GWAH
...
THAT'S SOME RADAR
WHY DON'T YOU LOOK FOR IT? TAKE CARE OF IT NOW!
DON'T SCREAM! I'LL DO IT!
YOU'RE HOPELESS.
* WAFT *

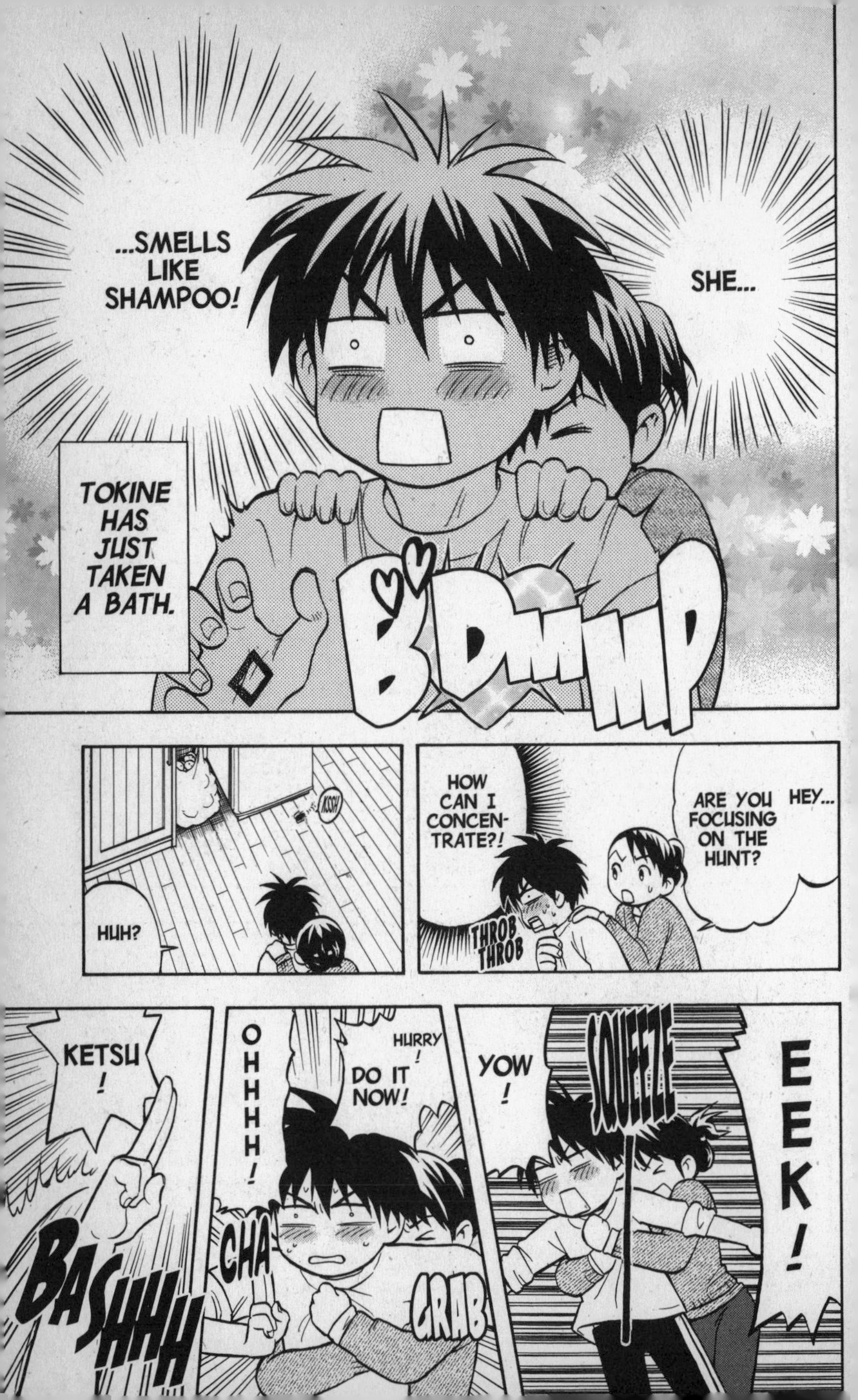
SHE...
...SMELLS LIKE SHAMPOO!
BDMMMP
TOKINE HAS JUST TAKEN A BATH.
HEY...
ARE YOU FOCUSING ON THE HUNT?
HOW CAN I CONCENTRATE?!
THROB THROB
KSSH
HUH?
EEK!
SQUEEZE
YOW!
HURRY!
DO IT NOW!
OHHHHH!
CHA
GRAB
KETSU!
BASHHH

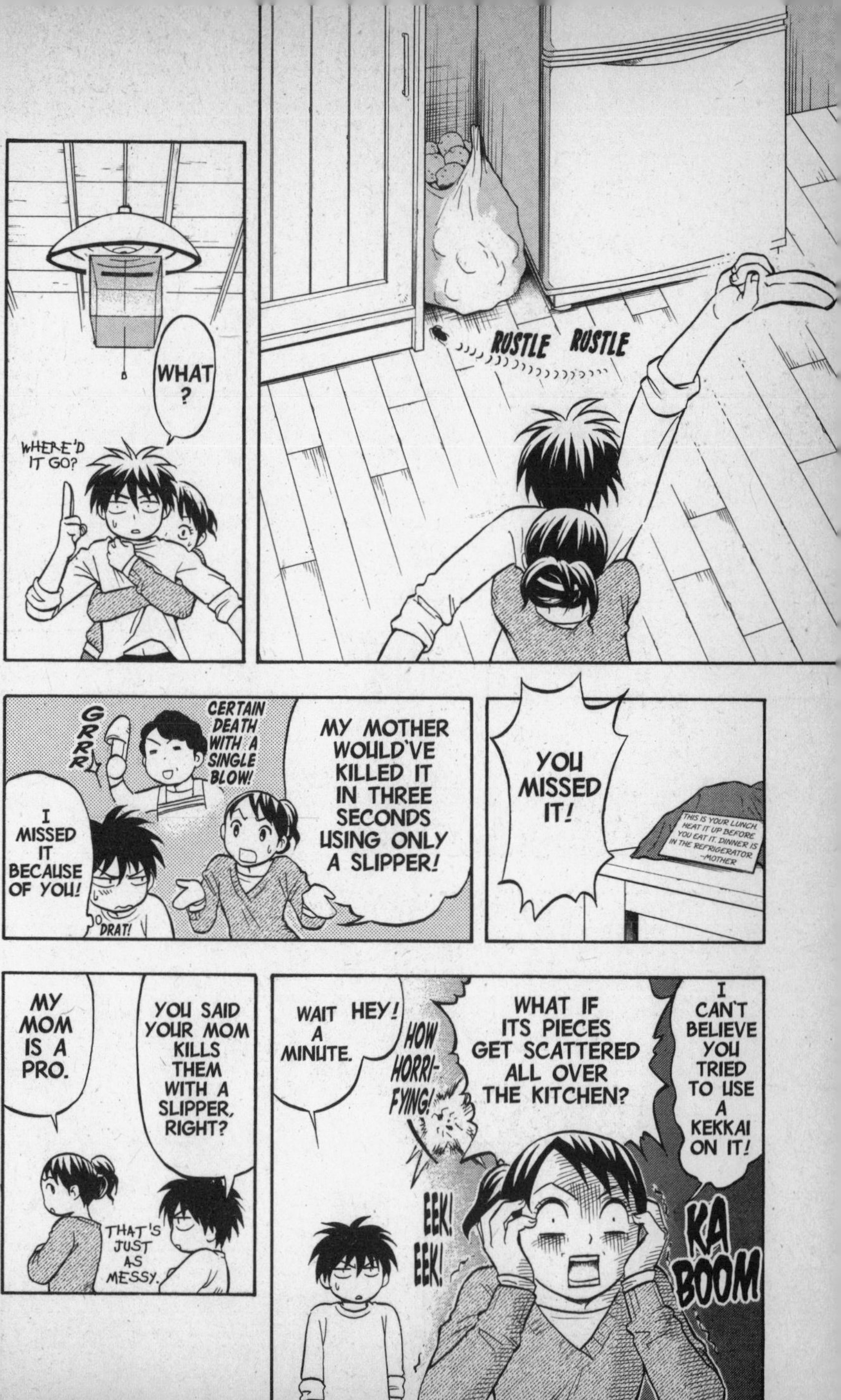
RUSTLE RUSTLE
WHAT?
WHERE'D IT GO?
YOU MISSED IT!
THIS IS YOUR LUNCH. HEAT IT UP BEFORE YOU EAT IT. DINNER IS IN THE REFRIGERATOR. ~MOTHER
MY MOTHER WOULD'VE KILLED IT IN THREE SECONDS USING ONLY A SLIPPER!
CERTAIN DEATH WITH A SINGLE BLOW!
GRRR
I MISSED IT BECAUSE OF YOU!
DRAT!
I CAN'T BELIEVE YOU TRIED TO USE A KEKKAI ON IT!
WHAT IF ITS PIECES GET SCATTERED ALL OVER THE KITCHEN?
HOW HORRI-FYING!
HEY!
WAIT A MINUTE.
EEK! EEK!
KA BOOM
YOU SAID YOUR MOM KILLS THEM WITH A SLIPPER, RIGHT?
MY MOM IS A PRO.
THAT'S JUST AS MESSY.

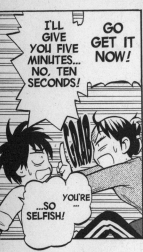

SHE...
...CAN CONTROL HER FORCE SO SHE WON'T MAKE A MESS WHEN SHE SMASHES THEM...
SIGH
HOHOHOHOHOHOHOHOHO
A PRO.
SHINING
I'M SCARED!
HOW FRIGHT-ENING!
YEEK...
GO GET IT NOW!
I'LL GIVE YOU FIVE MINUTES... NO, TEN SECONDS!
GRAB
YOU'RE ...
...SO SELFISH!
...
I'M SORRY.
BUT I REALLY CAN'T...
...STAND THEM...
ALL RIGHT.
LET ME SEE WHAT I CAN DO.

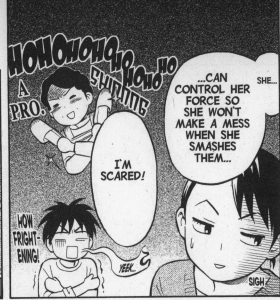

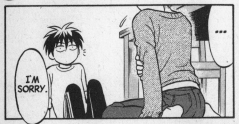

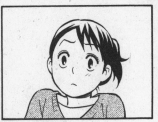

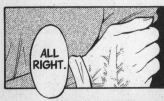

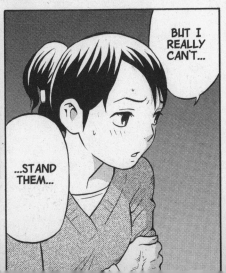

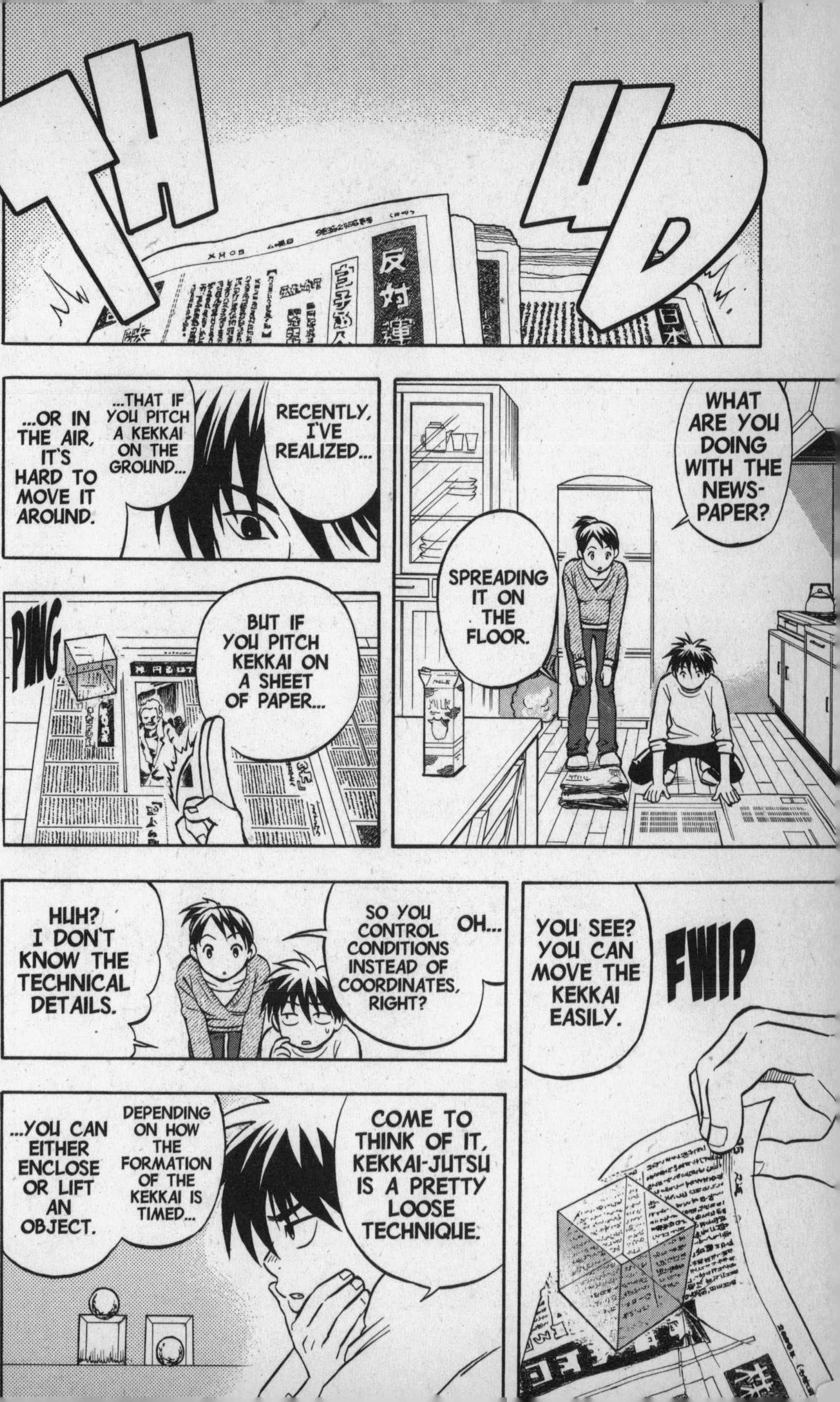
THUD
WHAT ARE YOU DOING WITH THE NEWS-PAPER?
SPREADING IT ON THE FLOOR.
MILK
RECENTLY, I'VE REALIZED...
...THAT IF YOU PITCH A KEKKAI ON THE GROUND...
...OR IN THE AIR, IT'S HARD TO MOVE IT AROUND.
PING
BUT IF YOU PITCH KEKKAI ON A SHEET OF PAPER...
YOU SEE? YOU CAN MOVE THE KEKKAI EASILY.
FWIP
OH...
SO YOU CONTROL CONDITIONS INSTEAD OF COORDINATES, RIGHT?
HUH? I DON'T KNOW THE TECHNICAL DETAILS.
COME TO THINK OF IT, KEKKAI-JUTSU IS A PRETTY LOOSE TECHNIQUE.
DEPENDING ON HOW THE FORMATION OF THE KEKKAI IS TIMED...
...YOU CAN EITHER ENCLOSE OR LIFT AN OBJECT.

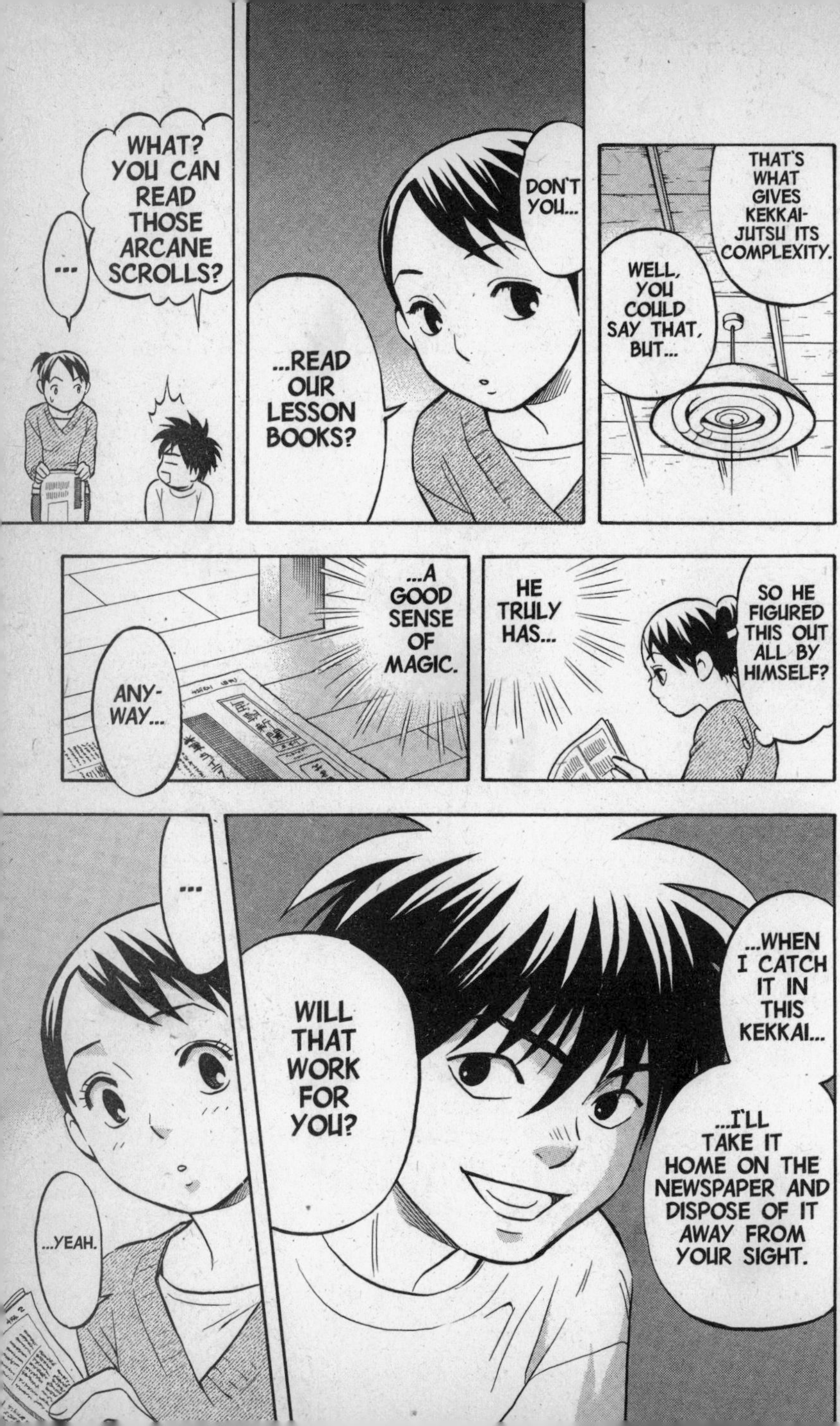
THAT'S WHAT GIVES KEKKAI-JUTSU ITS COMPLEXITY.
WELL, YOU COULD SAY THAT, BUT...
DON'T YOU...
...READ OUR LESSON BOOKS?
WHAT? YOU CAN READ THOSE ARCANE SCROLLS?
...
SO HE FIGURED THIS OUT ALL BY HIMSELF?
HE TRULY HAS...
...A GOOD SENSE OF MAGIC.
ANY-WAY...
...WHEN I CATCH IT IN THIS KEKKAI...
...I'LL TAKE IT HOME ON THE NEWSPAPER AND DISPOSE OF IT AWAY FROM YOUR SIGHT.
WILL THAT WORK FOR YOU?
...
...YEAH.

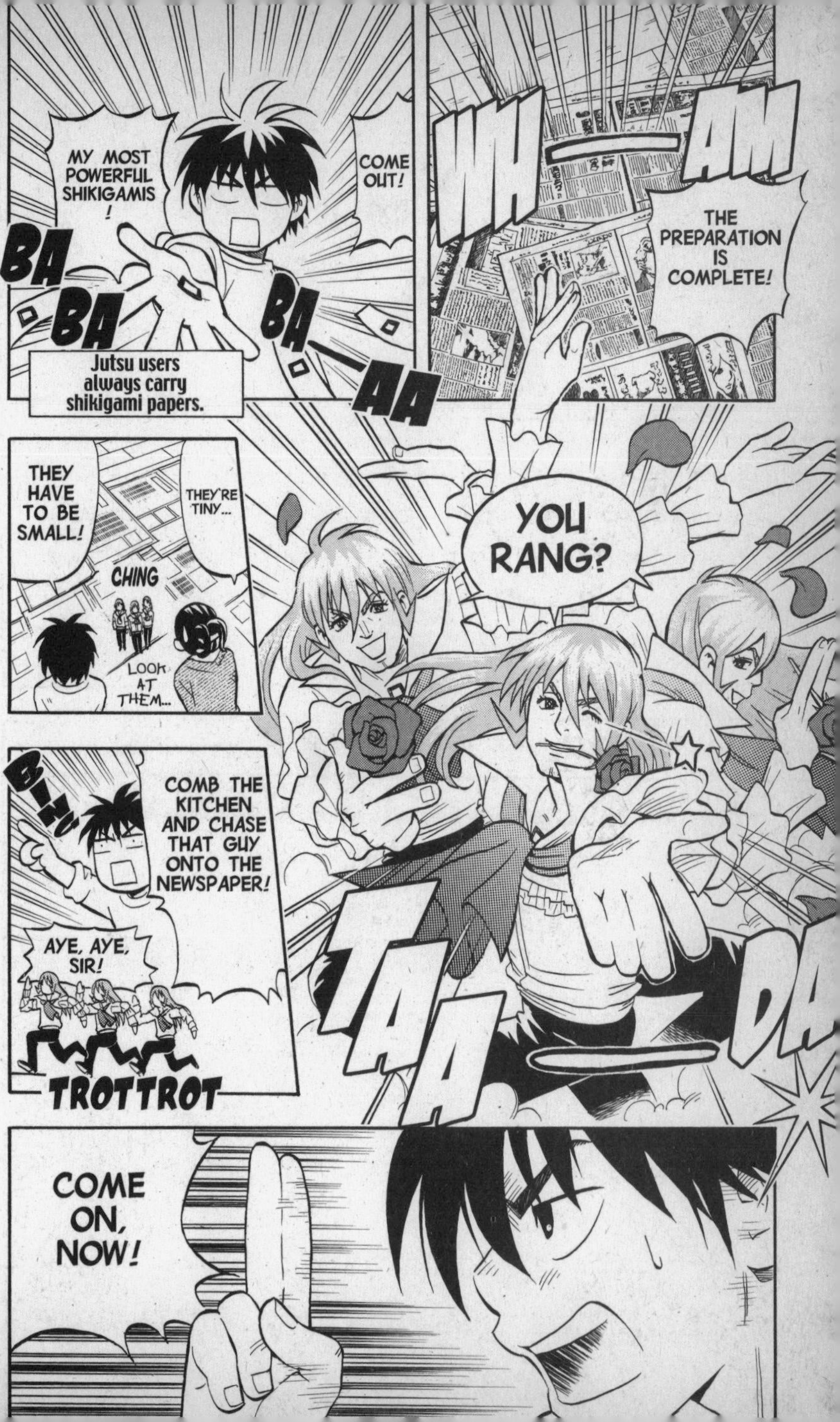
WH—AM
THE PREPARATION IS COMPLETE!
COME OUT!
MY MOST POWERFUL SHIKIGAMIS!
BA BA
BA—AA
Jutsu users always carry shikigami papers.
YOU RANG?
TAA—DA
THEY'RE TINY...
THEY HAVE TO BE SMALL!
CHING
LOOK AT THEM...
COMB THE KITCHEN AND CHASE THAT GUY ONTO THE NEWSPAPER!
AYE, AYE, SIR!
TROTTROT
COME ON, NOW!

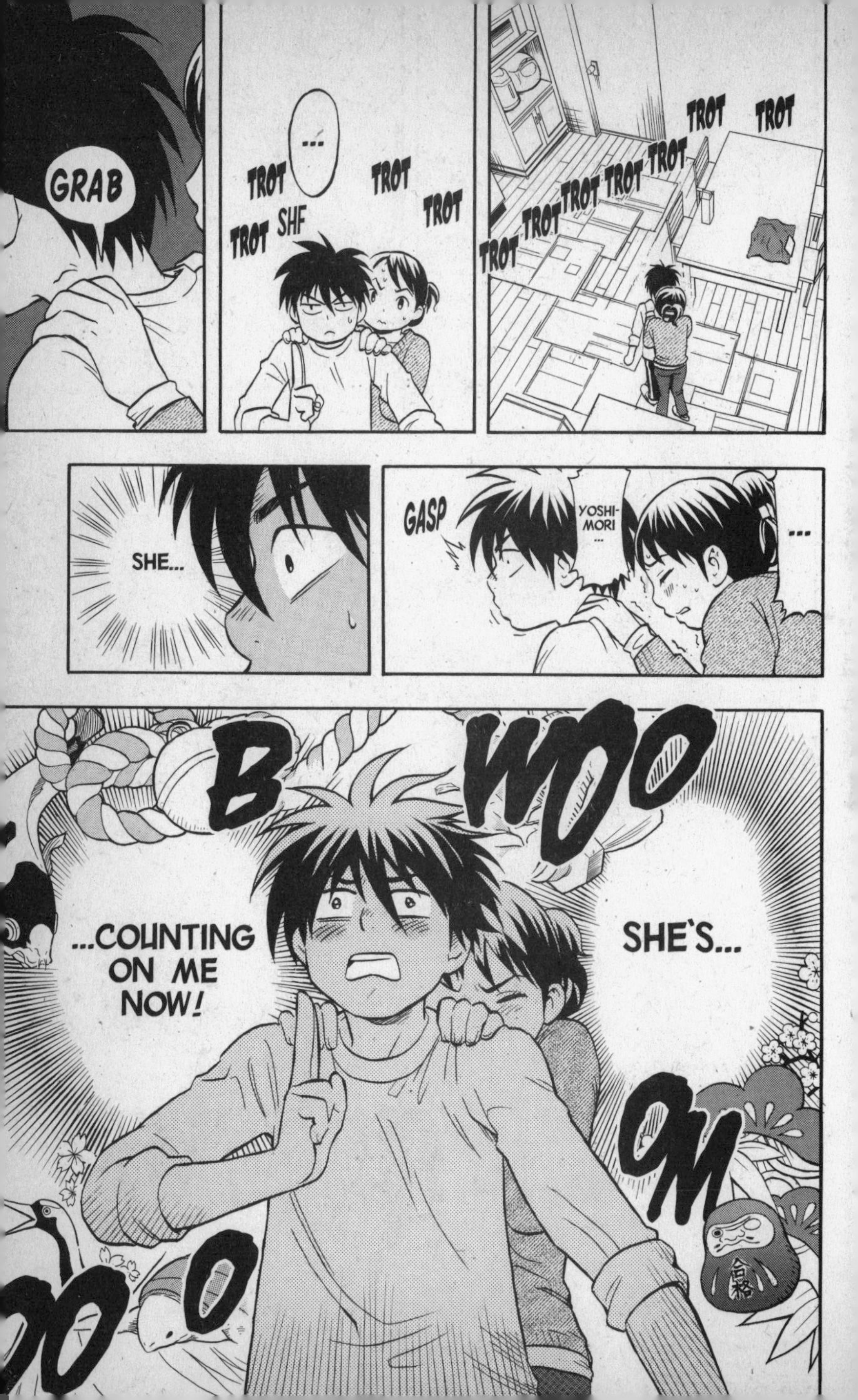
TROT TROT TROT TROT TROT TROT TROT TROT
TROT
...
TROT
TROT
TROT SHF
TROT
GRAB
...
YOSHIMORI...
GASP
SHE...
SHE'S...
...COUNTING ON ME NOW!
BWOOOM
OOO

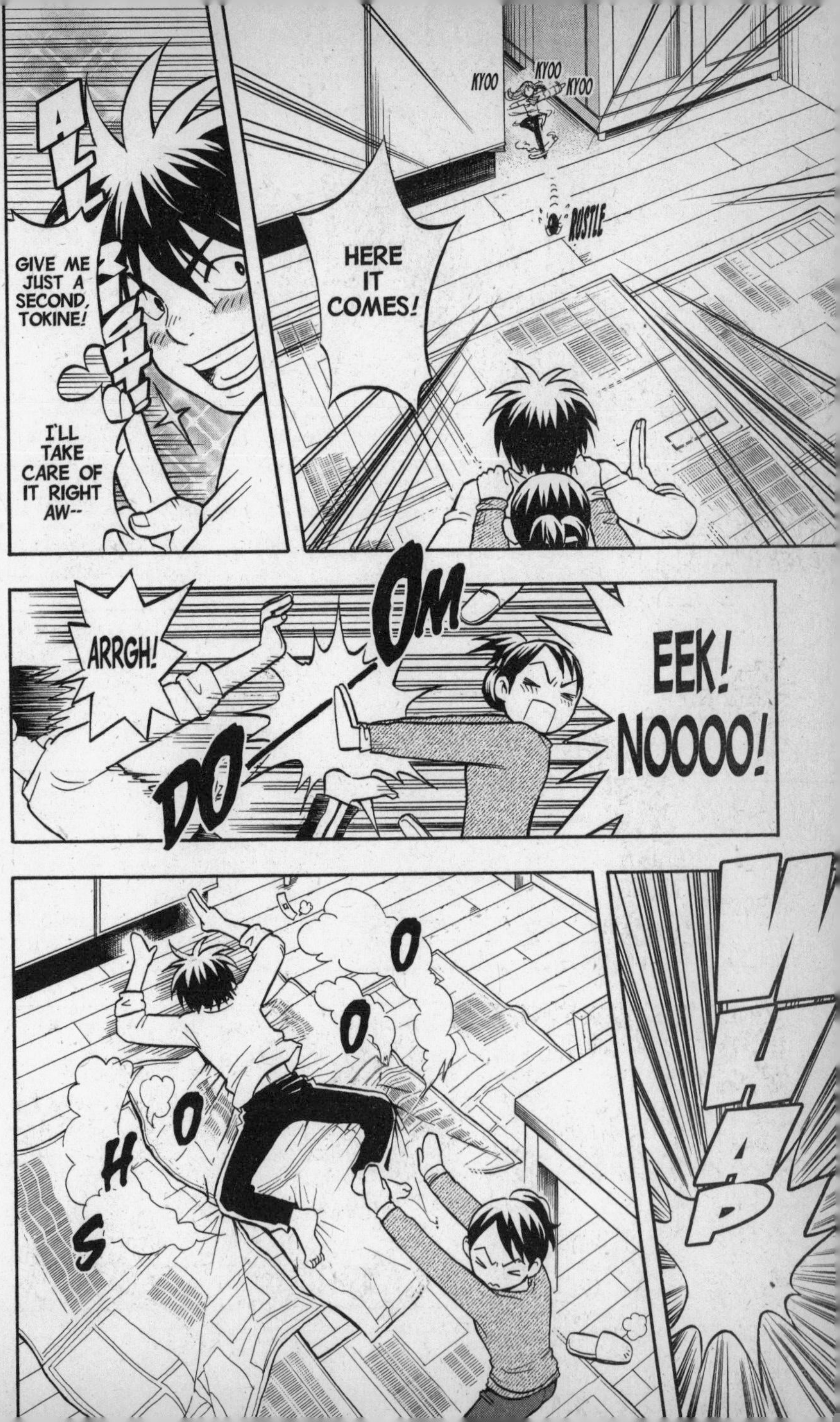
KYOO
KYOO
KYOO
RUSTLE
HERE IT COMES!
ALL RIGHT!
GIVE ME JUST A SECOND, TOKINE!
I'LL TAKE CARE OF IT RIGHT AW--
EEK! NOOOO!
DOOM
ARRGH!
WHAP
SHOOOO

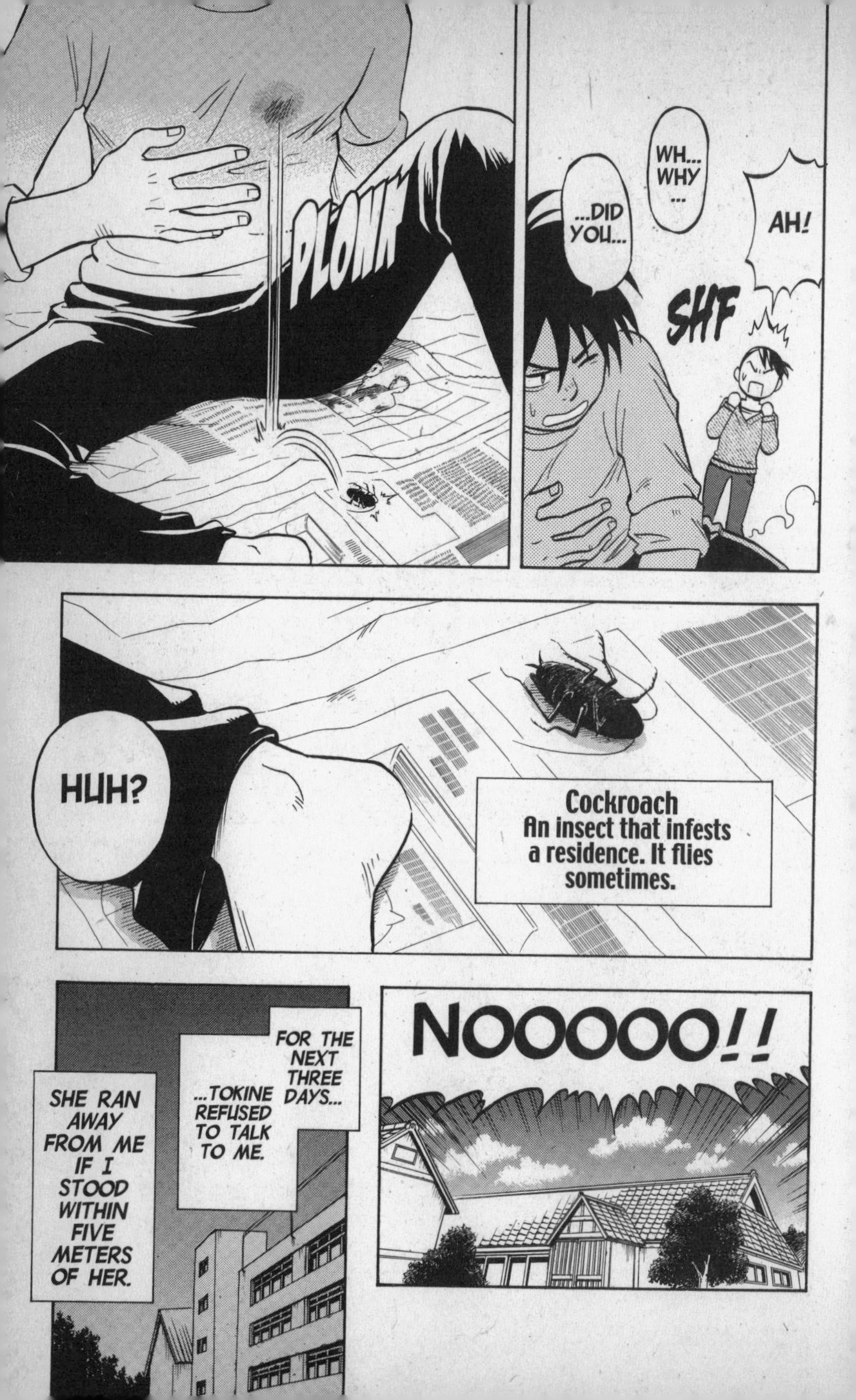
AH!
WH... WHY ...
...DID YOU...
SHF
PLONK
HUH?
Cockroach
An insect that infests a residence. It flies sometimes.
NOOOOO!!
FOR THE NEXT THREE DAYS...
...TOKINE REFUSED TO TALK TO ME.
SHE RAN AWAY FROM ME IF I STOOD WITHIN FIVE METERS OF HER.

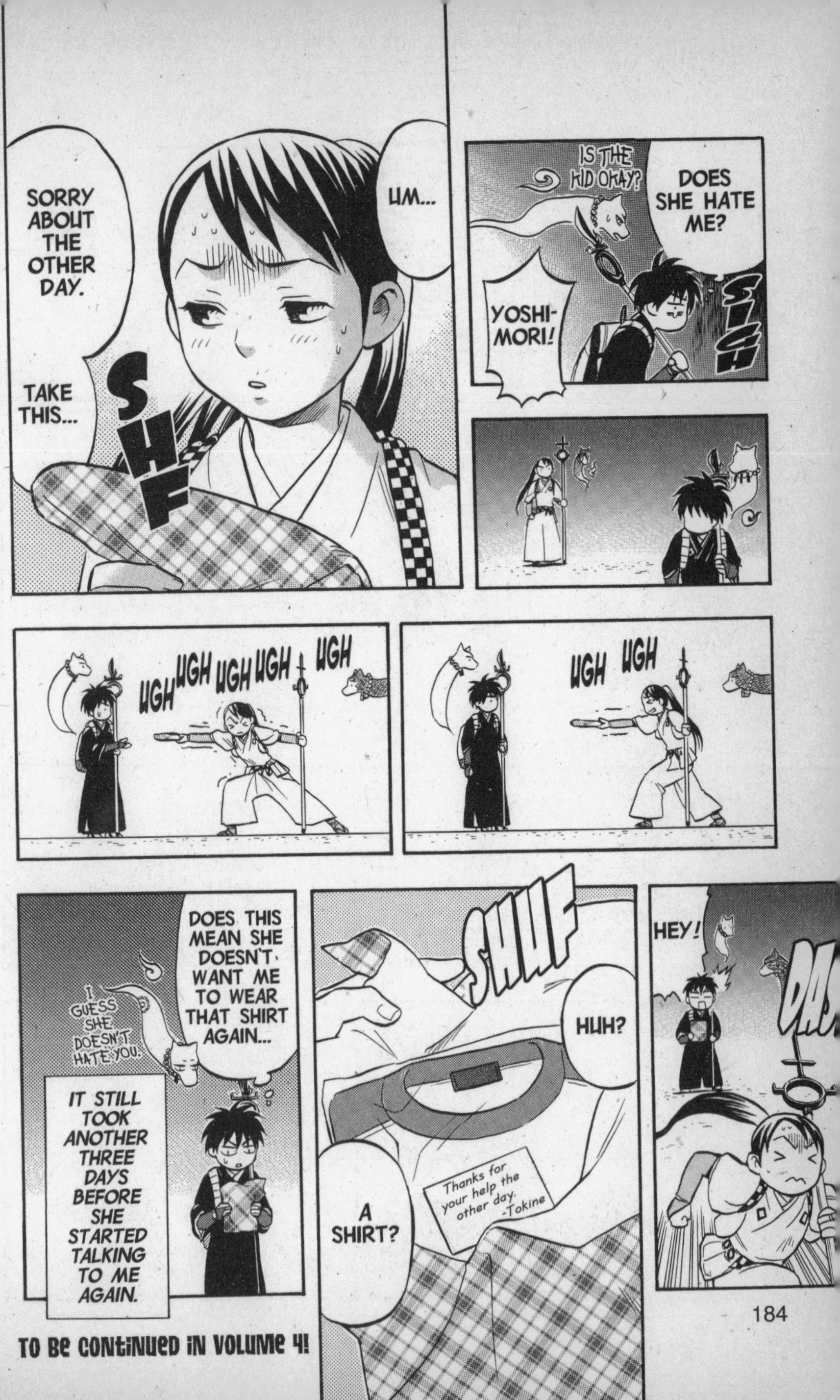
DOES SHE HATE ME?
IS THE KID OKAY?
SIGH
YOSHI-MORI!
UM...
SORRY ABOUT THE OTHER DAY.
TAKE THIS...
SHF
UGH UGH
UGH UGH UGH UGH UGH
HEY!
SHUF
HUH?
A SHIRT?
Thanks for your help the other day. -Tokine
DOES THIS MEAN SHE DOESN'T WANT ME TO WEAR THAT SHIRT AGAIN...
I GUESS SHE DOESN'T HATE YOU.
IT STILL TOOK ANOTHER THREE DAYS BEFORE SHE STARTED TALKING TO ME AGAIN.

TO BE CONTINUED IN VOLUME 4!

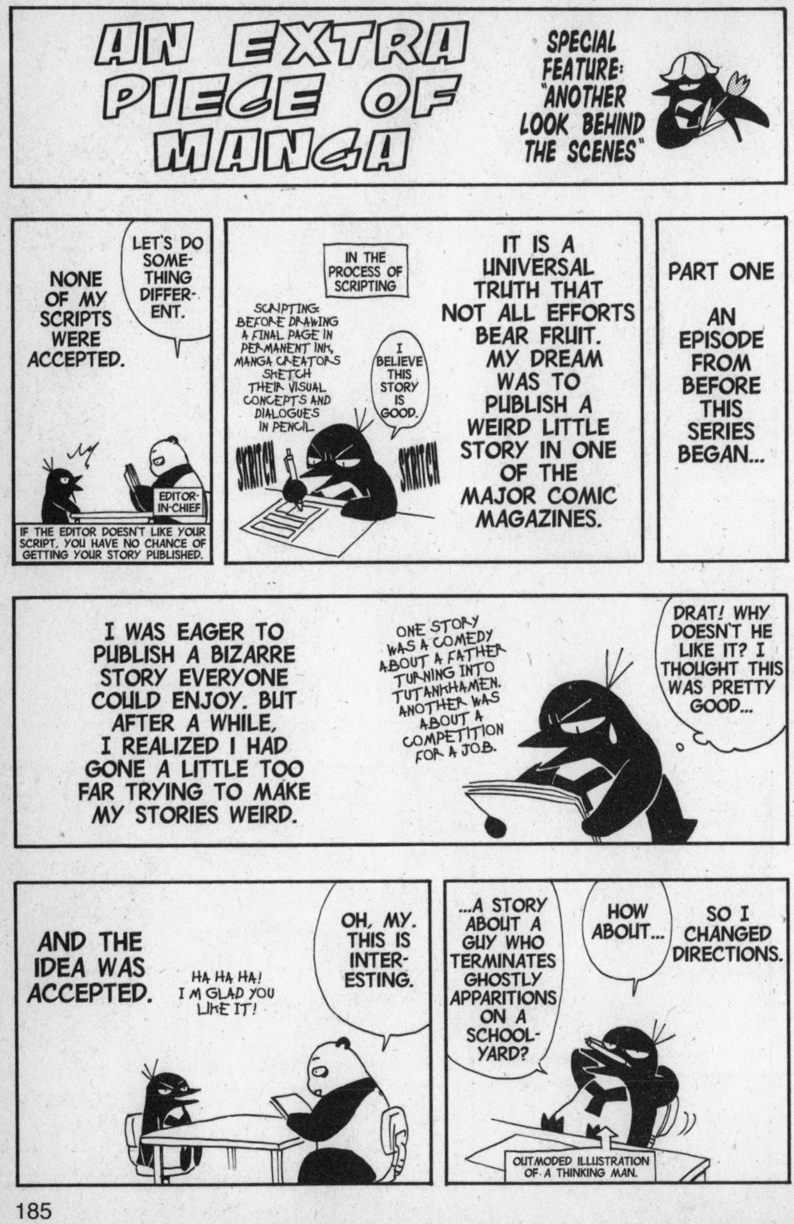
SPECIAL FEATURE: "ANOTHER LOOK BEHIND THE SCENES"
AN EXTRA PIECE OF MANGA
PART ONE
AN EPISODE FROM BEFORE THIS SERIES BEGAN...
IT IS A UNIVERSAL TRUTH THAT NOT ALL EFFORTS BEAR FRUIT. MY DREAM WAS TO PUBLISH A WEIRD LITTLE STORY IN ONE OF THE MAJOR COMIC MAGAZINES.
I BELIEVE THIS STORY IS GOOD.
IN THE PROCESS OF SCRIPTING
SCRIPTING: BEFORE DRAWING A FINAL PAGE IN PERMANENT INK, MANGA CREATORS SKETCH THEIR VISUAL CONCEPTS AND DIALOGUES IN PENCIL.
SKRITCH
SKRITCH
LET'S DO SOMETHING DIFFERENT.
NONE OF MY SCRIPTS WERE ACCEPTED.
EDITOR-IN-CHIEF
IF THE EDITOR DOESN'T LIKE YOUR SCRIPT, YOU HAVE NO CHANCE OF GETTING YOUR STORY PUBLISHED.
DRAT! WHY DOESN'T HE LIKE IT? I THOUGHT THIS WAS PRETTY GOOD...
ONE STORY WAS A COMEDY ABOUT A FATHER TURNING INTO TUTANKHAMEN. ANOTHER WAS ABOUT A COMPETITION FOR A JOB.
I WAS EAGER TO PUBLISH A BIZARRE STORY EVERYONE COULD ENJOY. BUT AFTER A WHILE, I REALIZED I HAD GONE A LITTLE TOO FAR TRYING TO MAKE MY STORIES WEIRD.
SO I CHANGED DIRECTIONS.
HOW ABOUT...
...A STORY ABOUT A GUY WHO TERMINATES GHOSTLY APPARITIONS ON A SCHOOLYARD?
OUTMODED ILLUSTRATION OF A THINKING MAN.
OH, MY. THIS IS INTERESTING.
HA HA HA! I'M GLAD YOU LIKE IT!
AND THE IDEA WAS ACCEPTED.

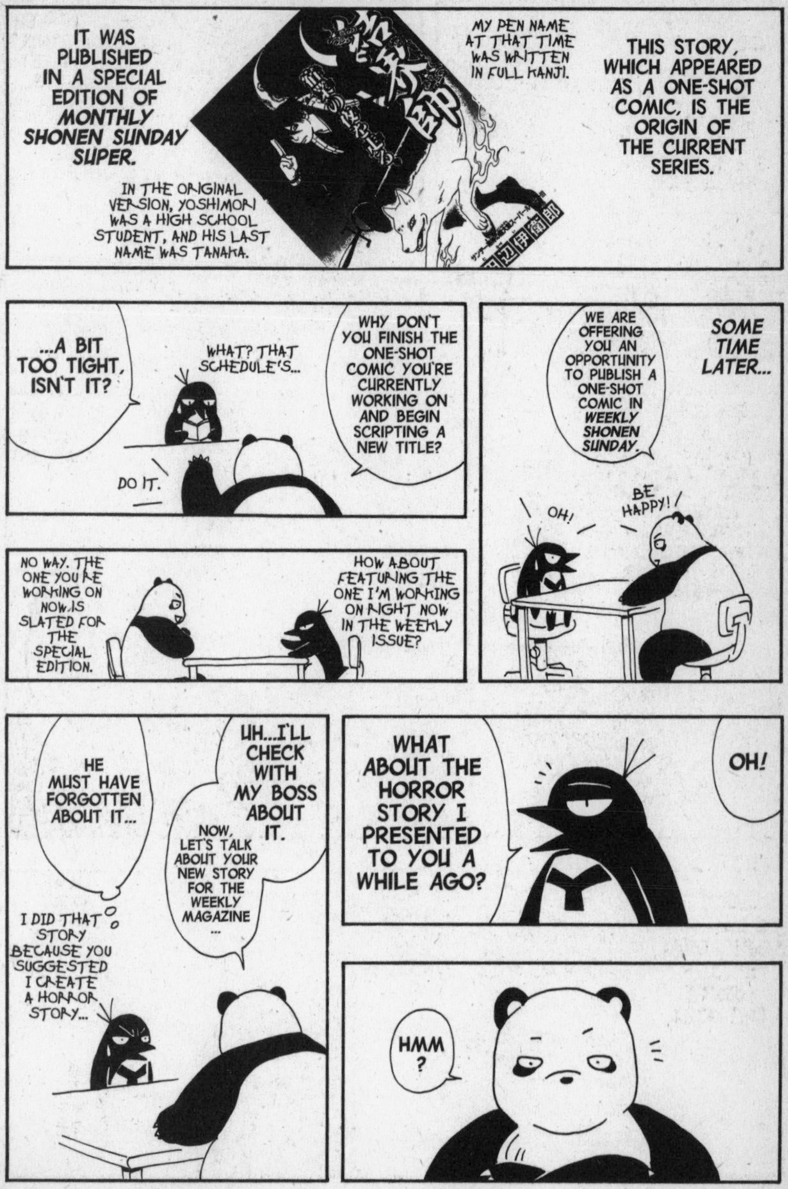
THIS STORY, WHICH APPEARED AS A ONE-SHOT COMIC, IS THE ORIGIN OF THE CURRENT SERIES.
MY PEN NAME AT THAT TIME WAS WRITTEN IN FULL KANJI.
IT WAS PUBLISHED IN A SPECIAL EDITION OF *MONTHLY SHONEN SUNDAY SUPER.*
IN THE ORIGINAL VERSION, YOSHIMORI WAS A HIGH SCHOOL STUDENT, AND HIS LAST NAME WAS TANAKA.
SOME TIME LATER...
WE ARE OFFERING YOU AN OPPORTUNITY TO PUBLISH A ONE-SHOT COMIC IN *WEEKLY SHONEN SUNDAY.*
BE HAPPY!
OH!
WHY DON'T YOU FINISH THE ONE-SHOT COMIC YOU'RE CURRENTLY WORKING ON AND BEGIN SCRIPTING A NEW TITLE?
WHAT? THAT SCHEDULE'S...
...A BIT TOO TIGHT, ISN'T IT?
DO IT.
HOW ABOUT FEATURING THE ONE I'M WORKING ON RIGHT NOW IN THE WEEKLY ISSUE?
NO WAY. THE ONE YOU'RE WORKING ON NOW IS SLATED FOR THE SPECIAL EDITION.
OH!
WHAT ABOUT THE HORROR STORY I PRESENTED TO YOU A WHILE AGO?
HMM?
UH...I'LL CHECK WITH MY BOSS ABOUT IT.
NOW, LET'S TALK ABOUT YOUR NEW STORY FOR THE WEEKLY MAGAZINE...
HE MUST HAVE FORGOTTEN ABOUT IT...
I DID THAT STORY BECAUSE YOU SUGGESTED I CREATE A HORROR STORY...

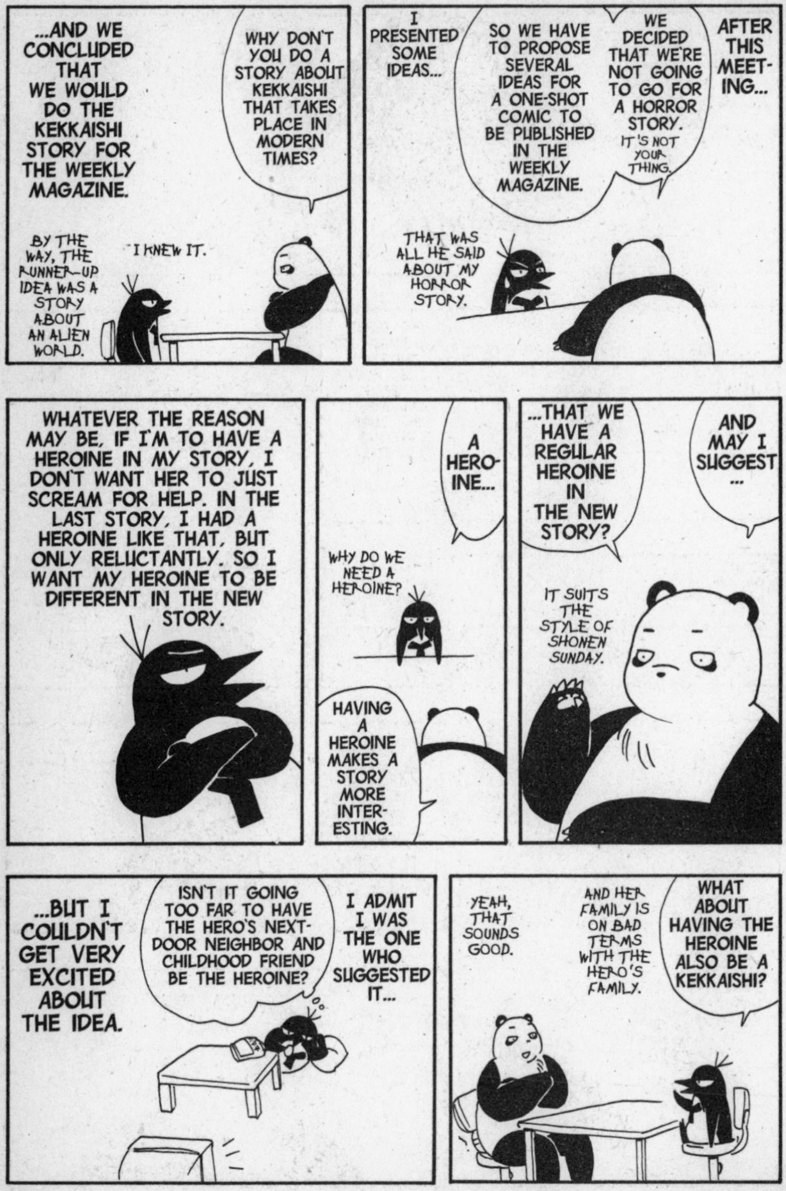
AFTER THIS MEETING...
WE DECIDED THAT WE'RE NOT GOING TO GO FOR A HORROR STORY.
IT'S NOT YOUR THING.
SO WE HAVE TO PROPOSE SEVERAL IDEAS FOR A ONE-SHOT COMIC TO BE PUBLISHED IN THE WEEKLY MAGAZINE.
I PRESENTED SOME IDEAS...
THAT WAS ALL HE SAID ABOUT MY HORROR STORY.
WHY DON'T YOU DO A STORY ABOUT KEKKAISHI THAT TAKES PLACE IN MODERN TIMES?
...AND WE CONCLUDED THAT WE WOULD DO THE KEKKAISHI STORY FOR THE WEEKLY MAGAZINE.
I KNEW IT.
BY THE WAY, THE RUNNER-UP IDEA WAS A STORY ABOUT AN ALIEN WORLD.
AND MAY I SUGGEST ...
...THAT WE HAVE A REGULAR HEROINE IN THE NEW STORY?
IT SUITS THE STYLE OF SHONEN SUNDAY.
A HERO-INE...
WHY DO WE NEED A HEROINE?
HAVING A HEROINE MAKES A STORY MORE INTER-ESTING.
WHATEVER THE REASON MAY BE, IF I'M TO HAVE A HEROINE IN MY STORY, I DON'T WANT HER TO JUST SCREAM FOR HELP. IN THE LAST STORY, I HAD A HEROINE LIKE THAT, BUT ONLY RELUCTANTLY. SO I WANT MY HEROINE TO BE DIFFERENT IN THE NEW STORY.
WHAT ABOUT HAVING THE HEROINE ALSO BE A KEKKAISHI?
AND HER FAMILY IS ON BAD TERMS WITH THE HERO'S FAMILY.
YEAH, THAT SOUNDS GOOD.
I ADMIT I WAS THE ONE WHO SUGGESTED IT...
ISN'T IT GOING TOO FAR TO HAVE THE HERO'S NEXT-DOOR NEIGHBOR AND CHILDHOOD FRIEND BE THE HEROINE?
...BUT I COULDN'T GET VERY EXCITED ABOUT THE IDEA.

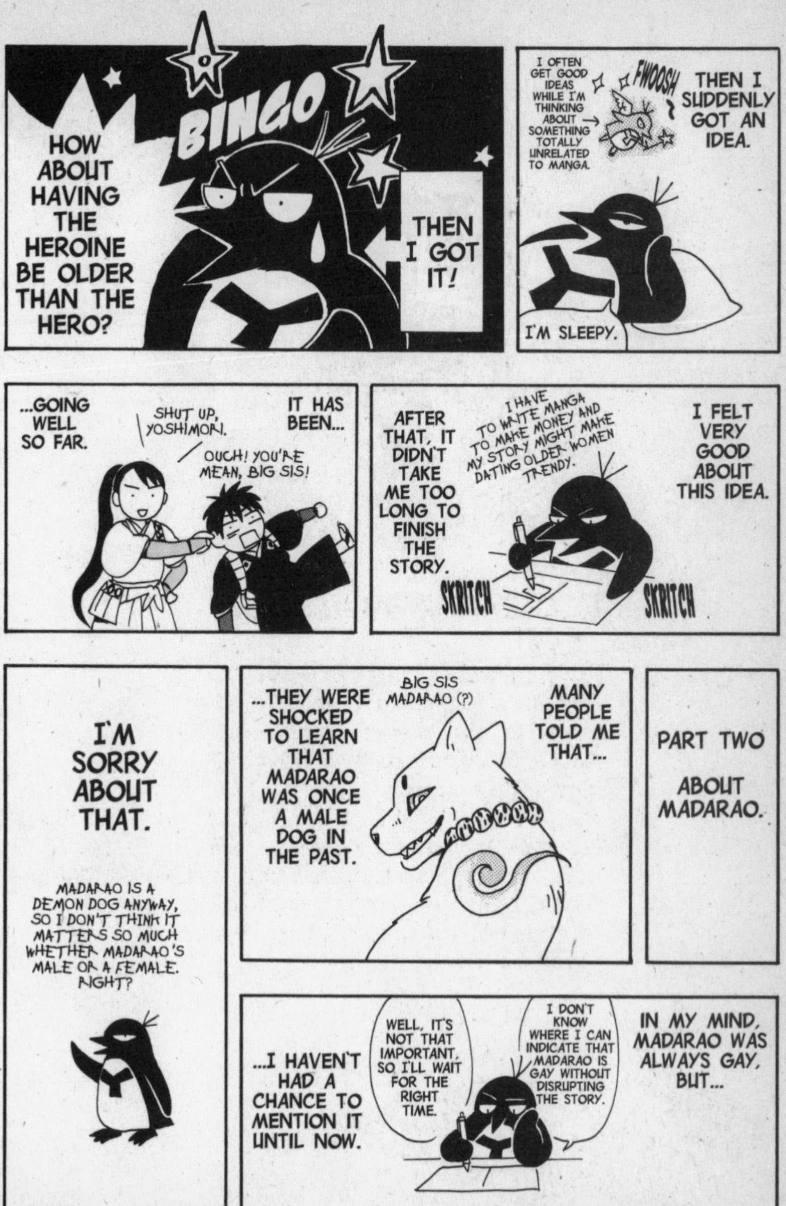
THEN I SUDDENLY GOT AN IDEA.
FWOOSH
I OFTEN GET GOOD IDEAS WHILE I'M THINKING ABOUT SOMETHING TOTALLY UNRELATED TO MANGA.
I'M SLEEPY.
BINGO
THEN I GOT IT!
HOW ABOUT HAVING THE HEROINE BE OLDER THAN THE HERO?
I FELT VERY GOOD ABOUT THIS IDEA.
I HAVE TO WRITE MANGA TO MAKE MONEY AND MY STORY MIGHT MAKE DATING OLDER WOMEN TRENDY.
AFTER THAT, IT DIDN'T TAKE ME TOO LONG TO FINISH THE STORY.
SKRITCH
SKRITCH
IT HAS BEEN...
SHUT UP, YOSHIMORI.
...GOING WELL SO FAR.
OUCH! YOU'RE MEAN, BIG SIS!
PART TWO
ABOUT MADARAO.
MANY PEOPLE TOLD ME THAT...
BIG SIS MADARAO (?)
...THEY WERE SHOCKED TO LEARN THAT MADARAO WAS ONCE A MALE DOG IN THE PAST.
IN MY MIND, MADARAO WAS ALWAYS GAY, BUT...
I DON'T KNOW WHERE I CAN INDICATE THAT MADARAO IS GAY WITHOUT DISRUPTING THE STORY.
WELL, IT'S NOT THAT IMPORTANT, SO I'LL WAIT FOR THE RIGHT TIME.
...I HAVEN'T HAD A CHANCE TO MENTION IT UNTIL NOW.
I'M SORRY ABOUT THAT.
MADARAO IS A DEMON DOG ANYWAY, SO I DON'T THINK IT MATTERS SO MUCH WHETHER MADARAO'S MALE OR A FEMALE. RIGHT?

FLUFFY

This sofa is heavenly. I feel like an angel!

But the first thing I need to buy is a TV table.

MESSAGE FROM YELLOW TANABE

There are always things that we don't immediately need, but we think it would be nice to have. There are also those things that we don't necessarily need but we want to have anyway.

Right now for me, a sofa is one of those types of things. I think it would help me to relax. Actually, what I really want is spare time to sleep. I would sleep three days a week if I could.

KEKKAISHI

VOLUME 3

STORY AND ART BY YELLOW TANABE

English Adaptation/Shaenon Garrity
Translation/Yuko Sawada
Touch-up Art & Lettering/Stephen Dutro
Cover Design & Graphic Layout/Amy Martin
Editor/Eric Searleman

Managing Editor/Annette Roman
Director of Production/Noboru Watanabe
Vice President of Publishing/Alvin Lu
Sr. Director of Acquisitions/Rika Inouye
Vice President of Sales & Marketing/Liza Coppola
Publisher/Hyoe Narita

Printed in the U.S.A.

Published by VIZ Media, LLC
P.O. Box 77010
San Francisco, CA 94107

Action Edition
10 9 8 7 6 5 4 3 2 1
First printing, October 2005

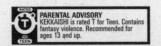

viz media
www.viz.com

RATED T FOR TEEN
PARENTAL ADVISORY
KEKKAISHI is rated T for Teen. Contains fantasy violence. Recommended for ages 13 and up.

store.viz.com

Editor's Recommendations

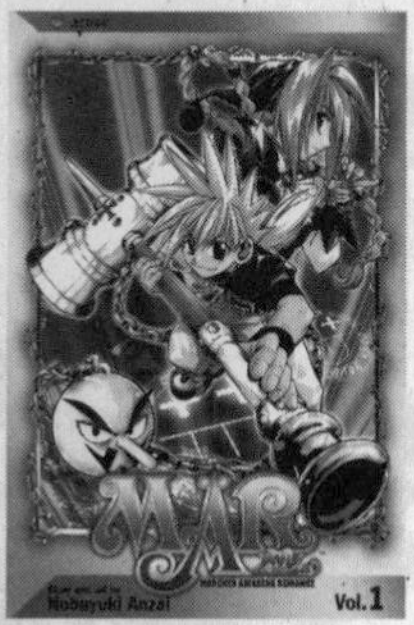

MÄR
Nobuyuki Anzai
Vol. 1

MÄR

Ginta Toramizu is a 14-year-old kid who doesn't have a lot going for him: he's near-sighted, doesn't do well in school, sucks at sports, and to top it off—he's short!

Then one day a supernatural figure appears at his school and summons him to a mysterious and exciting new world! In this strange universe filled with magic and wonder, he is strong, tough, agile—and he can see without his glasses! Thus, Ginta begins a mystical quest in search of the magical items known as "ÄRMS," with his companions Jack and the talking iron-ball weapon known as "Babbo."

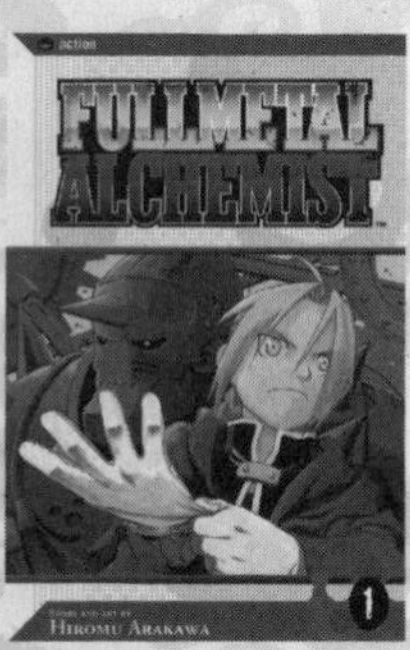

FULLMETAL ALCHEMIST
1
Hiromu Arakawa

Fullmetal Alchemist

In an alchemical ritual gone wrong, Edward Elric lost his leg. He was lucky…his brother Alphonse lost his entire body. At the cost of his arm, Edward was able to rescue his brother's soul and preserve it in a suit of steel armor. Equipped with mechanical "auto-mail" limbs, Edward becomes a state alchemist, serving the government on deadly missions and seeking the one thing that can restore his and his brother's bodies…the legendary Philosopher's Stone.

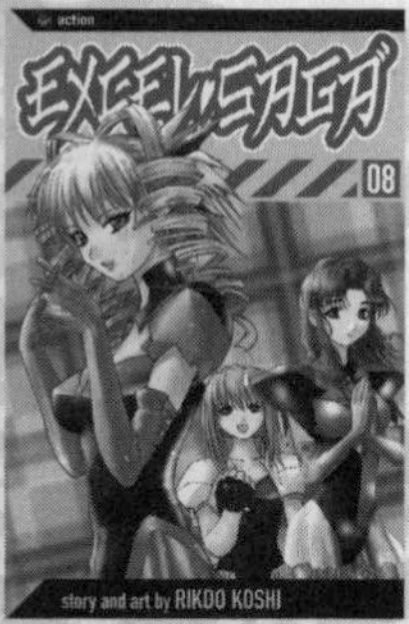

08
story and art by RIKDO KOSHI

Excel Saga

Today the city—tomorrow, the world! That's the plan of Il Palazzo, the haughty leader of ACROSS, a secret society based somewhere deep beneath the streets and sewers of Fukuoka, Japan. It's a good thing he's starting small, because ACROSS begins its bid for global domination with just two members—Il Palazzo and Excel, the teenaged girl smitten with him.

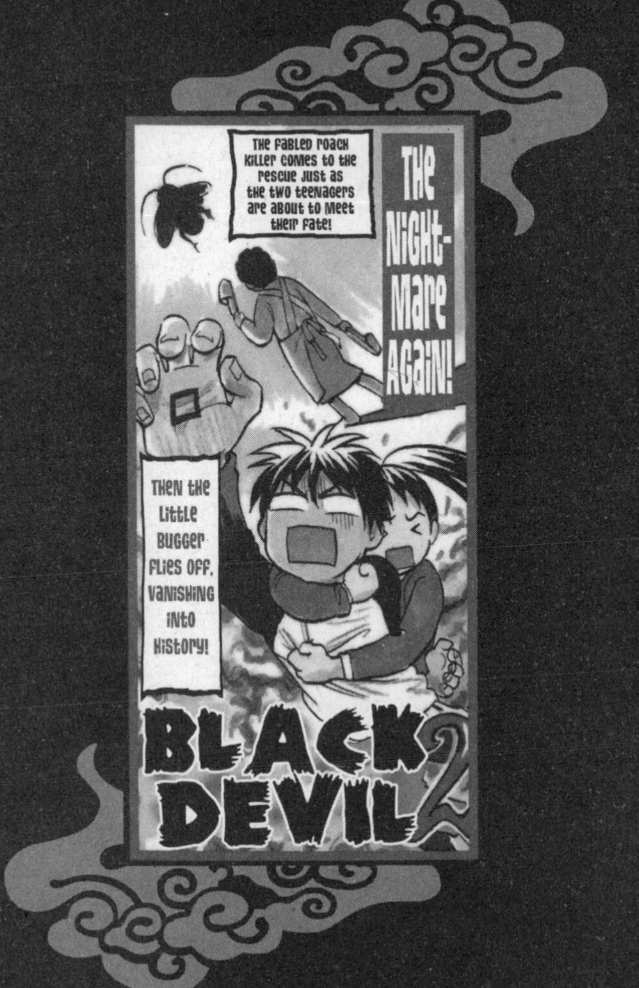
THE NIGHT-MARE AGAIN!
THE FABLED ROACH KILLER COMES TO THE RESCUE JUST AS THE TWO TEENAGERS ARE ABOUT TO MEET THEIR FATE!
THEN THE LITTLE BUGGER FLIES OFF, VANISHING INTO HISTORY!
BLACK DEVIL 2

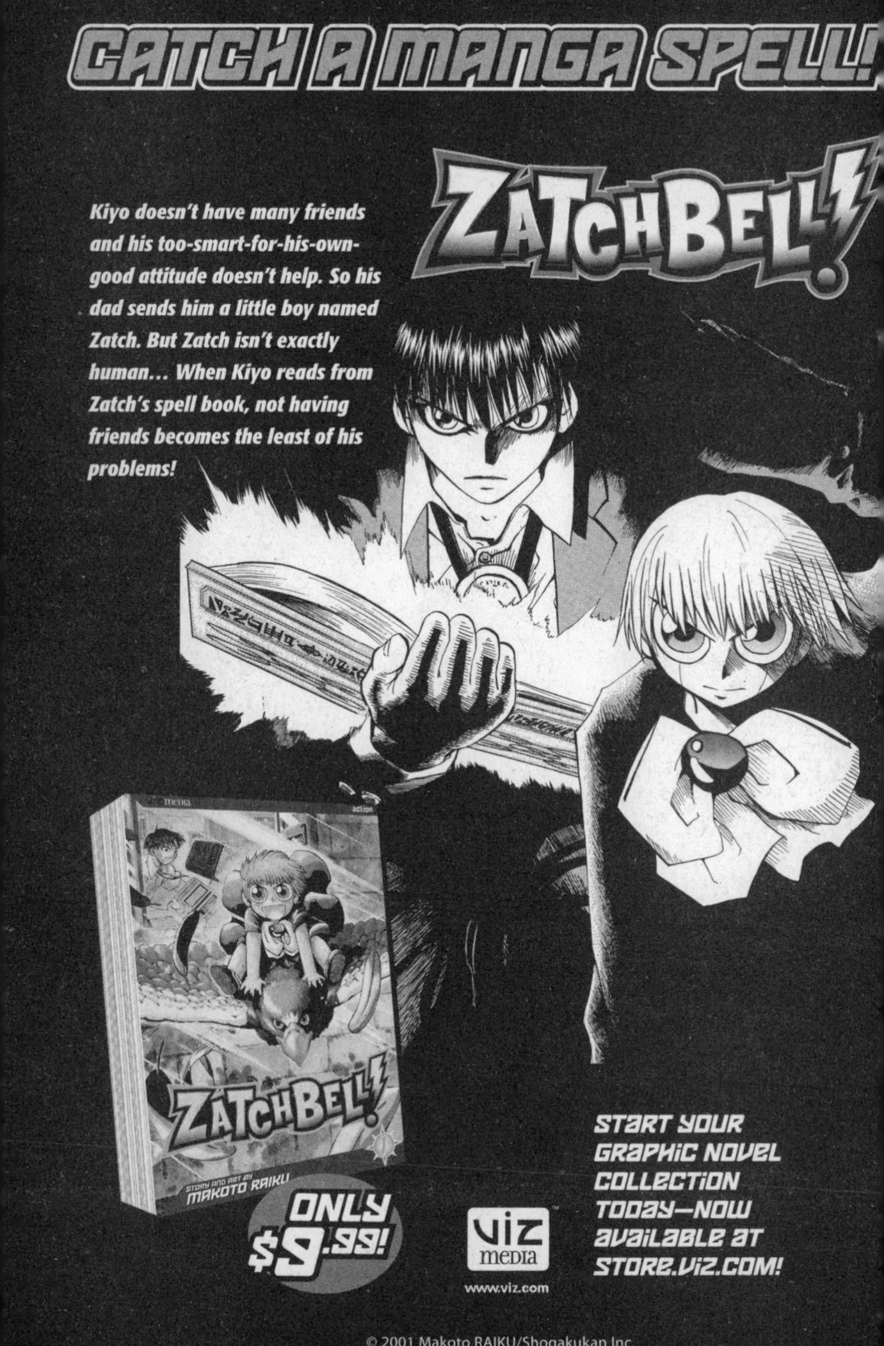
CATCH A MANGA SPELL!
ZATCH BELL!
Kiyo doesn't have many friends and his too-smart-for-his-own-good attitude doesn't help. So his dad sends him a little boy named Zatch. But Zatch isn't exactly human… When Kiyo reads from Zatch's spell book, not having friends becomes the least of his problems!
ZATCH BELL!
STORY AND ART BY MAKOTO RAIKU
ONLY $9.99!
VIZ media
www.viz.com
START YOUR GRAPHIC NOVEL COLLECTION TODAY—NOW AVAILABLE AT STORE.VIZ.COM!

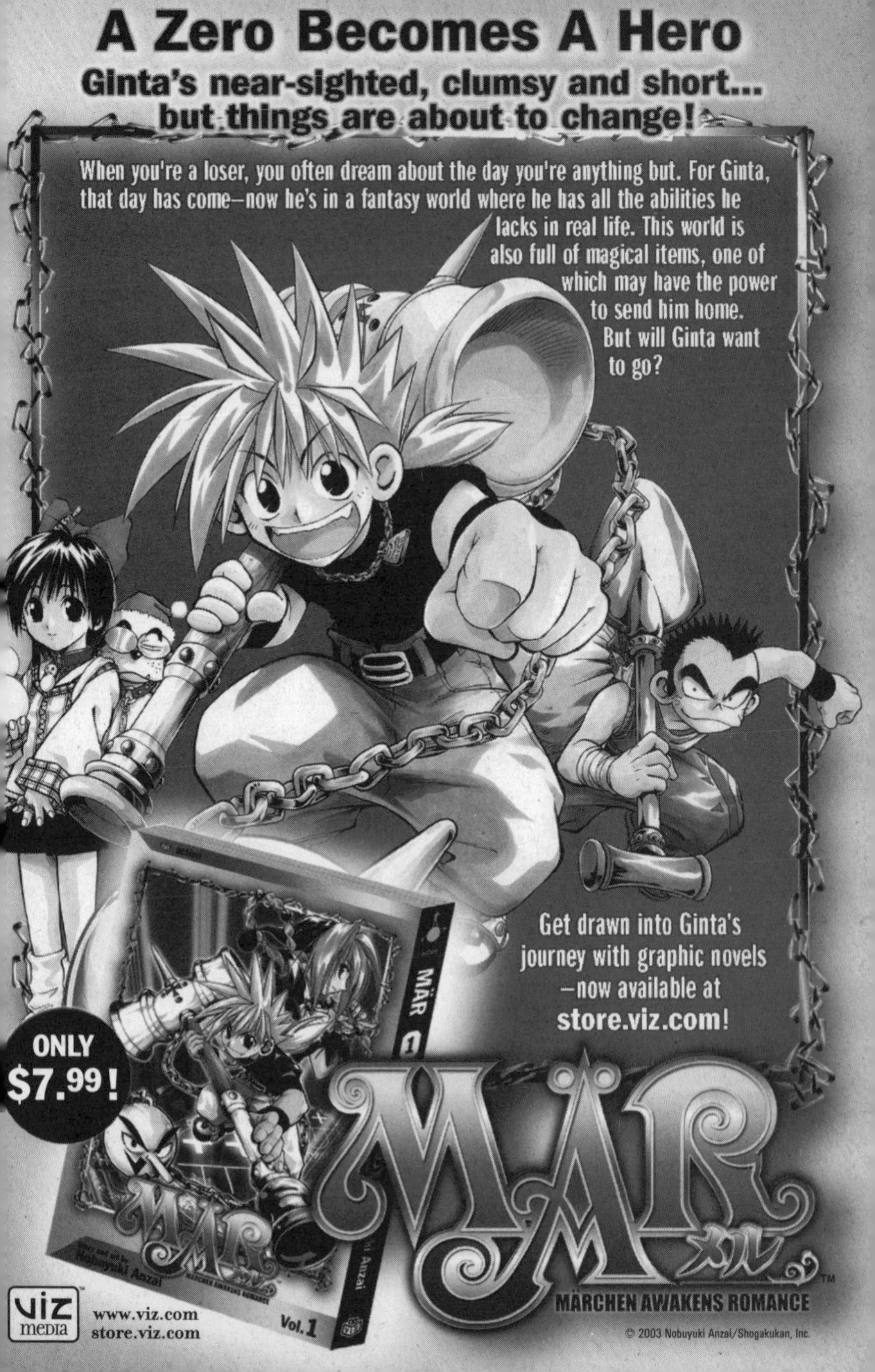
A Zero Becomes A Hero
Ginta's near-sighted, clumsy and short...
but things are about to change!
When you're a loser, you often dream about the day you're anything but. For Ginta, that day has come—now he's in a fantasy world where he has all the abilities he lacks in real life. This world is also full of magical items, one of which may have the power to send him home. But will Ginta want to go?
Get drawn into Ginta's journey with graphic novels —now available at store.viz.com!
ONLY $7.99!
MÄR
MÄRCHEN AWAKENS ROMANCE
Nobuyuki Anzai
Vol. 1
viz media
www.viz.com
store.viz.com
© 2003 Nobuyuki Anzai/Shogakukan, Inc.